THE YENAN WAY

THE

YENAN WAY

BY

EUDOCIO RAVINES

NEW YORK
CHARLES SCRIBNER'S SONS
1951

To All Friends of Freedom

CONTENTS

CHAPTER I

Initiation

1

I WAS born in 1897, in the sleepy little highland city of Cajamarca, Peru. My native city was a place in which everything happened in the same way, one day and the next, so much so that the town seemed static, immobile as the Andes, changeless as the curves in the paths over the hills. On occasion, the great landowners of the region might come down from their *haciendas* accompanied by regiments of Indians leading the beasts of burden, the "Lord's animals." This was an event, but the people seemed not to want to notice it. And then, after their departure, everything became the same, as if the city of Cajamarca were renewing the dreams of a thousand years.

Our town could indulge in long dreaming, if it would. In the place today occupied by the public square, the most powerful empire in ancient America had fallen. The Inca's army of 30,000 Indians had been confounded there by the most amazing cavalry charge of all time, carried out by 170 horsemen protected with culverins and armed with lances and swords. Four kilometers away in the evergreen heart of the landscape, steamed the wells of thermal water where Atahualpa had taken his last bath and entertained his nobles at his last feast. In our square was the place where the Inca captain offered gold in great basins to the Spanish horses, thinking that those monsters munched metal and could be nourished only by the most precious.

In the midst of modern wretchedness and backwardness, and the marshy bogging down, it yet seemed that over the lives of our people blew at least the breath of Pizarro's heritage. It was as if the inhabitants of Cajamarca felt themselves descended from a line of heroes—for Atahualpa, the Inca, and Francisco Pizarro were heroes, each in his way. Pizarro is the man who when close to seventy, hungry and sick on the Isla del Gallo, saw himself forced by the rebellious discontent of his men to return to the Isthmus, abandoning his dreams of conquest, his immense and mad adventure. Don Francisco took

1

one step forward, drew a line in the sand with the point of his sword, and like a great actor in an epic drama exclaimed: "That way to Panama to be poor; this way to Peru to be rich! Let him who is a good Spaniard choose to be a better." And he, old Pizarro, crossed the line; but of all his men only thirteen followed him, and with them he began the conquest of the Inca empire.

This heritage was a part of the people of our city. The traditional families of the place were proud of their lineage. They bore themselves well, for all the sickness of their society. It was not a legend, but history, that a time had been when, along the roads which left Cajamarca for the points of the Roads of the Winds, thousands of llamas and thousands of Indians had come laden with gold and silver, with all the treasures of the empire, for the ransom of the Inca. As witness to this, the stone building still stands in which the Inca Atahualpa was a prisoner, and where he drew with his great arm that other line; the line which marked on the wall the height to which the vast enclosure must be filled, once with gold and twice with silver, to buy his liberty. History and legend became one in that dreaming city which vegetated in a quiet as profound as that of its convent and its Franciscan monastery.

In their shadow I passed my early childhood; and here, when I was seven, I witnessed the exciting electoral campaign of 1904, in which contended Pierola, the democrat, the people's choice, and Pardo, the *civilista*, who represented the big landholders. My mother came of an old *civilista* family which had very much deplored her marriage to my father, whose family were democrats to a man and who had actually fought for Pierola in 1895 when he defeated Caceres. Now this father, whom I adored, was marching by at the head of the *Pierolistas*, and the city was shaken for once out of its usual lethargy. I can still remember snatches of the grownup conversations that reached my ears when the parade was over.

"Pierola is the solution for our problems. He is the man the country needs. The country needs a change and that change is Pierola," said my father.

"If we should win now, the country would take a great step forward. But I am afraid we shall lose. We have not the forces we had in '95," said my uncle.

"Pierola is popular; we democrats are in the majority. If they steal the election, we will have to raise the highland forces of '95 again."

"What we ought to raise is our children's future," my mother said.

"There is no future here. These pigs of landholders are incapable of undertaking anything. Buried in laziness and filth, maintaining unproductive lands, they are incapable of digging a canal or building a road. They cannot even exploit their lands, as they do the Indians. All I ask is that they work the lands they inherited, instead of letting them lie idle, year after year. Dogs in the manger while the people starve!" said my father.

"They don't even know how to give themselves a good life. They understand neither seeds nor fertilizer, nor animal husbandry, nor dairy cattle. The poor people are born on the ground, eat on the ground, mate on the ground, defecate on the ground, die on the ground, like beasts destroyed by filth, mange, and carrion," my blind grandfather added.

"One must be a good Christian, not coveting the goods of others," said my mother. "They have their *haciendas* because God willed it."

"God sends us into the world hairless. Why would He give anyone a *hacienda?*" said Aunt Adela tartly, adding, "*She* makes the poor little children get out of bed at four o'clock in the morning to kneel on the damp bricks during Mass. One of these days they'll get pneumonia."

"The Lord is pleased if we come to him by the road of mortification. To go to early Mass is a way of mortifying the flesh which is agreeable to God. And mortification is much more agreeable to heaven when it is done by little innocents."

"That seems to have been Herod's view," said the judge, my uncle's friend.

"Things have always been like this and always will be," said my grandfather, summing up. "This country's too hard, too difficult. It keeps its riches buried in entrails of stone. But young men always want to change everything. There is nothing like youth—faith and youth."

My mother led us to the bedroom. Through the window shone the luminous sunset. On my knees I repeated the words of my prayers mechanically. My soul was drunk on that marvel of twilight, which seemed to me a highland army commanded by Pierola himself.

My parents had conflicting notions of the education that I ought to receive. My father's dream was that I should be an engineer; my mother's, that I should be a Franciscan friar. She taught me to read

3

before I can remember and her first texts were the parables. My father brought home geography and history books, and talked to me about science. This disturbed my mother, who would say: "The poor child will be confused—there will be conflict in him between these readings and his religion."

"To live is to have entered a conflict. What he must learn is not to fear them, but to resolve them with a quiet heart," answered my father.

"The only road to happiness is the one that goes through the Mount of Olives, where the soul is offered up as a sacrifice and drains the chalice of bitterness."

"Happiness is being at peace with oneself, in accordance with one's best instincts."

"Man was born to fight against suffering, not to seek it out. What children should learn is to face life with courage."

They differed, my father and mother, on many things besides education, but they loved each other very much.

I never attended a grammar school and had in these early years no contact with other children aside from my younger brother and my two little sisters. My only world was my family and I observed the life around me somewhat as one might a pageant.

The city with its cataleptic life gave neither work nor bread to one who must live by the sweat of his brow. The land of that region was fertile, but the system was sterile. It was a rough land, bristly in its isolation, without roads, without ties to the world whose movement passed by it, along the coast and the sea. An enchanted, marvelous land, mother of a depressing atmosphere which enveloped man, clinging to him like wet leather, binding, constraining his muscles, his skin, his bones. The luminous radiance of nature accentuated the contrast with the misery, the beaten-down quality, the duskiness of the people. It was a brilliant natural world within which moved a dark people; it was a joyous world in which wandered people who were always sad.

In this world there was no work for my father, once the *civilistas* had won the election. Now new legends filled my mind, more modern ones than the old tales of Pizarro and Atahualpa.

Our home was peopled anew with marvelous visions. In the Amazon jungles there were not only souls to be won for Christ (as my aunt the nun had taught me), but other wonderful things as well:

4

rubber, precious woods, washes of gold, more rubber, miracle herbs, great rivers—the greatest in the world—and more rubber, a torrent of rubber that flowed down the rivers of the jungle towards the factories of Europe and of the United States.

Our sleeping city was invaded by the bewitching and everlasting fever of the forest land; the hot breath of the jungle reached the highland; the enchanted vision of fabulous wealth obsessed it. Every day, more fantastic news reached us from the interior. The son of Chavelita, the gaunt laundress who mourned without ceasing for her dead husband, had returned to the town rich after three years as a *cauchero* in the Napo. Don Sergio, who had left town without a cent four years ago, had returned from the Putumayo to buy a pharmacy and establish a flourishing business. Napoleon Gil had become a millionaire from rubber, from indigo, from the straw hats which were woven under water to keep them pliable and by the light of the moon to preserve their snowy whiteness.

To all this suggestive and seductive legend was added a patriotic motive. All the jungle was in dispute; in every river the Brazilians had to be fought for the land they were trying to claim; our heritage had to be fought for, not foot by foot, but kilometer by kilometer. My father was carried away by the rubber fever, by the witchery of the jungle. He dreamed of the great adventure that the jungle offered in every thicket; of the rich possibilities awaiting him at every bend in the river; of the handful of gold which was hidden in the trunk of every rubber tree.

He paced the floor without tiring. Sometimes he took me in his arms, that great man, with fists as big as my head, with a giant's shoulders. He would stroke my hair, and crushing me to his breast, murmur: "You will be a little man. I see it. You will watch over your mother and the little ones."

I felt as if something were twisting my heart like a wet rag; something which was like a great fear.

The morning came when he had to leave. I embraced him. I felt on my skinny body his big embrace, his large strong hands, and on my head his hot tears. I was shaken by his sobs. This hug, which was his last, gave me the measure of all the adoration my father had for me. Through my tears I saw the green eyes of the mule in the doorway, the mule which was to carry him away. He loosened my grip on him gently, kissed my mother and left us. As I heard the hoofbeats of his mule disappear in the distance, I felt a new life begin, a life with-

5

out a father. We were alone—my mother, and my younger brother José Manuel, and my sisters, Leonor and Ana Maria who was only a few months old.

I was eight years old when my father left and we became very poor after that. But I had not yet become aware of reality, for I was still living in the world of fantasy.

My mind was a theological cauldron; my imagination a mystical whirlwind, peopled with prophets on whom fire fell from heaven or stones from the hands of the Pharisees, with martyrs who drank boiling lead or fought wild beasts in the arena, or who, like Dionysius the Areopagite, beheaded by proconsuls, walked afterwards, carrying their heads in their hands. And in the midst of this imaginative world, grave, austere, and high in majesty walked the magnificent figure of Jesus, human archetype, the highest example for mankind to follow.

My mother loved the Christ of Calvary, of the garden of Gethsemane; she delighted in the sufferings of his Passion, his Seven Last Words, his appearance before Pontius Pilate. But I loved the Jesus of Bethany in the house of Mary and Martha, the Jesus who laughed at Peter, who sat by the roadside saying parables, who spoke on the Mount the most beautiful and human sermon of all time.

As our poverty increased my mother took in the laundry of some soldiers who were quartered in the town. This brought us more to eat but it was hard for us both. I filled the irons for her with hot coals and fanned them with the straw fans made by the Indians, and then sat beside her, reading aloud from the *Lives of the Martyrs*. Hour after hour I watched her, who seemed to me the incarnation of resigned fatigue. Her long, fine fingers curled over the hot handle of the iron. Sometimes she used both hands to make a stronger pressure, and her arms became tense. Before my eyes, her pointed shoulder jutted out of her curved back. Her head was bowed, a lock of damp hair falling over the wet forehead, her neck stretched out and tense as though an executioner stood beside her. Sweat rolled from her forehead, down her cheek, along her upper lip towards the chin, and fell at last in drops on the rough uniforms.

My father's letters came always from a greater distance. The last one was six months old and had been postmarked in the high Purus. He was getting out some rubber, but the transportation was difficult and every rubber tree, every pail of rubber, above all every canoe loaded with rubber, had to be defended from the Brazilians at the point of a gun. He said it was his duty to defend them and our Peruvian frontier.

One day my mother said happily: "We are leaving here, my son." "For where?" "For Matara. I have been named teacher at a girl's school there. They will pay me thirty soles a month."

Matara, a town of some two thousand inhabitants, had a little mud church with stumpy bell towers and two little bells all stained by the rains. In the atrium stood a big wooden cross; there was also a little grassy square enclosed by one-story houses. The school had a large courtyard and four rooms, one of them a kitchen, one a classroom, and the others bedrooms.

In this little town, as in Cajamarca, nature was luminous and unalterably springlike. The distant mountains were blue and the nearby hills multi-colored. It was a symphony of light and colors; it was saturated with calm and a feeling of peace. The adult population went out into the fields at dawn to work. There were a few who had their own small lands, but the majority were lessees of the great landholders. The lords gave them the right to sow certain pieces of land in the less favorable sections, and pasture the herds duly entered in the *hacienda* register. For this the lessees had to pay a certain price in currency, and in addition surrender a portion of the harvest and give free personal services in whatever work might be indicated to them by the managers.

It was a peaceful town of mixed-blood peasants, who all spoke Spanish, variegated with rich archaic words. And there, as my grandfather had said, people were born on the ground, mated on the ground, died on the ground. They lived in filthy hovels, blaming every illness on witchery and the evil eye—drunkenness their only diversion, a hole underground their only future. They lived in fear that the harvest might fail because of storms or frosts; that the lord might demand more grain than he was entitled to; that the patron saint of the town might not send the rain which the seeds needed to sprout and mature.

Contact with the people and the schoolgirls of this town, learning of their customs and their problems, their superstitions and their way of life, constituted my introduction to the world. Until then I had moved only within my family circle.

The two thousand inhabitants of that little town lived in adobe huts with straw roofs and earthen floors. The doors had no latches and the rooms no windows. On every side stretched the great lands of the lords, who worked them in the ways usual in Spain at the time of the conquest. These great landholders in four centuries had learned nothing; they burned tallow candles in their houses, sat on earthen seats, made no use of the wheel, and had no plumbing of any kind.

The dream of every man was to escape to the coast to work on the sugar plantations, where they would receive a salary and eat meat. The landholders disapproved of this notion. They said that life corrupted the young men, who returned without any manners and wished to be paid for their services. Schools were also bad in their opinion. The girls learned to write love letters and the boys to add sums correctly, which could be very disadvantageous to the landholders when it came to reckoning their portion of the harvest.

Seed-times were sad and silent in contrast to the harvests which were noisy, gay, and often drunken. The greatest feast day was that of San Lorenzo, on the tenth of August, harvest time, when the two statues were taken promenading in the streets and the young people were dressed in gay colors, and wore fantastic masks, and danced in the square. It all inevitably ended in drunken stupor for most of the population.

One day Tia Adela came all the way from the city, bringing news of my father's death. They had killed him on the border; he had died defending the riches of the jungle.

I felt a piercing pain. I remembered his great boots, his leather jacket, the cross that hung at his neck. I saw him bent over me saying, "You must watch over your mother and the little ones." I saw him at the head of the parade for Pierola, who had lost the election; I saw him walking ahead of the green-eyed mule. All night I dreamed of him, leaning his big body over me as I lay in bed and saying, "You will be a little man."

I never in my life had the slightest feeling of maternal protection. My mother was so weak, so little; she walked with such tiny steps; she knew so little of what was in books, except her religious ones. She was so bowed down by grief and had such fear of the future, that from the first I felt I was her protector. I began to feel there was a great distance between me and those of my age. I watched their play from a long way off. And I faced life from then on as an enemy. I could not enjoy or pass on; I had to fight.

The courtyard of our school was peopled with hens who fled out to the street when the pupils came in. Don Venancio, father of one of the pupils, got some lambs for us and pastured them on the lands of the lord. One morning his daughter came before dawn to say that the night before, after dark, they had been carried off to the big ranch house.

"To the ranch house, and why?"

"It is the roundup," she answered. "They have taken ours too. And my father says you must go with him to get them back."

In that region, every so often, the great landowner ordered a roundup. His men, mounted on horseback, brought in without exception every animal that was pastured on his lands which included often those of the small ranch owners as well. Then the animals were compared with the listings in the *hacienda* register, and those which were not in the books were considered his property and were so marked.

The little Ludmila was my guide, and we set off towards the hills beyond which lay the valley where the ranch house stood. It was a long walk; the ridge was steep and had taken on the blood-red light of dawn before we arrived. Far away in a diaphanous light could be seen the golden waves of the wheat fields, and beyond, the little rivers were visible, flowing down green slopes into a valley. I was absorbed in the overwhelming silence and a sense of triumphant life.

It was a completely new sensation. On those heights the soul became clear and hard, small cares disappeared and there arose instead a feeling of eternity. The light was quiet, like rest, and fell vertically on the land. It was a clean light. The silence was absolute; the distant land took on the colors of hallucination, and in that cold air we were the only creatures that seemed to move. I stood a long time watching on that height, so lovingly tranquil, so delicately silent. The smell of the earth had changed; it smelled of time. And beneath that fragrance, that intoxication of light and color, wrapped in that august silence, I felt, for the first time, in my veins and in my bones, that in living itself there was a vast glory.

Don Venancio's hut was reached at last, and after we had eaten we went on together. The descent into the valley was easy. Shortly after midday we reached the ranch house where were chained great mastiffs who must have eaten more meat than all the peasants in the valley. Already standing by the gate were a motley crowd of Indians and *cholos* waiting, like us, to claim their animals. After a long time we were admitted and stood before the table where the employees of the *hacienda* were dealing with the people's claims. Don Venancio explained to them who I was and why we had come, and after much conversation we were admitted to an inner room where the landholder himself received us quite amiably. He questioned us at length about my mother, my father, and all my other relations. Eventually it was decided to return our animals, and Don Venancio and I made our way to the corral.

We spent a long time in finding Don Venancio's flock and my mother's, only to discover (Don Venancio mocking and I indignant) that all of our sheep had been closely shorn; there was not a bit of wool left on them.

"And only yesterday," my companion said, "they were so woolly that there was enough for two mattresses; and now look at them! That's how the land owners get tens of thousands of kilos of wool each year."

We heard cries behind us and saw one of the stewards coming towards us, dragging behind him a little goat as a present for me.

"That," said Don Venancio, "is so you will say nothing about your wool."

I walked along in silence. Finally I said, "And every year is there a roundup?"

"Sometimes twice a year."

"And why do you let them do it?"

"That's funny!" he laughed. "What can we do? The land is theirs, and everything on it must be theirs. The houses, the trees, the grass, everything—even the men. And if the men belong to them, how much more must the sheep that eat their grass."

I was disgusted. I could see that the man had lost his capacity for indignation and that in his spirit there was no rebellion, no protest.

Night was falling and the earth was getting black; the light was like smoke. The mountain range had lost its colors and looked like the firm line of a flat picture. Only much later did I realize what I had learned that day—that the soul of the Andes is caught only by him who walks among them.

The roundup, the shearing of the sheep, proved to me and made me feel in every nerve the existence of a harsh and infamous social reality—the regime of serfdom, the wretchedness which it brought, the debasing filth and rampant villainy which was its core. Those landholders who, when it suited them, made fine speeches about social justice, forced even women and children to work without pay, took part of their harvests, made them milk the *hacienda* cows, and then sheared the peasants' sheep. And to prevent this there were no authorities, nor judges, nor human powers, nor Divine Judgment.

I dreamed that it was this which made Jehovah angry in the Old Testament, this that the prophets anathematized, and the Scriptures condemned. It was because of this that Jesus had suffered and died. My father had been right. What my country needed was a change. Of what would it consist? Who could do it and why? My thoughts went round and round looking for something, but I knew not what.

Where was the Lord God? What had become of his prophets? I whistled little Indian melodies to myself in order to scare away my thoughts, because they might be sinful.

2

When I was about fourteen, my maternal uncle Augustin, who was rector of a school in Cajamarca, wrote asking that I be sent to live with him and his wife, and complete my secondary education in his school and at his expense. I understood that this would make a deep and important change in my life, and I welcomed the idea, resolved to get as much out of it as possible. So I set off happily, even in the midst of my tears at parting with my family. I reached the city by evening.

Although my uncle and his family received me coldly and did nothing to make me feel welcome, the life of the school itself opened before me like an enchanting surprise. Here I met and formed friendships with boys who were to become important in the life of the country. The studies gave me no difficulty; they seemed as natural as breathing.

The history professor was a Negro, with eyelids as bulky as two nuts under which his bright eyes shone. He had travelled through Europe, Asia, and Africa and had read a great deal. We called him *zambo gallinazo* (turkey buzzard); he knew that we did and told us so.

"If a man's value depended on the color of his skin," he used to say, looking at one of the blondes in the class, "you and not I would be history professor. But no, my son; talent has no color."

"I know," he added on another occasion, "that you call me *zambo gallinazo*, but you may as well learn now as later that what counts in a man is not the color of his skin but his mental capacity, his spiritual powers and his vision. Toussaint L'Ouverture was black and a great man. Herédia and Alexandre Dumas were *zambos* and, let us face it, so was Simon Bolivar."

He exalted Socrates with devotion, cursed his judges and recited in a hoarse voice exquisite bits from Aeschylus and Euripides, Sophocles and Plato. His two great loves were Martin Luther and the

Jacobins. When he spoke of the Reformation he was so enthusiastic that his admiration became contagious. So, Martin Luther, from being a proscribed heretic became a genius in our minds and the instrument of one of the most important spiritual movements in history. These lessons were a break in the iron fortress of my religious faith.

So went four years in tears and in laughter, studies and games, readings forbidden and recommended, escapes to the country and examination worries, friendships and a greater knowledge of the wretched social reality which surrounded me. Then a political change brought the democrats in and my uncle the rector lost his job, while my father's brother, the Colonel, was made prefect. I then went to live with him, to browse in his library and read passionately, voraciously, everything I could lay my hands on. It was here that the faith I had learned at my mother's knees appeared no longer valid to me. I discovered Renan's *Life of Jesus*, and a man less like my mother's God than like a heroic and human person, who yet seemed to me too divine to approach the pain of man, the tragedy of my own doubting adolescence, and the social mysteries which gnaw the flesh of the disinherited. Nietzsche was next, and he, like Renan, destroyed for good my mother's work.

It would have meant a great deal to me to go on to the University, but this the family fortunes would not permit. Accordingly I went to work for an Italian storekeeper, Capelli, who was very kind to me until his death at the hands of a stranger who passed through town one day. I had all the problems of adolescence, the conflicts of sex and religion, to solve alone. The city where nothing ever happened and there seemed no future for anyone, depressed me more and more. I left accordingly for Lima, the coastal capital, to look for work and more money with which to help my family.

It was 1917 when I came to Lima, hungry for some faith and doubting my own destiny. Work was hard to find; time passed slowly, and so I devoured the news:

"A bloody revolution has broken out in Russia. The Tzar has been dethroned and the socialist, Alexander Kerensky, is the head of the government of the Russian Republic."

New names appeared in history—Milukov, Rodzianko, Tseretelli, Chernov. The French revolution has reached Russia, I thought, pleased by the downfall of Russian tzarism whose tyranny was familiar to me from my wide reading of Russian literature. I walked the streets looking for work, little guessing that this revolution which was shaking the world would have so deep an effect on my life, shaping my entire future.

After I had found work at last with Felix Leon, more names appeared in the news about Russia—Lenin, the Bolsheviks, the communist party, Trotsky, the Red army, Zinoviev, Bukharin, Kamenev, Dzerzhinsky. All the events taking place in Russia went straight to my heart. Every morning I read the news avidly, and in it I saw gradually a possibility of believing in something again, of constructing for myself a new faith. It was the possibility of believing in Man, in his rise, and in the creation of a better world for everyone.

As I read about it in classic literature, Russian life had seemed to me grievous, similar to that of my own highland country, and that of the dusty seacoast towns. I could find genuine analogies between the Indian and what I imagined the Russian *muzhik* to be; the bloody Russian insurrection and the mute protest of my own people—who were born, lived and died on the ground—seemed parallel expressions. Gradually I began to believe that the Russian revolution would show us, too, a way out. The Bolsheviks said they were ushering in the dawn of a new day.

Meanwhile my fortunes improved. I obtained a new job at Fort Hermanos and was able to bring my mother and the other children to Lima. At this time, I became interested in the socialist movements in my own country. These were as yet unorganized, vaguely anarchist, and completely ineffective. The social reformers who were at that time timidly making their appearance were almost unnoticed. José Carlos Mariátegui, Carlos del Barzo, Luis Ulloa, Pedro Bustamante Santisteban, proclaimed themselves the mouthpieces of socialism and proposed the organization of a political party with a strong inclination towards the paths of the Bolsheviks and the Russian revolution.

Meanwhile the people and the workers, roused by anarchist agitators, set up barricades in the streets and proclaimed strike after strike. The government police were able to control them, but the times were singularly unquiet. My sympathies were all with the people and the striking workers, and I soon determined to see what I could do to organize white-collar workers in a drive for better living conditions.

It was thus I first came to know José Carlos Mariátegui, director of *La Razon* and one of the advocates of the organization of a socialist party. He welcomed me and my friends warmly and gave space to the articles we had written on the situation of the white-collar workers. "Come whenever you like," he said. "Here you are welcome.

13

You must be opportunists. What you are attempting is a public service; no one has ever paid any attention to the white-collar workers or defended them."

Mariátegui had a rich persuasive voice; his eyes, clear as an eagle's, were large and black; his great nose was arrogant and commanding. His hair fell over a wide brow, yellowish and sickly. When he walked, he limped noticeably as the result of an unfortunate and ill-advised operation, so that his friends called him "the lame one," which did not seem to disturb him in the least.

In the offices of *La Razon*, every evening there were long discussions of religion, national and international politics, the Russian revolution, Wilson's Fourteen Points, the treaty of Versailles and the treaty of Brest-Litovsk.

Meanwhile an outstanding *civilista* had raised the banner of revolt against his own class. He got into power by a *coup d'état* and assumed control of the government. Most people were for this Augusto Leguía, but I was against him because he had at one time persecuted the democrats, and, even more, because he had yielded the territories of the Purus and the Aracá which my father had died defending. Events proved me right, for Leguía's first cabinet was a reactionary group.

"There is only one way open to us," said Mariátegui at that time, "Socialism!"

Encouraged by this man, who had some influence on all the socially conscious youth of that period, a group of us went ahead. Mariátegui himself went off to Italy and we were left alone, but we started a small paper of our own, organized the Lima white-collar workers, called a strike and won. In those days I had also found time, without leaving my job, to attend classes at the University of San Marcos, where, while I found the professors mediocre, the methods archaic, and the studies thick with pedantry, the atmosphere and my fellow students were exciting. The red group was full of young men of poor families, who were all for revolution. Among these was a man who was later to play a vital role in Peruvian politics; his name was Victor Raúl Haya de la Torre. He was a boy of good family from Trujillo, the coastal city founded by Francisco Pizarro, a city whose society still prides itself on its family escutcheons. He had, however, no means except the small salary he received for teaching in the Protestant School, run by Pastor John MacKay; and so could not associate with his peers, or those whom he considered his peers, in Lima.

INITIATION

When Mariátegui returned from Italy, Haya de la Torre was drawn into his circle; but the two, although on the surface they maintained friendly relations, were not really congenial. Mariátegui was an intellectual, a theoretician; Haya demanded action, and was impatient of the other's thoughtful approach to the questions of the day.

"Excessive intellectualism," he would say, "confuses the workers and instead of clearing up, actually darkens the issues in the unprepared mind."

"I can't see why it's intellectualism," retorted Mariátegui, "to let people of little culture know what is going on in the realm of ideas. If some fail to understand, there will be plenty who won't."

3

It was not long after this that President Leguía decreed the official consecration of the country to the Sacred Heart of Jesus. To this the country reacted violently, and the *civilistas* and the reds, the Protestants and the anarchist workers all made capital of it. There formed a spontaneous and powerful opposing coalition to Leguía, which included a great many devout Catholics and practically the entire student body of the university.

Workers and students joined in the demonstration at the University. The police intervened; fighting broke out in the streets; two demonstrators, one a student the other a tramway operator, were killed. The cause had two martyrs. After the government troops had withdrawn, defeated temporarily by the workers and students, there was a great popular meeting at the Plaza de Armas. Here, Haya de la Torre addressed the crowd and became a hero overnight, because as soon as the demonstration was over, with a real genius for publicity, he went around to all the newspapers with his version of the affair.

Next day the university became the barracks for the insurgent group. There was a general strike; the city was paralyzed; and the bodies of the student and the tramway worker lay in state in a university hall. Haya de la Torre, in the name of the students, delivered a funeral address. For the moment, the government was in real danger. But four months later Haya de la Torre was exiled, along with the other prominent leaders of the disturbance, and José Carlos Mariátegui took over the leadership of his followers and of others who had not belonged to the original group.

This group became firm around him; it called itself "communist" and "bolshevik," but it was really just a group of young men learning demagoguery. We made fine speeches and took dramatic

15

stands, but the gentle teachings of Mariátegui weighed less with us than the tradition Haya had left. How things might have turned out if our movement had been allowed to develop will never be known. Leguía's police, however, intervened. I was arrested as a communist, which I was not, and sent to the political prison on the Isla de San Lorenzo, from which I was later shipped off with other trouble-makers to Chile. It was not long before the Chilean police arrested me as a spy (a border dispute was raging hotly between the two countries) and exiled me to Argentina.

4

In Buenos Aires, in a boarding house run by Spaniards on the corner of Tucuman and San Martin, I found congenial company with several other exiles, among whom were Luis Fernan Cisneros (director of *La Prensa*), Luis Heyssen, Manuel Seoane, Enrique Cornejo Koster and Oscar Herrera. We talked for hours on end about the social problems of our country, its backwardness, its technical deficiencies, the poverty of the people, the Indian communities.

"The country is traditionally agrarian," Cornejo Koster would say, "and it has a communist tradition. Actually, the only people who understood the land were the Incas. A memory of those days is still fresh in the Indian villages. Once we break up the big landholdings and bring modern techniques into play, there will be a great revival."

"The country must be industrialized," we would answer. "The Indian must become a worker who receives wages; one who buys soap and washes."

One day a group of us were invited to meet the writer, José Ingenieros, who was considered in those days a great leader and teacher of youth. He greeted us cordially, and listened carefully while we told him of the social problems that troubled us, of the dictators, of the Indians. Finally, when we asked him what our country most needed, he replied:

"White race, my son! White race."

We left the house depressed, angry, and completely disillusioned. The great master had regarded our preoccupation as material for jokes. My own disappointment led me to seek out communists, anarchists and socialists, and I soon found myself in a motley group of students, workers, and professors who were trying to organize an anti-imperialist league. It had some success and even launched a paper *Revista del Oriente*, which kept people abreast of the events taking place in Russia. It was decided to arrange for an act of solidarity with

16

other leftist groups in support of the English miners who were about to declare a general strike. With this end in view, we went to visit Juan B. Justo, the leader of the Socialists.

He received us cordially but questioned us closely. "Anti-imperialist," he said. "That means against imperialism, eh? You're the Peruvian?" he asked, turning towards me. "Well, they tell me you are active and willing to sacrifice. That's good. When a man gives himself he should do it ungrudgingly. But they say you don't sleep, and that's bad. You'll work better if you sleep. Now, about imperialism. What is imperialism?"

"The last stage of capitalism."

"Says Lenin," answered Justo, "but what do you say? Don't merely repeat bad translations from the Russian. If we are living the last, or as the Russian really says it, the highest stage of capitalism, what comes next?"

"Socialism," my friend Kaufman answered firmly.

"Ah, but socialism and bolshevism are not the same things. Socialism is, above all, freedom, the rights of man, respect for his life and dignity. If this is lost it isn't socialism." Then he turned to me again.

"Does imperialism hurt your country?"

"Yes," I answered, "as it has hurt Panama, and Cuba with the Platt amendment—Mexico, Santo Domingo, and Haiti with war and occupation."

"Have you read Marx?" he asked.

"No."

"And Lenin?"

"No, I haven't."

"Well read them and you will learn that for Lenin imperialism is an economic phenomenon. Are there many foreign businesses in your country—imperialistic ones?"

"Yes, there are several."

"Do they pay salaries?"

"Yes."

"Well, well. And do the great landholders pay wages?"

"They do on the coast."

"Well, those are the capitalist *haciendas*. What about the highland ones?" asked Justo.

"There, they don't pay salaries."

"Well now, tell me which seems to you better for the people?"

"Neither," I answered.

17

"So both systems seem bad to you?"

"Yes, because in neither case do the people live decently."

"Well, you'll make a good socialist some day. But don't talk about imperialism: that's not the problem."

When we left him, Kaufman was angry, because Justo had seemed to believe in the progressive role of imperialism in backward countries. This, Kaufman thought, was absurd.

"This man," he said, "is an intellectual. A student of Marx. A liberal, perhaps. At any rate, we have succeeded since he has agreed to participate in our demonstration. Codovila and the communists will be furious."

"And why should they be annoyed by the success of something along the lines they have been following? It seems to me that you dislike the communists."

"Dislike them, no. Despise them, yes. Because the communists here are failures; they are cynical and play with people's hopes. You'll get to know them. You'll meet Vittorio Codovila some day, and you'll see what he's like. He knows only one thing—to dance to the tune that Moscow plays. He's a rogue; but you'll find that out for yourself."

When the day of the demonstration came, Codovila got up to speak—a chunky man with no waist and no neck, with wide hips and short legs. He spoke with a strong Italian accent and used vulgar words, speaking ill of the English, the French, the Belgians, and the North Americans; indeed, he did not have a good word to say for anybody but the Russians. He said that the communists were the only true anti-imperialists, that all the others were weak and vacillating. He made himself thoroughly unpopular with the non-communists present, who shouted him down. But from that day I was on friendly terms with the communist leaders, and I became more interested in learning from them.

I drew three conclusions from the new political circles that I had penetrated: First, that my ignorance was abysmal; second, that there was little hope of repairing it in this *milieu;* third, that I was tired of working for Mayon, Limited (where I had a job as an accountant) and must go to Europe where I could study socialism at first hand and learn some effective way of helping my poor people. I had saved money during my years in Buenos Aires. It was 1926. The franc had fallen. I bought francs. Then I went to see my employer and told him I wished to leave, and why. I thought he would be angry, but he was not. He seemed to understand.

"Go," he said, "and if the day comes that you want to return, write to me. You shall have your return passage and your job back." My fellow exiles gave me a great send-off. They said that since I was going to Paris, I must get in touch at Oxford with Haya de la Torre, to whom we all looked in those days for leadership, and see if, with Mariátegui's group as a cornerstone and Haya as a leader, a strong national movement could be formed to bring some semblance of democracy to Peru. The only fear some of us had was that Haya would not use democratic methods in his organization of such a movement. Heyssen and Herrera believed that he would, but Seoane at this time doubted it. I myself did not know. I could only hope. In any case I would soon be in a position to find out.

5

I reached Paris in 1927 and my first task was to learn to speak a French that could be understood. My knowledge of the language had been acquired so far only from books. Then I wrote to Haya, who after a trip to Russia and a long stay in Switzerland was now settled in Oxford, sending him the greetings of the Buenos Aires exiles. And after a few months, during which I had made friends with some forty young Peruvian students, Haya arrived in Paris.

We went to meet him of course.

We stationed ourselves in the neighborhood of the second-class coaches; the train arrived, the passengers descended, but there was no Haya. Then, typically tardy, Rozas, a Negro from Cuzco, joined us.

"Don't you know better than to watch second-class," he laughed. "Haya always travels in style." Sure enough, from a *de luxe* compartment, far beyond even the first-class coaches, alighted Victor Raúl Haya de la Torre, surrounded by porters carrying shiny leather suit-cases. He was dressed in the best English fashion and wore a trench-coat straight from Piccadilly. No one would have taken him for a penniless student from a backward South American country. One would have thought him, rather, the son of a rich Argentine cattle rancher or even a Milanese or Catalan industrialist. Smiling, with that warm contagious gayety that was so characteristic of him, his head proudly high, his walk sure and almost triumphant, he came toward us, adjusting the brim of his hat with a trimly gloved hand.

Haya greeted his followers, embraced them, slapped them on the back. He recognized them all, and had a smile and a special greeting for each.

"You look well, but your left eye is red. You must see an

oculist." And to another: "You are better, much better than when I saw you last. Have you been taking that cough medicine? And no liquor, I hope. That's bad for you."

I thought what goodness there must be in him, and how fine it was, preoccupied as he was with great social problems, that he found time for the little problems of each of his followers. His friendly, affectionate attitude towards them erased the disagreeable impression that the *de luxe* compartment had made on me. Where did he get the money? had been my first reaction.

He greeted me warmly and said that he would forgive me for not consulting him before coming to Europe, though he would have advised me not to make the trip.

"And why?" I asked.

"Europe has grown old," he said. "She has brought forth all she can; she is too old ever to conceive again. What is to be, is over there, in the world you have come from, the world you have abandoned for this."

"But," I objected, "the great teachers are here, the lectures, the galleries, the culture, the life of the spirit."

"You are sick with literature," he laughed. "But you are here; you will grow out of it."

"And you then, what are you all doing here?"

He hesitated, and the others, who had been laughing with him, were silent. He took my arm and drawing me away from the group, answered:

"I came to see Russia. I had to visit the home of the most gigantic social experiment of our time. I had to see for myself, so they can't lead me up the garden-path." He slapped me on the back and laughed again.

"This is one of the reasons I came to Europe," I said. "I too hope to go to Russia. I want to see what you saw. Then, too, I had to talk to you. We must organize an effective group; we must begin working for lasting reforms. And in this, your word—the word of Haya de la Torre—seems to us all decisive."

He glowed with pleasure. "We must talk," he said. "I am glad you have come." And indeed he seemed so in the numerous meetings that followed, during which our political comradeship grew to what was almost friendship. Even so, I still had certain reservations, and though I would not admit their existence they grew in the dark. I could not help wondering how Victor Raúl financed his expensive stay at Oxford, the fashionable teas he gave, his trips to Switzerland

and to the Salzburg festivals, his whole way of life so incompatible with the means of a poor student. In any friendship one is always afraid of knowledge that might cause a break. One avoids discovery, questioning, even curiosity. This was my attitude, reinforced by my knowledge of my friend's personality. His psychology was not that of an ordinary man; his behavior was not that of a person one might meet every day. There flowed from him, from his bearing, from his words, the almost juvenile gayety, fresh, warm, contagious, that I had noted at the train. He was charming and brilliant; he made each person he talked with feel specially loved, apart from others; he was clever and understanding about everyone's personal problems. On the other hand, he had a great capacity for hate, and he loved himself inordinately, his ideas, his opinions, his own position on any question. He had a sublime love for Humanity and a vast contempt for human beings. Behind his kindness there was cruelty. He was, above all, feverishly ambitious; but he was without courage. He had an almost obsessive fear of physical pain and no capacity to bear suffering. Incidentally, he hated women sexually. He used them only as instruments for his plans. He had a gift for guessing at once what he could gain from each one, and towards them all, blond or brunette, old or young, beautiful or plain, he had the same utilitarian attitude. Perhaps he felt the same way about men, but if so it was never evident, so sympathetic were his friendships. What impressed me most unfavorably about him was his anger when anyone proved him wrong, or even disagreed with him. He felt himself an exceptional man, marked by destiny for the execution of a great plan.

Beyond my awareness of this complexity, beyond my fears and doubts, remained my conviction that, whether in political action or in any other sphere of life, we must take men for what they are, and not for what we would wish them to be. Therefore, I put aside whatever qualms I had, and let our friendship, born of our joint interest in a political ideal, grow deeper and stronger.

Meanwhile, the German social democrats and communists, frightened by the rise of Hitler and the implications of the Versailles treaty for the future of their country, had joined with the Soviet Union in sponsoring an anti-imperialist Congress in Brussels. The Anti-Imperialist League in Argentina asked me to attend as their representative, after which my first act was to write and request an invitation for Victor Raúl Haya de la Torre as an anti-imperialist student leader, exiled as a result of his political activities.

21

Haya had veteran adversaries in Julio Antonio Mella, the Cuban communist leader, and Carlos Quijano, the Argentine lawyer. Finding my request ignored, I wrote again, mentioning Haya's journey to Russia, his friendship with Zinoviev, Lossovsky and Madame Kollontay, and his participation in one of the world congresses in Moscow. These facts impressed Willy Munzenberg, the German communist, who was official promoter of the Congress.

"You have triumphed magnificently," wrote Haya to me. "You must go to Brussels at once and wait for me there. They are sure to try to put me in the worst hotel. See to it that I get accommodations suited to my position. Let them remember that I am the leading anti-imperialist student of Latin America, whether Mella likes it or not. You have yet to meet that pretentious *zambo*."

I did indeed meet him in Paris, shortly afterward. Julio Antonio Mella was a bit theatrical and evidently had a high opinion of himself. But he was gay, frank and optimistic; his speeches, his conversation, his defense of his position radiated sincerity. He was a militant communist, and one of the few political leaders who had the respect of the people of Cuba. So great was his influence that when he embarked on a hunger-strike, the tyrannical government of President Machado was shaken. The Cuban communist party had expelled him for this, and he was now on his way to Moscow to be vindicated. Willy Munzenberg was disgusted.

"It is inconceivable that they should expel a communist leader," he groaned, "because he has waged an effective campaign against a tyranny so hateful to the people. It is they who should be expelled."

Mella hated Haya, whom he called a latin Chiang Kai-shek, and though I continued to make every effort, I soon became convinced that there was no hope of bringing these two together.

Shortly after my first meeting with Mella, I went off to Brussels to get a good hotel room for Haya. He arrived, was pleased with his accommodations (which were identical with James Maxton's), and embraced me affectionately.

At the time of my arrival, a sensational rumor was going the rounds among the delegates: Zinoviev was in Brussels; he had been seen at the Egmont Palace, where the Congress was to be held. It was not Zinoviev, as it turned out, but Vittorio Codovila dressed to look like him; the same high leather boots, the same black-and-white checked trousers and cap, the same corduroy Russian blouse. There was an extraordinary physical resemblance between the two men, and Codovila childishly exploited it.

INITIATION

Soon after Haya's arrival I met Codovila. We greeted each other pleasantly and talked of the Congress, of the Latin American delegates and of the need to agree on a common policy. This led to discussion of the disagreements between Haya de la Torre and Mella. To my surprise Codovila expressed great dislike for his party comrade, whom he called, among other things, "a fatuous intellectual" and "an ambitious *petit bourgeois*," and seemed on the other hand very eager to meet Haya. "The great weakness in the antiimperialist movement," he said, "is this rivalry between its leaders. That's all it is with Haya and Mella, rivalry without principles. It's the same in Mexico and Brazil, and the Comintern doesn't like it."

"What do you think can be done about it?"

"I would suggest a division of Latin America into sectors. One for the Caribbean, one for the Bolivarian countries, a third for Chile, Argentina, Uruguay and Paraguay, and a fourth for Brazil."

"Shall I sound out opinion for you?" I asked. Codovila seemed delighted at my offer, so when next I saw Haya, I discussed the plan with him. He seemed unimpressed. But the next morning, as soon as the delegates had arrived at the meeting, he asked for the floor and proposed the division of Latin America into four sectors. Codovila, amazed and delighted, seconded the motion, while Mella glowered at them both, strongly suspecting collusion.

That night Haya unfolded to me his own plans for our participation in the Congress.

"This Congress, as you know," he said, "is not going to solve anything. There will be speeches and discussions and arguments in which each will try to win his own particular point. They will agree at last on a set of vague, incomprehensible resolutions that nobody will pay any attention to. It's only when an order comes from the Comintern that the communists hasten to create some inconsequential clamor."

"What should we do then?" I asked.

"What we must do is to make our movement—the *Alianza Popular Revolucionaria Americana*—talked about in this Congress."

"How?"

"If we vote with the rest of them, approve everything they suggest, no one will pay any attention. We shall simply be lost in the mass of delegates. On the other hand, if we oppose them a bit they will be forced to notice us, if only to criticize us. Don't you see?"

"Alcibiades cut off his dog's tail, too."

Haya laughed. "Your pamphlet defining our movement is not yet

23

in circulation. Even in America, no one is familiar with the abbreviation "APRA." If we appear now in an international Anti-Imperialist Congress, voting 'with exceptions' for the proposals of the other delegates, we shall stand out among them and draw attention to our movement. And since you like classical allusions, all right; we'll cut our dog's tail off to get ourselves talked about. Cheap propaganda, isn't it?"

So at every meeting, in spite of all Codovila's pressure, we voted for the resolutions "with exceptions." And thus we called attention to the *Alianza Popular Revolucionaria Americana*.

CHAPTER II

Paris

1

TO THE newly-arrived seeker after knowledge, the Sorbonne presents a disturbing variety of courses, lectures on philosophy and individual studies of each philosopher. In room A, Plato; in room C, Heraclitus of Ephesus; in the corner on the right, a lecture on the trial of Socrates; elsewhere, the theory of relativity, the tragedy of Baudelaire, the monetary crisis in China, the morality of Spinoza.

I attended many courses and met many people, among them three who became my friends—Peng Yu Lang, a Chinese student of philosophy; Jean, a French boy who was studying languages and exchanged his French for my Spanish; and Paulette, a kindly girl with disheveled hair and nails bitten down to the quick. She smoked without ceasing, anything at all, so long as it was tobacco. She was taking courses on literature and art, and her conversation seldom strayed far from Corot, Monet and Picasso.

My friend Jean made fun of Man and Humanity. "I am not," he would say, "a pure Frenchman. I must have Norman blood or an English ancestor. I am learning Spanish to use when I go to South America. Imagine! A whole continent that speaks one language! I am also learning how to give injections, to suture wounds, to stop hemorrhage and to treat the bites of serpents; as well as to solder pots and pans and to draw up accounts. Do you understand?"

"Yes, you want to make money in backward countries."

"You can put it that way if you like. But I'm not really so selfish. I shall be bringing the light of civilization with me too, you know."

My Chinese friend was wonderful. He was attracted by complexity and his special delight was to analyze human feelings, reactions and conduct. "All religions are good," he said, "if they console the believer and make him kinder to his fellow man." His favorite philosopher was Hegel.

"Are you a communist?" I asked him once. He looked at me a long time, then answered slowly:

"All that is demagoguery—a betrayal of good faith."

"Have you no political opinions?"

"They are my own," he replied. "Not those of any political party."

Paulette took me to art galleries and theatres. She adored Shakespeare and abominated Racine. In literature her gods were Stendhal, Balzac and Flaubert. Of the contemporaries, she advised me to read Romain Rolland, Henri Barbusse, André Malraux. Many days of happiness and hunger, contentment and misery we shared, Paulette and I, Peng and I. Peng was soon romantically in love with Paulette and said he owed his happiness to me.

One day he asked me, "Would you like to meet Barbusse?"

"You think I could?" I asked breathlessly.

"Next Tuesday he will receive a group of us—Chinese, Annamese, two Algerians and a Bulgarian. Would you care to go?"

"I've absolutely got to go. Tuesday, you say?"

"That's right—Tuesday. I'm sure Barbusse will delight you. He is a fine talker and a man of universal knowledge. He takes great interest in the social problems of faraway countries, and will wish you to tell him about your America. Here they know only the other one—the America of Henry Ford, of chewing gum, of Morgan and Woodrow Wilson."

I went through the next two days in great excitement. I re-read *Les Enchainements* and *La Lueur dans l'Abime,* and on the appointed day I was waiting for Peng long before the hour he had set. He brought with him another Chinese and, smiling as always, introduced us.

"Sia Ting, representative in Paris of the Kuomintang." I greeted him politely and then asked,

"Peng, are you a member of the Kuomintang?"

"I would have told you before," he smiled. "I am not a follower of Chiang Kai-shek, although Sia Ting is my friend."

"He never wished to join us," said Sia. "As you know, Peng thinks politics is all a fair of mountebanks."

"No, it is not that. It is rather that, like Romain Rolland, I prefer to remain *au dessus de la mêlée.* Science has no party; art has none; nor industrial skill, nor the great satisfactions of the spirit. The discoveries of Pasteur, Bach's *Mass in B Minor,* the Horses of

San Marco, the law of gravitation do not belong to any party. Why waste one's energies to get a party card?"

The fourth of our group arrived, a ruddy, handsome German who clicked his heels together when he was introduced, and we set off by the Metro to visit the great Barbusse.

The interview was magnificent. The writer was a stimulating talker. In all his conversation there was one theme: There was no way to realize Total Man, free of contradictions, except by revolution. "For vital necessity, for the human imperative, for very pity—rebel!" He showed great interest in my American experiences and was well versed in the facts of the Mexican revolution; he spoke familiarly of Madero, Carranza, Pancho Villa and Zapata. He told us that he would like to launch a magazine for the intellectuals of Latin America, which would carry the message of revolution, and above all further what he called "the revolution of the spirit."

The German pointed out that the Russians mocked at this sort of revolution. Barbusse looked at him sadly and answered:

"I believe in the immense power of the human spirit. All social change, all political movements take place first in the spirit of Man. There can be no freedom until there are free men. In these troubled times, my friends, the spirit is strong precisely because the flesh is weak; for only the spirit can rise above this weakness."

When we left, Peng was skeptical. "The spirit," he said, "has its own field and it is not that of the sour insurgence of the mob. The spirit comes afterward, to give nobility and meaning to these savage explosions. The spirit is over and above all this, like eternity over any episode."

"He seems an idealist, a subjectivist," said the German.

Sia Ting made no comment on the interview, invited us to have coffee with him in *La Rotonde,* and when we were done he paid the bill and left us.

I left soon after, returned to my room and went to sleep. In my dreams, Barbusse's sentence echoed and re-echoed: "For vital necessity, for the human imperative, for very pity—rebel!"

2

After the closing of the Anti-Imperialist Congress at Brussels, Haya de la Torre went back to Oxford, happy about what he called "the triumph of the theory of the four sectors." In one of his letters he told me confidentially that he had asked Moscow, through a secret channel, for support in carrying out the revolution in Peru and in America generally.

"I have sent a clear and comprehensive description of our movement and our plans to Alexander Lossovsky, a great friend of mine and one of the gods of the communist Olympus. Lossovsky has a real understanding of Latin American, and more especially of Peruvian, problems. He is a rabid anti-imperialist who sees clearly that the revolution cannot succeed without diminishing to some extent the power of the United States. Whereas Zinoviev sees England as the ultimate enemy, Lossovsky believes that sooner or later Russia will come into conflict with the United States, and that the best preparation for it is a careful organization, beginning now, of the revolutionary forces in Latin America, which he calls the back door to the northern empire. Lossovsky has great prestige in the highest circles of the Kremlin."

I was much surprised by Haya's action, since I knew that he was not a partisan of the Communist International and that he was completely unwilling to become a party member, or to submit to the directives of Codovila, Mella, Ghioldi and company. I was equally sure that none of them would ever take orders from him. Haya wanted a command of his own, where he could be in complete control, and would never, I was sure, submit to the discipline of the South American Bureau at Buenos Aires. So I waited with interest for news of Lossovsky's reaction. Three months later Haya wrote joyfully, saying that he had received an answer from Moscow.

"When I come to Paris we'll go over the letter together. There is a magnificent chance of understanding, and consequently of the support we need. Our friend poses a good many problems and imposes conditions that seem perhaps a trifle excessive, but I feel that he wishes to cooperate, that he is trying to clear up rather than emphasize our differences." He was enthusiastic and optimistic about his negotiations with Moscow and the world revolutionary movement.

Later, when he visited Paris, we went over the letter together several times. Lossovsky was cordial without any doubt. He stated firmly and clearly, but diplomatically, the fundamental disagreements. He pointed out that in the anti-imperialist struggle in colonial and semi-colonial countries, the communist party made alliances with other groups only with the understanding that the communists would have absolute freedom to organize and grow, unimpeded, toward an eventual coming-to-power. He was violently critical of the United States, and advised Haya to awaken the ambition of other powers and thus force the internationalization of the Panama Canal. He declared it essential, that what he called "the throat of Latin America" should not be left in the hands of Yankee imperialism but administered by various countries, of which Russia should, of course, be one. He also suggested that the country in which the anti-imperialist revolution succeeded should be the anti-imperialist *state* and that within its borders positions of various types should be established. It was not clear to me what he meant by this, but Haya said that it had no importance.

"What matters more than anything," he laughed, "is the insistence of Moscow on the rights of the communist party. What do they care for the aims of the parties they assist, as long as it aids their struggle against Yankee imperialism. We can offer precisely that. It is to their advantage to cooperate with me. Of course it is!" And he paced the floor, stirring up the dust from the many-colored carpet. "The essential, to quote Lenin, is the question of power. Power —power!" And he pointed his finger at me as if he were haranguing a crowd.

"But what will the Russians ask in exchange for their help?"

"They won't ask much. They will help us, so as to strike at the power of the United States. Just as Canning, with the prestige of the whole British Empire, fostered the independence of the Americas to weaken Spain, so Russia will help revolutionary movements in Latin America today to weaken the imperialism of the north at its most vital point. And in this struggle we, the Latin Americans, will be the winners."

He returned to Oxford, to await a further message from Lossovsky. Meanwhile, the group headed by Mariátegui in Peru pointed out the defects and discrepancies in the structure and slanting which Haya wished to give to the APRA, the *Alianza Popular Revolucionaria Americana*. These criticisms were endorsed by the exiled Peruvian groups in Mexico and other places. Haya was furious at this mention of defects. When he talked to me about it, on his next visit to Paris, he said:

"All your contrary friends will see. That lame Mariátegui will see how much he counts for as a Marxist leader." And he threw himself on the bed, clasping his hands together behind his head. "You'll see what Lossovsky will say. I'm waiting for his letter which Miss Anna must have brought, but the damned old woman hasn't even called me."

Miss Anna was a woman past forty. She had met Haya at

Pastor MacKay's school in Lima and had become his friend, before the battle at the university. Since then, she had been the protector of the young student, whom she treated always with kindly affection in spite of Haya's harsh and sometimes even churlish behaviour towards her. She was a great traveler and made many trips, in comfort but without luxury, to eastern Europe and the Near East.

"I am interested," she used to say, "in the study of the various *mores* of Jews in the countries where they are numerous. I have studied them in Turkey (where there are many Sephardim), in Poland, Bulgaria, and Rumania; and I am eager to study them in Russia." And so she went to Russia. She was later forced to leave by the Soviet police, possibly because they thought her a member of the American intelligence.

Miss Anna meant very little to Haya. Women did not play any sentimental role in his life. "Women," he would say, "distract us from great objectives. Even the best of them are anchors which delay our progress. Revolution demands asceticism and is the enemy of all sensuality."

"Love and sensuality are not the same thing," I said with irritation, for I knew the hypocrisy in all this fine talk. "A woman can be a great help in the struggles of life; there have been many such in the lives of great men."

Such arguments always ended in a show of the anger which rose in him at any opposition to his opinions. He always took refuge in mystical theories, which he defended insincerely, with anecdotes based on the practices of anchorites, or quotations from the philosophy of Emmanuel Kant.

When Miss Anna finally arrived she had no letter from Lossovsky. This enraged Haya against the patient, gentle little lady, who was resigned to his humiliating treatment. Whenever such scenes occurred Miss Anna scurried away silently and saw to the mending of Haya's wardrobe and the replenishment of his wallet.

This was another of my disillusions concerning Haya's character. As I got to know him better I discovered that ordinary morals, especially those concerning money, seemed to bother him hardly at all. He not only ignored them, he openly despised them, imposing his own criteria of property rights, loans and money matters in general. Once I offered some mild criticism of his conduct and suggested that it might hurt his prestige. He was instantly angry but soon calmed himself and answered almost jokingly: "Have you read Goethe?"

"I've read a great many of his works. Not all. Why?"

He laughed, pulled out a notebook and read:

"Extraordinary beings overflow beyond morality. They operate like basic physical forces, such as fire or water."

"What do you think of that?" he asked gaily. "Goethe says that. I don't know where, but he wrote it."

"And of course you are an extraordinary being? One who overflows beyond morality, like fire or a volcano?"

"And why not? Don't you think so?"

"I think that you possess extraordinary qualities, Victor Raul. You have great gifts; you can be a leader of the masses; you have a talent for creating powerful propaganda. But I don't think you are Nietzsche's superman, and I don't think you have the right to ignore morality, or create one to suit your own purposes."

"Create my own morals, no. That is not the point of the quotation. Lightning is neither moral nor immoral. The effects it produces, whatever they may be, are beyond morality; overflow it, as Goethe says. The ocean, a storm, an earthquake, any cosmic force is the same. And you must agree that geniuses, extraordinary men, are like expressions of cosmic forces among other men."

"Living in society," I answered, trying to match his light tone, "men must act in accordance with *mores* which have grown up during centuries of living together. Men are not lightning, nor storms, nor volcanoes. We are persons, individuals, living in an organized society and consequently ruled by social *mores*."

"I was only quoting Goethe," he said.

"You have done more than quote him. You have caught at his statement as if it were one of the commandments, created especially for the extraordinary Victor Raúl. More than that, you wish to impose all this on our political movement. And that frightens me. You are leading us along a height and you may dash us into the abyss."

"Caesar, Alexander, Michael Angelo, Bolivar, all did the same. Do you think they followed social *mores?*"

"And are you Alexander or Bolivar? Listen, Victor, why not be Raskolnikov and kill the old woman?"

"What old woman?"

"In Dostoevsky's novel—*Crime and Punishment*. Raskolnikov saw the moral problem as you do. And so he robs and murders an old woman. Then in an anguish of remorse he goes to the police and confesses."

"That stuff about remorse, confession, guilt, all fits in a novel but it has nothing to do with life. Or if it does, it's just one of those odd quirks in the Russian soul, or some phenomenon of Dostoevsky's epilepsy."

"Then you don't believe in remorse or guilt?"

"Certainly I do. Just as I believe in rickets or tuberculosis or any other mark of weakness."

"So, in the last analysis, morals are a weakness?"

"Revolution and morals have nothing to do with each other. In Mexico, Pancho Villa—," and he related some anecdotes of atrocities attributed to the Mexican leader. This was always his way of ending a discussion. Once he had ascertained the position of the other man, he was not interested in clarifying his own, preferring to leave it vague.

From this time onward, our political collaboration, as well as our friendship, slowly deteriorated. I began to wonder if a movement of any real worth could be led by such a man. I began to fear that behind his overpowering ambition lay only amorality, cynicism and a willingness to destroy any social principle or ideal that barred his path to personal power.

I wrote to Mariátegui of my doubts and begged him to use his influence on Haya; to try to make him see the dangers of a movement that "overflowed beyond morality." I did not, however, mention at this time my fears of his dictatorial methods and his arbitrary and violently defended whims. Mariátegui answered many weeks later, explaining in detail his political differences with Haya and saying that he had written him repeatedly about them but had received no answer. As time passed, I was plunged deeper and deeper into an agony of indecision. I was torn between my growing doubts concerning Haya and an unwillingness to assume the responsibility for a break with him. I was even tempted at times to abandon all political activity, to forget the sorrows of my people, and to set to work to create a quiet and peaceful life for myself.

3

Henri Barbusse announced the launching of a new magazine, *Monde*, which he was to direct. His call was addressed to the *avant garde* intellectuals, and to all free men, French and foreign. Peng and I were invited to contribute. On the day of the first official meeting to discuss the policies of *Monde*, I went to see Peng at his rooms on the Rue Pascal. We arranged to meet later at the offices of the new magazine.

Peng had been washing while we talked. He scrubbed at his face with a towel, then turned to me, still smiling, and said:

"With Barbusse directing it, *Monde* should be a magnificent magazine. But you never can tell. He is so very sick. Then too, each time I see him he seems more won over to the political ideas of communism."

"And you believe this harmful?"

"I am sure that it circumscribes him. Everything that limits the spirit of man imprisons a man. It leads him first to condescension, then to compromise and finally to dishonesty. Moreover—how shall I put it?—as a Chinese, an Asiatic, I do not care for the hegemony of Moscow. I am repelled by the Russian interference. I am attracted neither by tzarism nor bolshevism, and I do not care whether the Romanovs or Stalin's police run Russia."

"Stalin's police?" I said, displeased.

"How else would you put it? The Russian people have always fought stubbornly for freedom but they have never achieved any concrete liberties. Russia has always been under the control of a police, the best in the world. Russia never really changes. Yesterday it was under the tzars; today it is under the so-called dictatorship of the proletariat."

When I arrived at the magazine office some time later, Peng was not yet there, and no other close friend greeted me. Barbusse seemed busy. I felt quite out of things and a bit uncomfortable until Peng arrived with a Senegalese named Goblan. Then we joined the others and took part in the meeting.

The Germans were the most voluble, for they had before their eyes the danger that threatened Germany and the world. Miguel de Unamuno made a speech against Primo de Rivera, the then dictator of Spain, which was translated by the wife of Joaquin Maurin, the leader of the Catalonian communists. Romain Rolland, the author of *Jean Cristophe*, was there too, that brilliant man who proclaimed that he was *au dessus de la mêlée*. He was pious in manner and very charming. He resembled an El Greco portrait, the thin face, the grave eyes, the pointed beard. Illness had bent his back; he seemed even more hunched than Barbusse and his voice was hoarse, his speech slow.

The aims and the point of view of the weekly were agreed on. We all promised to collaborate in its publication, to get subscribers and to bring in news. Barbusse closed the meeting and the group dispersed. At last, Peng, Goblan and I were left alone with Barbusse, Rolland and Unamuno.

Barbusse came up to us. He recognized Goblan and greeted him warmly. He thanked us for attending and said, "What luck to have a Latin American!"

"Hispano-American would be better," said Unamuno, "for he speaks Spanish, not Latin." He greeted me, and spoke hopefully of the magazine. "I shall contribute to it," he said, "and you must see that it reaches Spanish America. My name will assure it a market." Don Miguel was not being vain; it was true that anything he signed would be read in Latin America.

I told Barbusse how eager I was to help in any way I could. I offered to translate, to bring in news, to help arrange for American distribution, to organize sales campaigns.

Later, while Barbusse conversed with the others Rolland devoted himself to me, asking about my occupations and interests.

"It is an interesting life," he said. "Very interesting. What a time to be young! What a fortunate generation, and especially in your countries! So early you must fight for the liberties of men, for the bread of others. It is a heroic vocation, my son. It is one that consumes energy, the future, life itself; but never lose it, my son, never lose it." He was silent for a moment, then added, "You have the forehead of the conqueror and the mouth of the vanquished." He said goodbye to the others, and then to me. He kissed me on both cheeks, as the French do, saying, "Mon enfant—mon pauvre enfant!"

On the following day I began cataloguing news and addresses, visiting libraries and the offices of Latin American newspapers, collecting information. I edited circulars advertising the magazine. I wrote letters asking for exchanges and establishing contacts. I set up the files, using the methods I had learned at Mayon Limited, which won Barbusse's admiration.

"Will you help organize our work on the Balkans?" he asked.

"I would like to, certainly; but I don't know the languages."

"You can put the materials in order for the translators and you can file everything on the Balkans published in French and English."

I agreed gladly. A few weeks later everything was neatly arranged. Barbusse was very pleased. One night he called me into his office and said:

"You must be paid. We can not let you do all this without some recompense." His cough was better that night and it was easier for him to talk than usual. He asked me to sit down and we conversed at length on the political situation in various South American countries. I told him of my work with Haya de la Torre, of the foundation of the APRA and of the correspondence between Haya and Lossovsky. He was extremely interested and questioned me in detail. As I was leaving he asked me to collect information on the situations in Rumania, Bulgaria and Macedonia which had led to the pogroms there. He was to speak at a meeting held to protest against these atrocities and would need an outline of the facts.

In gratitude for my efforts, he gave me much of his time and helped me with advice.

"When young men ask in which political camp they should pitch their tent—what do you say?" I asked, on one occasion.

He was silent for a moment, toying with a Caucasian dagger which he used for a paper cutter; then he answered:

"Every man, no matter what his age, must choose his own position, must find his path by the light of his own conscience, without regard for the opinions of others. But if you want my personal opinion, I am convinced that the only place where a man can fight honorably, the only place where he has a chance to accomplish something important, is within the ranks of the communist party."

"The communist party?" I repeated, as if surprised.

"Have I shocked you?" he asked. "But what else is there? Anarchy, my son, is nothing more than social onanism. It is a generous dream, yes—an ardent sentimentality enriched by a brilliant imagination. For this reason the Spaniards, a richly imaginative people, are anarchists." He paused as if fatigued. I remained silent. After a while he continued:

"Social democracy? Too many deals, too much political trading. Its progress might be called the march of capitulations. The social democrats have not been defeated for a long time. They capitulate before fighting and so avoid defeat. They betrayed Germany and the world when they voted for the war in 1914. This was their great capitulation, their final renunciation. After that, one could never trust them again, could never again hope for anything from them. Only the communist party is left, my son, as a hope, as a possibility, as a promise, as a creative force. This is my opinion, but you must choose for yourself. You must think for a long time before deciding. You must study. You must ponder."

There was a long silence. At last I rose to take my leave. He took my hand in his and I found it difficult to remain calm and smiling, for his hand burned with the hot fever that was consuming him. With the palm of his left hand he balanced the Caucasian dagger, point downward on the desk.

"I think you are right. Perhaps that is the only path. But I must think," I said.

"There is no other," he answered. "But you are right. You must think about it before deciding."

I put my briefcase under my arm and left the room. It was very cold outside. No doubt I felt it more because the room I had left had been so warm, but I think I shivered because I was distressed; because I was afraid.

4

Barbusse introduced me to various communist intellectuals and party leaders—Marcel Cachin and old Charles Rappoport, Duclos and Florimond, Bonté, Cogniot and those heroes of the *surrealist* movement who were sympathetic to communism. I was drawn into the activities of this group, which included lectures on the splendid accomplishments of the Soviet Union; talks with communists and sympathizers just back from Moscow; films and dances; and, from time to time, street demonstrations—against the execution of Sacco and Vanzetti, for example, with clashes in the Boulevard Strasbourg and barricades in the Porte Saint-Denis.

When I told Barbusse about these adventures, he assured me with a pleased smile that, for a young revolutionary, all this was as good an education as the Sorbonne or the School of Higher Economic Studies. On reading my report on the automobile workers' strike, he called me in and praised me before the others for the precision of my data and my wealth of information. He then gave the report to one of my co-workers, asking him to correct my French. When the others left, he detained me and asked, "How are things with you? Do you have enough to live on?"

I explained my situation, my increasing poverty and my fear for the future. He listened in silence and dismissed me, murmuring, "We'll see, we'll see."

The next month found me working in the offices of the *Internationale des Travailleurs de l'Enseignement,* an international organization of teachers that decided many questions of socialist and communist policy. I was assigned a monthly salary of a thousand francs. It was my duty to see to the publication of their Spanish periodical and mimeographed bulletins, as well as the correspondence with Spain and South America.

"We can not let you waste your stay in Paris worrying about money," Barbusse said when I thanked him. From that day, I was sure I wouldn't have to write the letter my former employer expected —the request for my return passage.

I began my work in this organization under the direction of Vernochet and Cogniot. Vernochet was grumpy and sharp-tongued, spruce, a lover of good food, typically French. Cogniot accused him of being "rightist." He, in turn, accused Cogniot of putting other interests ahead of those of France. He never gave a name to these "other interests" but, as Cogniot pointed out, he was referring to Moscow, to the Communist International. "He's president of a Worker's International," muttered Cogniot; "he, a rabid French nationalist, who in the depths of his soul hates all internationalism."

Mariátegui wrote me, underscoring his disagreement with Haya de la Torre. The group he led indorsed his stand, and a good many Peruvian exiles expressed themselves frankly against the position of Haya and in favor of widening the breach which Mariátegui was opening. Haya refused to discuss the matter. I felt myself lost and confused. There were times when I was tempted to abandon all political and social reform and devote myself to the inner workings of automobiles and radios, to writing short-stories and novels, or even newspaper articles on the goings-on of Latin American millionaires in Europe. Then I could go on being friends with Haya, Mariátegui and everybody else. I confessed all this to Barbusse, without reservation, as if I were talking to myself. At the same time I told him the whole story of the correspondence between Haya and Lossovsky.

Barbusse was at his desk, cutting the pages of a book with a long Armenian dagger. He had a mania for collecting rare and artistic daggers. "I will write to Lossovsky," he said, letting his words fall one by one. "I will ask him for a frank answer. I know he will give it to me." I had run to him for advice, and he in turn was asking for advice elsewhere. When I tried to leave he detained me.

"Man carries destiny within him," he said slowly, through stiff lips. His voice was thick; his face an unchanging, sad mask. "It is not a force outside him as the Greeks believed; we carry it in our entrails, in the essence of our being. It is in the liquid whch flows in our veins; in the paste which fills the hollows of our bones. It is something in the fibers of our nerves, my son, something in that substance which stirs embryo-like within our skulls."

He fell silent, his brilliant eyes glazed with tears. He folded his hands, weaving his fingers together, and leaned his elbows on the greenish crystal of his desk. His lips were pale and dry and his tongue, when he moistened them, seemed too red in contrast to the pallor of his face. "If you fail this destiny within you," he went on, "you betray yourself. The self-betrayed are endlessly, hopelessly self-tortured. You may gain many material advantages but, in the words of Scripture, you will lose your soul. There is no contentment possible, my son, except in following our inner destiny; happiness is had only by living in harmony with it."

I started to speak, but he stopped me with a gesture. "As an automobile mechanic," he continued, "as a best-selling novelist, as a business man of one sort or another you might make money. And then? You would have cars of the latest model, good food, fine wines, perfumed women. But this is not enough. You would come at last to the *taedium vitae*, to a great despair, to the agonizing certainty of knowing yourself wretched. My son, my son, no one can go forward trampling on his own entrails."

There was a long pause. I could think of nothing to say. I felt maddeningly, hopelessly confused. "You will write to Lossovsky soon?" I asked at last, for no reason except to say something.

"Yes, tomorrow," he answered. "We'll see what he says. We must hope. I have unlimited faith in *them*. They walk, like the three magi of old, guided by a star—the star of mankind's liberation. We must have faith in their work, in their great dream."

I wanted to end this interview; I felt I could endure no more. I got to my feet but Barbusse detained me a moment longer. "The one cause for which one can fight honorably today," he said with profound conviction, "is communism." He accompanied me to the door and parted with me affectionately.

After that interview I abandoned the idea of being an expert on automobiles or radios, and concentrated on that task of unification to which I had pledged myself to Haya. I believed that if we Peruvians could be unified, if all of us could be welded into one group, Haya would become our co-worker and would be kept from becoming a dictator.

The copious correspondence from America that arrived in Paris as a result of my efforts was sent on to London. Haya answered with a letter full of congratulations. "You are magnificent," he wrote. "Your suspicions and misgivings had made me doubt you, but I see that you are my best friend and my most loyal companion. You have achieved a success beyond my fondest hopes; it is a real plebiscite. The only one missing is Jorge Basadre, but it doesn't matter; perhaps he is reconciled with Leguía. You have done an admirable job."

The attitude of Haya's friends in Paris changed again. They dropped their contemptuous manner and became affable. One day one of them, profoundly displeased with what he called "orders and counter-orders," showed me an earlier letter from Haya in which he called me an ambitious anarchist; one who wanted to supplant him and occupy his place and—who knows—perhaps serve the hidden purposes of the dictator Leguía. In view of this, the letter continued, they must defend themselves from me, going as far if necessary as a thorough dressing-down.

I felt no surprise—Haya was like that. To oppose his tendencies we must forge a strong team, capable of forcing him into less autocratic ways. Some weeks later, Haya announced his departure for the United States. Before leaving, he gave a lecture at Oxford on "The Internationalization of the Panama Canal." He wrote me, telling of the clamorous applause with which it had been received; and then he left for America, optimistic, full of plans for the future. His letters from the United States were even more optimistic and told of triumphs even greater. I wrote to him pointing out that the responsibility for anything he did must fall on his own shoulders. He replied, "Like the matador in the bull-ring, I say, 'Let me alone—Everyone outside!' "

The activities of the Worker-Teachers' International increased. It became necessary to find a new assistant and so I came to know Joaquin Maurin. Maurin considered Haya a naive politician (with which I disagreed), and told me anecdotes of Haya's Russian stay; how he had addressed an assembly of peasants from Kostroma, pompously and at great length; of the way in which the translator Shapiro made him say things he had never said. "And at the end," Maurin said, shrieking with laughter, "he kissed an old woman, just as if he were running an election campaign in South America. It's the truth; he kissed her, just like that—an old woman delicately perfumed with the fragrance of goat. He kissed her and called her *batiushka,* just like a novel." Maurin told many of these anecdotes in the presence of Vernochet and Cogniot who disapproved, but agreed that Haya was a political adventurer.

In America, Haya did everything he could to gain the support of any and every group. His complete lack of discrimination was sometimes amusing but often shocking. He who had been the friend of China at Oxford was entertained in Mexico by an anti-Chinese organization. He tried to raise funds in the most diverse circles and took tortuous paths along which no man of conscience could follow him. His letters became insulting, aggressive. "Reality rules," he wrote, "and reality is here, not in the Louvre or the Luxembourg. It is not important to stand open-mouthed before the Victory of Samothrace or the paintings of Corot, but it is important to see here the vital processes of American reality. It is not the same thing to stare at that "Olympia" you are always raving about, as it is to find oneself here in the presence of the United Fruit Company, Huasteca Petroleum, Anaconda Copper. Your opinions are very literary, very well-expressed, very learned, but a fragment of reality seen through the slit in my window-blind is worth more than all the literature you send me from Paris."

One day a bundle arrived from Mexico; clippings from newspapers and magazines, handbills, manifestoes published and edited by the "National Party of Abancay," a party that never was on land or sea. It was an organization that had no existence outside Haya's imagination. The "National Party of Abancay," these documents announced, was backing the exiled Victor Raúl Haya de la Torre for President of Peru.

I pointed out to him that this was a pointless and ridiculous procedure, a crude and grotesque farce. Haya answered with a rosary of abuse for his opponents and with the classic threat of the Catholic Church; "I will expel them from my party—I'll throw them out like dogs—traitors—judases—turncoats—I don't want to hear anything more from them or about them." He went to Panama, and then, shortly thereafter, appeared suddenly in Hamburg, explaining that the Canal Zone authorities had shipped him off by force on the *Bremen*. As soon as I learned his address in Berlin, I wrote him a pleading letter begging him to try to resolve his disagreement with Mariátegui. I received, in reply, an angry epistle, "If you and your friends continue to criticize me because I will not conform to your impotent intellectualism, I'll throw you out of my party, or get out myself. Yes, I'll get out; I'll go off somewhere for a rest and write a book about all this. But when I get out I'll throw away what is left of Mariátegui; I'll take him by his stump and hurl him into his own filth. Let him be king there! Then you will become a royalist and you can cry (in French, because it is more elegant) 'Long live the King.' And I shall answer you with the cry of Monsieur Cambronne (also in French, if you like) 'M——!' "

40

That, clearly, was that. I wrote no more letters to Victor Raúl.

Mariátegui, meanwhile, announced that he and his group would not follow Haya; and so the Peruvian exiles, despite their small numbers, were divided into two opposing camps.

Barbusse received an answer from Lossovsky. One rainy afternoon, as he was getting into his car, he said to me: "Our friends over there have replied to my letter." He never showed me any letter, nor made any reference to having received one; whenever he spoke of the matter he gave the impression that the message had been brought verbally. The next day he summoned me to talk about it; when I arrived he offered me a chair, closed the door and sat down at his desk. "I think I must begin," he said, "by repeating what I've said to you before: the only cause for which one can fight honorably is communism. Nowhere will your actions reach further, or cover so wide a field, or reap so abundant a harvest as they will with the communist party." There was a long pause. He seemed so exhausted that I wondered if I should ask permission to leave. Then he continued. "In the communist party, and nowhere else today, you will find the modern counterpart of the faith of the medieval mystics, the self-sacrifice of the Christian martyrs, the fierce spirit of the Jacobins of the French Revolution. It is, my son, the most beautiful human creation of these disenchanted times. Only you can descend into the obscure and treacherous caverns of yourself. Ponder—analyze —and make up your mind." And all the time he was speaking I was thinking, "What has this to do with Lossovsky's answer or with the message from Moscow?" Barbusse rose, came around his desk and stood before me. "You are going to be left isolated," he prophesied. "You will succeed neither in controlling your friend Haya nor in unifying this group of men whose characters and ideas are separated by chasms so wide and deep that you can not bridge them. Or, if you succeed in building such a bridge, or a hundred such bridges—they will break, all of them will break. Only one thing can unite men and that is faith in the same idea. And in your group that faith is lacking."

He was interrupted by a fit of coughing. When he had recovered he went to the window and, standing with his back to me, he continued: "For my part, and in spite of every effort to think differently, I am convinced that your friend Haya regards politics, not as a mission, but as an adventure—or perhaps as a business, which is much worse. For when politics is not a high human mission, my son, it

41

becomes a jungle fight, a conclave of traders. And you," he said, turning back to me, "you can not be a part of that kind of politics."

"No," I answered, "I could not walk that path. And unification may be impossible—Haya is excessively vain."

"So much the worse then," exclaimed Barbusse. "For to be vain is to be eaten away by a destructive modesty. Great vanity is modesty which is ashamed of itself. The vain man is a dangerous man."

There was another pause; he turned back to the window and brushed aside the tulle drapery. He stood looking out, as if watching for someone, or as if waiting for an idea to come up to him from the street. At last he turned to me again. "You are caught in a spiritual shipwreck," he said; "soon you will reach your island and know yourself a castaway. And a castaway, my son, is easily swayed by impulse, by art, by love; by a passion for gambling, for sports, for long journeys."

"Or for collecting daggers," I interrupted.

"Yes," he said, regarding his display smilingly, "by a passion for collecting daggers. On the other hand, a man who was part of a group, a revolutionary thinker, might collect daggers because they are easier to bring together than men are." He became grave again. "I am sure you will not remain a castaway; you are not one who can live apart. The fact of being *you* will force you to join your destiny to that of others. Therefore you must choose, and soon, on which side of the barricade you will stand. It becomes constantly more important to decide this, for at this moment in history—if you are on the side of the people—you must unite with the working class, with the militant proletariat. This movement, this growing power of the working class is not local; it does not develop in any one country; it is a world-wide process. Therefore, if you are on the side of the people, if you are on the side of history, no matter how diverse and zig-zag the path you take, you will come at last to the Communist International— that mighty movement which, beyond doubt, opens a new epoch in the life of Humanity."

He crossed to the fireplace, leaned against the mantel and stood regarding the busts of Beethoven and Lenin that decorated the narrow shelf. For a long time he remained silent and motionless; he seemed to have forgotten me. The silence grew heavy, pressed in upon me, all but crushed me.

I got to my feet, and I thanked him. I wanted to ask if Lossovsky had answered and, if he had, what he had said. Barbusse noticed my agitation and smiled. "I know that the future can not be decided in a day; I know, too, that you feel trapped. For you, this is one of those moments when the soul is open to all the winds that blow. But such moments are soon over. Soon you will have to make up your mind; then we will talk again. Today—now—I can only promise you that if some day you come to the ranks of the International you will be received as more than a simple recruit."

"Thank you," I stammered, "many thanks. Such a promise, such trust can be answered only with a great loyalty."

"A clean and disinterested loyalty," said Barbusse, "but that need not and must not be disloyalty to yourself. Many will come to you claiming loyalty. Loyalty to a friend, to a group, to an organization. They are always the same. Men who have no faith will demand that you be loyal to a faith. Men who comprehend no doctrine will demand that you be loyal to a doctrine. Spiritual parasites who have never defended the smallest plot of ground will demand that you defend vast fields. Never become the tool of such men. Be loyal to humanity by being loyal to that fragment of humanity, yourself."

I went out into the street, troubled and confused, feeling myself alien to the throng that surrounded me, to the street, to the world. The words of Barbusse echoed and re-echoed inside my head. I reached my hotel room, locked myself in and mused. I made and unmade plans. Thinking that I might be better able to put my thoughts in order if they were visible, I sat down at my typewriter and wrote at length about everything that had happened to me. Then I wrote letters to José Carlos Mariátegui, to Haya de la Torre and to the exiles in Argentina. I was exhausted but much calmer when the stars faded and the morning sun poured through my window.

5

Mariátegui answered me, enclosing a copy of the last letter he had written to Haya de la Torre. He said he had resolved to break with Haya once and for all and would not participate in the organization of the *Alianza Popular Revolucionaria Americana*—the APRA.

At this time a second Anti-Imperialist Congress was assembling in Frankfurt on Main. As before, the German Communists were in charge of the organization and the slanting of the agenda. The responsibility for its direction was assigned to Willy Munzenberg who, notwithstanding his bitter struggle against the authority of Thaelmann, was at this time one of the outstanding figures of the International.

To this second Congress I went as a delegate, representing Mariátegui's group. Barbusse sent me off armed with letters of introduction, particularly a very warm one to Willy Munzenberg, in which he spoke of me most kindly. He asked the German organizer to extend me a warm welcome and, in any case, to grant me the protection due a good friend. Cogniot provided me with a special credential for the communists, in which he said, "He is more than a sympathizer; he is not *yet* a party member, but he is a valuable and sincere collaborator."

With these documents I set off for Germany under the blazing sun of July, 1929. In Frankfurt everything went on as it had in Brussels, except that Nicaragua took the center of the stage and the Cuban and Mexican communists were constantly in the spotlight, as were the Chinese and the Hindus.

The minute the last session of the Congress was over I left for Berlin. I wanted to speak with Haya de la Torre; moreover I wished to take part in the great anti-war demonstration that the German Communist Party was planning for the first of August.

I went to Haya's house in Berlin at the first opportunity. He had the maid ask my name and then sent her to tell me to return at five o'clock. The message made it clear to me that his attitude was far from cordial. Nonetheless, I decided to return.

A few minutes before five, I found him at the door of his house mauling a great dog. He wore light trousers and a military shirt, the same style as the national socialists' but of a different color. We greeted each other as if we had met the day before, without coolness but also without affection.

"Do you come from Frankfurt?" he asked, still stroking the dog.

"Yes, I wanted to come here to talk with you, and to hear about Berlin."

"And why do you wish to see me?" he asked, laughing and thrusting his fist into the dog's mouth.

"There is a pledge between us. Before canceling it, I think we ought to speak out clearly."

"I don't like to waste my time on useless matters," he answered, still smiling.

"I don't think it so useless. At the very least I think we should do it in the name of the old and loyal friendship I had for you, and of my labors in your behalf. Moreover, it is a matter of conscience."

"Ah, true! I had forgotten your scruples, your moral reservations, your remorse—the confession of Raskolnikov." He underlined his words with sarcastic laughter. "That pleases you, doesn't it?"

"No, none of those," I replied seriously. "I wish only an understanding between us. You have taken your path; I wish to take mine.

But I do not want to do so without talking to you and dissolving, if we must, our old association."

"You haven't changed a bit," he exclaimed, folding his arms and planting his feet wide apart. "The same volatility, the same critical spirit, which is the only thing you have learned from the French, or from your own mystical tendencies."

"I wish I could say the same of you," I said, "but that is not what brought me here. I wanted to talk to you about our people, our movement, our disagreements even."

"That all important theory of the cripple Mariátegui?" he asked flippantly. "Don't waste my time with bad jokes. This German experiment, new, young, endowed with a miraculous dynamism, is teaching us that a hierarchy is essential to any political movement. There must be the power to command, and submission of all to this command—to the authority of the leader."

"With a difference in shading," I said, "this is the same thing practiced by the Latin American dictators—Leguía, Machado, Gomez, Ubico, all the rest. Why make this long trip to Germany?"

"You don't understand what is happening in Germany," he declared. "Here is a new political conception taking shape. I am learning things about the organization of the masses which will be invaluable to me. Something is rising here, more vital, more valid than this decadent thing of yours, this 'reasoned and reasonable freedom of free men.' Have you seen any of the national socialist demonstrations?"

"No, I haven't. I've read the French reports of them; and I've seen the newsreels."

"That won't do," he said, "you must see them. You must understand the explosive enthusiasm of these young people. You can be a friend or an enemy of national socialism, but you can not fail to respond to this awakening of Germany's mighty soul."

"Perhaps, perhaps—but what of us, what of our differences?" I insisted. "Can't we try to bridge this gulf between us?"

"Do you think that would be possible?" he asked. His voice was quiet, casual but somehow frightening.

"A lot depends on you, Victor Raúl," I pleaded. "If you will only try to achieve unity on the basis of principles that we can respect, then you will be our leader once more, our respected and beloved leader for whom we were always ready to sacrifice. You have been ungrateful, Victor Raúl; you have forgotten everything that we did for you, everything that we are trying to do for our country!"

He was silent, apparently in deep thought. I persisted, "For my part I would do anything possible."

"I know, I know," he said gently. "You were always the one with the most good will. You were closest to me and certainly the one who helped me most."

He seemed more cordial. He took me into the living room of his apartment; a very light, spacious room with enormous windows overlooking the Charlottenburg. There were many photographs of handsome young men, all wearing the Nazi uniform.

"We'll have tea outside," he said. "Sit down while I change my clothes; then we can talk at our ease." And he went into the bedroom.

I sat down, noting everything.

"The social democrats are done," he announced to me from the bedroom. "That's what people outside Germany fail to see. The social democrats are still thinking in terms of trade-union machinery. They are expecting a great general strike against the rise of national socialism—false gods—gods of clay!"

"Do you think the Nazis will come to power?" I asked.

"They have it already," he answered enthusiastically, "or, at least, it is within their reach. No one has any idea to what extent the Catholics and the Populists are going over to them, the Stahlhelm and the Socialists and the communists."

He emerged from the bedroom fastening his collar, his shirt tails out.

"Even the communists are going over?" I asked, horrified.

He laughed uproariously, contagiously, as he did when really delighted.

"Thousands of them," he shouted, "thousands!"

"The French press says nothing of this, though I've heard Barbusse express fear of it."

"Obviously Barbusse is a communist. He must be well informed and he knows where the shoe pinches. Are you working with him?" he asked.

"Yes, on a few things. A collaboration."

He finished dressing and we went out. Haya was faultlessly attired. He glanced at my suit, dark and too heavy for that heat, my wrinkled shirt.

"You always dress like a Frenchman," he sneered. "The French are amazing—the greatest creators of costumes for smart women, and the worst taste possible in their own clothes. How amusing."

In the café he was most cordial. He assured me that in Central

46

America all the common people were *apristas* (members of the
APRA), especially in Costa Rica. He spoke of his triumphs in Mexico,
in the United States and in the Caribbean. I didn't believe a word of
it. I let him talk.

We went together, that night at Haya's suggestion, to a great Nazi
meeting. He was so emotionally exalted by it that I was frightened. As
we walked back to his apartment, I asked:

"Have you turned Nazi then?"

"No," he answered, his voice calm, "but they have learned something that we haven't; something we should take advantage of. Can't
you imagine all this pomp, these trappings, these forests of flags, in a
political demonstration in Lima? You saw that crowd go mad tonight.
They didn't think about what was being said, or reason about what
was being proposed. They were persuaded by pure theatre. And if a
German crowd is like that, imagine what a crowd in Lima would be!
Our poor people who wait hours and hours to see the castle lighted
with fireworks!"

"But surely not everything can be reduced to that," I objected.

"And why not? The public must be treated like a child. Give it
toys—parades, demonstrations, marching men, bands, fireworks. The
important thing in this comedy is that each man feels himself a member of the cast, not just a spectator. Each poor devil must feel that
he is somebody; each unfortunate is an actor; each individual, lost
in the mass, is a hero on a lighted stage. The rest doesn't matter, man.
Don't worry about the ideas, the programs, the systems. Idle con-
ceits! Topics for ideologists, or in other words, those who will never
do anything."

He hailed a taxi, gave his address and whispered to me, "Be
careful; one must always be on guard!"

"I'm sorry for you when you talk that way," I said, paying no
attention to his warning.

"And I'm sorry for you. You, with your romantic determination
to reform people, to change their lives by improving their lot. Folly,
man, sentimental folly! The worst sort of folly because it puts absurd
illusions in people's heads. Aristotle was right. Some are born to rule
and others to obey."

"And you were born to rule and we were born to obey you? Our
mission is to satisfy your whims and applaud our little tyrant, no?"
I asked, laughing.

Victor Raul gave a great guffaw and exclaimed, "There is no

hope for you, you are beyond redemption, you will always be the same. You see what is happening here in Germany and you still dream of *Fraternité, liberté, and égalité.* How amusing, how very amusing."

I noticed that he stammered slightly, as if he were a bit drunk. Knowing that he was not used to liquor, I asked him if he were sick.

"Yes, I'm sick! Sick of the lot of you! I've already told Heyssen so. Hasn't he written you? I told him to. The movement I am organizing is based on the model you have just seen: the leadership of a hierarchy, a lifelong and unbreakable leadership, undisputed and indisputable. Exemplary penalties and punishments, within the party and without it; and violence, violence without scruple, for any adversary. Bludgeon, pistol, dagger, machine gun—what have you. And when these weapons can not be used, then strike at the enemy's pocketbook, at his wife, at his son, at his daughter; strike at his most vital parts, at his head, at his belly."

I didn't answer; he had worked himself up to the point where there was nothing to do but let him talk.

"I won't permit you people to manipulate me," he continued. "Neither you nor the cripple Mariátegui, nor any of you. It is I, I and no one else, who will make the movement; it will be formed around me, my name, my person, and I will do what seems best to me, without consulting anyone, neither the lame nor the handless, neither professors nor illiterates. And if I find you people in my way, playing little games of opposition—well, I'll not only run over you, but I'll grind you into powder, I'll tread you underfoot—so! so! so!" and he beat his heels against the floor of the car. The chauffeur slowed the taxi and asked if he should stop. Haya told him to go on.

I started to speak but he would not let me. "I'm through with all of you. If you've come to find out—well, now you know. The lesson has cost you a few marks but it is clear. Now you know. I want nothing to do with any of you. Write that to your friend Mariátegui; write it to the Mexicans; write it to all of them. Let them go to Hell! Now I have power behind me and you people signify nothing—absolutely nothing. One thing more! Be careful not to get in my way. Be careful!"

"Are you trying to frighten us?" I laughed.

"Frighten you? No. But don't take it as a joke. If you get in my way, a bullet will get you out of it. Do you understand?"

"I knew you had gone over to the National Socialists," I said, "but I didn't know that you hoped to outdo them in terrorism, in homicidal mania. I see you are an apt student."

Again he warned me that the chauffeur might hear. Then he continued: "I face reality. The movement I organize will be completely realistic. There will be no foolish scruples. There will be violence and there will be terror. He who does not bow down will be shot down. There will be one path, only one path to follow. There will be what you see now in Germany, a movement as violent as a natural force."

"There will be nothing to do," I said, "except oppose you."

"Who?" he mocked. "You? You oppose me? The toad who wants to be an elephant?"

"How you have changed, Victor Raúl," I said.

"You think so?"

"No, perhaps you haven't," I answered, calm again. "Perhaps you were always like this. Only now I realize what you are, and of what you are capable. We might have organized a vast and lasting movement whose action would have ennobled the whole life of our poor country. And now we will waste ourselves in a bloody struggle—a struggle that will accomplish nothing."

The taxi stopped in front of his house. We got out and he paid the driver. Then he turned to me saying, "Struggle? What struggle, man? Who is capable of opposing me? None of you, and you least of all."

I would not accept his challenge. "Think of all you can accomplish if you choose," I pleaded. He laughed. I stood silent; there was nothing more to say.

"Well," he said quietly, "this will be the last time that we will clasp hands. All political collaboration between us is at an end. Each must take his own path. You are the one who has divided us," he added. "I can not take your path and you have chosen not to follow mine."

We separated and I set out to walk off my grief, sure now of the future. Haya de la Torre would plunge Peru into material disaster and a moral breakdown. This was now quite clear.

As I walked away, he threw open a window and leaned out. "They'll shoot you down if you get in the way," he yelled. "They'll kill you like a dog."

I wandered like a sleepwalker among the gardens and groves of the Charlottenburg.

6

After this last interview with Haya, there was nothing to keep me in Berlin except my wish to take part in the German Communist

Party's anti-war demonstration. The Latin Americans from the Frankfurt Congress who were now in Berlin resolved to participate as a group, and march under a banner proclaiming the progress of the anti-imperialist leagues in their several countries.

Early in the morning on the first of August, the working-class quarters of Berlin hummed with activity. Crowds of laborers arrived on every train and on all the roads. Everywhere the youths of the Red Front, uniformed and armed, flaunted their pistols and daggers, their kepis and boots. They were as young, as strong, as enthusiastic, as numerous as the Nazi Storm Troops. The parade began, a series of compact groups preceded by forests of flags; and as it unrolled along the spacious avenue, toward the Lustgarten, a sky-shaking clamor swept over the city.

No, no, the Nazis would not come to power. These hundreds and thousands would prevent it. The Nazis must know this, must realize that any attempt, on their part, to gain control of Germany would be the signal for a civil war they could not hope to win. This was the unanimous opinion of all I spoke with that day; of the Latin Americans, of the Spanish-speaking German communists, of all those with whom I conversed in French or through interpreters.

German policemen, armed with pistols and white cudgels, marched in Indian-file on each side of the demonstrators. We, the delegates of the anti-imperialist leagues of Latin America, marched in a hollow square with our poster carried before us. They gave us as companions some Algerians and some Negroes from various French possessions, and from South Africa. I marched arm in arm with Barbusse's Senegalese friend, Goblan.

Heat rose from the asphalt as from a furnace; it radiated from the sweating bodies of the demonstrators; it fell diagonally from an almost tropical sun. The howls of the crowd hammered against my temples. There was speech after speech, and then suddenly the demonstration was over. The public fervor faded. The great mass of human bodies broke into many pieces, slowly dissolved like an iceberg that had entered tropic seas. Groups of people drifted off down various streets. We lowered our posters, furled our banners and waited for the crowd to clear away. Suddenly a platoon of policemen appeared on the corner. There was a confused outcry through which I could hear the officer in charge saying something, apparently ordering some paper read. The cries increased,

"Down with war!"

"Red Front! Red Front!"

The number of policemen increased; they mingled with the demonstrators. Then at a signal from their officer they began to swing their bludgeons. They fired a few shots and the fight became general; a moment later a "schupo's" cudgel caught me across the jaw. A sharp pain stabbed through my head. I tasted blood and everything went black. I no longer heard the cries.

When I tried to open my eyes, one of them remained closed. The lid felt as if it were glued down. My open eye saw electric light and the Negro, Goblan, watching me, half-sad, half-smiling. I tried to speak to him but pain drowned my voice. My tongue had swollen to four times its normal size, filling my mouth and choking me. The side of my head where the blow had fallen throbbed painfully; it was so swollen that I could not open one eye and could hardly open my mouth. My neck, my throat, my shoulder ached; and across the other side of my head, my other arm and shoulder, the length of my body, spread a livid, burning bruise. Goblan came to the side of the bed, put out his hand as if to touch me, and then thought better of it. "Rest quietly, comrade," he said. "They beat you up pretty badly."

On the third day I was better. My tongue was still swollen and injured, but I had been treated by a doctor and the pain was less. I could not speak but Goblan read the messages I scribbled on a pad.

"Where am I?" I wrote.

"Don't worry. In the house of a teacher, a comrade, an excellent man. He was the first we found after the "schupo" knocked you down. He hit you pretty hard, didn't he?" I nodded.

"Willy Munzenberg has been looking everywhere for you," said Goblan. "He got a letter from Barbusse and sent to find you. We have told him that you are here."

That same afternonon, Munzenberg and another doctor came. They dressed me and took me to the hospital for an x-ray. "There's nothing, nothing," Goblan told me happily. "You have no fracture."

"What we must do," laughed Munzenberg, "is repair the pavement where your head hit it."

I returned to the house where I had been staying and remained there until my wounds healed. I ate only ground meat and soups which my hosts prepared for me.

One morning Munzenberg telephoned:

"Have you a passport with you?"

"Yes."

"I'll send for it. Give it to the messenger who brings an order signed by me."

"All right, certainly, but——"

"No buts! I have a surprise for Barbusse. Don't anticipate it. Just send me the passport."

Two days later, Munzenberg came to the teacher's house and took Goblan and me away with him in his car. He introduced me to one Neumann, who spoke perfect Spanish. We went to a fashionable restaurant near the center of town. Neumann ordered a meal of *purées* and ground meats for me. We had an excellent red wine and a magnificent Rhine wine. At the end of the meal Munzenberg said, laughing: "Your friend Barbusse will be perplexed. He likes you very much, doesn't he?"

"Yes," I answered. "He has been very kind to me."

"His letter of introduction is a beautiful tribute," said Munzenberg. "He is a fine man."

Neumann spoke of Barbusse's work and of its three stages: The first, that of "Hell," with its crude realism and French sensuality; the second, that of "The Splendor over the Abyss," disenchanted, harsh, its accent that of a voice crying in the wilderness; the third, that of the message of the new faith, the heralding of a new world's advent.

The conversation was interesting, but I was curious to know what it was that was going to puzzle Barbusse. "Why do you say that Barbusse is going to be perplexed?" I asked, taking advantage of one of Neumann's brief pauses.

"Because you leave tomorrow," replied Munzenberg.

"For Paris?" I asked.

"No, comrade, for Moscow!"

My mouth dropped open and I sat motionless, staring at Munzenberg. Neumann laughed. Munzenberg watched me, half-mocking, half-triumphant, as if he wished to share what I must be feeling at that moment. Goblan applauded.

Munzenberg gave me my passport; it contained a transit visa for Poland. A page had been inserted on which was stamped, in Russian characters, the Soviet visa and permission to enter the Union of Socialist Republics. I felt as if I were bound to my chair. I could not even thank Munzenberg.

That was a night to remember; a night of rebirth. Happiness poured over my soul like a miraculous cataract. Goblan was as happy, as excited, as I was. We were to make the trip to Moscow together. We laughed, we drank, we sang:

PARIS

Arise ye prisoners of starvation,
Arise ye wretched of the earth!

Two days later we were on a train crossing Germany on the way to Poland and the frontier of the socialist Homeland. At last we were to see the country in which was forging the future of all mankind.

The river Oder lay behind us and the next day we crossed the Vistula. We passed through Warsaw, through Baranowicze, through Stolpce. Then, as sunset blazed in the sky above the immense plain, we arrived at the frontier that separated two worlds. I leaned out of the window, my breath catching in my throat. There was the wooden arch on which was carved the crossed hammer and sickle, and the phrase: "Workers of the world, unite!"

We were at Negoreloye. Here was the Promised Land.

CHAPTER III

The Holy City of Socialism

1

WHEN the leaders of the Crusades stood at last before the Holy Sepulchre they must have been shaken by an emotion which rose from the depths of conscience and instinct. Standing there on what seemed to them holy ground, they must have felt the breath of life itself, rising about them from the earth, from the trees, from the men, from the very roads. This was the emotion that I felt, the emotion that, from their confessions, hundreds of fervent communists have felt, on arriving at the frontier of the Union of Soviet Socialist Republics.

We changed trains and progressed a short way across the steppe. The train stopped at a platform on which were four or five soldiers of the Red Army.

The station was an enormous, wooden, barracks-like building. It was clean; on the walls were posters proclaiming in dozens of languages "Workers of the world, unite!" and pictures of Marx, Engels, Lenin and Stalin. There were little windows for changing money. There were crowds of people coming and going in every direction.

I changed ten marks and received close to eight rubles and a few kopeks. I then went to a restaurant and ordered tea and something to eat. They brought me two slices of bread, one slice of what looked like pressed fish, tea and one lump of sugar. When I came to pay, the price startled me. This meal cost more than twelve rubles; that is, more than fifteen German marks, the equivalent of ten or twelve meals in France, including wine.

On the train that evening, the travellers who spoke French and Spanish got together. It was as if each of us lifted the mask he had worn during the first part of the journey. A young Argentine communist (who was later secretary to Guralsky, the Russian director of the Comintern's South American Bureau in Buenos Aires), boastful, dogmatic and self-satisfied, talked of nothing but himself and always appreciatively. Karracik, a Brazilian communist, knew everything and

54

gave immediate and detailed explanations for everything we saw, everything that happened. According to him, the exorbitant price of things was due to a deliberate intention of the Russian government to clean out the pockets of the foreigners who came to Russia. The Mexican poet Litz Arzubide, a gay, demanding scoffer, was an incisive critic of this new society. A Canadian woman comrade was with us, perhaps in her thirties though her enormous size made her look well past forty. She had green eyes, a very pink face and tiny feet which contrasted oddly with her exaggeratedly thick legs. A tall skinny man who had said that he was a fur merchant from Vancouver turned out to be a communist delegate, too intimate by far with the Canadian woman.

Through the northern night the train wandered toward Minsk. In each of us arose a contagious enthusiasm, a gaiety with which we infected one another. We talked and laughed; some slept for awhile. Then we arrived at Minsk—a poor station, a poor city, poor houses. There arose from it a miasma of misery, compounded of poverty, fear, obstinacy and insolence. Vagabond children from three to twenty, swarmed over the train in search of an open window. If they found one, or managed to break a pane, they flung themselves into the car like cats and tore from the interior everything they could lay hands on. The train guards warned us to keep the windows shut and to leave nothing near them. It was the plague of the *bezprizhorni,* the wolf-packs, a product of the revolution.

Karracik explained that these children were orphans; that, lacking parents, they dedicated themselves to pillage. And that in a socialist state it was impossible to imprison or prosecute or maltreat such children; they must be won by kindness and persuasion. Though we laughed at this theory of his, we believed him in part. The presence of these waifs angered and distressed the poet Litz Arzubide and seemed to him a flaw in the revolution, a stigma on the socialist motherland.

The next day we reached Moscow. We saw the star of the Kremlin, the gilded domes of the Church of the Saviour, soon to be demolished; then the suburbs, the filthy streets, the Alexander station. Here at last was the sacred city of world revolution.

We alighted and went into the station as a group. Two men appeared from somewhere, grabbed our luggage and carried it to an antiquated car with wide fenders and high running-boards, a car like those undertakers provide. It must have been an elegant limousine in the days of the October Revolution. We settled ourselves in it and our guide said to the chauffeur:

"Ozhod-Niriat—*Komintern*."

This great word, pronounced in Moscow, by a Russian, seemed something in a dream. We were on our way to the very heart of the revolution of the proletariat. We passed down Tverskaya Street, then turned toward Ozhod-Niriat. The car stopped at an enormous, old house with absurdly small doors and a strong smell of rosin. We were given a cordial welcome. Astrogildo Pereyra, communist leader of Brazil was there; Humbert Droz, Lenin's friend, who was said to have studied theology in Switzerland before the Russian revolution changed the course of his life; Stirner, the official translator from Russian to Spanish, a Swiss who would never use his real name and was a devoted friend of Haya de la Torre. We were later joined by Alexander Lossovsky, broad-shouldered and bearded, extremely cordial. Still later Ricardo Martínez arrived (a Venezuelan who whined and screamed rather than spoke) representing the Venezuelan labor unions, which existed only in the minds of Vittorio Codovila and the humbug representations of Martínez. They served us tea, fish, ham, bread and a few lumps of sugar, the scarcity of which was notorious. The meal was sprinkled with questions and answers about Latin America.

During the days that followed, the situation in various countries was discussed. We began with Peru and Bolivia where there were no communist parties. Humbert Droz possessed a wide and deep knowledge of these regions. He declared that he had never been there, but his information was so extensive that I did not believe him. Droz was a suave, gentle man, anxious to hear the opinions of others; it was a real pleasure to discuss things with him, to exchange ideas and even to differ with him. He always sought for the truly important, for what was beyond opinion. He had vision and a passion for teaching.

Ricardo Martínez, the Venezuelan representative to the Profintern, was a man who had reached his position by fraud. He was an uncontrollable charlatan. He spoke affectedly and very solemnly. His conversation and his speeches were unbearably self-righteous. He quibbled about details but had no precision in his ideas, no definite knowledge about anything. He gestured extravagantly and everything he said was plastered over with Comintern terms and rude words. He was continually saying that one must go to the devil, that capitalism was going to the devil, that it was obligatory to let oneself be carried away by the devil. One day, irritated by all this, I asked, "Do you believe in the devil?"

"To the devil, my boy, is a saying. But how amusing you are, my boy; you caught me out, the devil take you. But that doesn't mean I believe in the devil."

The presence of this faker in Moscow, as a functionary of the Red Syndicalist International, had murky origins and involved a bloody drama. Julio Portocarrero and Armando Bazan (who had been in Moscow at the time, sent by Mariátegui as representatives of the Peruvian unions) told me about the events which had preceded Martínez's rise to his present position, and which had, at the same time, brought about the tragic death of Julio Antonio Mella, the Cuban communist leader.

When the anti-imperialist congress of Brussels closed, Mella went to Moscow. Both Cubans and Mexicans thought that he was in serious danger if he returned to America. His friends were desperate, sure that if he returned, the dictator Machado would have him killed. They were determined that he should stay in Moscow. At this time, Alexander Lossovsky, supreme leader of the Red Syndicalist International, asked the Latin Americans to designate someone to stay in Moscow to work with him and with the organization, taking charge of labor union affairs in Latin America. Mella's friends nominated him for this position.

Vittorio Codovila, who was also in Moscow on this occasion, determined to prevent Mella's election. He knew Mella to be intelligent and energetic, and undoubtedly feared that if he remained in Moscow he would gain the sympathy and good-will of the gods of the communist Olympus and become one of the great figures of Latin American communism.

When the Cubans proposed Mella's candidacy, Lossovsky said: "If the South Americans choose him, I shall be delighted to work with the boy. He knows, and so does everyone else, the liking I have for him. Make up your minds. Decide what seems best to you."

Codovila began his campaign to prevent Mella from remaining in Moscow. He attacked the candidacy, quarreled with the comrades who defended it, launched all sorts of accusations and attacks against Mella. Codovila intrigued and lied. At last he made a house-to-house canvass of the Latin American delegates and discovered that the majority would vote for Mella and against some Uruguayan whom he himself supported. Codovila's opponents accused him of favoring the La Plata region as against the Caribbean, and as this was not for him the root of the matter, he immediately abandoned the candidacy of the Uruguayan in favor of that of the Venezuelan, Ricardo Martinez.

At their first meeting to consider the matter of the appointment, the delegates were strengthened in their support of Mella by the remarks of Portocarrero and Bazan—witty speeches which shot Codovila's arguments full of holes. Codovila, however, maneuvered a close of the session before a vote could be taken.

Codovila was not one to accept the decision of the majority if it ran counter to his own ideas. Realizing that he could not win enough of the votes to gain his ends, he resorted to another maneuver. He told those whose votes he could count on, that the next meeting would begin at a certain time; those who were more or less indifferent were told that it would begin a quarter of an hour later; those who supported Mella were told to come half an hour after that. Thus, by the time these latter arrived, the vote had been taken and Martínez named as Latin American representative to the Red Syndicalist International. The delegates who arrived late were accused of not taking their work seriously enough to be punctual.

Codovila laughed at his success and made complicated jokes about the magnificent funeral which we must immediately prepare for Mella, so that it would be ready in time for his death. Martínez remained in Moscow, a monument to the trickery of Codovila. Mella went to Mexico to die at the hands of Machado's gunmen.

Such was the foundation of Martínez's position in Moscow. Everybody knew about this treacherous intrigue; everybody knew that he was a blood-stained incompetent, representing nobody. When his interference in our discussions of Peruvian and Bolivian affairs became unbearable, there were allusions, in his presence, to Mella and to the tragic lack of labor unions in Venezuela. After this, his long and empty interruptions became fewer.

Humbert Droz, in contrast to Codovila, was a sincere admirer of Mariátegui, though he was opposed to Mariátegui's theory of the organization of a socialist party with a secret communist fraction at its core.

"I don't believe in subterfuges," he declared. "If a socialist party is organized with a secret inner core of communists, it will end by one of them absorbing the other. The party will become communist, with our group triumphing, in which case we shall have lost time; or the party will become socialist and the communists will be absorbed, expelled or executed."

Lossovsky approved of this statement.

"Let us begin," suggested Humbert Droz, "by composing a detailed political statement to be sent by the International to the workers of your country. It will be a kind of open letter to be distributed on as wide a scale as possible. You yourself can help circulate it."

While we were composing this letter, Humbert Droz mentioned Haya de la Torre and the APRA. "I do not believe," said Lossovsky, "that this alliance of our friend Haya is effectively revolutionary nor particularly popular nor in any way American. But while I do not believe that he will be able to organize an effective political party, I do believe that he will create a very important movement. He is brave, ambitious, stubborn. What is more important, there is in his country, at this time, no organized political party. His alliance, therefore, will answer a need and when one supplies something that people lack, one is successful. No doubt about it."

"Haya," I observed, "is at the moment very devoted to the German national socialists."

"Naturally," Lossovsky assented, "but when he comes in contact with the Peruvian reality he will change. Fascism is impossible in backward countries. Peru, for example, could not support the elaborate machinery, economic, political and social, necessary to a fascist regime. It may be possible later to get along with him. We must not discard him."

"He is too fond of terrorist methods," I objected.

"Terrorist?" Lossovsky asked, surprised. "Why? It would be stupid to use such methods since there is no need for them. If he will work, and if he knows how to wait, power will come to him as naturally as ripe fruit falls from a tree."

"I do not believe he thinks so."

"Then he is less intelligent than I thought," said Lossovsky with a shrug.

Humbert Droz drew us back to the task of preparing the statement to the Latin American workers, and discussed the organization of communist parties in those countries where there were none. Lossovsky argued for their necessity with evident desire to convince.

"The march of world revolution," he declared, "demands the existence of communist parties in all these countries. He who serves the revolution, he who works for his peoples' freedom, he who wants to raise his countrymen's standard of living, must help create the only means to these ends, the communist party."

"Throughout the world, at this moment," he continued, stroking his beard, "a great danger for all humanity is arising. Fascism. Don't you see it; don't you feel it? Yet in the world today nobody wants to fight against fascism, only against communism. And isn't this a most important reason for being a militant communist, to be part of the vanguard against the greatest danger which has menaced humanity in all history? Or am I wrong?"

"You are not wrong."

Vasiliev, Bela Kun chief of the Hungarian party, Astrogildo Pereyra and Anetka, Bukharin's secretary, joined us. They read and approved our work. The Communist International would send out our open letter. As the discussion was ending Zinoviev entered. We all stood up to greet him and Droz gave him a resumé of what we had been talking about, and of the agreement we had reached.

"Are you the comrade who asked for this discussion?" he asked me.

"Yes, comrade Zinoviev."

"Good. But what seems to me essential in these matters is the question of men. Who are the men who are going to carry out the resolutions adopted here? Without them, these resolutions will be nothing but a scrap of paper. Have you thought of that?"

"Of course we have," answered Droz. "In Peru, Mariátegui and his group are very close to us; and now we have our comrade here who has come with the recommendation of Henri Barbusse."

"The comrade has come to visit the Soviet Union," said Zinoviev, "to talk with us, to compare his opinions with ours. But that doesn't mean that the resolution we adopt here will be carried out. It seems to me we must face this fact."

"I beg permission to interrupt," I said, with a tightening of my throat. "I would like to amplify the statement of comrade Zinoviev. I have come, as he says, to visit the Soviet Union, to compare my opinions with yours, but I have come also to join the ranks of the International and to work for it."

Zinoviev applauded, Lossovsky followed, then all the others. "You intend, then, to return to your country; to work there to collaborate with Mariátegui and the others in the founding of a communist party?"

"Yes, comrade, I am determined to do this," I replied with conviction.

"Excellent, excellent," said Zinoviev, "But think it over, ponder it, count the cost. Don't forget that in your country the government has spies and police, rifles and machine-guns. You must stop and think of all these things."

"I am prepared to return to my country and work in the organization of the Communist Party," I repeated. All were silent. Zinoviev signaled to Droz, who brought the meeting to a close. Then Zinoviev called me to him and embraced me effusively.

"Very good, my boy, very good. You have taken a great step."

Lossovsky embraced me too, scraping my cheek with his whiskers. He slapped my back and said, "Barbusse was right. I knew he was right."

Bela Kun, Droz and the others also embraced me as if I were an old friend. When I went to say goodbye, Zinoviev spoke to Lossovsky in Russian, then invited me to dinner. "You will enjoy meeting some Russian friends," he said.

A quarter of an hour later we were on our way to the country house in the suburbs of Moscow, where Zinoviev was staying. Droz sat next to the chauffeur, and in the back seat were Zinoviev, Lossovsky and I. Zinoviev spoke of the obstacles in the way of Russia's economic recovery and of the struggle against poverty, and discussed with Lossovsky and Droz what he called, "the heritage of the past." Later they talked of my stay in Russia and agreed that while the leaders of the International discussed the wording of the open letter, a trip should be arranged for the Latin American delegation to the southern part of Russia, the Crimea, the Sea of Baku and the Volga region. Humbert Droz was appointed to organize the trip as soon as possible.

It was getting late when we arrived at the country house. It was a *dacha*, simple, comfortable, surrounded by gardens and groves. There were a great many people there when we arrived, and after the commotion caused by the arrival of Zinoviev and Lossovsky had died down, I was introduced with very complimentary speeches from both.

"Comrade Bukharin, author of *The A B C of Communism*, you know him, don't you? Comrade Radek; comrade Tomsky of the labor unions; comrade Rykov and comrade Kamenev." My knees trembled. My eyes went from face to face; I did not know what to think or what to say. This was too much for me. A week ago, two days ago, I would not have dreamed of meeting these men.

Ham, cheese, various sorts of bread, great bowls of fish and butter were brought in; then vodka. In spite of their urging I could not eat. Everyone asked questions and tried to make conversation (all except Tomsky and Kamenev spoke French), but I could only answer in monosyllables. Radek took a glass and said he would teach me to drink vodka. "This drink is not sipped," he declared, "nor savored as the French do their cognac or the English their whisky. It is drunk at one swallow—the whole glass—thus!" And he emptied the glass, after which he made me drink to the health of Barbusse.

Later a typical Russian supper was served, with tea and vodka. There was a great deal of conversation in Russian and French; everyone rejoiced at my decision to return to America and help organize the communist party there.

After midnight I was taken to the Hotel Lux. I could not sleep. I lay awake trying to sort out the ideas and impressions that crowded my mind. I thought of my return to America; of the great poverty that reigned in Russia; of the difficulties of revolution and the shockingly low standard of living in Russia; of the *dacha*, its gardens, its modest furnishings; of these men who occupied the central place of command in the world revolution. Barbusse's prediction had come true: "If you reach the ranks of the International you will be welcomed as more than a simple recruit."

2

The trip that Zinoviev, Lossovsky and Droz had talked of was arranged. The Latin American group was to travel to the Crimea, to the Caucasus, to the basin of the Don and to the oil fields. Maria Casanellas, who was chosen to accompany us as guide and translator, was a thin little woman, her face sprinkled with freckles. She spoke Spanish with a good knowledge of the common words and idioms, but with so strange an accent that one could never guess in what part of the world she had learned it. She was the wife of Ramon Casanellas, the Catalonian who killed Dato, and who was serving the Soviet Union as an aviator. She had a small son, who accompanied us on our trip and proved a valuable courier, because he spoke both Russian and Spanish fluently.

We left Moscow by train; our first stop was to be Tula. Maria installed us in a passenger coach, using our special privilege to get us the best seats. The autumn was still mild. The trees were not yet stripped of their leaves and the fields breathed to the clear skies a fresh and loving fragrance.

Late in the afternoon of that day an accident occurred. Maria would not say what it was and the rest of the people spoke in Russian. The train stood for some time at the outskirts of a small village. We took advantage of the delay to look over the encampment that had formed alongside the tracks and to visit the village. I think I have never seen so frightful a pageant of misery. An accumulation of rags, of thousands of bodies; an ant-hill of filthy creatures, emaciated, dejected, infuriated. We had not expected this Dantesque vision; it was as if these people were living in the direct path of a war. It did not seem possible that this could exist twelve years after the revolution and the coming-to-power of the Bolsheviks.

While we waited, little Casanellas became sleepy and thirsty. I got him a bottle of pop and talked with him. When I asked about what we had seen, he looked about and seeing that his mother was too far away to hear, he said with contempt:

"This? All Russia is like this."

"How do you know?"

"Well, because everywhere I've been, it is always the same."

Throughout the long journey Maria always showed us the best: the best foundries, the best farm-equipment factories, the best rest-homes, sanatoriums and clubs. But even these were touched with the same grime of primitivism, of sordidness, of misery; the absence of even the most elemental good taste. This was an immense sad land where hundreds lived out their lives groveling in the dust.

Each time, in each new place there was a new scene of grinding hardship. In the country through which we passed there was taking place what was called, in communist circles, "the battle against the Kulak" or as Maria, and the presidents of the soviets who received us in the villages, preferred to call it, "the liquidation of the Kulak as a class." The agricultural regions of Russia were passing from a condition of private property to that of collective property and work. The kolkhoziens were replacing the kulaks.

In the cities, the campaign against the Kulak consisted in fomenting hatred against the rich peasant and inspiring sympathy and respect for the poor peasant. The kulaks were termed egotists, counter-revolutionaries, incorrigible enemies of socialism. While there was some exaggeration, much of this was true. The poor peasants, in urban opinion, were an immense mass of unfortunates who had suffered sub-human treatment under the tzars and were willing, even eager to collaborate with the new regime. The workers in the cities hated the Kulak and attributed to him all or most of their own misfortunes.

"You were detained? An accident?" the officials of the soviets asked us. And they always added, "You see, Yuri! You see, Natacha! The comrades didn't arrive on time because of an accident! The kulaks molested them! Ah, the wretches, the counter-revolutionaries, the bandits!"

We knew this wasn't true although we hadn't the slightest sympathy for the Kulak, nor did we analyse very deeply this business of "The liquidation of the Kulak as a class." It was represented to us as necessary, and we did not realize that it was in reality the beginning of the blood bath in which Stalin's regime has sunk Russia.

In the country, there were other and more pressing problems. We arrived, in the company of a party official, at a newly established collective farm. A ramshackle thresher, with every appearance of being home-made, was working on a heap of grain. Men and women surrounded us, examining us curiously, suspiciously. But as soon as they discovered that a party official from the city was among us, they ignored us completely and fastened themselves on him.

All the women talked at the same time, as if they were going to die in a few moments and must say all they could in the little time they had left. An old man tried to bring them to order; the young men sneered. The only quiet one of the group, a tall, bony, middle-aged man, laughed sadly, watching them, and shook his head as if he were thinking, "Time wasted."

Though I could not understand what they were saying, it was clear that they were protesting, complaining about something. They showed the official a dish of fish; they made him smell it; they screamed. One girl fell to her knees, wrung her emaciated hands, wept and kissed his hand, saying something in tones that suggested desperation.

At first, the official was embarrassed at our witnessing this scene, but very soon he regained his composure and began to deal with the workers. He cajoled, he laughed, he rebuked and he repeated incessantly those words which must be the first words every Russian learns: "Right away, presently, very soon." An expression very similar to the *mañana* of the Latin Americans.

That night at the hotel, I took care of little Casanellas. Since I had entertained him all day, he talked to me at length of what the people had said to the party official.

"Now don't go say anything to mother or the comrades," the little boy warned, "but the Kolkhoziens were saying horrible things to Petrov. They insulted him. They told him the food he gave them was garbage; that it was months since they tasted a lump of sugar; that the bread was sour and water could be wrung out of it as from a rag; that the fish was rotten and had made many of them ill, and there it was in the bowl getting rottener as all the party members and the government ought to rot too. They said they worked hard and lived worse than dogs."

The boy interrupted his story to say, "But swear to me, comrade, that you won't tell Maria." I promised again and he went on:

"Well, when we were leaving they told him that he had a head like a cabbage; that he was a knave; that the directors of the party had a fine life for themselves while others starved. They said that some day they would pay out the party as they had the tzar." He added laughing: "And Petrov, when they said such things to him, he played dumb; he pretended not to understand and talked to you people about other things. If you hadn't been there, well, he would have got into a fistfight with them because they were so insulting. But as it was, he played the fool and laughed as if it weren't meant for him. But when you leave here he will go back and settle accounts."

"Why, what will he do?"

"I don't know what they do, but they do something."

Maria called to the child through the open window and he went to her.

Conditions, and the state of mind, in other places were not very different—misery, hatred of the kulaks, masses of literature on industrialization and the Five Year Plan, and yet more misery. Great maps of Russia on which, when one moved one lever or another, colored lights appeared in spots where great industrial centers were to arise. And everywhere, in the midst of everything, a thick, hard discontent. From what we saw and what we sensed, we could understand that these people had no reason to feel content.

At Tangerova we visited a summer station on the shores of the Black Sea. It was a clean, modern, comfortable establishment, but somewhat crowded by men with their hair cut very short, women dressed simply but not poorly, people who enjoyed a standard of living far higher than that of the working people we had seen in city and country.

"Who are they? What do they do? To what group do they belong?"

"They are skilled workers. They earn more because they work harder and better," Maria explained casually, but a later conversation with little Casanellas gave her the lie.

As a guide Maria left much to be desired. She delayed and wearied us with her economies, her haggling over every kopek. Worse, she lied constantly. Knowing that we did not understand the language, she told us whatever she chose and explained things as she pleased. All the journey was unpleasant.

In a farm-implement factory, next door to a State wheat farm, we met a group of people with whom we could converse frankly. In charge of the farm was a young technician, a descendant of the aristocracy. He lived with a woman much older than himself, a faded blonde very careless of her appearance but not of her house which was neat, very clean and filled with vases of flowers and embroidered rugs.

We had dinner at the technician's house with the president of the village soviet, the director of a neighboring foundry, and three other men who seemed to be helpers, workers from the farm or bodyguards to the president.

The technician told us of his experimental work in the selection of wheat, the proper preparation of the soil, the use of fertilizers, all matters hitherto neglected in Russia. He directed the cultivation of a great tract of land. He had divided the tract into zones crossed by asphalt roads for the trucks which took the peasants to work, brought seed, fertilizer and tools to the fields, and later carried the harvest to the big consumer centers.

The technician's companion spoke French beautifully. The foundry director spoke it too but with an accent. The technician himself spoke English, German and Danish. He had studied in Denmark and Sweden. That evening after dinner, and several glasses of excellent wine from the Crimea, we told these men all we had seen and heard on our trip. The discontent that boiled over everywhere; the misery, which to us had often seemed unnecessary; the mass of filth which could surely be reduced with a little effort.

The foundry director, whose name was Dorogan, put out his cigarette in the ash-tray. Hooking his thumbs through his belt, he spoke casually but firmly:

"Russia has been one of the most backward nations on earth and one must remember this to understand her. She was involved in the Great War which hurt her economy profoundly, much more than England's, France's or Italy's. The more backward a country is, the more severe the effects of any crisis are. Then, after that," he continued, lighting another cigarette, "came the revolution. Only those of us who lived through it know what it cost in poverty, in loss of security, in profound human disturbance. The worst was not the revolution. Far worse were the invasions. Today white, tomorrow red. In the morning the Cossacks of Kolchak, in the afternoon the brigades of red militia, in the evening the squads of the anarchists. And before dawn the bands of pillagers, who, taking advantage of the panic, carried off the little that was left.

"All that was twelve years ago, my good Dorogan," I objected.

"Not twelve years, my friend; much less. As a matter of fact we have had peace for only five or six years; and in that time it is very difficult, impossible even, to remake everything. We have made a beginning." He paused, put out his cigarette, grinding it nervously into the ash-tray. He asked for another glass of wine and said that he hoped he was not boring the technician, who begged him to continue.

Comrade Dorogan proceeded:

"Socialism is the child of industrialization; you know that. In Russia industrialization is not far advanced; this is just not an industrial country. To achieve socialism it becomes necessary to industralize Russia and this is the task that confronts us—industrialization, plus heavy machinery, plus modern production methods. We must make Russia over. We must make her very nearly a second United States of America. Can you imagine that? The technical progress of the United States plus socialism?"

"Utopia," one of us answered.

"Exactly, comrade, or at least, very nearly. Hope and happiness for these millions of men and women you have seen these last few days, crawling in filth. But this will not come to us as a present, nor as a gift from Heaven. We must achieve it ourselves, with our own arms and brains. By our capacity to organize and to rise above this immense Russian inertia. I'll tell you the truth; we Russians like to work little and dream much."

He finished his wine and urged us to drink ours; then he continued:

"It is clear, my friends, that the people of the collective farms, do not, can not know or understand these things. All this is a great conception, an enormous and complicated enterprise. This is why they complain, protest, insult the party officials. If they did not behave so, they would be either angels from heaven or leaders of the revolution. They don't understand why they suffer, nor why we must pass through this difficult period. We know. They can not. It is not so some technician may get rich, nor that my wife may wear diamonds. It is so everyone may be part of a really new life."

I tried to comprehend this vast problem. The faith and conviction of Dorogan were almost hypnotic. He was so sincere a reformer, so sure that he was building a better world that this faith of his gave extraordinary power to his arguments.

"Then you think, comrade Dorogan," I asked, "that this great grief is only temporary?"

"It has a term," he answered. "It will be conquered. It will end someday, and sooner than many think. After two Five-Year Plans, every Russian will be able to buy as many shirts as a North American and eat beefsteak in the morning and a pork-chop in the afternoon. There will be no more rotten fish," he finished, laughing.

Early the next day Dorogan came and carried us off to his house. His wife was attractive and pleasant. She received us with exquisite kindness and introduced her three children, Lena, Natacha and Alyosha. We discussed a great many things, ate together and became friends. When we left, I embraced Dorogan as one of the builders of socialism and left him optimistic, happy, full of hope. Ten years later I was to find him crushed, hopeless, a spiritual ragamuffin.

Tired from our long journey, tired from examining and inquiring, grieved by this Inferno of sorrow and misery, and yet certain that all this squalor was only temporary, that there was a fixed term for its liquidation, we returned to Moscow—to the Soviet capital, with its narrow streets forming a gigantic cobweb around the Kremlin, paved with rough stone and smelling of rosin, livery stables and human filth.

We were back in the Hotel Lux. And we carried, mirrored in our eyes, an exact and detailed picture of what was at that time the homeland of socialism.

Ah—but tomorrow!

3

On my return to Moscow, I was given an appointment with Piatnitzky, one of the old Bolsheviks, co-worker of Lenin and leader of the October Revolution. Grumpy, always discontented, and in spite of all charming, Piatnitzky was Russia's most important theoretician on questions of organization. It was he who had created the Communist International.

When I arrived, Piatnitzky was not in his office. I was asked to wait. A short time later Zinoviev appeared, dressed as always in checked trousers, a black corduroy hunting jacket and a checked hunting cap.

"Have you finally seen a bit of Russia?" he asked, after greeting me. "What do you think? Come, you can be frank."

"It seems to me that the region we saw is a trifle backward."

"Only a trifle? Oh, no. It's very retarded and it's no worse than other regions. On the contrary, in fact. We showed you the best, of course. So now you can draw your own conclusions as to the general state of Russia. Surely it doesn't differ much from South America's less developed sections?"

"But Russia has immense wealth. She is immense in size, and Europe is next door."

"Europe next door! Exactly. That's the trouble. We are merely Europe's neighbors."

"Oh, but I didn't mean that," I said, embarrassed.

"I understand, comrade," he interrupted. "I know what you mean. I know you didn't mean to call us Asiatic, but I know too that you do not feel yourself in Europe. Your comment is just. As for the backwardness, it couldn't be more obvious. Perhaps the Russian who has always lived here is used to it, and can ignore it; but not the foreigner, or the Russian who has known Europe. But will you agree that since our revolution we have come a long way? And do you believe that we are determined to overcome this backwardness that you have seen?"

"I do agree, and I understand at least part of the problem."

"Good, I am glad. Remember that when we took over we found nothing but mud, and that from this mud we must mold socialism. We must make slaves into free citizens. And to transform slaves into free men," he said, taking a deep breath, "will not be easy. No—not easy."

He remained silent a few moments; he picked up a ruler from Piatnitzky's desk and struck the palm of his hand with it.

"No, not easy," he continued slowly, "because, though we Russians have fought heroic battles for freedom, we have never had it. That is the flaw in our present society. We are backward in many ways but the fact that we are retarded in this way is the most dangerous. Liberty is not a habit with us. Our lack of experience of freedom is the cause of most of the misery you have seen. But this too we shall overcome." And again he struck his hand with the ruler. "In a few more years, when we have succeeded in overcoming our material difficulties, when there is a decent standard of living in Russia, when we no longer need be afraid of starvation, liberty will become a reality in Russia, and will no longer be only a word and a dream."

"Don't be disheartened by what you have seen," he continued. "The revolution has added no new misfortune, no new injustice and has removed many. Perhaps we are not advancing as fast as the disorganization and misery of Russian life demands, but we do go forward. Once this heritage of the past is liquidated, then everything in Russia will change. You'll see when you return in a few years. You will find a vast and profound change on all levels when you return to report your successes and the progress of the communist party in your own country."

He dropped the ruler to the desk and wandered across the room to where a great globe stood, balanced on a copper ellipse in a corner.

"Yes, of course, that's how it will be," I said at last, to fill the silence that had lasted too long.

Zinoviev set the globe spinning. "In your country," he said, "the important thing is to create and develop a national movement. Your country, like Russia, has been standing still too long. You must convince your people that progress and well-being are possible. The *bourgeoisie* of your country is, as Mariátegui has said, 'a rickety plant growing in the soil of feudalism.' Well said, eh?"

He put his hand against the globe and stopped its spinning. Then he turned it with his finger tips and was silent, looking at the map of South America. At last he faced me and spoke:

"Give my regards to Mariátegui. Tell him how grateful I am for what he has written of me and other comrades in his *Contemporary Scene*. I'll send you a few copies of Russian magazines in which those articles are reprinted. Mariátegui has a brilliant mind; he is a true creator. He doesn't seem like a Latin American; he doesn't plagiarize, he doesn't copy, he doesn't parrot what the Europeans say. What he creates is his own. Defer to him and work with him."

There was a knock at the door. A very fat woman, with a mannish haircut, intensely green eyes and a gay smile, entered. "Comrade Piatnitzky sends to beg you to return tonight. He can not come today as he had planned. Tonight, please." And she was gone as quickly as she had come.

"Piatnitzky is like that," said Zinoviev. "He makes engagements that he cannot keep. But no matter; you will be with us a day longer." He took off his cap, smoothed his hair and continued:

"We will meet again before your departure, but in case we don't, remember to give my most affectionate regards to Barbusse and, when you get home, to Mariátegui. One thing more—don't go without seeing comrade Bukharin. He has information for you. I assure you that it is not bad news."

He clasped my hand, embraced me and left. I remember Zinoviev as I saw him then—broad-shouldered, his hair threaded with grey, the checked trousers. For this was the last time I was to see him. When I asked for him on my return, he was no longer in the International. He had been accused of being a *saboteur*, a spy and an enemy of the people. Not long after that, Stalin had him killed.

That night I returned to Piatnitzky's office. The interview lasted until dawn. Piatnitzky explained the form in which the party should be organized; the structure and the activity of the factory cells and the neighborhood cells; the organization and functioning of the committees. The old man enjoyed himself thoroughly, salting his lecture with recollections and anecdotes. He talked of Lenin, told of their discussions, their disagreements, their quarrels and their common struggles. It was almost dawn when he took me in his car to the Hotel Lux.

"I wish you success," he said as we parted. "I recommend courage, both moral and physical. It is our most important weapon in this struggle. Every good wish to you and yours. We'll meet again. Goodbye."

This vigorous and austere old man still had many more years of useful living in him. I could not, then, have dreamed that this man who took his leave of me in that mild Muscovite dawn was already marked for death. Stalin had not yet begun the purges and the slaughter of the old Bolsheviks. His policy of murder was already set in motion; the terror was unrolling in the country; but no one suspected the countless assassinations that he would order when he had achieved "the liquidation of the Kulak as a class."

Stalin did not apply to Piatnitzky the spectacular methods that he used later—the mock trial always presided over by the cynical and pitiless Vishinsky, where the accused was always assumed to be guilty, and his guilt proven by confessions he himself proffered to save his family and friends from merciless extermination. To the "great old grumbler" as Lenin affectionately called Piatnitzky, Stalin applied a mere "administrative process"; that is to say, a secret court-martial in which the police acted as investigator, prosecutor, judge, jury and executioner.

I did not see Zinoviev again, nor Bukharin, nor say goodby to Radek. "In Moscow," Humbert Droz had said, "you will never be able to be formal in your friendships. One night you will go to bed at the Lux and you will wake up on who knows what frontier of the world." And so it was. That night Droz appeared at the hotel to say, "Our best regards to Mariátegui; embrace Portocarrero; work hard."

"I beg you," I said, "to say goodby to everybody for me. Tell them that it was impossible for me to do it myself. And if you see the Negro, Goblan, when he returns from his trip, give him my regards.

Tell him how sorry I am not to embrace him before leaving. He was always very good to me."

One could ask such things of Droz. I never knew this tall, pale, priestlike man to be too busy for courtesy. He smiled and nodded, promising that he would give my messages to everybody and embrace Goblan when he returned from the trip the French-speaking group was making along the left bank of the Volga.

That same night an unknown, silent man conducted me to the station and put me on the train. A few minutes later the train-whistle sounded, the cars joggled and I was on my way. The train ran on past Minsk; on to Poland.

Acting on my instructions, when I reached Berlin I presented myself at a dress-shop on the Französische Strasse. A beautiful woman who spoke French like a Parisian received me amiably and advised me to go to Paris to await the sailing of my ship. "We have taken a passage," she said, "giving you forty days leeway. If you wish, you can go sooner simply by requesting the company for an earlier sailing. Or you may go to Paris where you have friends, and where the delay will be less expensive for you than in Germany."

I had to arrange for someone to take over my work in the Worker-Teachers' International and I wanted to say goodby to Barbusse and Vernochet, to Cogniot, to old Rappoport, to Florimond and my friends Peng and Paulette. Also, it was possible that Goblan might return before my ship sailed. What impressions would the African bring back from the left bank of the Volga? Would they be as painful as those I had received in the Crimea and the basin of the Don? So I returned to Paris, to await there the sailing of my ship from Antwerp a month later.

CHAPTER IV

Peru

1

WHEN I arrived in Paris, Barbusse welcomed me warmly and listened with delight to my account of my pilgrimage. "For Goethe, for Beethoven, for the illustrious men of that time," said he, "the great journey in life was to Italy; in our time it is to Russia, this journey that you have just made—the journey to Moscow."

Ten days later Goblan arrived, pessimistic and depressed. "The Russian workers who live best," he said bitterly, "have worse conditions than Algerians in France. They dress badly, they eat abominably, they have no shoes, they sleep huddled like animals. What a horrible sight! Did you see them? Eight, eleven, even fifteen in a little room. It is frightful. They can't get married because they haven't a place to sleep in alone." And Goblan buried his dark face in his pale palms. He was silent and motionless for a moment; then he continued:

"Only in Africa have I seen similar human misery. Only there is man sunk in such filth. But—you know something? One feels free there, in spite of French imperialism and its police and its soldiers. In the Soviet Union they aren't free at all. It is strange."

I repeated what Dorogan, the foundry director, had said and what Zinoviev had told me about the heritage of the past.

"Yes, of course. I can understand that," he answered. "That is the philosophy of the matter, but the hungry man doesn't want philosophy. He wants something done. And in this I am with the hungry man."

"Action will come later," I said. "But it will take time. It must grow slowly from an embryo to a foetus and then to a living creature. After all it takes nine months to produce a few pounds of human flesh."

"The reasoning is general," he said; then added, "but it is not bad to reason so. Often it helps one to see things more clearly. We must speak of this confidentially to Monsieur Barbusse. But my impression was a grievous one. And yours?"

"You know," I said, smiling, "that it could not be a pleasant one.

73

There are whole cities that stink as if the people were rotting alive."

"That's it," exclaimed Goblan, "as if one were rotting alive. And there is no freedom; confess that you noticed that. They aren't free like the French, not even as I am free here. They were kind to me; they gave me special privileges; they tried to show in every way their affection for Negroes, for all oppressed races. I cannot complain, but that is not the point. They are just not free."

"Is your faith weakening?" I asked sardonically.

"No. But I don't walk in the jungle with my eyes closed, especially not at night. That is my position."

We went over various notes we had taken and decided which matters were most important to bring to the attention of Barbusse. It was several days, however, before we could see him. The winter weather had driven him out of Paris.

"I have become a swallow," he had told us, smiling, the day Goblan arrived in Paris, "and I must follow the path of the sun. I shall have to travel to the Midi."

When he returned he sent for us, received us alone and we talked for some time. Goblan was clear, eloquent and moving. He described the misery of the Russian scene, the despair of the people, their want of liberty, the housing shortage. He told of their wretched wages, their hard work, their scarce and poor food, how they lived always on the margin of life.

Barbusse tossed his head, flinging the hair out of his eyes. "France was in the same or worse condition after Valmy," he said. "There was very little bread here then, no decent housing nor any liberty. There was a revolution going on, a fierce and cruel revolution, which devoured its own progenitors. But the historical process continued. The Republic advanced triumphant, overcoming the obstacles the past had left, overcoming those that her birth had created. In Russia, as Zinoviev so well said, they are liquidating the heritage of their past. The great realization will come later—socialism—free men, masters of their lives and of their tomorrow. We must have faith and know how to wait. We must have hope and know how to work, my sons."

Goblan and I left, comforted by this interview. He was staying on in Paris, and one snowy night he saw me off at the station. We embraced like brothers and I left.

Forty days later I arrived in Lima. That very night I met José Carlos Mariátegui on Washington Street, at a corner which he called the "Red Corner."

Socialist party or communist party? That was the question we put to ourselves that night. Mariátegui conversed brilliantly, with great simplicity and constant laughter. Each time he turned his clear, honest eyes toward me, those deep eagle eyes, unclouded by the illness that bent his body but could never bend his soul, I became aware again of the terrifying paradox of this maimed man. Though he could not hope for a single day free from pain, there was in him a marvelous joy of life and a desperate desire to stretch out the days which he knew to be numbered.

Early in our discussion we reached one clear conclusion. Whether our party was called socialist or communist would not alter in any way the character of the movement, nor change its doctrine or its program. Under either name, the purpose would be to organize a Peruvian section of the Communist International.

"This is self-evident," Mariátegui declared. "Now let us analyze the effects each name will have. If we call our party communist, the police will persecute us more. If we call it socialist, perhaps they will persecute us less. It all comes down to this. Don't you think so?"

We agreed on this, and a few days later held our first meetings with workers, intellectuals and trusted students. Most of this group were ardently in favor of adherence to the Third International; three young lawyers withdrew, fearful of what might happen. Mariátegui read the famous twenty-one conditions of Lenin. We drew up a program and elaborated on the statutes. We began to recruit new followers.

Then came the day when all work had to be abandoned. Mariátegui had become dangerously ill. A suppurating ulcer had formed on his stump; he was covered with boils. He had a high fever; then he became delirious. We took him to the Villaran Hospital. He had just passed his thirty-fifth birthday yet his life was burning out as if he were an octogenarian. The doctors held consultations, argued, prescribed and were mistaken. Mariátegui was dying and there was no help for it. I watched the end draw closer and closer, with a knot in my throat. I looked toward the future with terror. In my political work I had counted on the shelter, the great comforting shade cast by this man. When he died, I would be alone, with nobody to turn to for advice, without authority, without prestige and with an overpowering responsibility.

The end came one warm, sunny morning. Mariátegui lay, stretched out on the hospital bed, his stomach enormously distended. He was entirely conscious. He knew us all, but to me it seemed that already he looked back at us from the shadows. I could not bear it. I went out to the Avenue and flung myself down on a bench. Why, why, why was he dying now, just when he was needed so terribly? Why, just when I had come, bringing him the message he had waited for; why when we had just made our plans, traced a path, set a goal?

I went back to the hospital at last. The doors of the room in which Mariátegui lay, stood open as if they wished not to keep Death waiting. There was no longer any fear of cold or draughts. It was as if there were not only resignation but surrender.

"I don't want to go," Mariátegui cried hoarsely, "but what can be done?" He was silent for a few moments. Then he said slowly and distinctly: "Nothing will stand if it is not built on a great principle." And a little later he cried out, heart-breakingly, "Goodbye—goodbye, comrades. Goodbye, Anita."

And that was all. We had lost our greatest comrade, great, not so much for what he had accomplished, but for what he had begun. We were crushed by the sad event and felt that Death had never stolen a life so precious, so useful, so clean.

On Good Friday, with a great procession, revolutionary songs and red flags, we buried José Carlos Mariátegui, covering his bier with a huge scarlet banner. That march was the first in those latitudes to be captained by militants of the Communist International.

Now, without this man who had given us inspiration and authority and prestige, we had to continue our work. New converts were being made, new leaders were being trained, the first cells were being formed, just as Piatnitzky had directed. Information was going out to the factories and the villages, to the farms and mines. We told the poor and downtrodden to hope, to have faith in themselves. We told them that, with their help, the Communist International could bring peace and freedom and prosperity to all. And the people believed that this miracle was possible and sang hopefully:

Now Justice thunders condemnation,
A better world's in birth.

One day I met Hugo Pesce in a dark little alley as we were leaving an indoctrination lecture. "We have a new convert," I said.

"Or an *agent provocateur* from the police," answered Pesce. "You never can tell."

"Why do you say that?"

76

"No special reason. In Italy, one out of every three new members was a stooge sent by the police. Of course things are different here."

But they were not. Early one morning agents from the secret police invaded my home. They searched every room, split open all the mattresses, took up the floors, struck my sisters, and at last took me away with them.

"You are an agent of the Comintern," Fernandez Oliva, the chief of police, accused me angrily. "How did you get in?"

I had decided that the important thing was to show no fear, to remain calm. I was determined to give them no information.

"How did you get in?" he repeated, raising a silver-handled quirt.

"Through the door," I answered making every effort to appear calm and serious.

"No, no," he said more quietly. "I don't mean that. How and where did you enter this country?"

"Ah," I said with pretended surprise. "I entered the country legally, with a consul's visa and with my passport properly stamped as the police require."

"Police, police!" he snorted and seemed at a loss what to say next. I saw that on this point I had defeated him.

"I must know," he said very solemnly, "what transpired at the Congress in Frankfurt. Tell me."

I was astonished that this man should ask so stupid, so pointless a question, but I was reassured by his seeming ignorance of my trip to Russia and of what I was really doing in Peru.

"Everything that took place in Frankfurt," I answered calmly, "has been published, printed at any rate. If you wish you can send to Berlin for a complete report. If you like, I can give you the address."

Oliva's face became the color of ashes; his skin was too dark to turn pale. He came toward me.

"I won't stand for jokes at my expense. I'm damned if I will!"

I was sure he meant to strike me across the face with his whip. I knew that if I endured the blow, this man would destroy me. I jumped to my feet, took off my glasses and tensed myself for the attack. My one thought was to grab him by the collar, to get my hands on his throat. Of course the other policemen would reach me before I could do him any real harm, but if I attacked Oliva they would beat me into unconsciousness. And this was the best I could hope for; to lose consciousness. Then I could tell them nothing and I would not know or care that they were beating me.

But Oliva stopped, relaxed, lowered the whip and said quietly, al-

most banteringly: "Don't take off your glasses. Look me in the face."
I stepped back, put on my glasses and saw his face smiling and placid.

"Sit down," he ordered. I obeyed slowly.

"The police know everything," he said. "We use scientific methods. You have come here to cause the downfall of the government by promoting strikes. But we are smarter than you are. The only one of you who could read and write was Mariátegui; the rest of you are just poor devils, including Haya de la Torre."

He talked on for more than an hour, making very little sense. He talked of the economic crisis. He told me of a munitions shipment to a southern port, about which he had been forewarned. He was eloquent on the subject of all the information at his command on communist plans for Central and South America. He was sly and stupid and fantastically misinformed. I listened and said nothing. At last he ordered me sent to a cell.

The floor of the cell was muddy, the walls dripped water and were set too close together. "Here you will learn to sleep standing up," the jailor said, cheerfully.

"Perhaps I will learn not to sleep at all," I answered with a smile and in what I hoped was an indifferent tone.

After that the days and weeks passed slowly. Then early one morning they took me to the island prison of San Lorenzo.

Meanwhile, my friend and comrade, Henri Barbusse, had been informed of my imprisonment and was mobilizing a protest in France, Spain and Belgium. The Peruvian dictator received message after message from Europe, the signatures a resounding roll-call of authors, painters, musicians and political leaders, demanding my liberty or at least a public trial. The dictator was impressed. The police became more gentle; the guards servile. One of them told me confidentially that Barbusse had just sent a second message to Leguía, threatening to denounce his methods and explain to the civilized world how arbitrarily he denied liberty to citizens of Peru; how he refused them public trial and any opportunity to defend themselves.

Although my case was in no way unusual, although no judge had ever intervened in matters of this kind, the government was intimidated and decided that it would be wiser to exile me rather than to keep me in prison any longer. So one rainy afternoon I was conducted to a ship that was sailing south. It was a journey I now knew by heart —Valparaiso, Santiago de Chile, Buenos Aires. This was the year 1930, and my second exile. But already the communist seed was in the furrows, and no one could know how, nor when, nor where it would sprout, nor what harvest it would yield.

2

A carefully selected group of communists of various nationalities had begun to operate in South America, as a South American Bureau of the Communist International actually controlled and directed for the first time by the Soviet Union.

A large delegation had arrived, headed by Guralsky. His comparative youth notwithstanding (he was only forty), Guralsky was a Bolshevik of long revolutionary experience. A disciple and companion of Lenin, he had fought as an officer in the Petrograd insurrection of 1917, later in the civil war, and finally as a political commissar in the wars against the invasions. Guralsky held a leading position in the ranks of the party, was an intimate of Zinoviev, and a friend of Rykov, Bukharin, Kamenev, Trotsky, and Rakovsky. He had never been a Menshevik. "I was always on the side of our great old man," he used to say referring, of course, to Lenin; but he had been one of the leaders of the opposition in 1927. It was believed in Russia that he had organized the demonstration of protest against the Stalin regime that occurred in Moscow on the tenth anniversary of the revolution, which had shaken Stalin, his police and his whole oppressive system. The Georgian was forced to retreat; to soften his procedures and postpone his purges.

The French communist "Cremet," who had eluded the police for months (during this time the French Communist demonstrations displayed posters that asked ironically, "Have you seen Cremet?") was in fact Guralsky. In the South American Bureau of the Communist International he went under the name of "Rustico."

A young man called Pierre acted as Guralsky's immediate advisor. His French was peppered with Parisian idioms and slang expressions but his accent betrayed him as one who had learned French as an adult. Pierre was in fact very proud of being Russian, of being of Soviet stock and mentality. When he spoke of the Russian revolution he always mentioned "those of us who were twelve years old then." Though he was one of the youngest men in the Bureau of the Comintern, he enjoyed great prestige. His opinions had influence in the most important matters; sometimes he even vetoed resolutions that had been approved by the others. But he recognized Guralsky's leadership at all times, treating him as his superior even when their opinions had equal value.

Pierre was athletic, with a ruddy boyish face and crew-cut hair. He spoke Spanish with a marked Brazilian accent and occasional Portuguese words. He was as familiar with the Brazilian coast as with the Avenida de Mayo of Buenos Aires, where he spent most of his time. He had organized a chain of secret cells in every port, in every coastal village, in every Brazilian cove. He maintained direct control over the communist groups in every ship that sailed from Brazil to foreign ports, and declared that no ship had ever escaped him, not even the Italians.

Pierre was astute, intelligent, with a lively imagination and a quick sense of humor. He almost never laughed. When he made fun of anything he did so unsmilingly and in a serious voice. In spite of his youth he was in the confidence of Stalin, and had close contacts with the inner circle of the government and the Bolshevik party. "Orestes" the Italian and "Nemo" the Tunisian, both members of the South American Bureau, used to call Pierre "the eyes and ears of the Kremlin in the South American segment of the Comintern."

The majority of this policy-making group of agitators in South America was composed of Russians and Poles, together with the Czech, Frederick Glaufbauf, the Tunisian, "Nemo," and the two Italians, Marcucci and "Orestes." We, as the leaders of the South American communist parties, composed the minority. South Americans also formed the phalanx of functionaries who did all sorts of diverse tasks —office and editorial work, and propaganda.

The South American Bureau of the Comintern had no fixed site of operations; it acted as a flying brigade, moving from one place to another at a moment's notice. On Sunday, it would be meeting and working in the city of Rosario; on Tuesday, it would join a delegation from Chile in Cordova; on Wednesday, it would be in Montevideo working with Paraguayan delegates and preparing to leave for Santa Ana do Livramento to confer with the Brazilians. Guralsky himself was prodigiously active. He maintained a magnificent control over the most complicated situations, and over his own nerves. He was clear-sighted, kind, always warm and gay.

None of the Soviet group ever let us know his true name—the name by which he travelled officially. In general, we called them by designated names. "Juancito" was the representative of the Red Syndicalist International; "Inez," an enchanting representative of the Comintern, worked with Guralsky. "Mauricio" was the organizing expert. Marcucci, leader of the Italian communist youth, changed names with every place. Guralsky was "Rustico" in Argentina; "El Viejo" (the old one) in Montevideo; "Juan de Dios" in Chile. The others were Luis, Panchito, Manolo, Julian. No one knew where they lived. They could call us up on the telephone but we could call them only through an intermediary who, though he did not call them himself, received regular calls throughout the day. We could communicate also through the "contacts"—young men and boys who brought messages, made appointments, arranged meetings in the cafés, in the public squares, at the art exhibits and in other public places where there was a good deal of casual coming and going.

After my arrival in Buenos Aires, the first person of Guralsky's group I got to know was Inez. She gave me general information—the password for telephone calls, the way in which I would be summoned, and so forth.

Doctors' and dentists' offices, it appeared, were the favorite places for summons to a meeting. At first I thought that the doctors were party members or sympathizers, but this was not so. Often our unwitting hosts were outstanding conservatives. "Panchito," a Soviet citizen who spoke perfect Spanish, preferred as meeting places the socialist libraries, the reunion centers of the Radical Party, and buildings owned by the Catholic associations. In Chile he had even met people in churches. "They are very comfortable," he used to say, "especially in summer. You can talk as you like with no one to bother you. When some priest comes along, you just get down on your knees and pray devoutly. You ought to see the gratified and happy faces of the padres!" He boasted of never having been arrested and of having escaped persecution in a dozen countries, including Portugal.

Before I had been in Buenos Aires forty hours, the Bureau met to hear what I had to report. Guralsky listened attentively, asked intelligent questions, clarified for himself and the others the meaning of my remarks, and drew from what I reported some unexpected but logical conclusions. He had practical intelligence, a realistic point of view and a grasp of the size of the tasks before us. Even more, he had sound judgment in estimating difficulties and weighing the importance of what each of us was doing.

Guralsky was, from the first, understanding and honorable with me. He was a great student and always ready to learn from others. He encouraged curiosity, suggested new paths of action, used all his extraordinary talent to induce growth in those with whom he was associated. He liked philosophic discussions, and often invited me on long jaunts during which he discoursed on such things. Notwithstanding the intimacy and trust that was established between us, he never spoke of the disagreements within the party, nor mentioned Zinoviev, his close friend, nor any internal Russian matter.

After my report to the South American Bureau of the Comintern and the discussion that it occasioned, I began my daily work. I drew up the Manifesto entrusted to me, breaking completely with the old patterns that Codovila and the Argentine communists had imposed, whereby all the documents were written in the confused and unreadable jargon that results from translating Russian directly into Spanish. The barbarous grammar, the absurd misuse of words were removed from the texts I edited. When I presented my work for discussion, Codovila rejected it indignantly. He called it "intellectual bungling" and delivered a diatribe against writers. He didn't argue reasonably; he merely said that these were not the proper "formulations" (Soviet jargon for words).

I listened to Codovila's violent and offensive speech and came away like a whipped dog. Rodolfo Ghioldi was the only one who had defended my modifications of the wording. I decided that it was useless to make an issue of the matter; that they had best rewrite the Manifesto to suit themselves. Perhaps Codovila was right in saying that what I wrote would be incomprehensible to the workers, and even more so to the country people.

That night there was a plenary session of the South American Bureau. All the Soviet and Polish leaders were there and a discussion of my Manifesto was first on the agenda. I was ready to withdraw the text and make the changes that Codovila had suggested, since he seemed so sure that these were necessary if the workers were to understand our program. Besides, the entire political bureau of the Argentine party always sided with him.

"What the hell," one of the young contacts said to me. "Codovila controls the cash. It's poor policy to quarrel with him."

"Whose cash?" I asked.

"Oh, don't talk like a fool," the boy answered. "The cash from the Big House, of course." In our jargon, the Big House meant Moscow, that is, the Comintern.

So, when the meeting began I felt already defeated. But before anyone had expressed any opinion, Guralsky took from his briefcase a copy of the document in question. "At last," he said, "the South American Bureau is going to put out a Manifesto that is intelligible and written in a Spanish that is a pleasure to read. This Manifesto is clear, definite, brief and well written. At last we have got away from our usual style of Danish translators putting Russian into Spanish, or putting into Spanish what some Greek had previously translated from the German."

The Soviet delegates burst out laughing. Codovila took notes in a little book; Ghioldi looked at me, smiling and nodding. Guralsky produced a notebook and went over the Manifesto in detail. He underlined its strong points and pointed out its weak emphasis on certain ideas that it seemed to him important to stress. He drew his pencil through a few repetitions and read from his notes what he considered were its omissions.

Codovila then spouted incomprehensibly in answer. He seemed to have no control over the words that poured from between his lips. He agreed with Guralsky in the main, but said he had a point of view which he would communicate to me before the final revision. "State your position right now," Guralsky said pleasantly, "so that we can discuss it."

"I don't want to lengthen the meeting," said Codovila.

"This is a good time," Guralsky said, emphasizing each word, "for comrade Codovila to express his opinions before us all. Don't be afraid of prolonging the meeting. Don't worry so much about our sleep. If we don't sleep tonight we can sleep tomorrow—and if we don't sleep tomorrow, then all the better for the comrade chambermaids who will be saved the trouble of making our beds. Come on, Codovila! We are all listening."

"I refer merely to the formulation," Codovila said, glaring angrily at Guralsky. "I am the first to recognize that the Manifesto focuses the problem and that it will reach the workers, but it seems to me that the formulations are incorrect."

"Which formulations?" Guralsky asked, holding out the document to him. "Point them out."

Ghioldi interrupted and attempted to change the course of the discussion, while Codovila pretended to read, but Guralsky would have none of it.

"No, no," he said, "let us stick to the point. Let comrade Codovila point out the changes he wants made."

The silence grew. Codovila was as red as a lobster. Drops of sweat beaded his forehead and his ears were dark vermilion. His pencil ran rapidly along the lines of the document and Guralsky laughed.

"I haven't before me the corrections I think should be made," Codovila said. "But it is only a matter of small changes in formulation."

"Large or small, the changes must be pointed out," insisted Guralsky.

"It has no importance, no importance at all," repeated Codovila, throwing up the sponge. "You may count on my vote."

"Your vote doesn't interest us," interrupted Juancito. "What interests us are the changes you declared so essential. Earlier this afternoon you called this document a hopeless mess; now you say that no important change need be made in it."

"Now we have got to the heart of the matter," Guralsky exclaimed grimly. "I have come to America for precisely this; to end these perpetual intrigues, to put an end to this monopoly of wisdom in the hands of a few. I have come to ring down the curtain on this farce. I see no reason for enduring any longer those who, before they dare speak, repeat 'Moscow says!' and 'Moscow says!' thereby, before they have even presented their opinions, imposing an unbearable silence on all the other comrades."

The Russians and Poles were laughing. Inez's calm glance rested on me as if she were looking through me. Codovila tried to say something but Guralsky spoke authoritatively:

"All who are in favor of the text of the Manifesto as written?" A moment later he struck a sharp blow on the table and said the one word, "Approved!"

After this incident, the work progressed in its usual manner but we shifted from city to city. We read, we discussed, we wrote, we analysed reports which came in by the most surprising routes from diverse points in South America. A report on Cuzco came by plane from Panama; a large chart, and data on a Valparaiso strike came from Montevideo; a brief manuscript on communist activity in the left wing of the Colombian Liberal Party came wrapped in a newspaper from Santiago de Chile. Packages arrived from various business houses in the city, brought by sailors, aviators, tourists, sportsmen.

"This is the system Guralsky has organized," Glaufbauf told me proudly.

One afternoon, while we were holding a meeting in a Montevideo basement, the siren of the newspaper *El Dia* blew. Guralsky asked for someone to go out and make inquiries.

Larrobla went out and returned a few minutes later.

"A hug of congratulation!" he shouted, and embraced me effusively.

"What has happened?"

"A military *coup* has overthrown Leguía, in Peru."

"This is the first of the series," said Guralsky. "The crisis, my friends, the crisis!"

I was puzzled, not knowing what to think.

"I must go see," I said. "I must!"

"Good. Go ahead," said Guralsky. "Investigate everything you can. Prepare a report for today at six. Tea on the Carrasco beach. Wear your best dark suit."

That afternoon I reported everything I had been able to find out and to conjecture.

"Who is Sanchez Cerro, the leader of this *coup d'état?*" they asked me.

"When Mariátegui was still alive," I answered, "he invited me to visit him one day. I arrived at nightfall. He told me that he was expecting Pedrito Bustamante Santisteban, who was bringing with him a soldier who wanted to talk with us. Soon Pedrito arrived, and with him a small man who wore mufti awkwardly—a man who had the appearance and manners of a soldier. This man was very dark; he had high cheekbones; and since he had no fingers on one hand he was nicknamed "el Mocho." It was Sanchez Cerro, and he swore to us then that he would overthrow Leguía.

"Mariátegui looked at me with surprise and Pedrito urged the soldier to explain himself further. He talked for a long time. He detested Leguía, but above everything he was determined to be President of the Republic. 'I must be president,' he repeated, pacing the floor while we sat listening. 'I must be. You'll see. I'll go to Arequipa and I'll work like a dog, but if they don't kill me, I swear to you by my mother, I'll overthrow Leguía!' And then, as if he guessed what we were thinking, he added, 'No, I'm not bluffing. I'll do exactly that, though you may not believe me. It won't be more than a year; perhaps only a month if luck is with me. Maybe two months, but I swear by my mother, you'll hear of me.' "

"Well we're hearing of him," said Guralsky. "It is clear that we have here an ambitious and stubborn man, strong and rash. He has no principles; professes no doctrine. He will go along with anyone who supports him; he will follow any path, accept any gang that furthers his ambition. He will not be able to keep a hold on the working class, for the crisis will not permit it. And this will bring about an uprising that will wreck all his plans and bring about his downfall sooner or later. We must put no trust in him. We must oppose him in so far as he opposes the workers."

The discussion continued and it was decided that I should return to Peru. "It's too bad," Guralsky confessed. "I was looking forward to working with you in Argentina and Uruguay, and later in Chile and Brazil. But I agree that you must return to your own country. We must have a communist party there that we can count on."

3

Meanwhile alarming news reached us from Buenos Aires, of an impending *coup d'état* against the government of President Irigoyen. There were predictions of all sorts. It was clear to us all that, whatever happened, our South American address lists must be removed from Buenos Aires at once. In these lists were the names of hundreds of people who served the party in one way or another—names of people who acted as contacts, names of committee-heads in ports and on ships, names of trusted sympathizers. If this list should fall into the hands of the military police, the secret machinery, so carefully and laboriously worked out, would be exposed. "Above all," said Pierre and Guralsky, "the lists for Brazil and Chile must not fall into the wrong hands."

"You go," Guralsky told me. "They don't know you in Buenos Aires and the police there have never seen you. You will go with perfectly faked papers. You will find Codovila and tell him that he must remain at the head of the secret work, and that he must give you the documents to bring at once to Montevideo. Do you understand the importance of this mission?"

I answered that I did. And after a thorough briefing from Pierre, I left for Buenos Aires.

The city was in great confusion when I arrived, but by evening of that day the military held Buenos Aires, Irigoyen had been deposed, and the radical government had been swept from power.

It would be a long story, were I to tell in detail how I managed to secure our membership lists and carry them out of Argentina, packaged up with a bundle of old architectural sketches. Only one fact in this adventure was important. Vittorio Codovila, as usual, had blundered. He had distributed the lists broadcast among the comrades when the trouble began, and he had given no clear orders what was to be done with them. He had then cleared out of Buenos Aires, and left his collaborators to be taken, should they be, with all the incriminating evidence in their hands.

An hour after my return to Montevideo, Guralsky had all the lists. He was furious with Codovila. "He is a charlatan and a coward," muttered the Russian. "What a revolutionary! That greasy, fat, cabbage-head never works at anything except impressing Moscow!"

"I thought he had been given orders to leave Buenos Aires at once," I said.

"Who would give such orders? He left because he was afraid. All he ever does is run away from the slightest danger."

At a meeting two days later, the Russians berated Codovila for his behaviour. The fugitive declared that he was persecuted and conspired against, that they were trying to destroy him. He begged to be sent to Moscow; there they would see his worth and give him the great work for which he was destined. After various consultations, Guralsky decided to send him to "the House" immediately.

"Let him go. It will be much better for our work. Let him go, and make sure he never returns to America. They ought to send him to Italy. But no! This fat creature will never go where the firing is heaviest."

Codovila thanked Guralsky with tears in his eyes and begged him not to send an unfavorable report to Moscow. He promised not to return to America, even if they offered to send him, and added that he would ask to go to Italy. At this Guralsky burst out laughing.

"No, no, don't say that, or I won't believe anything you say, Vittorio. If you say you won't come back and bother us here; if you say you'll stay in Moscow, or go to England, or Indochina, I'll believe it. But you, ask to go to Italy! Oh no, Vittorio. Benito is there, and the Ovra police. You'll never go to Italy, Vittorio."

So Codovila left Montevideo and went to Europe.

During the next few days I conferred with Guralsky and the Russians about various phases of our work. We talked through the nights and into the early hours of the mornings, on the warm beaches by the light of the moon.

"If possible, remain a few days in Bolivia and send us as complete a report as you can on the political situation there; on the possibilities it offers; and on what trends seem likely to affect the future." This I agreed to do.

"I want you to meet Luis Carlos Prestes," continued Guralsky, "the most important convert I have ever made in all my career as a revolutionary. He is intelligent, brave and thorough. And he is, what you so well express in Spanish, a *caballero*. In his own country he is known as 'The Knight of Hope.'"

"What a wonderful nickname! He must be very happy to have earned such a title."

That afternoon I met Luis Carlos Prestes. Guralsky, proud of his convert, was already preparing to send him to Moscow. Captain Prestes was to become one of the prominent figures of the Communist International and leader of one of the four Muscovite "columns" in America. Lean, delicate, brilliant, quiet and stoical, Prestes was a man of vast culture, of a mystical temperament, altruistic and courageous. He is, without doubt, the most outstanding figure in American communism. Psychologically, he is the perfect antithesis to Codovila. And this makes his *prestismo* far more dangerous than *codovilismo*.

Our first conversation was cordial and interesting. We discussed many subjects other than politics, for Guralsky led the conversation into various channels as if he wished us, in this brief interview, to get to know each other as well as possible.

After that I did not see Prestes until four years later in Moscow. He had become by then one of the important leaders, one of the best organized and powerful minds in American communism. For Prestes, as for Earl Browder of the United States and Lombardo Toledano of Mexico, there is, and always has been, respect and special attention in Moscow and the Kremlin. These men are not put up at the Hotel Lux. They receive the same privileges as the most devoted Stalinists—Mao Tse-tung of China, Ho Chih Minh of Indochina, Gottwald of Czechoslovakia, Pieck of Germany, Kuüssinen of Finland.

Luis Carlos Prestes in Brazil, Vicente Lombardo Toledano in Mexico (without being inscribed as party members), Blas Roca and Candelaria in Cuba, and Vittorio Codovila in Argentina, constitute what might be called the four "columns" of the Soviet Fifth Column in Latin America.

After the meeting with Prestes, I took leave of Guralsky, of Pierre, Juancito, Mauricio and the others, and sailed out of the La Plata River. My destination was the Andes—La Quiaca, Tupiza, La Paz. I travelled now with my own passport and my own legal identity.

4

One cold morning in October, by the beautiful waters of Titicaca, one of the highest lakes in the world, I felt again the thrill of seeing my native land. Only one who has been exiled by force can know such emotion on his return. It is like a stiff wind arousing all one's memories of the land that gave one birth. I thought again of Don Venancio, of the roundup, of the sheared sheep, of the eclipse of all justice, all law, all human principle in these mountain regions. Remembering all this, I began my mission.

The poet, Gamaliel Churata, a friend of Mariátegui, was the intellectual pontiff in the city of Puno. He became a valuable assistant in our communist proselytizing—an appeal based on the Inca traditions of primitive communism which embodied the aspirations of these people; their hunger for land—the hereditary dream, passed from generation to generation, of owning a plot of earth. Thus the elemental and primitive egoism of the peasant served as a prime means for organization of a movement which had as an essential principle, the abolition of private property.

The fall of a dictator in a Latin American country is followed always by a period which has been called "the democratic springtime." For a few weeks or months, the citizen feels liberated and for the most part gives free reign to his tongue. The press is uncensored. Judges recognize the *habeas corpus*. But this lasts only a short time. The new government clinches its position, organizes its police and grows into a new dictatorship, imposing the same restrictions as did the preceding tyrant. All this takes place against a background of ornate speeches in praise of democracy, and proclamations in which the new dictator gives lip service to democratic traditions and principles.

In the "democratic springtime" which followed the downfall of Leguía, Haya de la Torre's first emissaries arrived in Peru. The young men of Cuzco who had played the *quena* at his Paris meetings arrived, converted into the leaders of the APRA—the *Alianza Popular Revolucionaria Americana*. They brought with them the fruit of Haya's visit to Germany; the marching ranks "preceded by forests of flags," and the Roman salute (but with the left hand).

The communist party began its conquest of Peru in the city of Cuzco. At the ruins of the fortress of Sacsayhuaman, exalted by the emotion of the high places and the magic of old legends, and feeling themselves the heirs of Incaic communism, the people of Cuzco pledged their loyalty and proclaimed the establishment of the Peruvian section of the Communist International. The silence of the heights was broken by harangues and declarations; then the workers went down to Cuzco prepared to fight, to give their blood if need be, in defense of the communist cause.

"We shall follow the path of our fathers," the workers repeated with enthusiasm, "the path of the Incas."

A depression had crippled the economy of Peru. Its effects, as always, fell most heavily on the poorest inhabitants. All building stopped; industrial activity languished and hunger fell like a shadow across a country already poor. We had to organize quickly in Lima the nuclei or cells which would direct the campaign in the rural regions. There was no time to create an efficient group. Living in the midst of this convulsion, there was no way but to take the bull by the horns.

The "General Federation of Workers" which Mariátegui had founded, had been until then but a lofty aspiration and a pompous name. It was only in the upheaval of the depression that it was really organized and a National Labor Congress convoked. Throughout the country the workers responded. The success of his Labor Congress delighted Guralsky and the South American Bureau of the Comintern. We began organizing communist cells in the ranks of labor, especially in the mining zones.

The mine workers had never had a union; had never combined to defend their rights. The North American mining companies permitted no organizations except sports or fraternal clubs. The successive governments and the companies had crushed every attempt to organize the workers. Taking advantage of the "democratic springtime," we communists stormed the mining fortress. Tumultuous meetings drew thousands of men who, for the first time, heard talk of human rights. They learned, for the first time, that the managers, the directors, the engineers, the foremen were not by a law of nature the masters of the men who worked under them. They heard, for the first time, that in other countries miners organized unions and bargained with management. Surprised and jubilant, these miners discovered that they too were men —citizens and members of the human race.

The mining company was frightened and asked for soldiers. The new government sent troops armed with machine-guns. The managers talked at length with the young officers in command, while the congress of miners continued its peaceful meetings. Then one night police and soldiers invaded houses and hotels, beat up the delegates, arrested us, and piling us into a freight car carried us off to the capital. The miners woke the next morning and learned of the night's events. The town was shaken with anger. Men and women swarmed out into the muddy paths that served as streets, and armed with sticks and stones, invaded the homes of directors, managers, engineers and foremen. They captured the bosses (without taking into account that these were foreigners and North Americans) and shut them up in the *casinos*. The Mining Federation, which had just been organized, declared a strike which spread over the whole region.

The imprisonment of the North Americans at Cerro de Pasco

frightened the government and electrified the workers of the country
and of all Latin America. As propaganda, it was without doubt a mas-
ter-stroke. The police released us, the strike was lifted and the situation
returned to an unquiet but relatively normal condition. But the police
had been checked, not defeated, and very soon they struck again. They
had the workers of Mal Paso invited to a demonstration at Oroya. The
miners set off, and as they crossed a narrow bridge, found the police
behind a parapet on the other side. A few volleys at close range took
care of the situation. Fourteen killed. Several hundred, including
women and children, wounded.

The miners' attempt to organize a union was crushed with machine-guns and rifles. The union organizers and members were treated
like bandits. Homes were repeatedly invaded by the police and each
visit left a deeper scar. A sadistic savagery was exercised on the poor
chattels of the workers and their families, as defenseless as they were
unfortunate. Filthy straw mattresses were split open by bayonets; furniture was reduced to useless splinters; earthen pots were ground to
dust under the soldiers' hobnailed boots.

Latin American police are stupid to the point of genius. There
are times when it is hard to say which is the greater, their ignorance,
or their servile and cynical corruption. One morning the chief of police
will order the imprisonment of all those who have written or signed
articles in a given magazine or publication which is considered not
too loyal. In one such case a magazine carried articles signed by Henri
Barbusse, Harold Lasky, André Malraux and Paul Nizan. The arrest
of these men was ordered. "Bring them in by the scruff of their necks,"
shouted the chief of police. "Bring me in that Barbusse and that Lasky
and they'll get what they deserve here. Boot them in. We'll teach that
Malraux to write stupid articles."

Someone suggested timidly:

"If the superintendent will pardon me! I beg the permission of
the chief of police to interrupt, but——"

"Yes, yes. What is it? Speak."

"Well sir, those writers are all French, except for one who is English."

"I don't care if they're Chinese, I want them brought in. They'll
see who they're up against, they'll see." And the officer laughed and
repeated, "Dragged, booted, it makes no difference here." Then turning to his informant he asked pleasantly: "Where do they live, these
writers?"

"Sir, in France, and——"

"The Plaza de Francia," cried the superintendent. "It's a small square, fortunately. Search every house. Send all the men you need, captain."

And so Barbusse, Lasky, Malraux and Nizan were hunted assiduously in every house on the Plaza de Francia and in all its neighboring streets.

Added to this ignorance is a fierce system of torture which in brutality, if not in refinement, is similar to that used in Germany yesterday or in Russia today. To such *regimes* the dictators give the pompous name of democracy, in messages, speeches, proclamations and laws. These are the *regimes* that one fine day are recognized by the State Department in Washington, and greeted with a fine speech from His Excellency, the American Ambassador, and the personal representatives from the White House. In all these speeches there is talk of democracy, the mandate of the people, human rights and free speech. All this is said in honor of military bandits, specimens of the mangiest totalitarian stock.

This permanent cruelty serves as yeast in the ferment of popular discontent. The best allies of the communist campaign have been these seekers-after-power, the autocratic generals, the petty tyrants who think of themselves as providential. They and their gendarmes, and the cuties and prostitutes they raise to positions of power, are the most effective aid to communist propaganda. The dictators and their children, and the scandals they are involved in; the sudden wealth of the dictator's relations and friends and protégés, and of the lovers of his girl friends, and of the procuresses for all the debauchery that swarms around the government palaces of so many Latin American republics, all swell the popular hatred. Every year this hatred grows. Every year there are new initiates to this hatred—people without party or ideology, groups without any definite tendency, unified only by discontent and disgust, whose sole desire is to change their position on the Procrustean bed to which they are bound. Communism seems to this disconsolate and desperate human mass simply a way of changing their position.

After three years of combat in defense of the primary interests of the working people, I fell into a snare that the police had prepared for me. My arrest was hailed as one of the greatest victories of the government, its police and its press. The Minister himself questioned me. I was taken to his office; he was surrounded by the highest officers of the police. I knew them. Among them all, there was not a particle of intelligence or integrity. A crew of cynical sadists; nothing more.

"Who are the members of the communist party?" the Minister asked me, soberly.

"The members of the communist party," I answered, equally soberly, "come from the most unsuspected places. They are bosses, great mountain landholders, exploiters of the Indians, who run to join us because they are tired of this succession of knavish dictators and thieving generals."

"I absolutely forbid you to speak so," said the Minister, banging on the table.

"If I am silent, the stones will speak for me. I am answering your question. To the communist party come engineers who have lost their contracts through political favoritism; doctors whose work is taken by quacks protected by the dictatorship."

"I must reprove you again. You have no right to speak of the government in such a way."

"I beg your pardon, Mr. Minister. Your own police recruit hundreds of workers, peasant, students and professional men to the ranks of the communist party."

"What are you saying?" screamed the chief of police.

"It is as I say. Every day your police, as inefficient as it is villainous, takes off to prison hundreds of innocent people, unjustly accused of communism. We make many converts among these prisoners, and for this purpose have very effective indoctrination courses in all the jails."

The Minister had mimeographed copies of the indoctrination courses taken out of a cupboard. They were lessons in which important points from *Das Kapital* had been put into the vernacular and applied to actual situations.

"These are the indoctrination courses?" he asked.

"Yes, sir."

"Well, you had best be shut up in the cisterns of Real Felipe, and be left there *incommunicado* until further notice."

The Castillo del Real Felipe, "King Philip's Castle," is an old fortress, built in colonial times to defend the city from pirates. The cisterns are subterranean wells, built to store water for the use of the defenders in case of siege. These had been converted under the "democracy" of the dictators into prisons. One went down into them on a fire ladder; their floors and walls were always wet, and no light penetrated their dank obscurity except at high noon.

The barracks of this great edifice were also full of political prisoners who wore their lives away, waiting for the trial that never came. In the Latin American countries that live under the cynical rule of such "democracy," judicial power is a mere cog in the oppressive machinery of the dictator. The *habeas corpus* is an abstraction—two latin words without meaning in real life. When they are pronounced before judges, they occasion the same mocking smile that greets any mention of human rights.

The great majority of political prisoners shut up in the Castillo del Real Felipe and the island prisons were members of the APRA. One day, made desperate by their long imprisonment, they declared a hunger strike. They had previously, however, accumulated in each of their barracks a supply of food; chocolate bars, condensed milk, tinned meat and crackers. We prisoners in the cisterns, strangers to this preparation, found ourselves faced with the *aprista* hunger strike and the motto, "Liberty or Death." Though it had been organized by the *apristas*, we communists felt ourselves bound to this strike and would not break its solidarity.

Twenty-four days without food in those damp, dark cisterns, surrounded by absolute silence, enduring the long slow approach of unconsciousness, was not a pleasant experience. During the first days, hunger produces waves in the body that beat against the brain and nerves, a torture which strikes at definite times. Later, the need for food becomes constant. Hunger becomes painful. After that comes a gentle slow fever, which quiets the whole body. Lulled by this fever, one dreams, wakes and drifts back to dreams again. They are always childish dreams, of food tastefully prepared, of favorite soups, steaming and appetizing. These dreams grow dimmer; then comes complete eclipse. One loses the power to dream, or even to sleep for very long. Sleep is interrupted, full of parentheses that open and shut without reason; there are brusque jumps from sleep to waking, and from waking to sleep.

Vision becomes miraculously clear; the images evoked acquire a brilliant precision of outline; the angles and contrasts are sharply perceived. I began to see remembered phrases inscribed on the stone vaults of the cistern—then remembered scenes. The policeman who had hit me in Berlin appeared as clearly as if reproduced in technicolor; the station at Negoreloye, the forests of hemlock, the somber brick walls of the Kremlin, passed before my eyes. In my ears sounded the strokes of the clock in the Red Square, ringing out the *Internationale*.

As the days went by, the border between sleep and waking faded.

There remained either a blank or the passage of images; either total blindness or the luminous vision of an extravagant parade. Later there was no color to the images, no angles, no contours, no shapes—only a fixed idea that hammered incessantly and persistently, a phrase inscribed everywhere in dancing letters:

> *Chocano, permit one who loves you well*
> *To pin a laurel leaf to your lapel.*

These two lines that Ruben Dario wrote when he was drunk on cognac, as homage to José Santos Chocano, were like a pliers that closed on my head, crushing my skull. I could never understand why, of all my memories, this alone should endure. Beyond this obsession and under it, I noticed a great silence in the cistern, as if in preparation for death.

One night, with fire ladders and torches, the police, the informers, the officers came down into the cistern and put me on a stretcher.

"He doesn't weigh anything!" cried one of those who managed the pulleys.

"He's still alive," said another; "his skin is firm."

In the hospital the doctors gave me injections of serum and oil and fed me juices and broth. A month later, in the ancient and unhealthy infirmary, a close bond had linked me to the most conspicuous *aprista* leaders. Our common misfortune made us brothers in spite of our ideological differences. The community of suffering unites men beyond their grudges and overcomes the deepest divergences. To escape the endless, unbroken boredom we were obliged to talk; that is, to argue. We compared ideas, methods, situations, aspirations. And at the end of each argument I came to the same conclusion; what was drama in communism, was in *aprismo* a farce. What the Communist International held up as the banner of a revolution born of social tragedy, *aprismo* hid as Nestor hid the Greeks in the belly of the Trojan Horse.

Haya de la Torre had convinced his lieutenants of that "overflowing beyond morality" which he had preached in Europe. They felt themselves protagonists of a great revolution, and considered terrorist action an integral part of the policy they had come to carry out. The leaders of the APRA, imprisoned in the castle, were a motley crew; some were philosophers and ideologists, others were incurable rogues. Some wished to accomplish a real social transformation; the rest to get easy jobs or a chance to get rich. But all were united in readiness to do violence, to kill, to treat their opponents as cannibals treat their prisoners. "An eye for an eye, a tooth for a tooth," they said,

95

"is an antiquated law. The *aprista* law is both eyes for an eye, both jaws for a tooth!"

While the majority of the prisoners killed time with card games, chess and checkers, a small group established a sort of Socratic academy.

"We are not interested enough in ideas to have an ideology," said Orrego, the official philosopher of the APRA. "Only one idea is important and that is clear to us all. We must seize political power. To attain that end we must use any means, any method."

"Even Nazi means and methods?"

"If it gains our end, why not?"

"But that is immoral. There is no justification for it."

"What do you want? Politics or morals? To take over the government? Or write a prayer book? Besides, the communists look at it the same way."

"The communists are opposed to terrorism."

"Of course you are opposed to the sort of terrorism where the terrorist risks his skin, as did the old nihilist. Bolshevist terrorism is safer. It is carried out from above, by the police. When it comes to terrorism, the *aprista* risks his life; the Bolshevik police agent augments his pay. That is the difference."

"The *apristas* make use of racial enmities. We try to unite; you try to divide."

"We are not responsible," answered one Secada, a Chinese, "for the fact that there are two or three million pure-blooded Indians in the country who carry in their souls an explosive resentment that may break out any day. It's not our fault that there are hundreds of thousands of negroes, and mulattoes of all shades, who are discontented and embittered."

"Embittered by what?" asked Herrera, a communist leader.

"Embittered by the color of their skins, that brands them inferior in a white man's world."

"But don't you understand that the fault for this lies——"

"No, no," interrupted Secada, "the APRA doesn't waste time looking for faults. We take the facts as they exist and deal with them. There is resentment among the negroes and mulattoes, and among the Indians. There is a virus of rebellion among the mixed group with too much Indian blood, among the *cholos*. Well, we use all this as fuel for the locomotive that pulls our train to victory, to our destination— Power."

His companions cheered his speech. The guards drew near to see what was going on. "Quiet there, or you will go to the cells," said the corporal. We lowered our voices and continued the argument.

"I don't understand," said Herrera, "how you *apristas*, even if you do take power, are going to be able to pacify the racial resentments of Indians, *cholos* and mulattoes. Within the APRA you have all the big landholders in the mountains, the most reactionary and primitive gentlemen in the country. I can't understand it; honestly I can't."

"The communists are fools to end all fools," screamed Secada so loudly that we had to silence him. "There is no doubt in my mind. Haya always said so. He is a genius. He is the Torch Bearer, with capital letters."

Antenor Orrego interrupted: "The bosses, the feudal cavemen do a great political service. They employ, not workers, but serfs. The serf earns no salary; he works for nothing on the land of his lord. The lords pay no social security, obey no labor laws, or for that matter laws of any kind."

"And does this seem good and just and progressive to you?" asked Herrera.

"I tell you again that we are not moralists; we are politicians. And our politics consists in this, that these feudal lords, these cavemen, become with our support, senators and deputies in Congress."

"And what good does that do the Indian?"

"Oh naive one," mocked Orrego, "these feudal bosses who don't pay salaries or obey labor laws, who pay no insurance for those who work their lands, when they become senators and deputies, propose, carry out and impose laws in favor of the city workers. They authorize bonuses. They are in favor of profit-sharing for salaried workers. Why? Because none of these advanced laws affect them. On their own lands, none of the laws they approve have any application."

"But this is madness!"

"All right, if you like. But this madness leads to power. The workers don't see it as you do. They welcome these laws; receive these bonuses jubilantly. They are fervently grateful to us, and beg us to dig deeper still into the pocketbooks of the rich."

"But this way," I argued, "you ruin industry; you discourage the industrial revolution and close the path to the economic development of the country."

"It's all the same to us. I tell you, neither morals nor industrialization interests the APRA. Power is the only thing that interests us. Once we have power, then we shall see."

"But that is dangerously cynical."

"Dangerously cynical or cynically dangerous, as you like; but it is very much what the communists propose with much less success, and for a much later date. The communists promise a heaven on earth after 'the triumph of the revolution of the world proletariat' and after a dozen Five-Year Plans. That is, after this generation and the next are dust. The APRA does not hope for so much. It invites the bosses and the mountain lords to Congress *today* to make laws that will benefit the workers. We practice that old adage, 'He who doesn't cry doesn't suck.' "

"And since the millions of Indians don't cry——"

"Then they don't suck."

"And all the pro-Indian talk of the APRA? And the propaganda that is used to appeal to the foreigners' sentimental love of the picturesque?"

"That," said Orrego, smiling, "that is fuel for the locomotive which will carry us to power."

"With intentions like these," I said, "the only ones who will benefit will be the most reactionary, the most primitive—those who use no machinery, who pay no salaries, who obey no labor laws——"

"And a few groups of workers," interrupted Secada. "Those who cry loudest, which is what counts."

"All right, and a few workers. This way you are at once against the proletarian revolution and against the development of capitalism in the country. You are against the landholders who pay their workers, who use machinery on their ranches, who comply with the labor laws. You are against industry and the industrialists. You benefit no one except the feudal lords."

"We are not opposed to your revolution," declared Orrego. "We have told you that. If Russia wins out, if your proletarian revolution succeeds in the world, when the thing is sure, then *zas!* A turnabout and here we are, friends and allies of our dear comrades, the Russians. If, on the other hand, fascism comes out on top and defeats your dear Papa Stalin, well, what do you want? Shall we still look to Moscow? Oh, no, we are not like you. We don't put all our eggs in one basket. Look! In politics you have to be like the peasant who went to offer a candle before the Archangel in the statue where he is shown killing the devil. Just to be on the safe side, the peasant pretended not to know which was Saint Michael and which the devil, and offered a candle to each."

PERU

"And this is wise," said Secada, "for if one candle goes out the other may stay lit."

"And if fascism wins?" asked Herrera.

"If fascism wins? Fine! They salute with the right hand, we with the left. They have their storm troops, their *arditi* or what have you. We have our brigades of *búfalos*. They have their Duce and their Fuehrer; we have our Companion Brother and Chief who is one of those men born once every five hundred years."

"Barbarous!" exclaimed Herrera.

"Barbarous?" Orrego asked, surprised. "No. We are men of our time, that is all. The world is faced with the alternative of fascism or communism. You have taken a side; you work for the triumph of one, the defeat of the other. We take no side; we are waiting to see who wins."

"While you become martyrs," interrupted the *aprista* draftsman Esquerre, "we capitalize on the martyrdoms. Haven't you noticed that all the communists they torture and kill, we turn into *apristas?*" A burst of laughter greeted his words.

"But that is fraud," said Herrera.

"Perhaps it is, but the people don't know it and we profit by it," answered Secada.

"Then what you are organizing," said Herrera, indignantly, "is not a political party but a political swindle."

"The swindler who puts the swindled in prison," Orrego said smiling, "is not a swindler. He is a great and admirable citizen, perhaps even a hero or a saint."

"It's still a political swindle," I said, "that every honest man must denounce and combat."

"We are invulnerable," replied Orrego contemptuously. "Every attack on us from the Conservatives presents us to the hungry, discontented, resentful people as revolutionaries, that is, as true friends of the downtrodden. When they attack us, call us progressives, they light in the heart of the masses a great love for the APRA and for Haya."

"Let's have a drink to the most efficient propagandist for *aprismo*," said Secada.

Esquerre brought in glasses full of liquor. We drank two, five, ten swallows of the burning spirits; transparent, caustic, smelling of grapes. As we began to get drunk, a sergeant appeared. He was fat and pockmarked. He objected because we had introduced liquor into the prison. He was very angry. Finally, he decided to have a drink with us. "Just a little one."

99

He was a poor man and not a particularly bad one. He got drunk and talked about his wife. Later he swore to us that he did not torture, had never tortured. "It's those informers," he whispered, contemptuously. "That flat-nosed Flores, that villainous Mustiga, that braggart Alegría. They are the ones; they are barbarous. I don't know why they do it. After all, the political prisoners are our neighbors. Don't you think?"

We agreed with him; drank to him; to his wife; to the liberty of the next one to be released. The poet Spelucin took from his miserable pallet a package of coca leaves and a little gourd filled with powdered lime.

"I invite you to join me," he said, opening the little packet reverently. Until dawn, half a dozen of them sat chewing the leaves and talking on esoteric themes. The chubby sergeant was the first to fall asleep.

5

Meanwhile, a series of very important changes had been taking place in Europe. The German Communist Party, light and hope of millions of communists across the world, was crumbling. The great bulwark of the Third International was falling, and the burning Reichstag lit the triumphal march of Nazism.

Again and again, the imprisoned communists asked me to explain why this was happening. They had been promised civil war in Germany. Not only was there none, but the communist colossus was surrendering like a coward, without resistance, without a single shot. I didn't know how to answer them, nor how to explain to myself this break, this capitulation, this moral bankruptcy.

"Why haven't they fought?" my comrades asked.

"Why have they surrendered in this cowardly way?" asked the *apristas*.

I could give no answer. The imprisoned communists were shamed in the eyes of the *apristas* who taunted them with the surrender of the German party.

"We hoped," said the poet Spelucin, "that the German communists would form the first rank in the battle against Nazism. But they have surrendered like cattle and they are being slaughtered as if they were."

To reinforce their arguments and to encourage their own follow-

100

ers in the long prison vigils, some of the leaders of the APRA uprising in Trujillo told stories of that tragically bloody week.

"Búfalo was a man—not like Thaelmann," laughed the Negro, Esquerre. "He didn't surrender or put out his neck for the axe. He fought like a lion. He was a man who didn't know the meaning of fear."

"Every night," said a workman, an older man who had taken part in the drama of Trujillo, "he got us to unite again in the ruins of Chanchan. Búfalo was convinced, and he convinced us, that we must make the revolution that the *aprista* party had come to this country to accomplish."

"Some of us didn't agree," said a hoarse voice, from a pallet in a shadowy corner.

"Yes, of course, a few. There are always those," answered the old man, "but Búfalo said it had to be done. He had courage and he was convincing. How he talked! You remember friends? He was a man!"

"A great man!" came the enthusiastic chorus.

"There, in those meetings, Búfalo planned the attack on the barracks—remember? He knew where the doors were, the windows, the corridors——"

"He knew where every officer slept," interrupted Salaverry, a hoarse-voiced mulatto, "where they kept the bolts of the guns and where you had to go to get the belts for the machine-guns."

"That's how it was. He prepared everything. He knew how many men must go to the main gate, and how many should attack through each window; which was the easiest spot, and which the most difficult. And he took the most dangerous for himself."

"So they would shoot him?" said a little blond boy. "I think he was wrong."

"At the zero hour," said Salaverry, "the place for the chief is in front of his men if he wants them to follow."

The old man continued calmly:

"Búfalo directed the attack on the barracks and put himself at the head of the attackers. He was in shirt-sleeves, very pale, tight-lipped——"

A long cheer interrupted him.

" 'Forward, *canejo!*' shouted Búfalo. 'Go in and get them all out! Be men, *canejo*, kill them all! We have suffered like idiots long enough! Get the sons of bitches! Kill every bastard there!' "

"And you should have seen the boys!" put in Salaverry. "That's when we found out who was a man! When the bullets whistled and we had to break windows and doors to get in."

"Were you armed?" someone asked.

"The arms were in the barracks. A few had revolvers. Most of us had nothing but sticks and stones and a few crowbars. Not so, my friend?"

"Yes, that's how it was. Those men were brave, not like they are today. God, how brave they were! The pity of it was, that right there, at the big gate, lay Búfalo. They killed him in the first few minutes."

"They say it took many volleys."

"He had one in his forehead. That's the one that stopped him. That finished him."

"You should have heard the shouting. We won by shouting. The soldiers were paralyzed. Inside, some of the sergeants and corporals began to help us. In less than a quarter of an hour we had taken all the officers prisoner. We tied them up and shut them up in a hall. The soldiers ran around the barracks like chickens. They came and went; some of them leaned against the walls and others went to the kitchen and ate everything they could find. They didn't seem to care what happened. Some of them asked if we were going to kill them on the spot. Our men grabbed the guns and filled their pockets with cartridges; they took out the machine-guns—what a mess, by the Virgin! —no one knew what to do with the cannons or the big cannon balls. Everyone tugged at them as if they were going to take them home for their children to play with."

"The pity of it was that Búfalo was dead," insisted the mulatto.

"Yes, but there was our companion, the army officer," interrupted a man with high cheekbones and piercing eyes. He looked mongol, a kind of living copy of those effigy jars that are found in pre-columbian graves. We waited for him to continue but he was silent.

"Our companion the army officer arrived much later," said the mulatto. "Quite a while after the barracks were taken and the officers captured."

"I was with the officer," retorted the *cholo*, "and *I* did not arrive after the barracks were taken and the officers captured. I helped take the barracks and, if you remember, it was I who tied up the major and I tied the rope to the cannon to drag it out. Don't you remember?"

102

"It was the *cholo*, Yako, who hauled the cannon," said the blond boy. "The officer didn't wear a uniform, did he?"

"No, he had an overall. And I pulled the cannon out and the rope left its mark on me and that's why I'm alive today!"

"What mark? Why did that keep you alive?" we asked.

"When we lost and the troops took the city afterwards," Yako answered, "the officers examined the shoulders of every man for the mark of the rifle-strap. And every man who had that mark was shot."

"And you didn't have that mark?"

"I had one all right but it was under the mark of a braided rope."

"I don't understand about the mark," said another man, a professor from the southern highland.

"Well listen," said the old man, "if you carry a gun for weeks, slung by a strap over your shoulder, it leaves a mark on you. That's what the officers were looking for. And you'll never talk to anyone who had that mark."

"Why not?"

"Because their tongues are underground," said the mulatto. "Because everyone who had that mark was shot then and there. Now do you understand?"

There was a tense and bitter silence. The room was now in total darkness. Outside, beyond the bars, we could see the silhouettes of the guards, armed, their bayonets fixed.

"Why do they carry fixed bayonets?" asked the blond boy.

"Well, what happened? What did they do with the cannons and the rifles?" asked the professor.

"For Christ's sake, where have you been all your life?" asked the mulatto. "Did you fall on your head when you were a baby?"

"I never belonged to a party. I know nothing of such things."

"Then why are you here?"

"Someone wanted my job. And I was courting a girl in the town. The sub-prefect liked the girl, so he reported me as subversive. I've been here for two years."

"Well," the old man went on, "we took the city that same day. Everything fell into our hands. We took the officers we had captured to the city jail and left them there. Forty of them, from second lieutenants to majors."

"And what did they do?"

"What could they do? They did as we said. They still had their uniforms, their gold braid, their insignia, but we had their revolvers.

The truth of it is, we were the ones who didn't know what to do. We had no leader. We ran around like chickens, just as the soldiers did when we took the barracks."

"What do you mean?" asked Yako. "We took over the prefecture and put in an *aprista* prefect."

"And what good did that do us? We waited like idiots for the government troops to come and exterminate us. I tell you we didn't know what to do. I was there, I know what I'm talking about. I wanted to fight on until we won, but how? Look—we were running around the streets with one of the cannons, and the children followed us around with the cannon balls. Then suddenly someone said, 'Let's attack the *hacienda* of Casagrande,' and—I don't know why—just for something to do, I said, 'Let's go.' So we went to the station and got hold of a locomotive and a freight-car."

"And was it hard to get that cannon into the freight-car!" added the mulatto.

"You remember? You were there. We got it on finally and put wedges under it and we took along twenty big cannon balls."

"And you went to the *hacienda?*" asked the professor.

"Sure we did," said the mulatto. "Remember, old fellow?"

"How could I forget? We got there, stopped the locomotive and loaded the cannon. We had an Indian with us who had been an artillery sergeant. He finally said he was going to fire, so we'd better all cover our ears."

"And then he fired the first shot—God, was it funny!" laughed the mulatto.

"That shot hit everything. The cannon shot itself off the freight-car. The wedges flew, the wheels slipped and the cannon fell off into a ditch full of mud; you couldn't see any of it except the mouth, smoking. We'd have needed an ox-team to get it out of there. We couldn't think of anything else to do, so we went back to Trujillo on the freight-car with the cannon balls."

"And the cannon balls?" asked the professor.

"This fellow did fall on his head when he was young," said the old man. "They stayed at the station, my friend. Do you want to go and get them?"

"No," said the professor. "I just wondered. And then?"

"Then the government troops came. The airplane dropped bombs and scared everyone. That night all hell broke loose. They started taking prisoners and shooting people. They killed men like flies. Didn't they?"

We were silent.

"Why have the guards got fixed bayonets?" the blond boy asked again.

"That's true," the old man heard him for the first time. "They have got fixed bayonets. What's going on?"

"Something's up," said Yako. "Something has happened."

"And the captured officers?" asked the professor.

"We had to kill them," said the mulatto, "because if they were left alive they would denounce a lot of us. Anyhow they were army officers and the army was killing our companions. So we hesitated a while and then we killed them all, that same night. We shot them through the windows. I held the lantern and the others shot them, trying to get them in the head. Some clung to the wall screaming; others fell to their knees and begged to be spared for the sake of their children. They tried to keep out of the light but in half an hour we got every one of them."

No one spoke. After a while each man went to his bed. The mulatto lit a cigarette. By this light I saw his face; he was smiling. He seemed to find this bloody tragedy pleasant to remember. The other prisoners begged a drag from his cigarette. This he granted, but he did not let them take it in their fingers. He held it to each in turn, keeping his fingers pressed together so that the smoke escaped with difficulty.

"There they were, by Christ," he said with satisfaction.

"Something has happened," Yako said from his bed, "if they're carrying fixed bayonets."

Aprista terrorism, I was thinking, was now in full swing. The boastful words of Haya in Europe were here translated into blood and corpses, into senseless and cowardly cruelty. Here were the followers of the *Alianza Popular Revolucionaria Americana,* convinced that they could cure the grief of the people by washing misery with blood.

The barracks remained dark and silent. Every half-hour the whistle of the sentries sounded outside. In the first hours of dawn the guard was doubled and the prison flag was raised to half-mast. Sanchez Cerro was dead!

The President-Dictator had been assassinated. It seemed impossible that this was the true explanation of the fixed bayonets; it seemed rather, a dream born of the yearnings of thousands of prisoners. But it was true. The President had been shot as his car drove through a public square. The *aprista* worker who had done the deed had died on the spot, run through by a hundred bayonets.

The government changed and there was the usual result—the democratic springtime. Jails opened and poured forth their political prisoners. Exiles returned. The press was free. Weeks, months went by; but I remained in prison, without trial or sentence of any kind. The new cabinet of General Benavides' government was headed by Jorge Prado y Ugarteche. His political reputation for supporting democratic forms was justified, for he emphasized respect for the constitution and tried to keep his acts within the law. The jails were emptied of political prisoners. Yet I remained confined. For me alone the democratic spring of 1933 remained winter. To all attempts to obtain my liberty, or at least a trial, the police officials answered, "Mañana, mañana."

At this time an emissary from Moscow was traveling through Latin America, calling on the communist parties to send representatives to the seventh Congress of the Communist International, which was to be held in the Soviet capital. So now, once more, I had an appointment in Moscow. I seemed to see, beyond the bars of my cell, the Red Star, blazing above the spires of the Kremlin.

6

The physical and mental torture inflicted on the prisoners, the frightful food, which was actually rotten at least twice a week, together with the hunger-strike and its consequences, had destroyed my health. I looked like a skeleton, my skin was peeling hideously and my eyes were big with fever. One night I was shaken by chills; I shivered on the pallet that served me as a bed and my teeth chattered. A policeman who had once been a medical student came to see me and, taking my pulse, diagnosed my illness as malaria, the classic tertian fever.

Some days later, accordingly, I was moved to the prison of the Guadalupe Hospital in Callao, where I was given dozens of quinine injections. The former medical student had diagnosed correctly and a few weeks later I felt better and was free of fever.

The prison was large, very cold, with a yellowish tiled floor, a very high ceiling and walls that needed whitewash. It had no doors but was closed off instead by a huge barred gate. Alfredo Elias, the *aprista* leader, was my companion in this imprisonment, in the discussion of the books we read, and in endless talk of the day when we would be free. We planned fantastic escapes.

From these half-joking conversations I went on to real planning, for I was now sure that the Benavides government was not going to release me. I read; I talked; I spoke French with Sister Margarita; I answered the doctor's questions; but all the while the idea of escape went round and round in my head. Not only was I eager to be free; not only did I wish to attend the Congress in Moscow. I was heartily sick of the prison food—especially the soups so heavily laden with camphor. In the opinion of the police and the prison doctor, camphor decreased the sexual desires of the prisoners—desires which they seemed to think insatiable. I had to escape. But how? I would have to get help from outside. How? A letter to someone? But they would never let it go. A courier. But who? Then I thought of Sister Margarita.

This Sister of Charity of the order of Saint Vincent de Paul visited us every day. A Parisian, still young, thin, sensitive, with beautiful eyes, she was always very kind to her patients. It made her very happy when I spoke to her in French of Paris, of the left bank and the book-stalls along the Seine, of the Mont Ste. Geneviève and the Luxembourg. At these times she would look at me kindly and ask, with maternal tenderness:

"Why have you committed the grave error of becoming a communist? You have gone off the narrow path that leads to God." And to this I would make no answer, for fear of wounding her through her faith.

"You must be so unhappy," she often added. "It makes my heart bleed to see you in so terrible a situation."

"And why unhappy, Sister? Do you think the early Christians were unhappy when the emperors threw them to the lions?"

"How can you make such a comparison? It is not the same thing at all."

"All of us who suffer for the sake of justice are of the same kind," I said. 'Blessed are they who hunger and thirst after righteousness.' "

At this the Frenchwoman shook her white coif till it fluttered like a great frightened bird, and urged me to finish my dessert. "I made it myself; it is not prison food." I enjoyed the sweet and thanked her.

"You don't know how grateful we are, little mother. This dessert you have made should be eaten only by Sisters of Charity and communists like me, for we're both in the odor of sanctity."

Sister Margarita pretended to be angry and said she would not come again if I blasphemed. But she always came again, announced by the rustle of her starched, blue habit, the white wings of her coif like a cool shadow. She listened to our confidences, but never gave us any in return. She talked of the French countryside, the cooking and the flowers of France, and at these times she became radiant; but she never spoke of herslf. What memories, what nostalgias, what dramas, I wondered, slept or stirred restlessly under that starched white coif. Little by little we became good friends; so much so that at last I dared ask her to carry a letter for me to the outside.

"I am here," she said with emphasis, "to serve the Lord and his unfortunate creatures; not to carry papers for communists."

"This has nothing to do with communism, dear Sister," I said, just as emphatically. "It is a matter of health and perhaps a bit sentimental. But if you don't want to do it, it's all right. Please forget that I asked you."

On subsequent visits she chatted with me, as she had before, about Notre Dame, the Tuileries, and of Louise de Marillac, foundress of the Hôtel Dieu. Then, three days later, she fell silent, stirring the dessert she had brought, and at last asked, "For whom is the letter?"

"For one of the internes of this hospital."

"If you had only told me that—" she murmured, smiling her gentle smile. "I'll be back this afternoon and I'll take it for you then."

She left me overwhelmed with gratitude and with every hope. This third-year medical student was a party member; and with his help, I thought, something could really be done. His answer was that he must discuss the matter with two of my cousins who had recently arrived from home; which meant, in our language, two men from Moscow or the South American Bureau of the Comintern. Shortly afterward, injections were prescribed for me and I was not surprised to see my comrade arrive with a hypodermic syringe. He was accompanied by a member of the secret police, but we managed, in spite of his presence, to exchange notes.

The "cousins" were, as I had suspected, messengers from the Bureau who agreed to my escape, provided that it could be carried out without too great risk of my being shot, or of any bloodshed whatever, and with nothing, absolutely nothing, left to chance. An abortive attempt would complicate my situation very much.

The first and perhaps greatest difficulty was to get past the two sets of barred gates, watched day and night by guards who changed every six hours. The first gate closed off the room we were confined in from the corridor which led to one of the courtyards. The second gate closed off the corridor from the courtyard. How to get past them? The more I thought about it the more impossible it seemed.

Then one night, by chance, hope appeared. My companion, Elias, the *aprista* leader, became seriously ill with a throat infection. The next day Sister Margarita demanded a doctor for him.

"My poor children," she said, "you have caught cold in this room that I call the room of dereliction; for only derelicts come to this. It is cold enough here to freeze the very soul. These tiles make you cold just to look at them; and these great high ceilings and no proper doors! Who ever saw a room without a door?"

The doctor came, accompanied by two assistants, both communists, who had changed their shifts so that they could come. The doctor mistook us for patients with the same disease and examined both of us carefully. He painted our throats and said that Elias might have to have his tonsils out. In any case the treatments must take place in the nose and throat clinic, and authorization for us to make daily visits to the clinic was obtained. At the same time the doctor recommended a visit to the dental clinic.

If I was to use this opportunity to escape, Elias must be my accomplice; and we must act quickly, before our throats were well and the daily permission to leave the prison rescinded. When I approached him on the subject, he agreed enthusiastically, and from that moment we both made every effort to arrange things so that there should be no slip. Thursdays and Saturdays, I was allowed visitors for an hour. I told my mother and sisters to stay away so that this precious time could be used by the daughter of a general, whose party membership made her a perfect messenger for communication between me and my friends outside.

Every step that had to be taken from the clinic to the street was carefully measured and timed. The hour for our appointment was miraculously changed from morning to afternoon, when the guard was often sleepy from the effects of a full meal and, more often than not, a drink or two. Finally, the day before our escape, my "cousins" visited me on passes issued to other people so that I would recognize them as allies the next day. Miguel was tall and robust and had a slight limp; Camilo was shorter and younger, more agile and less noticeable. (Needless to say, their names were not Miguel and Camilo.) The plans were made. The thirty communists who were to take part in my escape were armed with blank cartridges. Only the six who were to flank me, as I walked down the passage and into the street, were to carry loaded revolvers, which they were instructed to use only in case of extreme need.

The great day arrived, and as I lay on my pallet waiting for the guard to take us to the clinic, I thought how those barred gates were to close behind me for the last time. Alive or dead I would escape from them forever that afternoon. I tried to think of some tiny detail which might have been forgotten, but all was lost in a disconcerting vagueness. My mind wandered, without control, from reality to fiction. It came to rest at last on the decapitation of Julien Sorel, the wilful hero of Stendhal's *Le Rouge et le Noir*.

Alfredo Elias spoke to me and I consigned him to the devil, just as Sister Margarita entered. The prison clock struck one. The hour had come. I was trembling from head to foot when the Sister of Charity approached me and began to pray.

"Exaudi nos Domine—miserere nobis," she recited tonelessly. Can this nun suspect something? I wondered. Why has it occurred to her to pray, this day of all days?

"What ails you, Sister?" I asked, almost angrily.

The locks turned, the bolts clanged. The sergeant arrived, fingering the sheath of the great broadsword which hung at his waist and seemed to be his pride and joy.

"Both to the clinic!" he ordered. He clicked his heels, did an about-face and left. Alfredo Elias rose from his bed at once, but I dawdled, pretending to look for a prescription that I needed, hoping in this way to use up the five minutes that it always took the sergeant to reach the street. Elias helped me search.

We passed the first gate, followed by Sister Margarita, still praying, as if she would have us die well or escape successfully. This woman must know something, I thought. She must be praying to quiet her fear.

We reached the second gate. I thought of those condemned to death who walk between high walls with a priest beside them mumbling Latin phrases. We passed the second gate and turned toward the second courtyard.

"Au revoir, ma soeur," I said to Sister Margarita.

The nun's lips trembled with prayer. Or was it fear?

"Has she gone crazy?" asked Elias.

"She just felt like praying today," I answered with a calmness that surprised me.

At that moment the lookout posted in the second courtyard made a wide gesture with his arms; the signal was passed on to the first

110

courtyard, to the waiting-room of the clinic, to the outermost garden and to the street.

On a bench in the corridor a man whom I knew to be a member of the secret police was sitting, his oily black forelock hanging in his eyes and his head fallen forward as if he were asleep, or pretending to be. A few yards away, two men leaned against the wall, watching him. The two exchanged a meaning look with me. I was still haunted by the thought; did Sister Margarita know something or was she psychic? I noticed that one of our policemen had been changed. The one next to me was more athletic; he had scabs on the backs of his hands as if he had ichthiosis. The other one was older, fatter. It would be harder for him to run.

In the corridor we met a big man with a shaggy head of hair, wearing a woolen undershirt and a Salvation Army cap. It was Miguel, the slightly lame one. Where had he got hold of that hat? A little way behind him walked a boy, wearing a great white apron, and carrying a tray laden with dishes and slung from his neck on a strap, thus leaving his hands free. As he drew near I saw that one hand was significantly plunged in his apron pocket.

We had got as far as the waiting-room. My knees were trembling and I was walking very slowly, almost staggering. Suddenly two men near us began to scream insults at each other. The larger seized the other by the throat and seemed about to strangle him. The athletic policeman who accompanied us threw himself upon them to separate them. At the same instant a tall boy came out of one of the clinics and threw a handful of flour in the eyes of the fat policeman, whom it was then easy to disarm. Meanwhile the men who had pretended to be fighting (two comrades, of course) had managed to disarm the other policeman and lock him in an empty office.

Elias and I were flanked by half a dozen armed men who appeared as if from nowhere. As we went down the corridor a nurse came toward us; a shot was fired and she threw herself on her knees. We passed two members of the secret police standing with their faces toward the wall and their hands up as if they were hanging pictures. Needless to say, their revolvers had been appropriated. In a matter of seconds we had reached the street.

There Juan Barrio and a group of comrades were waiting for us in a car with its motor running. Nearby was a more powerful car, toward which a policeman and a guard were moving. I warned my friends of this danger in time, and Miguel dashed off to puncture its tires. We had to leave him there and clear out at once. As we turned the corner a shot rang out and then another. We followed a zig-zag route for a while until we thought ourselves safe enough to stop in a little square. The chauffeur changed the license-plates on the car. Elias and I had stripped off our prison clothes and put on others that our liberators had brought. Then we drove on, being careful to keep within the lawful speed and to stop for traffic signals. We arrived, at last, at the door of a house almost directly across from the police station. Here a safe shelter had been provided for us.

Meanwhile, the police were giving out the story of our escape. They gave the number of the license-plate (which had been stolen from a private car half an hour before our rescue), and correct data on Elias and me, but completely incorrect descriptions of the comrades who had delivered us.

There had not been a single wound; only one policeman had received a temporarily disabling blow on the head. The police never caught any of those who had cooperated in the rescue, and all the people they arrested (including a dozen communists who had in truth helped) were able to prove that they were *bona fide* patients at the clinic.

"No blood! No prisoners!" Miguel shouted triumphantly when he arrived after dark, minus the shirt and cap.

The afternoon papers were snatched up by the public. They carried long accounts of the noonday escape, enriched by the imagination of the journalists. The papers compared the story to the deeds of Chicago gunmen. But it was, in fact, more like the moving-pictures —spectacular, noisy and totally bloodless.

"It has been a terrific *coup*—with rose-water," said Camilo. "A *coup* which is worth more than ten thousand indoctrination courses and a million manifestoes. This event will be engraved on the hearts of thousands of workers. By now, half the population of the country is celebrating as if it were a holiday."

I was to go to Lima, accompanied by the general's daughter and one of her enchanting little friends who had helped in carrying out the rescue. My two "cousins" were arranging my departure from the country, as they had been directed. I was on my way to Moscow.

CHAPTER V

The Yenan Way

1

MY ESCAPE from prison was hailed by the Latin American Bureau of the International, and later by Moscow, as impressive and lasting propaganda. Agents of the Bureau stowed me away aboard a Grace liner sailing south, and so I managed to get from Peru to Chile where, in Santiago, I met Guralsky (or Juan de Dios as he was known there), and our associate, Inez. Guralsky left for Russia, but I stayed in Santiago long enough to receive medical treatment. Then I flew to Buenos Aires, and from there went on to Montevideo where I took ship for Moscow, via Barcelona and Paris.

2

I reached Paris in the spring of 1934. My first duty, in view of the deep affection I bore him, was to see Barbusse and thank him for the effort he had made (for a second time) to free me from prison, and perhaps even from death. I was sure that he would be glad to see me again, and so he was. But he was appalled by what he called, "The Tragedy of Humanity."

"Germany is Nazi," he said sadly, "and the former members of the communist youth will march against the socialist homeland. National Socialism has on its side the machinery of organization, the habit of discipline and the anti-liberal spirit of the German people. I see war again on the horizon."

"What do you think we ought to do, Master?"

"With Romain Rolland, we have begun a vast movement to unite all those who love freedom. At this time it is no longer a question of fighting for the emancipation of the workers, but of saving the liberty that is still left us. We must unite everyone in Europe who is aware of the meaning of fascism and its danger. The 'Amsterdam-Pleyel Movement,' as I call it, will bring together all who know the danger and who love freedom—socialists, communists, laborites, democrats, liberals, catholics. That is the only task before us today."

113

Barbusse then turned the conversation to Peru and the possibility of a vast union of Latin American countries along the lines we had been discussing.

"And what does the International think of all this?" I asked.

"It will declare itself in this next Congress. At present there is a sharp division. The French party is in favor of our policy; the German party is not. The Chinese are with us and so is Earl Browder. The Latin American position is not yet clear, and the Russians are by no means convinced. It is encouraging that George Dimitrov is on our side, but I am disturbed by the lack of enthusiasm on the part of men like Manuilsky. We must remember that he always expresses the opinions, or at least the suggestions, of Stalin."

"And what about Stalin?"

"Ah, comrade Stalin," Barbusse smiled. "We have talked about this with him fairly frankly. He values the collaboration of Romain Rolland, because he knows that he has great influence over the best intellects, not only of France, but of the world. But Stalin is reserved in his opinions, even with his friends. He has never given us any real support, but it seems that he does not consider our plans inimical to the interests of Russia, or too far from the party line. At any rate, I think he wants our movement to broaden and become stronger."

With these bearings I set off for Moscow, stopping off in Berlin on the way to verify Barbusse's observations. Nazism had indeed won the people, including the young laborers and thousands of former communists. And it was obvious that all these people were back of Hitler because they wanted to be, and not because something had been put over on them.

The following week I arrived, for the second time, at the Soviet border. There I was put into a first-class compartment and served a generous supper. Minsk had not changed since 1929—rags, misery, vagabonds, thieves, the people badly dressed and shod even worse. And yet the literature that I had been receiving during these years had boasted of the success of the Five Year Plans, the socialization of more than eighty-seven percent of the Soviet economy, and the removal of the restrictions on food and clothing.

The next day we reached Moscow, and there I found changes. Tverskaya Street, which led from the Alexander Station to the Comintern was now called "Maxim Gorky" and was paved with asphalt. In Ozhod-Niriat, many tall buildings were in process of construction. Also, I was given a far warmer reception than that I had met with on my first visit. Two people met me at the station with a car, just for me and my scant baggage. In the Comintern building, the functionaries were very solicitous, especially when the young man who accompanied me whispered in their ears. The faces of the stenographers (infallible barometers of the Comintern) made it clear that I was welcome in the city of socialism, and in this house from which the world revolution was directed.

Manuilsky himself received me that night. The old man with his pink cheeks, his bright eyes, his white moustache and his grey forelock, received me with open arms.

"You are one of those one must greet with a hug," he exclaimed, and clasped me warmly. "You are well spoken of. We must talk a great deal."

In the friendly conversation that followed, we talked of the more important aspects of the world situation and then came to the problems of Latin America, of which it was clear to me from the first Manuilsky had no great grasp. He generalized too much, taking South America as a single entity, as a vast territory inhabited by people completely in the grasp of the big North American bankers. His picture was vague, oversimplified and therefore erroneous. I refrained from even hinting this opinion to him, since he was one of the most important people in the Comintern and trusted by Stalin.

Manuilsky asked me a great many questions about Guralsky and my personal opinion of each of the men in his group. After several matters had been discussed in detail he asked me pointblank: "Do you have a high opinion of Guralsky?"

"Yes. He seems to me one of the most valuable men in the Comintern."

"Have you talked with Sinani yet?"

"No. And I don't know him personally, only his writings. I know that they differ on certain questions concerning the problems of Indian communities."

"Correct. On these and on other points Sinani is not in agreement with Guralsky. All these things must be talked out and clarified. I think there will be time."

I did not understand him then. It was only later that I learned that an International Congress would be impossible, owing to the deep differences between the Soviet and the foreign leaders as to the path that their collaboration should take. There was ardent support for the Popular Front and equally strong opposition.

"Are you in favor of the Popular Front?" Manuilsky asked me at this time.

"Yes, I am," I answered. "It seems to me that such a movement will make the communist parties freer in their action, more flexible, and more apt to grow numerically as well as to increase in authority."

Manuilsky turned on me a fixed stare, hard and inquisitorial.

"Are you sure?"

"Yes, very sure," I answered firmly, though I knew from Barbusse that he would not agree with me.

"There is the danger of deviations, of the merging of communist parties with outside forces."

"Yes, there are those dangers. But the danger of Nazism seems to me greater and more urgent. Then too, I believe that isolation is proving more of a threat to the communist parties than would co-operation within a broad democratic movement."

"Do you know that in the Comintern yours is the minority opinion?"

"Yes, I know. But I believe every comrade should defend what he believes just and valid, don't you?"

Manuilsky smiled and changed the subject to that of my health.

"You've had a very bad time," he said. "You must have proper medical attention. A healthy communist is a fighter; a sick communist is just another invalid. Meanwhile, come tomorrow afternoon at five to meet our comrade, George Dimitrov."

"Is it true," I asked, "that he will be proposed as president of the International?"

Manuilsky laughed and did not answer; I took this to mean yes.

I met Dimitrov the next day. Tall, robust, with a serene serious face, and a calm manner, he impressed me as a man who was sure of himself, a man of great will-power and honesty. Unlike Manuilsky he answered questions directly, concretely and without evasions.

"The Latin American question is of the greatest importance," Dimitrov said to Guralsky, who acted as translator, "because the policies adopted there will serve as a precedent for other similar regions. There will be no world Congress this year and perhaps not even next year; the disagreements are too deep. But as almost all the Latin American delegates are here, or on the way, let us take advantage of it to have a Latin American Congress. What you decide will serve as our course of action."

"What do you think of the Popular Front?"

"That project of Barbusse and Rolland? I am heartily in favor of it, but there is little sympathy for it. What do you think of it? Do you know it?"

116

"Yes, I know the general plan and am in favor of trying it."

"Well then, defend it at the Congress. But for the present, you must take care of your health. You look very sick; you must be careful."

As he took his leave he said to me: "If you are for the Popular Front you should talk with the French comrades. See Thorez when he arrives, and Raymond Guyot of the French youth movement."

Two days later I was a patient in the Kremlin Hospital, taking a rest-cure that lasted two weeks. I was then sent to a sanatorium near Sochi, on the coast of the Black Sea. There I was able to meet and make friends with hundreds of party leaders, Soviet authorities and various persons very close to the Kremlin. For three months I stayed in close contact with members of the *élite* of the party and of the government. I noticed that within the sanitorium a very tight spy system functioned, which carefully supervised the conversations, the movements and even the correspondence and friendships of every person there. It was then that I began to understand the essence of the form that life in Russia had taken, and to realize that all resistance to Stalin's purpose of imposing a personal and police dictatorship would meet with harsh opposition. The sanitorium was a seething cauldron of political antagonisms. The party was like a boiler, subjected to too high pressure. Stalin was not absolutely sure of his party, but he had the police meticulously organized under his personal control; a police much more numerous than the party itself, well fed, well armed, and which enjoyed privileges superior to those of many party dignitaries and to the upper category of government functionaries. The police power stretched across the whole Soviet Union.

During a stay of more than two months at the sanitorium, I noticed that not a single factory worker or miner ever came to its comfortable pavilions and dormitories. A disturbing majority of the patients were members of the police; some were party leaders or Kremlin functionaries, and a few were factory or *sovkhoz* directors. The regime was, we were told, for the benefit of the workers, peasants and soldiers. But in that sanitorium where I was carefully tended there was never a worker or peasant. The soldiers probably had their own sanitoria.

I discovered that medical science was extremely retarded in comparison to the West. The doctors were unselfish, competent, and sympathetic to their patients, but they lacked the advantages that modern techniques have put at the service of medicine. They were short of instruments, drugs, specifics, sometimes even of cotton. This shortage was attributed, by the doctors and nurses, to the great need of certain materials for the manufacture of armaments.

"Armaments?"

"Yes, of course, armaments. Can't you see there's a war coming? Don't you know that the capitalists are drumming up war against our beloved Russia; that they are going to attack us; that they want to encircle us first and destroy us afterwards? Eh—the bandits!"

I listened with interest and was rather shocked to find that the people who talked in that way really believed it. The war psychosis was developed in the average Russian to an extraordinary degree, amounting almost to a collective paranoia nurtured and cultivated by the Kremlin and the secret police. Out of fear of war, the Russian who was neither a policeman nor a government employee put up with hunger, misery and terror. He sacrificed himself so that the country and the government might be well armed with tanks, airplanes and bombs for his defense. The armament race against which we, the communist parties in capitalist countries, were incited to fight without respite, was an everyday concern for the government and for the Russian people. In the immense vastness of the Soviet Union, the scarcity of the most essential things was routine. Russian homes in general had a shockingly low standard of living, touching on misery in millions of cases. According to popular belief, this shortage was due to the desperate armament race. It was the price the Russian had to pay every day, to keep his country from being invaded by the capitalist pirates and the nazi bandits.

At the end of my ninth week of rest and pleasant idleness, I prepared to return to Moscow. Barbusse had arrived but he would be in Moscow only a few days, leaving shortly for the south—Georgia, the Republic of the Kirghizes, Azerbaijan and the warm Black Sea. I could imagine what a collection of artistic daggers the great writer would make on his trip. I felt that I must see him; to talk with him about the reality around us, about the future of the gigantic Five Year Plan, now in full swing and celebrated as the dawn of a new society, now springing beyond the realm of the idea, now a solid accomplishment built of steel and concrete.

The kindly and caustic old doctor, who made fun of everybody and everything, authorized my departure. His young assistants repeated their instructions about diet and rest and warned me against emotion at mealtimes. The nurses were very kind. The severe matron let me break my rest routine, and leave my wheel-chair to go to the beach to bid my numerous friends goodbye, especially the children whom I reduced to helpless laughter by my peculiar pronunciation of Russian.

In the Hotel Lux in Moscow, they had prepared for me one of the new apartments on the top floor. Manuilsky had commanded it, with the result that the hotel manager himself ran to open the car door when I arrived from the station. Never had the translators and stenographers been so cordial.

3

The Moscow press had given a warm homage to Henri Barbusse, hailing his arrival in the Soviet Union as a unique event. He was called "a noble and sincere friend of Stalin," and, along with laudatory adjectives for his person and his work, "the companion in arms of Maxim Gorky." It was obvious that great political importance was attached to his visit.

In Russia, autumn is the most beautiful season. The harshness of the winter has not yet come and the atmosphere is agreeably mild. The rains, the thaw and the frightful mire that must be endured in the Russian springtime all are lacking. The autumn was the best season for Barbusse's miserable lungs, and by arriving at this time he could become acclimatized so that he could endure the first cold. On the anniversary of the October Revolution, he was to take part in the parade on the Red Square (past the railing of Lenin's tomb) marching next to Stalin, and in company with the high dignitaries of the *Valst*. The Soviets designate with this word a concrete category of power, making an abstraction of the persons who compose it. It is something like "the throne" in absolute monarchies, or "the court" of Louis XIV in France. Barbusse was the foreigner who was to share with George Dimitrov, the highest honor accorded by the Kremlin to its distinguished guests.

It was not easy for me to see Barbusse. Not only was Moscow not Paris, but he did not sleep in his apartment in the Hotel Metropole; he only came there for a few hours when the temperature was warmest, to receive the visits of his friends and the greetings of important Soviet personages. I left him a letter in which I greeted him and begged him, if he would, to give me an interview. Inside of forty-eight hours we were together. He was excited about the imminent ending of bread and other rationing.

"They have almost overcome the greatest difficulties, those that have weighed heaviest and lasted longest. Now the people will be better fed, they will have a different standard of living." He spoke of the successes of the Five Year Plan and of the changes its achievement would cause in Russian life, above all in the lower strata of the working class. Several times he referred to cordial conversations with Stalin.

One afternoon he called me aside and said in a low voice, "I think you are about to have a great opportunity. Within a few days comrade Stalin will accord a friendly interview to a small group, not more than fourteen people. Thinking you would like to meet him and hear him, I have included your name." I was deeply touched and thanked Barbusse for this new kindness, whereupon he smiled with his usual sweetness.

"I was sure it would please you. Bring me your Comintern documents and two photographs for identification. If you wish to ask any questions, bring them to me, typed, in Spanish. They will translate them. You may ask two questions if you like, but under no circumstances more than three."

He left me to receive several Annamese who were in Moscow accompanied by the French communist youth leader, Raymond Guyot.

Two days later I received a visit from a tall man with an enormous round face, pink and fleshy, and a shorn head. He gave me a questionnaire in Russian to fill out, translating the questions for me, one by one. Name, surname, social origin, income, professions, etc. etc., which I had many times already sent in to the Comintern. I pointed this out to the man with the shorn head, but he shrugged his shoulders and continued to fill out the questionnaire.

"Why do you want to see Comrade Stalin?"

"You can guess, comrade, that it is no mere curiosity. I am no tourist."

"Is it then a political interest?"

"Well, yes, political interest and personal satisfaction."

"Have you any journalistic interest?"

"Properly journalistic, no."

The moon-faced man made notes in a book which he had taken out of his briefcase. I wondered if the secretaries, guardians and supervisors would in the end cancel Barbusse's offer.

"It is Barbusse who is sponsoring this interview."

"I know, I know, or I would not be here. You must give me your documents and the text of the questions you wish to ask. We must examine them and let you know if they are proper questions, or such as may not be put."

"All right. Now, comrade, may I come to the interview?"

"I don't know. I cannot tell. It is not up to me. They will let you know."

"When, more or less?"

"I don't know. Soon, comrade, soon. And you know—Barbusse will have told you—whether you come to the interview or not, absolute discretion. Not a word to anyone; absolutely not a word."

The man with the shaven head went away. At suppertime I received a fairly young couple; a man wearing a silk *rubashka,* black riding-breeches and black, shiny, custom-made boots. The girl was tall, her hair parted in the middle and caught at the neck. She wore no stockings, only sandals, and a foreign dress. This couple treated me more cordially than had the moon-faced man. They questioned me about the date of my joining the party, the number of times I had been imprisoned, the contacts I had had in the political field before joining the party, my intellectual preferences and finally, over and over again, if I had ever had any nervous disease.

At last they were through with the questions. I asked them if I were sure of the interview.

"We cannot tell you. We do not know. They will notify you. Since it is comrade Barbusse who has asked, it is almost certain that you will be considered."

They went off, smiling and gay, taking their leave most cordially and with good humor. Two days later, I had a call from Barbusse saying that I should not leave my room during the next official day of rest. It was forty-eight hours away.

Very early on the day of rest the moon-faced man appeared in my room. He was very respectful. Not content to call me simply comrade, he said "dear comrade," "esteemed comrade" and "my good comrade." I was to go first to the Metropole to meet Barbusse and the others. We would enter through the Moskva gate, by the bridge along the flank of the big old house of the Comintern. My heart beat violently, as it had the first time I went up in an airplane, or on the day of the flight from the Guadalupe in Callao.

I went to the Metropole with the moon-faced man and I waited a good half-hour for Barbusse. When he arrived he asked us to breakfast; it lacked two hours of the time for the interview. With Barbusse were Guyot, the leader of the French communist youth, two Annamese whom I saw for the first time and a Malay, probably a communist from Indonesia. We all spoke French, meanwhile enjoying an excellent breakfast. I pondered the systematic separation that was being made in Russia of the Asiatic communists and those of Europe and America.

121

While Barbusse and Guyot talked with the Annamese, I thought of the special attentions given to certain people; of how Earl Browder, for instance, Foster, Ford and the North Americans never stayed at the Hotel Lux but at the Metropole; and of how the Chinese, Indonesians and Indochinese were housed in special homes outside of Moscow. Only on occasions like this was it easy to see and talk with them.

After breakfast we left for the Kremlin. The car went down to the Moskva to get to the other side of the brick walls. Under the arch we were detained by Red Army soldiers who examined our papers, looked at each of us and asked in correct French if any of us bore arms. After a brief consultation we were permitted to pass.

The car went up a slope and crossed a wide courtyard where we were detained again, this time by officials of the uniformed state police. After the examination of our papers we had to abandon the car and go on foot behind a guide.

The Kremlin within is like one of those World's Fairs at which many countries and industrial firms build pavilions. Gardens, court-yards, houses of various styles, churches, large and small. We were taken to a vast hall, soberly furnished with antique pieces. There we waited for a long time, until various persons came out to talk with us. Barbusse was admitted to an inner room.

A young man, gaunt and austere of face, called me by name and said my questions would not be taken up either because other people had already formulated them or because they touched too closely on the international policies of the present day. I must limit myself to lis-tening, and abstain from any interrogation. This I promised to do. We were then admitted to the next room, where Barbusse was talking with several individuals to whom we were introduced. One of them was Mao Tse-tung, leader of the Chinese Communist Party.

A man, whose gestures and speech were serious to the point of stereotype, indicated the places each of us should occupy. Barbusse was to be at Stalin's right and Mao at his left. Then came the translators and secretaries. The other fourteen of us were to stand facing them. A few minutes before eleven, one of the functionaries announced in a low voice the arrival of comrade Stalin. We were all standing.

Stalin came in through a little door at the side. He wore a white cotton *rubashka*, khaki breeches and dark brown boots. With his right hand he supported the pipe in his mouth, exhaling a bluish smoke. He smiled pleasantly, although the smile seemed to give his face an expres-sion of mockery. He shook hands cordially with Barbusse and Mao, and after that we approached, one by one, to clasp the hand that he held out to us across the wide table.

Stalin is not a tall man. Indeed, I was struck by the difference between the living man and the many statues and portraits that form the iconography of modern Russia. His face is pale, yellowish and pockmarked. He has a very large belly which seems to annoy him, since his effort to hide it under the folds of the wide *rubashka* was obvious. When he laughs his sardonic laughter, he shows two rows of pointed teeth, with evidence of caries. His hair and moustache are grey and bushy and he has many fine lines from the eyes to the temples. He stood throughout the interview, on legs that seemed to me too short for his trunk.

His glance was astute rather than intelligent. Mistrust and suspicion showed in it more than sharpness and perspicacity. He forced himself visibly to appear kind and condescending, but from his general appearance, as from his gestures and inflections, I sensed that his affability did not flow spontaneously but arose as if for the occasion. Stalin, from the first instant, showed special cordiality for Barbusse as well as for Mao. Barbusse seemed a bit tired. Mao was hard-faced, deliberately severe and, at the same time, obsequious to the point of devotion. When Stalin said something, Mao nodded insistently, and once or twice when Stalin said that a question someone asked had already been answered, Mao adopted an attitude of reproof and displeasure.

One of the translators asked the first question, on the subject of racial discrimination.

"All racist ideas of discrimination or racial segregation," Stalin said, "are the product of chauvinistic hatred but they can be very powerful." Without actually mentioning the name, he referred to the United States, and exalted the great fraternity that existed among races in the Soviet Union. He told how in the factories, the unions and the workers' clubs anyone who used a racial insult like "jew," was severely and publicly reprimanded. He spoke with emphasis, taking his pipe out of his mouth, especially when he used words like *first, second, third, fourth,* which he did often to divide the periods of his exposytions. While the translators gave a version of his words, he looked steadily at us, one by one, standing as we were before him across the vast table covered with an embroidered cloth. In all his answers he used rounded clauses, pausing with deliberation at every transition. To a question someone asked about Indians in South America, he answered that the South American natives lived under conditions like those which predominated in the Colonial period, at the time Fray Bartolomé de las Casas made his famous denunciation to the Crown. He declared that racial discrimination in South America was more diffuse, primitive and unconscious than the organized discrimination in North America. Then he spoke of the racial question in a more general fashion, and said that the Chinese were victims of discrimination by the white men. "Isn't that true, Comrade Mao?" he asked, turning to his left. With abject devotion Mao nodded respectfully and answered him, not in Chinese but in Russian:

"Da—da—da, tovarich Stalin. Da, tovarich—spasiva bolshoi— spasiva!" (Yes, yes, Comrade Stalin, thank you very much.)

The next question was on his policy toward the Popular Front, and this seemed to please him. He was glad the topic had aroused such interest and declared that it must be thoroughly studied and decided. After that an end must be put to sterile discussion.

The last question was with regard to the success of the Five Year Plan, the situation of the collective farms, and the future in store for the average citizen of Russia. Stalin repeated everything that the propaganda said. The second Five Year Plan was a great success; it ushered in the socialist regime; more than eighty-six percent of the Russian economy would be socialized. There would be no retreat in the field of economy towards the capitalist system of private property. He even went so far as to predict that within five or six years the average Russian citizen would be able to have everything that the average citizen of the United States or the most advanced European countries had today. "It is a matter," he added, "of abolishing every vestige of capitalism in the life and consciousness of men by the end of this Five Year Plan." After this statement, the interview was brought to an end with a warning of the grave danger of war which threatened the Soviet Union and the need there was to intensify preparations. Since he was certain that it would come as an invasion by the capitalists, without any previous warning, it was essential that the vast country and its immense population be constantly mobilized, day and night. As for the sacrifices required for the sake of armament, he declared that what might seem excessive to other nationals would be accepted by the Russians, who had been accustomed under the tzarist regime to a very low standard of living. Lastly he spoke of the paradise on earth that the collective farms had become. He seemed really to believe it, so that I wondered if perhaps the facts were not distorted before they reached him through the seven circles which so perfectly insulated him. He took his leave of each of us cordially, calling us by our names, and speaking a few pleasant words to each.

After the interview, the translators, officials, guards and secretaries approached us, warning us in many languages not to repeat any part of the interview in private conversation—much less in any journalistic fashion. We left by the long series of courtyards, corridors and galleries by which we had come. Once in the car, we drove under the entrance arch where we turned over our passes to the guard, and went back to Ozhod-Niriat.

I tried not to confess it to myself; I avoided contrasting the memory with the previously imagined truth; but there was no doubt that the interview and the man had disappointed me. Stalin was far from being the superior archetype that I had dreamed; he seemed to me heavy, cold, contemptuous, suspicious. In the midst of all this, there came to me an idea, at once vague and concrete, an idea which has become firmer with time. Stalin is not a European. He seemed to me totally a stranger to occidental thought. I expressed this idea to Barbusse, when commenting on the interview and how my questions had been rejected. And the writer, loyal friend of Stalin, did not reply.

"What else drew your attention in the interview?" he asked.

"The submission with which Mao Tse-tung behaved toward Stalin; as a human phenomenon it surprised me."

"And the more so if you remember that Asiatics do not as a rule show their emotions. They are good friends. Stalin prefers him to all the other Chinese comrades. And there are many excellent ones."

We said nothing more about the interview.

A week later, Mikhail Kalinin, President of the Soviet Union, received a large group, mostly of non-communist Europeans—Englishmen, Belgians, Frenchmen, Swedes and Czechs. In all, about a hundred of us in a sort of auditorium waited almost an hour for his arrival. Entering to applause, the nominal chief and representative of all this vast Russia was jovial and good-humored. Tall and blond, with bright eyes and very white skin, he dressed like a European—trousers, a coat and vest, a hard collar and a French *beret*. Across his vest hung a great watch-chain, and for some reason that I could not fathom he put me in mind of an old watchmaker, although he said often and proudly that he was a metalworker.

As the applause died, Kalinin sat down at a wide table on a kind of stage in the auditorium. The translators began to put questions, notwithstanding the fact that none of the audience had spoken a word.

The first question concerned the Five Year Plan, and Kalinin answered it simply, lauding the accomplishments so far and quoting a British economist at his club dinner: "Either the Five Year Plan will smash us or we will smash the Five Year Plan." General laughter greeted this, but the Russian guards, translators and secretaries did not join in it.

The second question dealt with the situation of the collectives, and to this Kalinin declared that the Russian peasant had never enjoyed better conditions, and that collectivism in the country was amply protected by the government. He said, for example, that in one region on the left bank of the Volga the harvests had been entirely lost in consequence of a drought. Not only had the state cancelled the debts of the collective farms of that region, but it had extended them credit to purchase food, seed, fertilizer and everything that was necessary to start anew.

Finally a British worker in the audience stood up and said in English, that he would like to ask a question on the spot. There was a murmur of approbation in the hall. The Russian guards and secretaries had to yield because Kalinin gave orders for the translation of the question.

"How many Five Year Plans does the President believe will be necessary before the average Russian worker reaches a standard of living equal to that of the British worker?"

Kalinin did not deny that the standard of living in Russia was very low compared to that of the West; but this he ascribed to the heritage of tzarism and the hardships of the revolution. Furthermore, he added, the British worker profited, as the Russian could not, from the imperialist exploitation of the colonies. A new murmur ran over the hall. The British worker had set a precedent in speaking out. A Belgian metalworker now rose to his feet and asked:

"Comrade Kalinin, you are the President of the Soviet Union, that is, its first citizen, aren't you? Then why is it said in Europe that you take your orders from Stalin?"

"I am not a fool," answered Kalinin. "I am a metalworker and you know that they are not idiots. I am President of the Soviet Union, and as such I give orders to Stalin. He is the secretary of the Bolshevik party, and as a party member, I obey him. Is that quite clear?" The Belgian sat down amidst laughter.

"Why," then asked a French Catholic, "are Russian workers short of butter, eggs and bread, while in all the European countries Russian wheat, eggs, butter, fish and sausages flood the markets at such low prices as to compete with local products?" The translator had to re-

126

peat the question twice. Kalinin then answered with a long speech on the dangers of war, capitalist encirclement and the fierce threat of the capitalist sharks, from which we gathered that he meant that the Russian people must go without all these necessities to pay for the munitions factories. The old man did his best (and he had no mean ability) to cloud the issue by diatribes against capitalism and its agents.

A Swedish worker, asking the reason for the existence of so many different categories among the workers, received no answer at all. French and Czechoslovakian communist workers asked further questions about the Five Year Plan and the collectives, which were more agreeable to the Russians. Notwithstanding, in the midst of this return to Kremlin customs, one of the English workers, old and solemn, courteously asked: "Why does Bolshevik Russia make advantageous trade pacts with fascist Italy instead of with countries which are not enemies of labor?"

"The day that the English workers accomplish the revolution that their Russian brothers have accomplished, that day we will sign a trade pact favorable to British workers. But I shall not see that day," said Kalinin, "for the British worker is a great opportunist, without doubt the greatest in the world."

Gay laughter filled the hall. The old English worker sat down saying that his question had been evaded, but the translators did not seem to find a word in Russian for this. The interview came to an end and Kalinin withdrew smiling, amidst the applause of the audience.

I had now met the two most important men in Russia, seen them close and listened to them. My skin tanned from the Black Sea sun and the Crimean winds, my heart full of hope, I began my work in the Kremlin, there to defend the Popular Front in theory and in practice, encouraged by Barbusse and the French. Maurice Thorez who had just come from Paris, and with him Guyot, were as ardently determined as I was to organize a vast front of resistance against the fascist onset.

4

The delegations from Argentina, Brazil, Cuba, Mexico, Colombia and Uruguay were by this time arriving in Moscow, without knowing of the postponement of the seventh Congress of the Communist International. It had been decided that a Latin American conference would be held, in which the outstanding problems of the whole Latin-speaking part of the hemisphere would be treated by thirty of the most important communist leaders of that area.

Preliminary conversations had begun. The central debate hinged on the different, and actually opposed, positions of Manuilsky and Dimitrov and the theories held on the one hand by Guralsky, and on the other by Sinani—the two principal directors of the Latin American section of the Comintern.

One afternoon while we were warmly discussing these matters, Moscow was shaken as by an earthquake. From Leningrad came word that Sergei Kirov, second man in the Soviet high command, the Bolshevik leader picked out as Stalin's immediate successor, a prominent member of the Politburo and Number One man in Leningrad, had been fatally shot in the nape of his neck.

The Hotel Lux seethed from the roof to the basement. No one stayed in his room. There were questions on every side and all of us eagerly devoured *Pravda* and *Izvestia* and every English, French and German leaflet. There was equal commotion in the Comintern.

The assassin had acted with strange and extraordinary ease. At the moment of the killing the two men were alone. This in itself perplexed me, since no one could come up even to my room unless I authorized the visit by telephone, using a code password that changed from day to day. Every visitor had to present a pass which I must sign, indicating the hour that he had left my premises. I therefore could not understand how an assassin could enter so casually the office of the president of the Leningrad Soviet, carrying a loaded revolver, or station himself behind the victim when they were alone, and when there was no one else even in the adjoining corridors. It was inexplicable, absurd, inconceivable. I said so in the lobby to the other comrades, commenting on the precautions with which we were surrounded and the so-much-greater ones which must therefore have been taken for Kirov.

After supper I went to see Maurice Thorez. I talked for half an hour with him, and with Raymond Guyot, and as they had to go out I went back to my room. When I got there two men were waiting for me, wearing caps and black jackets. On the table, next to the lamp, was a very large pistol.

One of the visitors did all the talking to me; the other spoke only to his companion, and in Russian. The Spanish-speaking one asked me about my social origin, the date of my joining the party and a heap of information which I gladly gave them. I knew quite well that I was in the presence of the Soviet police. My visitor pointed out to me very insistently that I had shown very poor judgment in expressing my views on Kirov's assassination.

"I expressed no opinion," I said, "only that it seemed to me frightful that whereas communists like me are surrounded by such careful vigilance it could be possible for assassins to enter and leave the offices of men like Kirov; and moreover that they could remain alone with their victims."

"This would suggest ineptitude to you?" he asked.

"Perhaps. I don't see why my opinion should be taken seriously. And if anyone questions me, it should be the party."

The individual's voice turned wheedling and mellifluous. Very smoothly he asked me my opinions of Zinoviev, Bukharin, Rykov and others.

"Look," I said, laughing familiarly, "if you want to know my views on anything, go to the Comintern. As soon as they order me to, I shall be delighted to answer any question you feel like asking me."

There was an exchange of opinion between the two men in Russian. The Spanish-speaking one explained that I refused to talk without orders from the Comintern.

"It is not a question of an investigation, less still of an interrogation," he said to me. "Just a friendly conversation between comrades who wish to reach an understanding."

"Frankly," I said, "I am not trying to reach an understanding with you. I understand neither your visit, nor your attitude." The policeman sat down and spoke at length of the pernicious activities of the "opposition," praised the firm hand, magnificent talent and extraordinary vision of Stalin, and declared that if he believed in Providence he would say that it would protect the revolution. Now that Lenin was dead, a Stalin was needed. He repeated this like a creed. Then he went on and on, speaking of the opposition, saying that not one of them would remain alive, that that very night eighty spies had been shot in Leningrad who had been in prison for a long time, and that the avenging hand of Soviet justice would continue implacably punishing the deviationists, the enemies of the people. It was unpleasant to listen to him. He spoke in stereotyped phrases and used the same arguments, even the same words, as *Pravda* and *Izvestia*.

At last they both went away, taking their leave cordially but leaving me profoundly unquiet. Throughout the hotel there was a nervous agitation which contrasted with the indolent indifference of the man in the street, although the news was well known over the whole nation. Next day at the Comintern, every office had its rumor, every stenographer brought more hair-raising news. In the afternoon the story went the rounds: "Magyar has been arrested." Indeed the agent in charge of *International Correspondence*, one of the most competent Hungarian communists in the Comintern, was not in his office, nor was his secretary.

That night there was a great assembly of all the members of the Comintern. The conduct of Magyar was to be judged; or rather, he was to explain it. He was accused of having contacts with Kirov's assassin, and even of trying to protect him from implacable Soviet justice. We came into the vast hall and were seated in the same row as Manuilsky. Magyar was on the stage, quiet, defiant, eating a ham-and-cheese sandwich with frightening calm. The first row seemed to be filled entirely with members of the Soviet police.

Manuilsky was the first to speak. He ranted indignantly, flushed with anger; he harshly chided Magyar and all those whom he called "the friends of Zinoviev and Bukharin, who used to work in the Comintern." He demanded that they confess their crimes, and that Magyar in particular tell what were his connections with Kirov's assassin; why he had tried to help him and impede "the avenging hand of Soviet justice."

The whole assembly applauded Manuilsky. That is, in some sections the applause began faintly or did not sound at all at first, but as soon as the men in the front row stood up and faced the audience it rose to a general clamor. Magyar then rose upon the stage, with the unfinished sandwich still in his hand. He came forward and began to eat noisily. Between mouthfuls, he said: "I think you had better wait until I finish this sandwich, because otherwise I won't be able to talk."

We protested Magyar's rudeness. I could not understand how a man who found himself faced with so grave an accusation, one which might even cost him his life, could take the matter so lightly, needlessly adopting so grotesque and insulting a pose. Manuilsky and others hurled curses at Magyar.

"Don't be angry, Manuilsky," said Magyar, laughing cynically from the stage. "You are old and it may affect your kidneys. Not your heart, for you haven't got one. Calm yourself man, calm yourself." The men in the front row looked at one another and then at us in the back, wagging their heads as if to say, "What do you think of that?"

Magyar then made a long speech, rhetorical, affectedly theoretical, about the Hungarian revolution and the important role he had played in it. Finally, referring to Kirov's assassin, he called him a good man, his friend, and admitted that he had tried to help him. "Which of you," he asked, "has not a friend and would not try to help him in time of trouble?"

130

"But in trying to help him," said Manuilsky, from his orchestra seat, "you are defying Soviet justice."

"You are old, Manuilsky, to be repeating the foolishness coined by Stalin's secretaries. I am not defying——"

The noise was deafening. The men in the front row protested loudly. Others yelled and berated Magyar, who, from the stage, with another sandwich and a bottle of pop in his hand, laughed until he shook all over. When the clamor died down, he continued: "I defy no justice, nor you, Manuilsky, nor the idiots who are determined to have a drama this evening. Come now, why so much fuss over the death of Kirov? Has not almost every Russian and certainly every Hungarian here tonight killed at least one man? You can't tell me any different, because I know. And I ask you, were not those lives you took worth as much as Kirov's, humanly speaking?"

The shouts began anew, "This is unbearable." "What has got into Magyar? He is not himself." "He's crazy!—a comedian—a wretch!"

"Let him continue, comrades," said a man with a shaven head who was acting as president. "Go on, Magyar."

"I know," said Magyar after a large swallow of pop and a mouthful of sandwich, "that all of you have renounced human feelings and language a long time ago. I too; but it happens that I have a stubborn memory which still retains traces of the old tongue. I ask you, you cretins, what did Kirov have that any other man hasn't?"

A new storm broke out in the hall. "He is talking like a maniac! He's playing a comedy! He's crazy!"

"Neither crazy nor a humbug," yelled Manuilsky. "He is a counter-revolutionary, an enemy of the people, a zinovievist bandit." And the indignation against Magyar flowed over the hall like a wave, filling every corner.

I had known Magyar well. He was serious, controlled; he wrote brilliantly and clearly, and when he corrected the articles we contributed to *International Correspondence*, it was always with good humor and great pains. On seeing him pass along the corridors of the Comintern with his briefcase under his arm, one would have taken him for a university professor. In his writings he had been Stalinist. When he spoke, he did so amiably, pausing often, with a grave voice and impressive sobriety.

How could he be a bandit, this lucid interpreter of marxism, this quiet transparent man who had always kept free of violence and clung to logical reasoning? Suddenly, almost overnight, when some perverse creature (as the Soviet press put it) had assassinated Kirov, he was transformed into a man possessed by the devil. There, on the stage, eating his sandwich with studied coarseness, Magyar was like a monstrously deformed figure. Insolent, contemptuous, become suddenly a cur, he seemed in truth to be playing a comedy, carrying out an assigned role, rather than facing a terrible reality. When he had finished, he dusted off his hands elaborately and stood with his legs far apart and his arms folded, defying the assembly.

Three men asked for the floor and spoke in turn, rendering homage to Kirov, the great Bolshevik, fallen in the fight against the people's enemies, fallen in the cause of the world proletarian revolution. Kirov, the best friend, the most precious and intelligent collaborator, the most devoted brother of Stalin! Each time Stalin's name was pronounced, the men in the front row rose to their feet and applauded, turning towards the back and inviting us all to applaud too. Moreover certain men, posted throughout the audience, were noticeably regular in their cries and the energy of their applause.

"Stalin—Stalin—Stalin!"

From that night on, I never heard any word in Russia oftener than that one. On all sides, under all circumstances, in varying tones: "Stalin—Stalin—Stalin!"

Magyar asked for the floor to speak again. The president of the assembly, he of the shorn head and pink face, demanded silence and invited Magyar to say what he liked. Electric dictaphones were turned on to record everything he said. Magyar did not specifically accuse, but he made terrible insinuations against the closest friends of Zinoviev; Bela Kun, ex-president of the Hungarian republic; two of Bukharin's secretaries; the little old Finn, who called himself "Martens" in the Comintern, and who was one of Kuüssinen's rivals in the communist party in Finland where he was looked on as a venerable figure; the long, thin Chemodanov, president of KIM—Communist International of Youth—for whom Manuilsky bore a grudge which might or might not go as far as hatred; old Piatnitzky, and several of the men protected in the Comintern by Zinoviev.

I had the impression that all this was forced. It did not seem natural; it was the talk of an actor who didn't quite manage to play the role very well; it seemed a grotesque comedy destined, however, to turn into a horrid reality, a little later and offstage. We came out after three o'clock in the morning. It was not clear whether Magyar was a villain or a rogue. We were surprised that he had dared to mention comrade Piatnitzky, and to mix into his references comrade Helen Stassova, the enchanting old lady who had been an intimate friend of

Lenin and whom he had called "my beloved autocrat." Hearing us, Manuilsky interrupted with energy and some anger: "Piatnitzky," he shouted, "and Helen Stassova think that to have been a friend of Lenin is proof of talent, but their behavior only goes to show how by the path of sectarianism one can get to imbecility and banditry."

That pronouncement overwhelmed me with fear, a fear which grew when, on the following day, the absence of Piatnitzky from his offices was being commented on, and when we discovered that a dozen men of the NKVD were searching his files, paper by paper. We were all very much struck by the fact that the Soviet press announced the next morning a large number of executions without any trial, neither naming the assassin of Kirov, nor trying nor judging him in any normal way. No one ever saw Kirov's assassin or knew who he was.

I did not understand that, in those moments, one of the most hideous mass slaughters of all time was being unloosed in Russia. I did not realize that the assembly I attended was a kind of rehearsal of the bloody drama that Stalin's regime was preparing, and which would unfold itself implacably and fiercely through many years in the immensity of the steppes, drowning in blood, crushing under a mountain of crimes, the slightest symptom of opposition or of mere difference of opinion.

Perhaps for an instant it crossed my mind that Magyar was playing a base comedy—that the whole thing had been staged by Manuilsky, by the servants of Stalin in the Comintern, by the chiefs of police, to explain and justify to public opinion the pitiless repression which was from that moment turned against Zinoviev, Bukharin and their friends, and which was afterwards extended to all sectors of Russian life. But at the moment I did not succeed in getting the clear picture which came to me only slowly and painfully and after many years.

When we are possessed by an idea as a faith and an obsession, when we are in love with the path and dazzled by the goal, contrary ideas reach our mind and touch it temporarily but are not allowed to dwell in it consciously. It is as if some mysterious force built impassable partitions between our conflicting thoughts so that they can not join and fight. Only the lapse of time and the experience of living can slowly break down these defenses, letting in the antagonistic notions which may crumble what we once supposed a tall and solid structure of belief. Only many years later, did I dare even to think that Kirov had not been killed by the zinovievists, but that the candidate for succession to Stalin had been liquidated by Stalin himself, and that the assassin was a member of the NKVD. In this way only could be explained the logic of events of that time, to which I was a witness.

After that assembly of the Comintern, the members of the Moscow machine of the International, the friends of Zinoviev, and almost all those who, resisting the leadership of Manuilsky, had approved the candidacy of George Dimitrov for the Presidency of the Communist International, disappeared from their offices one by one. There came a day when ugly, chubby Bela Kun did not come to work. Juancito, my Polish comrade of the Latin American Bureau, to whom Magyar had referred in his speech, disappeared also. Another day, Chemodanov, President of the KIM, was missing; then the gay and amenable old Piatakov; then the translator Smirnov; the stenographer Anetka, and the assistants Shapiro, Goldenberg and Cheliabin.

Along the corridors of the ancient house of the Comintern an icy wind of terror was sweeping. Entrance to any office might cause sudden dread to whoever worked there. People began to walk hunched up and terrified. Fear swept especially over the Russians, Finns and Poles. It was as if the focus of the conspiracy which culminated in the assassination of Kirov had been the Comintern—the organization where the Old Bolsheviks were entrenched; where Zinoviev and Bukharin, two of Lenin's great collaborators, had held the presidency. It seemed as if the behavior of Magyar had been a signal, a justification for the NKVD to begin the pitiless persecution which it had for a long time planned.

It was a methodical persecution which ran like a complex machine, well greased, on fine and hidden gears. Day by day, the outstanding directors of the various departments of the Comintern kept disappearing. The Hotel Lux became a center of operations for the secret police. The NKVD installed a special office in the building and there were taken, for identification, the persons who were snatched from their beds and later carried off in the closed wagon which took them away forever.

Simultaneously the Soviet press, the resolutions of the communist party, and the government departments, announced that bread rationing would end, that the butter ration would increase and that its distribution would be extended to workers who were not then receiving it. Abundant and optimistic reports of the success of the Five Year Plan were published and it was even suggested, though vaguely, that the restrictions on clothing and shoes would be appreciably diminished. It was dramatically announced that workers might procure bicycles, radio sets and even aluminum kitchen utensils. The radio sets were of the "Soviet type" on which the listener could not choose or control the stations. They served exclusively for listening to government and party programs.

Popular comment on the end of the bread lines, plus fear of the police, effectively prevented whatever might have been said about the political persecution let loose in the bosom of the Bolshevik party, and carried out against the highest figures in its command. New *chiskas*, or political housecleanings, were announced, and new charges brought against very important people. The name rang out now of Sinani, director of the Latin American Bureau of the Comintern.

Sinani was a tall man, thin, always shod in very clean boots and dressed in a European sack coat with narrow-waisted riding breeches. He had a military air, left over from his army life. At the start of the revolution he had been a lieutenant in the tzar's army; he had fought on the side of the White Russians, and had later been captain in the armies of Kolchak. Not until 1920 had he gone over to the Bolsheviks; later he had joined the communist party. Sinani was a very stubborn man who argued calmly but defended his ideas with obstinacy, even after they had been refuted. When he had a strong argument he harped on it until he tired his hearers. He never yielded without a fight, which might, in some cases, go on for weeks. A great student with prodigious analytical power, Sinani was of value in any theoretical discussion of Latin American problems.

Sinani had been chosen now for accusation. His past was spoken of, his origins, his early life, his wife Ossia's blond hair, her tempting beauty and the extraordinary fact that she was not affiliated with the party. We were all called to an assembly in the public room of the Lux. It was called a "cell session" and the order of the day was "The Sinani Case." It was a matter of purge.

Something was beginning that might end before a wall peppered with shots. We all understood this and were afraid, but we smiled and pretended to be gay. It was a routine gayety, such as we displayed during sessions in which themes like "The Relative Stabilization of Capitalism" or "Building Socialism in a Single Country" were to be discussed.

Sinani was already at the rostrum; no sooner was the meeting opened than he took the floor. In the front row sat the unmistakable NKVD with their long jackets, their fat faces and their shorn heads. I soon learned to pick them out in any gathering by their glance, by their superior dress, by their step, their laugh, their way of walking. It was clear they had no desire to be unperceived. On the contrary, they wished to impress, to show themselves, to give corporeality to the existence of terror.

Sinani was greenish except on his cheekbones where he had two livid violet spots. Tall, gaunt, he spoke rationally with accented energy, and one felt he was being very sincere.

"From a child I learned to love Russia ardently and passionately, perhaps because it was my lot to live simply on the eastern border. My father died in the war with Japan in 1904. He died for Russia and was one of her heroes. I was only a boy."

"Less literature!" cried one of the NKVD.

"*Nous ne sommes pas dans une académie,*" squealed Manuilsky's French secretary.

"Let him speak," said others.

"I have been asked for my biography, comrades," Sinani said in a quiet voice, "and I am giving it. I know it by heart, for I have lived intensely and honorably, and moreover I have been asked to relate it so often." He spoke then of his education, of his adolescence, of his studies, until the time when, because he was the son of a man who had died on the field of honor, the doors of the Russian army were opened to him.

"Of the tzarist army!" screamed the woman who served us tea in the office and who had always seemed to me just a poor woman, without opinions or political ideas. And yet there she was, dishevelled and furious, accusing Sinani.

"Yes, comrade Shura," answered Sinani, "of the tzarist army. In those days there was a different army in Russia." The audience laughed and the president said drily:

"Don't chat, Sinani, and don't call the comrades by their names. Direct yourself to the chair, and try not to draw attention to yourself."

Sinani proceeded with his story and told how he had studied in military academies, and how he had been stationed in Petrograd, Kiev and Vladivostok and of his participation in the war.

"But your mother, comrade Sinani," interrupted the secretary of the cell, waving a sheaf of papers, "received a stipend from the tzarist government, which implies some sort of service."

"True, comrade secretary," Sinani answered, "my mother received the pension that the government paid for the blood my father had shed, defending Russian soil in an unfortunate war."

"Unfortunate war!" shrieked the comrade who cleaned our offices in the Comintern. "You are becoming chauvinist. What kind of communist is this turncoat?" The president imposed silence.

"My mother," continued Sinani, "received a small pension, such as widows of soldiers who have died for their countries customarily do. My mother gave no service in exchange for this."

"So she lived parasitically?" remarked the secretary.

"I think the term is unjust, comrade secretary. She lived on the blood of my father." Sinani's voice broke with emotion. As if it were feared that this emotion might touch the audience, one of the NKVD exclaimed: "Come on. Less pathos, less literature!"

Sinani told how he had fought at the front and the battles he had been in, his wounds, his part in the battle of Tannenberg. Then of the Kerensky revolution and his transfer to Vladivostok to convalesce. Then of his action against the armed bands of rogues who belonged to no party, professed no creed, and dedicated themselves only to pillage.

There was a loud buzzing of voices in the hall, but all from a small minority—among them, besides the police, the lowest employees in our section. Sinani's secretary was very pale, but she had energy enough to smile whenever he looked at her. Julio, the comrade with whom we worked in the Pacific sector for South America, said nothing, but looked at me with fear. He seemed angry or frightened, I couldn't tell which, when anyone insulted Sinani.

Those who screamed were almost rabid:

"He is insulting the proletarian class. He is blaspheming against the revolution. This character is a counter-revolutionary, a bandit."

The president made them sit down and be quiet. Sinani went on:

"No, there wasn't any question of a working class, because, where I was, there wasn't a single worker. And it wasn't revolution or communism, or a creed of any kind. They were just pillagers, assassins and incendiaries."

"They were the guerrillas of the proletarian revolution," the crowd screamed.

"No, no. I know what I'm talking about. They weren't guerrillas; they were individuals who practiced the most vicious forms of highway robbery. They were Russian bandits and Chinese bandits."

"He is using capitalist language," they screamed. "Sinani, you are a *bourgeois!*"

Sinani was impressive when he told of crossing over to the communist side, his entrance into the Red Army, his work as instructor of recruits, his campaigns against the invasions.

"Let him tell how many communists he had shot. Let him tell!"

The president repeated the question.

"I never had any of them shot," answered Sinani.

137

"How do you know?" asked the secretary.

"Because I never had anyone shot," Sinani replied.

"So you are a vegetarian soldier?" they jeered him.

"To kill in combat is one thing; to order people shot is another!"

"Well then, I ask you, how many men did you kill in combat?"

"If I killed any I could not know it, nor count them," said Sinani harshly.

"He is hiding the truth—he is lying—he is trying to deceive the party!" cried groups of people who had risen to their feet.

Someone hissed, others followed his example. Julio shouted, his voice trembling:

"Let there be order in the assembly, comrade president."

"The president is directing this assembly," came the answer from the chair, "comrade Julio does not need to point out my duties to me."

Julio was silent and the hall became quiet. The inquisitorial glance of the police went over it.

Sinani was less pale now and seemed surer of himself, or else of the subject he was talking about. He spoke of his work in the Communist International, his reports, his articles, the essays he had written for the Latin American section of the Leninist Academy. He cited his studies of Bolivar and the Spanish-American wars of independence; of Porfirio Díaz and the regime of the *cientificos,* of the dictatorship of Machado in Cuba, Gomez in Venezuela, Leguía in Peru, Ibañez in Chile. The president interrupted:

"One afternoon," he said, referring to notes the secretary had given him, "you were in the Red Square; Julio was with you, and your wife Ossia. You met Vasiliev, the friend of Piatnitzky, and Lenka, his secretary. You had a little talk, a political talk. Do you remember?"

"I do not remember very clearly," said Sinani, troubled. "I have met many people in many places; and my talk is always political."

"Try to remember," said the president.

"Try to remember," echoed the secretary. "Try to remember, Sinani."

"It may be. In any case, what is wrong with a conversation with a party comrade who is an active worker in the Comintern?"

"Ossia, your wife, could help you to remember," said the secretary, "but she must be at home, since she is not a party member."

"Ah," they cried in the hall, "so his wife is not a party member, and he a director of the Comintern! What sort of behavior is that for a communist?"

Sinani was completely upset. He tried to explain why his beautiful

138

blond wife, with her slanting eyes and strange vampire face, her startling dress and coiffure, had not joined the party.

"Comrades, she lacks political culture. We have lived together barely a year. I respect her personality and have not wished to press her, because I think one must come to the party without any pressure."

"*Petit bourgeois!*" screamed Henriette.

"A *petit bourgeois* marriage," added the woman who served the tea.

"Your wife doesn't belong to any union either, does she?" asked the secretary.

"No, she doesn't," acknowledged Sinani.

"Doesn't she work?"

"In a factory, no."

"How does she live?" asked the president. "Who supports her?"

"I support her," said Sinani firmly. "My salary permits me to do so. We live in an apartment at the Hotel Lux, as everyone knows."

"But," said the secretary, "let's get back to the conversation with Vasiliev in the Red Square. He said to you, Sinani—remember? 'Can you imagine what would happen if the party chiefs disappeared?' You were a bit surprised, as if you didn't understand. And then Vasiliev said more clearly, 'What would happen, do you think, if the great comrade Stalin should die?' Then you withdrew from the others, took Vasiliev's arm, and in the company of Lenka, the three of you went on talking. Do you remember now, Sinani?"

The man had received a blow. He paled visibly and clasped his hands desperately.

"Yes, now I remember. Vasiliev's question arose from our comments on the death of our comrade Gorky, on the merits of his work, on his friendship with Lenin, on the sad weight that had fallen on the Russian people at his death. It was then that he said——"

"That's how it was," said Julio, rising to his feet. "There were at least six people there."

"And why did *you* go with Sinani to the Red Square?" asked the secretary.

"To see that the placards for the festival were properly translated into correct Spanish."

"What Spanish does Sinani know?" asked the secretary.

"I read it fairly well," said Sinani, "but I wasn't there for that, particularly. I went with Julio to stretch my legs before returning to work at the hotel."

"He is lying," said an NKVD. "Let his contradictions be noted."

139

"There is no contradiction," said Sinani. "Julio went to look over the placards in the Red Square. My wife and I went along for the walk. Vasiliev and Lenka happened to be there, as were also several painters."

"But you spoke of the death of comrade Stalin," put in an NKVD man.

"We mentioned no names," said Sinani, "and certainly not that of comrade Stalin."

"You didn't point him out like Kirov?" screamed the NKVD man, hysterically and surprisingly.

Sinani was staggered.

"But why say such dreadful things?"

"Very well," said the president, "you spoke of the death of the party leaders, of what would happen, of how the Russian people would receive the news. You, Sinani—what did you say?"

"I said they were all in perfect health and we need not worry about them. That was all."

The president went on to ask a few important questions, looked at the NKVD, glanced at his watch. He then said it was late and he was going to close the meeting. Next morning Sinani was working at his desk as usual. On the following day he participated in one of our political gatherings and spoke at length on the Popular Fronts. By the third day, we had begun to forget the events of that night at the Hotel Lux.

The searchlights of the NKVD slipped silently from the figure of Sinani to that of my friend Guralsky. He was suspected of zinovievism. There were those who declared that Guralsky had been seen talking to Zinoviev in a café. It was even said that he was one of the people most esteemed by Zinoviev, and a favorite of Bukharin. In this case, I was much more closely connected with the accused. It was not as it had been in 1929, when I knew only at second hand of the battle against the Kulaks. Now it was the Old Bolsheviks, the friends of Lenin, the makers of the October Revolution who were the Kulaks. It was a question of their physical liquidation, of a Stalinian drive against the venerable patriarchs of bolshevism. I dwelt on this thought for a moment, only to dismiss it from my mind, as believers do temptations.

Two weeks after the Magyar comedy, the Soviet government had dissolved the Association of Old Bolsheviks, a kind of club or academy where the most experienced revolutionaries used to meet, Lenin's friends and the founders of the party. Stalin's police persecuted them as enemies, as *bourgeois*, as Kulaks. The organization's library was carefully expurgated, the furniture was moved to one of the NKVD offices, and the house where they met was made into a workers' amusement club. All this was commented on quietly in the Comintern. In the Lux there was the silence of the tomb. And fear grew from day to day.

I was resolved to fight in Guralsky's defense, if they should trap him as they had Sinani. I had worked with Guralsky. I knew him to be honest and if necessary I was prepared to speak out in the communist assembly of the Hotel Lux before the NKVD. I visited him more often than before, but we never spoke of the repression or of the wave of fear which had swept over those who worked in the Comintern. One day while we had tea, I said unexpectedly:

"It is being said that you are a good friend of Zinoviev and that you were seen with him in a café. They are recalling that you organized a demonstration against Stalin in 1927. But if they bring any of this up, I am prepared to defend you." Guralsky looked at me in surprise and then, smiling sadly, said: "Your tea is getting cold." There was a long silence broken only by the tinkle of our spoons stirring the sugar in our glasses. The telephone rang and Guralsky answered.

"Yes, yes—what?—when?— And——"

He hung up the receiver and remained seated, his hands between his knees, staring into space.

"They have arrested Sinani," he said somberly.

"Sinani? Ours?"

"Yes."

Sinani did not return to his office nor to the corridors of the Comintern, nor to the Lux dining room. The next day the blond vampire, Ossia, left the hotel also, taking her belongings away in broad daylight, much to everybody's surprise.

One night at dinner a young Cuban communist who had come with Blas Roca said to me, "Julio and our section secretary have both disappeared."

"And Sinani?" I asked.

"Don't mention him," he said. "It is like pronouncing the name of an evil spirit. No one knows anything about him."

On the following morning in the Comintern the rumor ran from one office to another, in whispers, secretly: "The NKVD has uncovered a plot. They were going to kill Stalin. It was a terrorist plan organized by Sinani."

"And Sinani?"

"They shot him."

5

The Russian misery of 1934 was perhaps not so great as in 1929, but in both cases it was the misery of a people living under wretched material conditions. The standard of living of a competent Russian worker, or of a farmer on a collective farm, was very much lower than that of an ordinary French worker, or an Argentine, or a Spaniard.

The housing crisis in Moscow and the other large cities was more acute than that endured in any city in the world. Men and women were jumbled together in an incredible fashion. Some over-talkative Russians said that to complain was only to draw upon oneself the attentions of the police, to cause one to be suspected of "rightist" tendencies and thus become a candidate for the purge as a "saboteur," a "deviationist," an "enemy of the people" and eventually a victim of what in Stalinist language was called "an administrative process." This last meant that a case was handled discreetly by the NKVD, from arrest, through imprisonment, to a secret funeral. If anyone in high circles criticized such action they were quieted with the promise that all this was but a temporary phase, and that in another year would appear the most progressive and liberal constitution of all time—the Stalin Constitution. Such talk acted like a drug.

Seventeen years after the October Revolution there was absolutely no liberty for any citizen, no matter how authentically proletarian he might be.

One of the most shocking things in Soviet life, and a reflection on the development of the Five Year Plans, was the terrible quality of everything produced in the Soviet Union. The canned food was dangerously spoiled in many cases; locks either shut and would not open, or opened and would not shut, or else neither opened nor shut. New doors fitted so badly that the cracks had to be filled with paper and rags to keep out draughts. The busses fell to pieces on the roads. The shoes were coarse, made of faulty leather and were always coming open at the seams. The men's suits were inferior to the most ordinary in South America. The coats people wore took on from the sweat of the owners an unendurable odor of sheeps' dung. Over the doors of elevators there were always signs saying "out of order." In addition to poor quality there was a scarcity of all the things essential to even a low standard of living in South American countries.

Guralsky, to whom I confided my distress, said that I suffered because I had too western a point of view.

"Industry needs workers," he would say. "They must be brought from the country to the cities; this causes congestion and the housing crises. Only in the last few years has there been any balance between import and export, ending in the blockade. It is only recently that we have been receiving the machinery from the United States and Europe which is needed for the heavy industry of socialism. It should be remembered that for its industrial development, the United States had millions of immigrants from Europe already trained. Soviet industry has had only ignorant *muzhiks* to work with, idiotic peasants, men who never before saw a machine. It is only a matter of time."

"And liberty? Socialism ought to guarantee liberty to the citizen —the safety of his life, his home, his correspondence, his wife and children."

"It will come. It will come. Next year the Stalin Constitution will be put into effect—a real political and judicial masterpiece. It is filled with the deepest respect for life, for liberty and for civil rights."

I was irritated to the point of nausea by the persistence with which the cult of Stalin was nurtured and spread. He was blessed and exalted as the miracle worker who cured all the evils in Russia. Everywhere were portraits of him; his name was written in every language used in the land, millions of times a day. His statues, arrogant, wrapped in a large Russian coat, stood in every public square, at every road intersection, in the halls of new offices and in the courtyards of the old, in the vestibule of barracks, in the corners above library doors. It was worse than Hitler in Germany. It was coarse, tawdry, vulgar, in thoroughly bad taste. Statues, portraits, flags, signposts, voices on the loudspeaker—everything was Stalin.

On political holidays, in workers' clubs, in schools, in unions, in the theatres of the Red Army, wherever we were invited to be guests, someone had always to speak for the Latin American delegation. No sooner did a speaker mention Stalin than the band broke in with a deafening triumphal march. This made me thoroughly sick, and I mentioned it confidentially to Lipo, a naturalized Lithuanian worker who was a directing member of the Argentine communist party. Perhaps I did it as much as anything to shock his affected fanatical devotion.

"If they make me speak today," I said on the way to a festival, "I will say the name of Stalin six times and I warrant they'll interrupt me six times for the band to play. In that way, mine will be the most brilliant speech."

"Don't talk foolishness, comrade," said Lipo.

The festival began. Speeches, more speeches, until it was my turn. The first time I mentioned Stalin, the trumpets and drums would not let me go on. When the translator came to the name they burst out again while the assembled people screamed: "Hurrah for the great Stalin! Thank you, comrade Stalin!"

In my speech I named him six times, as I had promised Lipo I would, and with the translation this made twelve interruptions from the band. When I returned to my seat I caught an indignant look from Lipo and was afraid he might really get me into trouble.

"That is not being a good communist," he whispered. I took the offensive.

"What makes a bad communist," I said, "is to be silent at the password, not to repeat the order, not to support the party. In a word, Lipo, to sabotage propaganda."

The man was silent and I thought I had really convinced him.

Later however, at a party at Lossovsky's house, Manuilsky led me aside and said: "To the cultivated man, with a high ideological conscience, some aspects of party propaganda may be distasteful. For example, the constant repetition of the name of our great comrade, Stalin. The propaganda for comrade Stalin," he continued when I remained silent, "is necessary for the revolution. The Russian people is politically very backward and its general culture is not up to Western standards. To uncultivated people, ideas must be presented in a tangible form. Catholics do not put images on the altars to inspire the faith of theologians. It has been found necessary to give a symbol to the Russian people. Idolatrous perhaps, but very wise."

"Yes," I said, "I can see that. I believe it is a good thing in the Soviet Union to exalt comrade Stalin in this way."

"No, no," Manuilsky said angrily, "not only in the Soviet Union or within the party. Everywhere in the world, in your country too, the great leader, loved by the people, must be comrade Stalin. And the duty of every good communist is to repeat everywhere, all the time, that for the workers there is only the Soviet Union and our great world director, comrade Stalin."

At this moment Rudolfo Ghioldi, the Argentine leader, approached us, a bit loquacious in his cups. He caught on immediately to our conversation, showing that he had heard something before.

"Oh, comrade Manuilsky," he exclaimed dramatically, "these are the cartesian doubts of the intellectuals. I too am an intellectual. I did not have the good fortune to be born in the proletariat. But I tell others like myself—like this man—I tell them, comrade, that to the phrase 'workers of the world, unite' must be added another very important— but very important—"

144

"Yes," said Manuilsky, "what?"

"Ah," exclaimed Ghioldi, "another phrase, an important, and imperative password, 'Communists and advanced intellectuals, unite and abase yourselves?' "

"How disgusting!" I exclaimed involuntarily.

Ghioldi looked at me as at a communist who was in disgrace. Manuilsky took us both by the arm and led us into the dining-room where a group quickly formed around him to discuss various things. Finally, the Argentine Lipo, raising his glass and scraping my nose with his arm as he did so said: "Three cheers for the great comrade Stalin!"

"Stalin! Stalin! Stalin!"

Several years later, in Buenos Aires, I ran into Lipo and dropped a casual remark to the effect that I would be ashamed to be an agent of the NKVD and spy on my companions in the delegations. Lipo changed color and I realized that my blow had struck close to home. By that time I was looking back to my second visit to the land of socialism, and realizing with horror what had been going on. But that was years later, and I a wiser man.

Meanwhile, in the Comintern, we were holding the last meetings of the Latin American Communist Conferences, under the direction of Manuilsky and Dimitrov, with the supervision of Gottwald of Czechoslovakia, Kuüssinen of Finland, Pieck of Germany, Kolarov of Hungary, Togliatti of Italy and Van Minh of China.

Throughout the discussions it was obvious that there were deep differences in the positions of Dimitrov and Manuilsky. Often, Manuilsky would retreat to the old concepts which had ruled the International from its inception, while Dimitrov criticized them. To any attentive observer it was clear that Dimitrov saw the problem as one of the western struggle against fascism, whereas Manuilsky was restrained by the rigid directives that came down from the Kremlin. Dimitrov was openly in favor of the Popular Fronts; Manuilsky, without actually opposing them piled up objections, pointed up dangers and weighed the magnitude of obstacles. He agreed that in liberal countries like France, Belgium and Spain, the tactics of the Popular Front might get results, but he felt that the possibilities must be carefully analyzed.

At any rate there remained the two points of view. Dimitrov was in favor of Popular Fronts everywhere, and Manuilsky was for armed insurrections in some places. Luis Carlos Prestes and his Brazilians, as well as the Argentines, agreed with him. Maurice Thorez, Raymond

Guyot, Palmiro Togliatti, Gottwald, Kuüssinen, Mao Tse-tung, the Annamese Ho Chi Minh, Guralsky and the important Latin Americans all had their say. Stalin had still not decided one way or another. And there lay the difficulty. The subject had come to be a gordian knot, and the only Alexander who could cut it was the great leader, Josef Stalin.

In the Latin American Conference this compromise was reached: Popular Front in some countries, more especially Chile; insurrection in others, especially Brazil. An argument in Russian went on between Manuilsky and Dimitrov, and no one bothered to translate it until Manuilsky complained that Dimitrov was trying to blame him for the serious political losses that the International had recently suffered, especially the collapse in Germany. Dimitrov gently denied this. He blamed the break in the German party on historical circumstances and on the world situation, as well as on the pressures in Europe and the internal weakness of the German party. The argument spread. All the foreign communists in Moscow began to frequent our meetings, especially the French and the Chinese who were on the side of Dimitrov. Barbusse followed it all with the greatest interest, since the original idea had been his.

Once it was decided, over the opposition of the Argentines, that Chile should be a field of experimentation for the Popular Front, Dimitrov requested that I should direct the new policy. When I managed to see Barbusse, I found him very enthusiastic.

"It is the right road, my son," he said. "I know with what fervor you have defended our point of view and I know you will carry out this idea in South America with great success. But listen to a word of advice. You must have immediate success in a short time. Your triumph shall be the banner of the Seventh Congress."

"I want to know some important things," I said. "You may count on my absolute discretion."

"What do you want to know?"

"What is Stalin's personal opinion of the general idea of the Popular Front?"

"He is not against it."

"Why then do Manuilsky, Kuüsinen and Gottwald, who are close to him, all pile up such objections to it?"

"It is not decided yet."

"All right, but if Stalin had shown sympathy for the idea they would be praising it from the housetops."

"You are right. And because Stalin knows this, he has withheld judgment. But he is not against it. A few triumphs anywhere in the world would incline the balance in our favor. The essential thing is speed."

"How long?" I asked.

"Oh, fifteen, twenty months. No more."

"Perhaps we shall have results sooner," I said, to make him happy. He put his hand on my shoulder, as he did when he was pleased. I took advantage of this mood to tell him all my doubts and worries—the wretched condition of the Russian people, the scarcity and the poor quality of everything, the dumb discontent, the terrorism, the persistent rumors of great concentration camps of forced labor for political prisoners, the suggestion that great public works like the Canal from the White Sea to the Baltic were being carried out by forced labor, slave labor.

Barbusse listened in silence to my outpourings but without surprise.

"This is not new to me," he said. "I have heard worse things even from well-informed Russian sources. But all this is merely a phase, the result of the heritage of the past of which we have spoken before. It is terrible. Yes, I know: Gorky and I often lamented it, with poor Krupskaya, Lenin's widow, tormented by the vigilance of which she felt herself the victim. But I assure you, it will end. I don't myself understand the essence of the Russian differences of opinion, but they were always like that. They take political life passionately and have no conception of compromise or of tolerance. Politics for the French is high comedy; for the Russians, Greek tragedy."

"All right, Master, but temperament can not justify arrest, imprisonment, judgment and execution so arbitrary, so tyrannical."

"You are right, and I have said so to Comrade Stalin, not as my opinion but as that of the whole liberal world. And he has promised me that all the accused shall be publicly tried. Do not worry, my son. There will be no Balkan methods or Latin American ones. There will be tangible and convincing justice."

I knew Barbusse would never lie to me. "I promise you, furthermore," he went on, "that next year there will be a new Constitution. I have read the outlines of the various chapters and assure you that it is without doubt the most advanced and most liberal of any in the world today. England, France, the United States will be behind it, in what concerns liberal theory and practise. It is admirable, my son, admirable!"

I was completely reassured. The promises of Barbusse were comforting. I had profound faith in their realization. We would wait for the establishment of that Constitution, the most advanced, progressive and liberal in the world.

The conversation turned again to the Popular Front, and he emphasized anew the importance of my mission.

"We need your success in South America. For this reason I have even asked Stalin for his opinion on the concrete case of Chile."

"And what does he think?"

"You understand that all this is absolutely confidential?"

"Of course I do."

"It was two days before he answered me."

"And what did he say?" I persisted, after a long silence.

Barbusse smiled again, paced the floor for awhile and then, very serious, as was his wont when he wished to place great importance on things, he spoke: "Comrade Stalin, two days after I put the question to him about the Popular Front in South America, answered me that in his opinion the way that must be used there was the 'Road of Yenan.'"

"The Chinese way?" I asked, surprised.

"Yes, the Chinese way. The tactics followed at present by Mao Tse-tung, Chu Teh and Li Li Siang."

"Then," I exclaimed, with great emphasis, "I cannot leave without talking with the Chinese comrades—with Mao and Li and the rest—about the Road of Yenan, the tactics of Yenan. Can I, Master?"

Barbusse, looked at me in silence, laughed a little and then said: "Stalin is of the same opinion. He thinks you must talk to Mao and the other Chinese. He thinks the conversation will do you a lot of good. Of course you must not copy, but create."

"I must get an interview with the Chinese," I said as if thinking aloud. Barbusse laughed again at this and said:

"Wait quietly in your hotel. If not tomorrow, then the day after tomorrow someone will call for you to take you to the country house where they are lodged."

I left, expressing again and again my gratitude to Barbusse.

"Don't leave Moscow without seeing me to say goodbye, my son."

6

Two days later I found myself in the big country house, surrounded with parks and hedges and fenced in with barbed wire, where lodged about seventy Chinese communist leaders. They were all absorbed in a bitter ideological struggle between the positions of Mao Tse-tung and Li Li Siang.

Li Li Siang spoke French fluently. He had been educated in Europe, an Asiatic with occidental ways of thinking, a marxist who had studied at the Sorbonne and at Heidelberg, at Louvain and Cambridge. Vehement, clear headed, with a good sense of humor, Li Li Siang was intellectually superior to both Mao and Chu Teh.

Mao Tse-tung was tall, robust, clumsy in his walk and in his manners. His large hands and feet bespoke his peasant origin; his idea of arguing was to say "Yes! Yes! Yes!" and "No! No! No!" He was dogmatic and poor at dialectic but could think clearly about what he wanted, or what he knew. He did not adorn his speeches nor watch his language; he was brusque and direct in his expressions and constantly asked the translator to repeat the equivalent of the interjections with which he compensated for his small vocabulary. And, indeed, even in translation, the interjections gave a special flavor, a typical slant, to the words or ideas that Mao tried to express.

Mao was devoted to Stalin. He named him at every moment; he did this also, no doubt, to give himself importance before the others, especially Li Li Siang, his rival and adversary in the party inner circle. Every two sentences, Mao would say that this luminous and magnificent idea was not his, but comrade Stalin's—that this other expression, that other suggestion, was not the child of the brain of the humble Mao. No. He had merely the talent to borrow them from comrade Stalin.

He had an astonishing memory for remembering Stalin's phrases with literal exactitude. And not only literally, but with a precise memory of the moment in which Stalin said them, the occasion, the reason and the circumstances that surrounded the pronouncement. An old pastor, an assiduous reader of the Bible gifted with prodigious memory, would not have quoted the psalms any better.

The differences of opinion between Mao Tse-tung and Li Li Siang had nothing to do with the "Road of Yenan"; they agreed on following this. Their differences were more abstract. When they argued, the large rough Chu Teh tended to go along with Mao, rather than with Li, whom he often contemptuously called "intellectual."

We talked of the Yenan tactics. Three Chinese acted as interpreters and kept correcting one another; and in this way the version was cleansed of error. I stayed in that quiet country house, in the midst of that Chinese storm, for three days and nights. Both Mao and Li seemed delighted to have me as a guest, and so to please comrade Barbusse and the illustrious comrade Stalin.

After the ample explanation I gave them of the APRA they were agreed that there were close analogies between it and the Kuomintang, and between Haya de la Torre and Chiang Kai-shek; but that it was possible to get the APRA to follow along with the Comintern. In this the tactics of Yenan might help, they said.

"The fundamental key to the Road of Yenan," said Li, "lies in the fact that our work does not consist in thinking exclusively in proletarian terms, or taking in account only the working class. We think in much wider terms, which touch on other social sectors and include other classes. In view of the menace of fascism, millions of people are disposed to fight on our side. We must make this count for us.

"But it is not only fear of the loss of liberty that clears a way before us. We can play on the ambition of thousands of politicians of all sizes, who have come from the *petite bourgeoisie,* both urban and rural; men who are unable to reach high positions, not so much suited to their abilities as in accord with their ambitions. If we, the communists, with the large or small forces at our disposal, offer our support to these politicians, they will come to our camp—not as registered members of our party, which would not suit them or us either, but as servants. Servants of expediency. It will be to their advantage to serve us. We will repay them always far better than their own parties would, or the sectors in which they operate.

"We have won in this way hundreds of officers of Chiang Kai-shek's army. The Chinese soldier is ambitious. He is hungry for power in a way the European soldier is not, and thirsty for riches, comforts, and luxury. There are Generals in Chiang's army who are poor and obscure provincials. If they had not gone into the army they would have been court clerks, proprietors of mule herds, or at most teachers in rural schools. And the one thing they long for is to get out of their mediocre economic *milieu,* to become rich men, powerful and fortunate.

"Serving the ambitions of these Generals, oftentimes putting ourselves at the service of these war-lords, we communists have won advantages and positions we could never have got by fighting. The fighting of masses does not always lead to political victory. Often, these procedures which at times seem those of the serpent achieve greater and more permanent triumphs. The talent of the communist is in knowing how to take advantage of them."

Mao arose, walked to an opening in the wall, and called for drink and glasses. He then spoke calmly, looking at me out of slanting eyes set in a sun-tanned face.

"The greatest talent in this work, comrade, is never to be associated with failure. Never to defend the weak, even when he is right. Never to attack the pillager of the treasury, if he is the owner of a great fortress. He might crush you and there is no use being a martyr."

I tried to speak but he stopped me with a gesture and went on:

"Our experience, the experience of the Road of Yenan, is this: People like doctors, generals, dentists, town mayors, lawyers who are not rich, do not love power for itself; much less for the good they can do with it. They want it for the wealth it can bring. They achieve power, and then they begin to call out like Napoleon for money, money and again money. Get this through your head, comrade! If we help these people, if we are a ladder for them because it suits us, well then it would be absurd for us to stay their hands, sew up their pockets or check their greed. If we did this, they would turn against us and try to crush us. That happened with Chiang in 1927—we tried to play the moralist and he hurled all his power against us."

Li Li Siang at this point interrupted, and for an hour the two men quarreled in Chinese without the translators giving me a French version. At the end Mao served drinks and proceeded:

"Let them get rich today. Very soon we can expropriate everything. The more help they get from us in their pillage, the more positions they will let us take and occupy; they will help us to capture them and even to extend them. Of course there are two important things to remember. Never participate in any fraud or plundering, which is more difficult than you might think; and carry out your collaboration without the people's knowledge, without leaving any proof of it for your enemies to find. This delights your robber friends of course. For your integrity leaves more for them to divide among a larger number of fellow rogues."

Mao smiled again, that enigmatic Chinese smile. I never knew whether he was laughing at the theory he preached, at the knaves he did business with, or at my astonishment and perplexity. He indicated to the translators that it was my turn to speak, but please would I keep to purely practical aspects. The moral question would be discussed later, "or not discussed," they added as an after-thought.

"I understand," I said, "the basis of your system. It is a matter of winning certain sections of the *petite bourgeoisie* over to your side to open a path for yourselves."

"No, no. You have not understood at all," said Mao. "It is not a matter of deceiving anyone about our position or ideolgy."

Li Li Siang interrupted: "Do you sincerely believe, for example, that we deceive anyone if we contribute to the victory of a radical politician of the lowest rank—one who has been passed over a hundred times by his own party perhaps because of his incompetence, but who has ambitions, is manageable, and may get to be elected deputy, say for a district of the Gironde or Britain, precisely where we communists can never elect one of our own people? Is that a deception?"

"No, in your concrete case perhaps not."

"It is putting your cards on the table—going in for the clean game that pleases the British so much—*a quid pro quo*—a giving and receiving. In such a case as I've cited we give this radical socialist what he can never achieve by himself, receiving in turn what is our due. Ah yes, we receive that, without doubt. The radical is elected deputy, but he will be effectively compromised to the degree that he must support one of our comrades for selectman or at least registrar. Such politicians don't mind much; it doesn't touch their sentiments or their pocketbooks; they are actually glad to do it. It seems a trifle to them and they remember that they may need us later. You let them understand clearly that they will keep going up the ladder, and that they can count on firm support to the extent to which they serve us."

Mao took up the explanation at this point.

"Here are two things. The first is that this tiny man, this communist who, thanks to our arrangements, is chosen selectman or municipal counsellor, will find the way easier when the party wants to elect a deputy or capture the mayoralty. Then, the public won't elect the radical, but the communist. The end remains the same; the means change according to our power. This method seems slower, but it is actually quicker and surer. That's the first point.

"Now for the second. Any person who receives our support and does not fulfill his part of the bargain must become the target for a frontal attack of pitiless ferocity. It is enough to make an example of one; once they see that we can bar the path to a man, that we have the power to destroy him utterly, the rest will be afraid not to play our game. We communists have never given this fear enough weight. I don't know why. The ambitious *petit bourgeois*, taken with the fever of greed, feels real anguish when we strike him hard. He must be really destroyed with every arm at hand, be left a wretched tatter at the end."

And then, as if he sensed my distaste, he added:

"Reality, life, this moment in the world, present us an alternative, sharp as a razor's edge. Ponder it, discern it, get it into your head. Either we must lay aside a few principles or we leave the way open to fascism. And do you realize what that would mean?" He unleashed an eloquent and dramatic description of the world subjugated by Nazism. Then at the end he added: "These are not the ideas of Mao. These are weak echoes of the clairvoyance of our distinguished and meritorious comrade Stalin."

Supper time arrived and Mao arranged for us to eat alone, with Li, Van Minh and two translators, instead of joining the other seventy Chinese in the large dining-room. After a delicious Chinese supper, the full moon over the immense plain and the warm air drew us to walk for awhile in the well-kept gardens. Later in my room, alone with my tormenting thoughts, I saw that wherever they led me, I came at last to that alternative, sharp, as Mao had phrased it, as a razor's edge. And before me arose the spectre of Nazi cruelty, Nazi sadism, bestiality unleashed over humanity. No, it was unbearable. Something must be done. Mao and Li went too far perhaps, balancing themselves on an inclined plane that might lead to the depths. But perhaps it was their Asiatic mentality and the violence and pitilessness for which Mao had quite a reputation. There might be a gentler way of using their principles. Perhaps—perhaps— And so the human spirit is led, little by little, to the downward slope of moral concessions. It bargains today, to yield ground tomorrow, to end at last in the inevitable retreat, the unconditional surrender.

Mao had used the argument for all it was worth—Nazism, or a worse evil. And he had laughed with a touch of the infinite contempt that the Chinese feels for the white man. "And humbly I must confess that all this is the argument of the great Stalin. Get this into your head, dear Latin American comrade, Stalin is always right. His vision touches on every country, not only Soviet Russia, but the gigantic Chinese horizon. His glance includes all Asia. Do not forget it, comrade."

Next day we renewed our conversations.

"We must capture the *petite bourgeoisie*," said Mao, "as the Nazis have done. We must work on politicians who have been passed over, as I said yesterday—on doctors mired in mediocrity, lawyers sunk in their narrow means. And it works, let me tell you, in the average strata, where ambition and corruption are marks of the official who goes on to be chief. But, my friend, it fails always with representatives of the powerful class—with financially successful people. They think of their own interests and are no longer greedy for wealth, since they know they can get it without our cooperation. They know very well, also, that the slightest collusion with us might do them irreparable harm."

"A very useful tool is the great lord who has lost his holdings," interrupted Li, "the aristocratic lady or gentleman from the highest social sphere who has come down in the world. If we offer him ever so little, he will serve us gladly. He will do what he is asked, lend precious aid, and give what is almost impossible for us to get. Of course, within the party you must always treat him as a great lord.

"When we communists offer the small or great power which we may have in any given country, we are really using the prestige that the Communist International and the Soviet Union have come to have in the world. Whether we use the ambition of the ambitious or the disinterestedness of the romantic, or the hope of the liberals left over from the nineteenth century, you would be surprised from how many sectors (except the very successful) we can get people to join with us and carry out our plans.

"And it is logical that it should be so. If you, in the name of the communist party, propose or sponsor the candidacy of a left-wing liberal, of a progressive radical, you are touching on several sensitive points; first the obvious disinterestedness of the communist party, and further, the sentimentalism of the man himself and the ambition that he is very often ashamed to show. There are hundreds of such men who have never thought, for example, of being president of their country. The communist proposal will fill him with joy, and as a natural result there will flow in his circle a sympathy towards communism. These communists who give so much, and seem to ask nothing in return, will seem very attractive. They will help to make the name of the party popular and they will protect us so that the party shall have men in office. And all the time remember that these progressive radical *bourgeois* and their leftist cliques pass, while the party remains. We are the eternal, they the ephemeral. Thrones totter, but the Church remains."

Li Li Siang paused, and the translators repeated to Mao and Chu Teh, in Chinese, what he had said. Then he invited me to give my opinion. "Tell us what you think. This is not an official party meeting, but a conversation among comrades. Manuilsky was very anxious for this discussion. He has a high opinion of you—with reservations, you understand. The Soviet comrades always have reservations. Dimitrov, on the other hand, is much closer to you politically. He said you would come."

When the translator got to this point, Mao broke in angrily, in a low hoarse growl. Li answered him crossly. Chu Teh spoke a few words and Li smiled, suave and sarcastic, saying in French:

"Mao and Chu think I ought not to have mentioned Dimitrov or Manuilsky. I maintain that there is no need of such foolishness. Manuilsky knew that you were coming to see us?"

"I let him know I would come. He asked who had arranged the interview and seemed satisfied when he learned that Stalin himself had suggested it to Barbusse." Van Minh vouched for the truth of this, and added that he had informed Dimitrov.

"The subject has no importance," he said, displeased, "since you spoke to Stalin himself about it." This angered Mao again, he stamped his foot and screamed in a high falsetto, the only word I could understand being, "Stalin—Stalin—Stalin——"

"Let us hear what he has to say," interposed Van Minh quietly. "Tell us frankly what you think. Here there will be no false positions since it is not a party meeting. Speak without fear."

"Touch on the practical aspects," said Mao, "leaving morals aside. In life there are no ethical victories. Morals are just so much dessert. When the animal is full he begins to worry about right and wrong, as if it were an accompaniment to digestion."

"I think that the Road of Yenan envisages a completely new kind of politics for us. If I understand you, it goes beyond the strict limits of the working-class and poor peasants and the poorest of the middle-class. We must go daringly into other fields, keep our eyes on the positions we want to win, and forget everything else; at any price, win friends, sympathizers and servants."

"That, especially that—servants," screamed Mao. "People who serve us, through greed, through fear, inferiority, vengeance, what have you, but who serve us. Serve the party, serve the designs of the Comintern, serve the cause of the revolution. Congratulations, my boy, you have caught the very essence of the Yenan Way. Now apply it."

"Yes, I think I understand. Now to take up individual points."

"That is easy," said Li Li Siang, "if you have the fundamentals. Come now, be specific."

"In Latin America," I said, "the dictatorial type of regime, be it civil or military, is too frequent. In dealing with people who impose themselves by force, yet all the time prating of democracy, how should we act?"

"They are a bit like our Chinese war-lords," said Li, "people who use the military academies, the gold braid and rank, as a spring-board to power."

"Is that it?" asked Mao.

"More or less," I answered. "But can we communists, the most advanced ideologically, the leaders of the working class, appear as friends or allies to such persons? The people will mistrust us. Our enemies will taunt us with it, and we shall be helping the very men who snatch the people's liberties."

"Oh, dear friend," said Mao, taking his head in his hands. "How deluded you are with respect to the political thinking of common people. You have a romantic idea of the revolution and of its politics. You think that workers and peasants and *petit bourgeois* are full of noble intentions and faithfully respect *mores* and principles. What an error! It's not like that, my friend. The immense mass of our friends and enemies is made up of opportunists. You must get that through your head—complete opportunists."

They all agreed. Chu Teh grunted angrily at what he called "lack of common sense" and added that, unlike Li Li Siang, he had no love for long discussions. Mao said something about Stalin which quieted Chu and then continued: "We are not even going to suggest that you should conduct a political campaign in favor of the dictators, or that you should hitch the party fortunes to the wagon of military victors. Not at all. On this point we must be very clear.

"There are social sectors, there are countries which have real party politics, a democratic life, real civil liberties. In such places one adopts the Popular Front, to attract the leftwingers and the leftist groups, good or bad, sincere or not. Tempt them, each through his particular weakness, as the devil tempts. You understand? Help them to get what they want; put pressure, first with offers, later with threats. Compromise them if you can, so that they can't get away. And this every day, without respite, one after the other with as deep a psychological study of each as possible. So much for places where a Popular Front is possible. That is the easiest to understand, isn't it?"

"Yes," I answered. "Now for the others."

"Now as to your dictators. They interest me particularly. It is this sort of thing, dear comrade, that has been my specialty. You know that in China one can not speak seriously about any form of democracy. In countries where politics has not developed even that far; where open or masked abuse rules; where elections are a farce; where the military leaders and the bosses do as they please; where a man isn't even a number—where do you expect to get with your political romanticism?"

"All right," I said before his silent stare, "then we shall have to fight."

When the translator read off my words in Chinese, Chu Teh got up, groaned, and went out onto the verandah.

"Chu Teh says you are like a child," said Van Minh, smiling.

"I suspected he had called me a fool," I said.

Mao began to speak again:

"Fight," he sighed, "fight and lose. The blow of the dictator will always land on your head; he will torture you and yours. His police will crack your skull. And what's in it for you? Nothing, absolutely nothing. You will be alone—for no one cares to share blows. No human ambition is nourished on misfortune, no greed satisfied by bad luck. Few and far between would be those who would come to our side, with only the anger of a dictator to look forward to. You are asking for heroes, not converts. And heroes are not recruited often. They are the divine exception!

"Your thinking is antiquated. Now that the Soviet regime is established, one way or another, in a sixth of the world, we must use other methods, other tactics. If you give tacit support to the dictator, he will give you political jobs in exchange. He may launch terrible diatribes against communism; he may even outlaw the party and legislate against it. But if you have been his friend, he will not touch a hair of your head. You can work away quietly. He will use you against his enemies and ask your support in critical times; he may even get you to call a strike somewhere that will hurt his enemies. And if you are useful to him in these ways he will give new positions to the party. What else matters?"

He stopped for a drink, offered some to the rest of us and continued: "There is one thing more—the business of the workers. What will the proletariat and the peasants say of all these maneuvers? What will the intellectuals and the white-collar workers who respect the party think? Ah, my friend, all of them, in your country and mine, are human; with the strength and weaknesses of men, with their virtues and vices, their egotism and their aspirations. The workers will be with you if you get something for them. They will abandon you if you do not, however lofty your principles. Get the dictator to give them advantages at your request and they will love you. Push them persistently to attack the well-off, and for the most part the dictator will conceal your demands and even satisfy them to gain popularity."

In all this explanation, so severely free from any doctrinaire principle or moral evaluation, in this shameless exposure, I felt a disheartening basis of realism. The Chinese were not very different from Latin Americans, although Mao maintained we lived in two worlds.

"There are three worlds," said Li Li Siang: "The Asiatic, with its millennial culture, but with immense technical ignorance; the European, with refined culture but a deficient command of technique; and America, the genius of technique, with only the vaguest notions of culture. Latin America is still a sort of limbo where everything is new-born, in formation, undefined and nebulous."

We ate the delicious Chinese food with its strange sauces and appetizing flavors. Then we talked about everything all over again, in spite of Chu Teh's disapproval. We travelled the Yenan Way in every direction, and after effusive demonstrations of affection they saw me to the car in which I was to journey to Moscow. Van Minh went with me, and Kuo Mon Jo who had never spoken a word throughout the long conference.

On the way we talked about methods of organizing a Popular Front in Latin America. I insisted on my disapproval of the tactics that had been adopted for Brazil—armed insurrection.

"Manuilsky and Prestes, as well as the leading comrades of Brazil, can not be wrong," said Van Minh. "Obviously the Brazilians know more about their own country than you do. Don't you think so?"

"No doubt about it," I admitted, as we drove into a populated area where the boundless wretchedness of the people, their rags, their bottled-up anger, struck me anew.

"Then too," said Van Minh, "you know there are very severe criticisms of Manuilsky's direction of the International. We haven't had a single success under him—not one—only disasters, large and small, all over the world. It is likely he wants one success, at least, before turning over the command to Dimitrov. That, perhaps, is why he is so anxious for the Brazilian insurrection."

"And it will be another failure," I declared.

"They can't be so wrong," Van Minh said dogmatically. "Manuilsky considers it vital."

"Vital for him," I said harshly.

"Yes," said Van Minh, displeased, "and also for the International."

"But do you think, comrade, that just to save face so much should be risked, as must be in this venture?"

Van Minh pretended not to hear. We spoke of the situation in Russia, the opposition and its absolute defeat, and the prosecution of the prominent zinovievists. We were coming into the city. I wanted to discuss his compatriots' ideas with Van Minh but I felt that I had no arguments against them. I had to think, to order my ideas and to build with them a logical scaffolding. For the moment I had lost my bearings.

I was not happy about myself. I didn't like the idea of the Yenan Way, and yet I saw no alternative. Sometimes I felt that a strange destiny, outside of myself and my will, was forcing me to go on compulsively, hurrying, and with the weight of all my doubts upon me. At other times I didn't even feel human, but like a sheep in the middle of the flock led against its will along the edge of a precipice. And above destiny and above the flock, above my doubts and scruples, hung the menacing spectre of fascism. And my faith in an idea which exercised over my spirit the witchery that dazzles, blinded and drew me on like a vortex.

It was 1935. The world was afraid: of National Socialism and the Gestapo; of the Duce's speeches and the growing power of the Wehrmacht, of the concentration camps and the torture chambers and the pogroms. I shared this vast human fear. The Road to Yenan seemed the only way out. It was a weapon, a dike to prevent fascism from overwhelming every human liberty. It is wonderful how rich the sophistication and how subtle the logic a man will use to justify his faith to himself. Compromise will be preferred to the rigidity that might mean shipwreck and failure. No one likes failure or will march towards it knowingly. When it threatens, we take any devious course to avoid it; and only when our faith has been mortally wounded at last by undeniable facts, then only—then there is no choice left but stoicism.

7

"Your interview with the Chinese comrades took a long time," George Dimitrov said, greeting me cordially when I arrived at the interview he had requested for the following evening.

"Yes, it was long," I answered, "and very interesting. But there were moments when the zig-zags of the Yenan Way were like a bitter draught."

"A bitter draught," he repeated. "How do you say it in Spanish?"

"Trago amargo."

"Trago amargo, trago amargo," he said slowly. Then he asked me to sit down, and offered me tea. As always he was dressed in black. He was pale, as usual, but happy and ready to talk.

"You are off to America," he said, "and you are going to be one of the first in the world to try out the Popular Front. Upon what you and a few comrades in other countries do, will depend the future of this new approach. If you succeed, your success will serve as an argument in the seventh Congress of the International. If you fail, perhaps all our Popular Front policy will fail too. And then the Russian comrades will have proved their point—or will enforce it. I wish you success if you can get it, for your work will open up new horizons and show how absurd it is in this struggle against fascism to call socialists, 'social fascists.' But the German comrades are hard—that Wilhelm Pieck—so dogmatic, so sectarian!"

"Can't he be brought around?"

Dimitrov smiled and said: "There is no man more deaf than he who will not hear, says Scripture. Do you remember? And our Pieck does not want to hear anything unless it is said in Russian. Well, let's get on to you. It seems Li spoke to you very frankly, and they were authorized to speak as they did. What about this business of," and he looked at his notes, "a *trago amargo?* You may be right to some extent, but remember my friend, that at this time we can not have political ethics or ethical politics. The world situation gives us only one alternative. Which do you prefer—a certain amount of immorality, or the triumph of Nazi tyranny?"

"Well—" I hesitated.

"No, no," he said. "There are not many paths or even detours which we can freely choose. This is a crossroad in history and we can go in only one of two directions—fascism, or a fight against it with every weapon at hand. You are free to choose, but there is no middle road."

"But," I said, "if we could find a path to preserve liberty by adjusting to the democratic system, making concessions——"

"Exactly!" he said enthusiastically. "That is what we are trying to do with the Popular Front—to preserve the liberty of the citizen, to prevent the shipwreck of the democratic regimes, imperfect though they may be. And for this, the tactics of Yenan are essential although they have, for palates like yours (and mine too, I assure you) a flavor of *trago amargo.*"

I leaned forward to escape the glance he fixed on me. I moved in the leather chair and kept my eyes on the door-knob which shone like an eye.

"A ghastly alternative," I said.

"A categorical alternative, with no way out. Am I not right?"

"Yes, you are right." And we were silent for a long time as if we had said everything but hoped that there were something more to say. Dimitrov finally broke the silence:

"You understand, dear comrade, that it is not my fault the outstanding members of the liberal *bourgeoisie* and the leftist or leftish elements of the *petite bourgeoisie* are politically and morally corrupt. It is not my fault that the most eager aspirants to parliamentary posts in Latin America are candidates without electors. And neither is it my fault that these are just the people who will pay most for our support, and who are disposed to serve us most unconditionally. The liberal politician, be he radical or socialist, who counts on popular support, who enjoys influence in his party and has an effective electoral contingent, will never seek us out to give us help nor to ask for ours. On the contrary, he will be our competitor, our adversary. On the other hand, the politician without party, the displaced man, will welcome our shelter and will be our most energetic defender. And for us he will have the advantage of not being a communist, of not being branded with the hammer and sickle."

"But among them," I said, "we should choose the least faulty."

"Oh comrade! You are going back to the cave from which I've tried to draw you! Most faulty? Least faulty? Free from defects? No, that is not the most essential thing. You must judge coldly who serves the party and who fails to serve it. This must be your only criterion. Remember that all our concessions are only temporary. Don't forget that we communists are fighting for the world revolution. When it triumphs the steel columns of communism will march over the bodies of those same people who now hasten to offer us their protection. It can not be helped. It is an inescapable consequence!"

He paced the floor with long, slow steps, stopping in front of the window.

"Our goal is to make ourselves strong, to acquire skill in mass action, to win positions and become capable later of striking blows."

We parted after he had wished me luck and embraced me. I had embarked officially on the Yenan Way.

After the conversation with Dimitrov I had a short talk with Manuilsky. I was deliberately sober, and he pointed out what a great responsibility rested on me. He insisted uncompromisingly on an ample and energetic and immediate movement of solidarity, at the moment that the popular insurrection should take place in Brazil.

"All recommendations are unnecessary, comrade Manuilsky." And so the interview ended with a farewell.

Once free of preoccupations, I went to dine at Guralsky's house. When I left the Comintern building, two letters were given me; they were from Dorogan, who had been transferred to Moscow to a heavy industry factory as a simple mechanic; he was no longer at the foundry of Cheliabinsk, where he had been director for several years.

Guralsky seemed very happy in his position but was skeptical about his own future. When I spoke to him of Dorogan, I told how I had met the man at the little foundry on the Black Sea and the efforts I had made to find him before finally receiving his letters.

"A foundry director who comes here as a simple mechanic?" he said. "Wouldn't that mean he has been demoted?"

"I don't think so—why?"

"Such strange things happen to people in the upper categories! It might be wise to find out first if he has been disqualified as director."

On the following day I went to the address Dorogan had given me. There were his attractive wife and his three children; all were studying French.

"Dorogan," said his wife, "will not arrive in Moscow for two or three days. You will dine with us of course. He is most anxious to see you. Come day after tomorrow, in the evening."

The following night there came to my room at the Lux a man I had never seen before. He was carefully shaved, with unusually good clothes, tall and self-satisfied. He came in without knocking at the door, which he closed, after looking up and down the hall first. He searched the bedroom and then sat down, lit a cigarette, and offered me one.

"Pack up. You're leaving tonight."

"Tonight? I should like to take my leave of a few comrades."

"Here in the hotel?"

"Here, and outside too."

"Neither here nor outside," he said dryly. "We'll be at the station in an hour."

While I packed my few belongings, he said, "You will go through Germany, because we require it."

"All right," I said, without accenting the importance that I gave to this journey across the Nazi country.

He took my suitcase and opened the door quickly, looking down the hall in both directions. When we got to the elevator marked "out of order" he swore and hurried down the stairs to the side street. I followed him to a waiting car and we went to the Alexander Station.

On the train, he made them change me into a compartment with another traveler in it. He asked for tea, we chatted of the future and he wished me well. Half an hour later the train began to move. The policeman got off, waving to me cordially from the platform.

I stayed in the compartment with a man of mature years, grey-haired, with a skin free of wrinkles. I was certain he was from the NKVD and he stayed with me to the border.

On leaving the Soviet Union this second time I had less faith than I had brought with me. Something had burnt out in me and the ashes stayed on the snow of the steppe where the winter was ending. I entered Nazi Germany by the Polish frontier and was surrounded by uniforms and brigades of blond boys who made their iron boot-heels click gaily on the pavement. I was amazed at how well everything turned out. It seemed no time before I was walking along Copacabana and by the shores of the heavenly sea of Rio de Janeiro. Then I went on my way to Buenos Aires—my destination, Santiago de Chile.

CHAPTER VI

Popular Front

1

THE experts of the communist brigade, which was to work in Chile, arrived one by one. Frederick Glaufbauf, the Czech, a professor in the Lenin Academy, was the only member of the former South American Bureau who was returning to America, this time to Santiago and under my orders. The others were: a German with an unpronounceable name and unmistakable accent, son of a Nazi professor at Bonn, who passed as Manuel Cazón, a Spaniard; the Russian Kazanov, who at my arrival already spoke like a native and had Chilean papers under the name of Casanova; Ricardo Martínez, the Venezuelan, who came as auxiliary of a union organization; and Marcucci, the Italian youth director, who was to be political advisor to the delegation.

This last was the outstanding figure of the group. In spite of his youth, he saw problems clearly, had talent as an investigator and rich experience in the legal end of our work. With his help, I screened the presence of the foreigners by opening offices which had every appearance of an innocent business, and laid out the plan by which our apparatus would function.

Once established, without any of the Chilean party members knowing of us, we proceeded to contact their principal leaders. Elías Lafertte and Carlos Contreras Labarca were out of the country—the former on his way to Moscow—so, for a long time we had to work without these two.

The President of the Republic, Arturo Alessandri, had declared that the communist party would never carry its red banner on the Alameda de las Delicias while he was President. The communist party, thus outlawed, was engaged in petty and sterile activity. The police watched everyone carefully and no real political action was possible in the country. This was our main problem.

We made our first contacts with the secretary of the Chilean party and finally met with a group in a little joint behind a fruit-stand, run by the girl-friend of a railroad comrade, Luis Valenzuela Moya. Marcucci would not join us, but the rest of us went in and found Galo Gonzáles, Chacon y Corona, Raúl Barra Silva and the union specialist Pablo Cuello, as well as the deputies Andres Escobar and José Vega, all happily eating slices of watermelon. This spectacle had something grotesque about it and seemed to me ingenuous, irresponsible and actually indecorous. We spoke with the leaders, refusing to hold any meeting in this place, where the police could enter at any time.

"We can go elsewhere," said Galo Gonzáles, sadly abandoning his watermelon.

"We will go nowhere," I answered. "When we are ready we shall call you. Neither your mother nor your wife nor your little daughter must know where you are going nor at what time. That is not advice; it is an order." They looked surprised but agreed to wait at home for the next twenty-four hours to await our instructions.

The meeting, when it finally took place, got us nowhere. "You think," said Barra Silva, "that we can come out in the open?" And smiling compassionately, he added, "You don't know this government and this police!"

"Before the year is up," I said, "we shall be marching down the streets of Santiago."

"You think you are in France!" mocked Chacon.

"I know where I am," I said with some asperity, "and I also know what difficulties I shall meet and the poor quality of human material with which I must overcome them. And I am not bluffing."

"At any rate," said Cuello, "we ought, I think, to cooperate with these comrades who have come to help us." Chacon answered with a long speech in praise of the Chilean fighter, his courage and his capacity for sacrifice, ending on the note that they needed no foreigners to give them lessons.

At this point the German, Cazón, exploded. This indolent slow calm of theirs was unbearable to him. He pointed out that they had spent ten days arranging a meeting, which through their stupidity could not then take place, and now at the first real contact they were unwilling to attempt any kind of action. Glaufbauf interposed with his usual tact to say that all this was quite natural; it was a result of the old techniques. We left, having accomplished nothing except to arrange for another meeting.

If the Chilean leaders understood one thing well it was passive

165

resistance. They proposed nothing, they opposed nothing, they did nothing. Finally I lost my temper.

"We are going to carry out our program with you, without you or against you. From now on every man will do his job in a responsible fashion. We shall accept no explanations or subterfuges or long tales about difficulties. The juggling is over."

However, things went from bad to worse. Within our own group, Martínez was a thorn in my flesh. He criticized plans that had been made and directives adopted with his consent. And so we went to work on him. The man was literally smashed, and his position ceased to exist.

When the Chilean leaders saw with what energy we intended to carry out the attack against the old position, they divided into two groups—one which accepted the new ideas and another which wanted to resign. Cazón wanted to consider these resignations as desertion in battle. I insisted on a national conference of the party to accept their resignations and name new leaders. It was called and met without incident; and so the heavy inertia of the Chilean leadership was finally overcome.

The application of the "Yenan Way" tactics in Chile demanded special attention to the sectors susceptible of approach, and the establishment, after that, of a *quid pro quo*. To find these people was much easier than I would have thought. They were men of good will, romantic, sensitive to human grief, ready to give us their collaboration as long as it remained a secret. All they asked was that the normal current of their lives should remain undisturbed.

As it was impossible to work with large numbers of sympathizers, we had to do it individually in some cases, and with very small groups, in others. There were some who had a passionate curiosity to know what was going on in Russia; and there were those who approached us as a consequence of their philosophical interests, or their desire to understand the theories of communism. Among the intellectuals, there broke out wars of words more violent than the wars of religion. They cursed at each other and called each other "incompetents" and "plagiarists" and "sterile toadfish." Pablo Neruda, allegedly a poet, received the combined assaults of Vicente Huidobre and Pablo de Rokha; these last also attacked each other with ferocity and perfidy. The party had to act as pacifier, trying to convince the intellectuals that their violence might be better used in defending communism and the Soviet Union. It was not possible to conciliate these warring party moguls, but a sort of armed truce was obtained.

The sympathizers were grouped according to their friendships, or according to the motives that brought them to us. There were those, for example, who dreamed of a journey to the Soviet Union as tourists. In a vague and unconfirmed way I had word that three people might be selected for such a trip, but the hope was encouraged in all of them. On their return, two of the three who went would have nothing more to do with the party, but meanwhile, we had obtained the services of more than a hundred.

The most numerous were those who wished to learn the fundamentals of our doctrine. Men and women of real culture and good social position began to join the restricted "circles" in which courses were given and lectures offered. All world affairs of any importance, as well as national events, were interpreted in these circles, giving always a favorable picture of the revolutionary process and presenting always to the growing audience the mortal dangers of fascism. The circles multiplied, even in the most fashionable parts of the city. Lessons were taught in houses that were little palaces, with sometimes as many as twenty expensive cars waiting at the door. No week went by without our conquest of new and firmer positions.

Marcucci, who had not approved of my efforts at first, was impressed by the ease with which proselytization went on in so short a time.

"You have the advantage," he said, "of knowing the *milieu* and the psychology of these people. For a European, it would be impossible. The *petite bourgeoisie* of Europe is a devoted and enthusiastic watchdog of the capitalistic system. The Latin American is more unprepared, more ingenuous. The Latin American is living in a political stage of terrestrial paradise; he is still in a state of innocence."

"These positions that we are gaining will increase," I said, "and will be used at the first opportunity, without forcing the issue, to get the party legalized and to get an organ for it—a legal newspaper."

"A newspaper!" exclaimed Glaufbauf. "The work is going well. Let's not start dreaming!"

"Without a newspaper—a daily, legal newspaper," I answered, "we can not construct a solid Popular Front. A political party that can not maintain a paper will never convince the public of its capacity to lead the people to power."

"Let's not talk of the faraway," said Marcucci. "Let us look at the immediate reality and see it as clearly as possible. I think we have put our best foot forward. The 'Road of Yenan' in Chile is now much more than a road. It is already a march. What I don't see yet is how you are going to develop this movement and put all these contingents to work. It is not only a question of having a newspaper, but of making all this function. How do you see it?"

"I don't know when an opportunity will present itself; I can't predict when favorable conditions will arise. It may be next week, or in six weeks, or in ten or fifteen months. I think it will be before the seventh Congress."

"A communist can leave nothing to chance," said Ricardo Martínez, sententiously.

"We are leaving nothing to chance, comrade," I answered, nettled. "Every day we gain positions; every day our subterranean influence grows; and what seems more important to me, we strengthen the faith of the party members in the possibility of success."

"That's it," shouted Marcucci, turning a cart-wheel in the middle of the room. "We must remember that the Chilean communists have had a long series of defeats. Now comes a renascence of faith in the Chilean convert; he feels that the wings that were plucked will be able to fly again, and he smells (for he cannot see it yet) the possibility of success."

"But what is your plan?" asked Glaufbauf. "What are you actually going to do?"

"First, a party conference, keeping the directing team we now have; next, new conquests in new zones, bringing the radicals into our sphere by holding out the hope that the next President of Chile may be one of their members; third, with the financial support of our sympathizers, we organize a press for the launching of a daily paper."

"All right," said Glaufbauf, "and then what?"

"Break the ring that fences in the party. Utilize more and more of the young radicals we have won. Sink a wedge between the components of the so-called Left Block, which is now united against us, and win positions there."

"How?" asked Martínez.

"Don't scream; I'm not deaf. Why, by feeding the ambition of a few, opening up new horizons for them so that they can get ahead."

"That's right," said Marcucci. "It's time to feed somebody's ambition and forge the first link of the chain."

In the bosom of the radical party was a latent schism. Although the radicals had supported Allessandri, the conservatives and liberals were given all the plums, and so there was a dumb discontent in a large sector of the party. The communist propaganda would have to turn this into a break between the radicals and the parties they had been collaborating with.

"The radical party deserves a better fate and the radicals have a right to more rewards. The historical destiny of the party is to win the presidency and to conquer power by a great popular alliance. The next president of Chile must be a radical."

This communist suggestion, slipped across quietly in small district assemblies, in restricted political circles of third and fourth category, had a surprising effect. Immediately the idea was sponsored by larger radical groups, and so, gradually, imperceptibly, in the foggy realm of ideas a subtle alliance grew up between the radicals and the communists.

Soon after, a *rapprochement* between the communist leaders and some active radicals, who felt overlooked in their party, became possible. There were friendly suppers and lunches, with chats around the table, washed down with the good Chilean wine, at which hints were dropped about future senators, deputies and directors of businesses dependent on the state. It was surprising to see with what eagerness these "innocent" suggestions were caught up by the young hopefuls. And even more surprising to see, a few years later, how they had been converted into fact.

"And you communists then," they would say, "what do you want?"

"Nothing, absolutely nothing!"

"Impossible! Nobody works for nothing."

"We are working against the triumph of fascism; to sponsor a government which will legalize the communist party, which will neither imprison nor murder nor beat up our leaders. Nothing more."

They were deeply stirred. This may not all be true, they probably thought, but if the communists give us a hand up we would do well to take advantage of it.

"If only you don't attack us it will be sufficient," said one young radical leader. "We would be grateful enough to thank you and leave you in peace. An attacking communist is like a bug in your ear. It would be a good thing to have you for our friends." That indeed was all we wanted; to be left in peace to work for strength later.

"It is incredible," said Marcucci on the eve of his departure. "What a land of promise for communists!"

That night we ate together; it would be the first and the last time anyone would see us, so it didn't matter. Marcucci was sad.

After a short trip to Argentina, Uruguay and Brazil he was to go back to Europe.

In our work with non-communists I saw examples of lawyers who spent the day defending special interests, corporations and imperialist business ventures, and the night anathematizing capitalist exploitation, the greed of business and the businessmen. These men helped the party financially, authorized credit from the banks, and aided the organization of counter-espionage within the police. They helped to weaken repression, making it sterile in effect for the government. The same thing happened with all sorts of doctors, public servants and even with some businessmen. It was clear, too, that the communist party had recovered faith in itself. We had to restrain the aggressiveness of our new contingent. These sad, defeated people had freed themselves from their sense of inferiority and were ready to fight.

The great opportunity arrived only two days after Marcucci's departure. Pedro Leon Ugalde died, the brave senator for Santiago, a radical leftist beloved by the people. The following day was set for the burial. This was it, our great moment! I called a meeting of the communist leaders and proposed a plan.

The communist party would attend and would unfurl its banners in the cemetery to honor the memory and labors of a great radical.

"But where do you want to take us?" demanded Galo Gonzáles. "What will it get us, when all the world knows that we attacked Pedro; that we have called him awful names."

"The people will say, quite rightly, that you are sorry for your foolishness, that you are anxious to admit your error publicly, even though so late. Only very brave politicians do that. And the public loves courage."

"They will never believe us," protested Chacon and Corona.

Before midnight the battle had been won inside the party. We had to reach people in all the nearby towns and factories, calling the workers to the funeral. Flags were sewn, posters painted, photographs pasted on placards. "It is as if the party were legal," said an old man. "Tomorrow at last will see us in the streets." Speeches were prepared. Marco Chamudez was to speak one, the worker Pilona another.

The day came. Leon Ugalde's bier was carried on the shoulders of workers and of the top leaders of radicalism. Tens of thousands of persons from every social stratum walked behind. Cordons of policemen armed with clubs escorted the procession which grew in volume and showed itself hostile to the government. The crowd was enormous. All Santiago was there.

There was tension, because handbills and manifestoes had announced the presence of the communist party. Most people expected the communists to be aggressive and virulent, not only against the government but against the radical party. When Chamudez stepped forward to speak, he was greeted with hostile cries.

"Outside! Make him get down! Wretch! Communist, outside! The communists were enemies of Pedro Leon! Outside!" In the growling mass someone tried to pull Chamudez back. The communists surrounded him, unfolded their flags; the handful of men showed themselves ready for anything.

"Let him speak," cried someone, and there was silence.

The words fell solemn and clear, ringing with emotion, from the mouth of Chamudez.

"Chileans!" The silence deepened. It was the first time any communist had opened a speech without saying "comrades." "In the name of the Communist Party I come to lower our banners before the tomb of a man who fought bravely for the freedom of his people——"

A thundering ovation rose to the sky. "Long live Pedro Leon Ugalde, battler for liberty!"

The wall of hate and of resistance had been broken; popular sentiment and the sincere grief of the people had been exploited; the psychologically favorable moment had been utilized.

Juan Luis Mery, director of the daily *La Opinion,* who was at that time under persecution by the police for having attacked the "Ross Calder contract," an arrangement between the government and an electric monopoly, was next announced. Mery hailed his dead friend and said he had not been able to stay away from his funeral even though by coming he risked his liberty. The warmth with which he was received showed him to be at the height of his popularity. And from this incident came the idea: Juan Luis Mery must be the successor of Pedro Leon Ugalde in the Senate for Santiago.

On our return we had a meeting. The atmosphere was completely different. The Road of Yenan was open at last.

2

Candidates to fill Leon Ugalde's seat in the Senate sprang up like mushrooms after a rain. The so-called Left Block went on constituting a barrier to the advance of the communist party, so it became essential to break it down, using every opportunity. Oscar Schnacke, the socialist leader, was one of the candidates. Schnacke was a stubborn adversary, and he knew the actual communist strength, which in Santiago did not reach to one thousand. So he was not disposed to make concessions. In the radical party, the name of Juan Antonio Rios (later to be President of Chile) was pronounced rather feebly. The Chilean communist leaders favored the candidacy of Lafertte. Juan Luis Mery had just been exiled to Argentina. The Left Block had announced in the morning papers that their deputies and senators would escort him, in honor, as far as the border.

In the next meeting of the communist party the Road of Yenan was discussed. "Schnacke is a hard fighter and it is desirable to defeat him. Lafertte is a communist whose candidacy will only demonstrate how few electors we control. Juan Luis Mery is at the moment persecuted, but he has just received the popular homage at the funeral of Leon Ugalde; he has a newspaper, and since he is a member of the Left Block as well as Schnacke, to support him would be to drive a strong wedge into this block."

There was a battle within the party. The Road of Yenan was too bitter a draught for some workers. Nonetheless, before midnight, Juan Luis Mery received notice in hiding that the communist party would support his candidacy with the slogan: "It is not a matter of accompanying Mery to the frontier, but of preventing his exile." The following morning, Chilean political life was surprised by the disguised communist inroad. Many began to wonder if the communists had not assumed direction of the political battle of the moment. Influence was brought to bear on the radicals, with the suggestion that Mery's candidacy might be a step towards the presidency. The daily *La Opinion* shifted towards its new allies; the Left Block was successfully split, and the socialists isolated.

Our sympathizers were immediately mobilized to work on Marmaduque Grove, a socialist leader, to restrain the "uncontrollable ambition of Schnacke," and to keep public opinion from putting the blame for Mery's exile on the socialists. Later, he would be accused of having given a cheap victory to Alessandri's regime, and would be blamed in addition for the defeat of the left.

Grove gave in, and the unification took place around Mery; after which the government decreed amnesty for the director of *La Opinion* so that he could carry out his campaign freely. In this way the communists won their demand and Mery's exile was prevented.

Mery called on his adherents to stage a big parade in the streets, and down the Alameda de las Delicias. It was led by the radicals, with the socialists and democrats following and the communist party at the end. It was the best place to be, since the crowd always seeks the tail of a parade whenever the head is made up of people from the upper classes. Our numbers, therefore, appeared double. The red banner *was* carried down the Alameda de las Delicias, giving the lie to President Alessandri.

Although the government put over its own candidate and Mery was defeated, it was natural that from then on, the politicians on the left should take the communist party into consideration. Every embryo politician, all who wanted a hand up, became our friends and were to some extent agents for us. The revolutionary movement of yesterday had become a bargain counter, which had nothing to do with the emancipation of the proletariat or the relief of the hard conditions suffered by the masses. But it was without doubt a success for the Communist International, and added to the glory of the Comintern, its agents, the Soviet Union and the great and illustrious Stalin.

After the electoral fight, we had long conferences with the more advanced radical leaders. Justiniano Sotomayor and Saco Lanfranco led the group which was to launch and foster the idea of the Popular Front in the radical assembly of Santiago. In the bosom of this assembly, the idea had already been accepted that the next President should be a radical. And so it was easy to insinuate the next step— a political force which might be capable of achieving that goal. Justiniano Sotomayor, Saco Lanfranco and their group put the thing over brilliantly. The top leaders of the radical party met with a concrete demand from within their own ranks. The communist party was behind it, but acting from afar, by remote control. And then a new opportunity came to favor our plans.

Polls to elect a senator were called for the district of Cautin and Bio-Bio. It was necessary to give a victory to the people; to find a point of least resistance and wage the battle in such a way as to defeat the government. Moreover, in the directing circles of radicalism there had arisen some strong opposition to the organization of the Popular Front. The young radicals were being sharply criticized. They were accused of serving as agents of the communists and playing their game. It was important to strike a hard blow at this campaign. So, to achieve this end, the communist party supported for Senator of Cautin and Bio-Bio, Dr. Cristobal Sáenz, one of the greatest landholders in the district, and one of the biggest wheat men in Chile.

Protests arose among the communists.

"What are the communists going to get out of a radical victory? What is the working class going to gain from the electoral victory of a millionaire?"

"In Cautin and Bio-Bio, dear *roto*," was the answer, "you are not going to change the radical's position in any case. At present, in that district the communists have, at most, seven votes. What sort of triumph can you attempt with seven votes? On the other hand, if we support this millionaire we get two things. First, we weaken the campaign against us within the radical party and gain the confidence of the most powerful among them; second, the number of converts will increase in this campaign and we shall soon be getting aldermen and mayors in Cautin and Bio-Bio where now we have nothing."

So the rich landholder marched to battle, supported by the party of world proletarian revolution. A few workers cried out, others went along swearing, but the party was on the Road of Yenan. The Popular Front won its first great victory in Cautin and Bio-Bio. The press announced the victory but said not a word of the substantial growth of the communist party.

The party had come out of hiding, practically on the shoulders of the radicals. It was leaving its illegal haunts like a Cinderella, drawn in a beautiful carriage, much to their disgust and in spite of their protests, by the socialist and radical leaders.

3

Politicians of every shade of opinion who felt or knew themselves to have been overlooked, were the first to draw close to the communist party as a result of the electoral successes. Just as we anticipated, there opened before them a horizon full of promise; the party could perhaps give them the lift they needed. The *"bourgeois servants,"* predicted by Mao Tse-tung, came in avalanches, diverse in morals, politics, economic circumstances and social position. There was the generous type, moved by the suffering of the people and hopeful for a new world. They had absolute faith in the Comintern's word and professed devotion for everything Russian, be it a book of Stalin's exquisitely printed in Spanish in Moscow, or a gaily-painted wooden doll. Compassion for human misery can be inconceivably strong in the average man. The wretched situation of the people and the communist determination to improve it even at the cost of sacrifice, moved thousands of people in the lower middle class. There was nothing revolutionary about such people; they were simply concerned for the sufferings of others. And to these, very gently, the communists played sentimental tunes, not even suggesting violence—on the contrary, condemning war, with which the great, international munitions makers were about to destroy the world. It was flagrant that the great prayer for peace on which the communists put such emphasis was in absolute contradiction to revolutionary violence, to the actual methods of the Soviet Union and to the desperate Russian armament race.

To all this emotional appeal there was a tremendous response, especially among the youth. Schoolboys and University students, adolescents looking for work, boys eager for adventure and dangerous living, all were drawn to the party, and embraced with fervor the struggle for communism and the directives given by our delegation of Comintern agents.

Another thing that always brought results was the offer of help to any candidate who had been defeated by the Conservatives. Such men accepted our offer with tears in their eyes and were helped in forms that ran from simple electoral meetings with propaganda in their favor, to strikes organized in the industries owned or directed by their opponents.

The communists on the Road of Yenan specialized in hate campaigns. Patiently and stubbornly, a cell would be formed in the village, in the suburb, in the district, which would snowball hatred against a marked person or entity. In this way the party made itself feared and exercised a sort of blackmail, from whose grip it was hard to get free and which was even harder to combat. The sympathizers were much more numerous than the converts, and more docile as well. They could afford to take greater risks since they could prove that they were not communists. So we learned, day by day, through the tactics of Yenan, to exploit neighborly love and the unworthy ambition of the defeated, the healthy idealisms of the young and the hatred of professional rivals. Above all, we drew like a magnet every candidate for senator, deputy, mayor or alderman who wished to be elected and lacked votes, prestige or competence. To obtain these "victories" the Chilean workers were making the greatest sacrifices. Those who had least were giving most; and the worst of it was that they were giving it to put knaves into influential positions from which they could then disperse favors to the party. In this way the communist party was becoming an exploiter of the working class, a parasite upon it, feeding on its blood.

The "Road of Yenan" went into the field of labor unions with the prestige given by its political victories. It was not our policy, as it had been in the earlier days, to impose communist directors on the unions. On the contrary, we tried to attract to our camp the leaders already chosen by the unions, to corrupt, convince and bend them to our will. Each case was studied. Services were rendered, ambitions aroused, greeds encouraged, positions assured. The leaders of the independent unions were offered expert accountants, special editors, people who understood the articles of the Labor Code and were experienced in the routine of the Labor Ministry. There are many problems, large and small, that the most competent labor union leader is stumped by. All these problems we solved for nothing. Men appeared who were the unionist's mere servants at first, but who grew slowly and in time to be the real rulers, almost one might say, the spiritual directors of the union leaders. In this way the union heads became putty in communist hands. Behind the secretary, the stenographer, the legal aid, a cell functioned, a committee or directing nucleus of the party. Gradually it dictated the notes taken, the speeches made, the positions held, by the union leader and the working mass. So the independent union leader became our puppet and served us far better than if he had been a communist; for he was known as a man without a party by the workers and his employers, and had more influence because of it.

Those who resisted met with difficulties of all sorts. Paths were closed to them; they were made to understand that they had no future; their friends were drawn away; they were isolated. A slow but relentless campaign was waged to persuade the workers that they had secret understandings with the bosses.

"Of course," it would be said, "he is a good honorable man who wouldn't be an employer's agent. But he doesn't want trouble with the bosses. He would rather compromise and thus sacrifice your interests." And little by little the workers' trust in the leader would be undermined. This policy was called "drilling the boat," not sinking it with a blast or dashing it against the rocks, but opening tiny holes so that the water might fill it gradually, and eventually it would sink by itself.

Making a strike fail was a good tactic. Then the independent union leader would be blamed, and we appeared as the real defenders of the working class. Or we sometimes increased the violence of a peaceful strike so that the leader would be compromised and fall, either because the police arrested him or the employer fired him.

But the method that worked best of all was to get the favor of the officials in the government labor offices.

Ministers as a class have no desire to complicate their lives, and even less to lose their jobs, their salaries, their fine cars or the attentions of women who go to ask them favors. In Latin America, a Minister of Labor is always a lover of compromise and "fixing." The interests of industry or the real needs of the workers have in such men no particular friend. And these Ministers know that communists are expert troublemakers. So, when a communist leader comes, suave and humble, to their offices, bringing with him the formula for a nice arrangement, the Ministers of Labor, the Directors of Labor, are very glad to see him and to be his friends and allies. Full success is assured when the Minister or Director is convinced that the party can favor the candidacies of a senator, a deputy, a mayor or an alderman. "What we must achieve," we agents of the Comintern said, hammering the table at the cell meetings of each union, "is that all the advantages the workers gain shall come through the communist party." And so all resistance disappeared. The workers grouped themselves with the winners, and the independents were left with only one course—to knuckle under to our demands and yield to the pressure we put upon them.

The socialist union leaders, with their own party behind them, were the hardest to do anything with. Here we had to seek a compromise, find a formula for understanding. And after laborious discussions, communists and socialists always reached an agreement. It was an immoral one, certainly, for it amounted to a division of the spoils.

In this way the Road of Yenan was succeeding in Chile. Moscow sent special informers to pick up the most complete information on the experiences, the results and the extent of the movement. And the Chilean communist party won a seat of honor at the seventh Congress of the Communist International.

Then the news arrived of the complete crushing of the insurrection in Brazil. There had been no time to organize the movement of solidarity that Manuilsky had requested. The insurrection took place in the midst of an incident deliberately created by the government. It was guided by illusions which (nursed in Moscow) had multiplied and grown; and so it took place under conditions that made the rebellion dangerous and absurd. The Brazilian revolt was quashed instantly; the great majority of the members of the new South American Bureau formed in Moscow in 1935 fell into the hands of the police. And Manuilsky's great undertaking to save face sank into mud and blood.

He had chalked up a new defeat, which he managed to survive politically, thanks to Stalin's favor.

The seventh Congress of the International closed, and Carlos Contreras Labarca and Elías Lafertte returned to Chile to assume the open direction of their party. In Chile, as in other countries, the quality of the leadership was not what the membership deserved. The working class was immensely superior to the group that declared itself the director of its destiny. These leaders were not chosen by the members, but rather imposed on them for obscure and often blind international considerations. "Don't change horses in the middle of the stream," was the principle followed and the leaders were in for life, unless some murky circumstance should put them in the category of saboteurs, enemies of the working class and the world revolution.

Contreras Labarca was a timid man of blighted personality, ambitious and mediocre. In his youth he had tried to be a lawyer but failed in his studies and so became a communist. When Ibañez' dictatorship in Chile unleashed a furious persecution of the communists which was then extended to all popular parties, Contreras Labarca became secretary of the party in its illegal period. When the repressive wave passed, he found himself in the top post and clung to it stubbornly. He was a thick-witted man of little general culture, without imagination and with no gift for polemics. He mistrusted every recruit who showed distinction of any kind. With the patience of a boa waiting for its prey, he laid traps for anyone he considered a possible rival. He lived obsessed by the nightmare of being ousted as Secretary-general of the communist party, as a result of which he developed a positive genius for selecting the most mediocre people as his collaborators.

Relations between the Comintern agency and the party directors were polite but without warmth. Indeed, an invincible chill permeated them. Whereas the native Chilean leaders throughout many years had only failures to show, the Comintern delegation had pulled the party out of its illegal position to lead it through success after success to a political position beyond its fondest dreams. Moscow had suggested that we should gradually turn over the real control to the local party, giving them faith in themselves and making them feel their responsibility. So one day I proposed to them our plan for publishing a newspaper which should make known the new policy of the party to the public.

The suggestion was received with mistrust and little enthusiasm. Contreras Labarca objected that the party had no funds for such an enterprise, to which I answered that I needed no help from the party, only the authorization to take up the matter with our friends and sympathizers.

"And what press will publish it?" asked Galo Gonzáles.

"The organization of a newspaper," I answered, "demands a printing press of its own. Otherwise one works for the printer." Finally in a long and boring session the authorization I wanted was obtained. We would found a press and publish a paper to be called not *The Scarlet Banner* but *Popular Front*.

The hour had now come for our numerous sympathizers to give a concrete proof of their devotion. Some were to give their quota just once; others were to pledge a quarterly amount by accepting discountable letters of exchange; others would offer the support of their credit for short-term loans. And so was born the journalistic venture of the Chilean communist party. Its founders were all non-communists who, without joining our ranks, founded the most powerful enterprise that the party ever had in Latin America. With the pennies of our members we never could have done it.

With the funds we raised in the name of *Editorial Press Antares*, Barra and Company, Limited, we bought some old machinery from a press which had gone broke—a linotype machine with a gas furnace, and two flat presses that could put out a thousand double-sheets an hour. The personnel was entirely communist and came in before dawn to go out after dark, physically exhausted by the rigor of their task. Seldom, I think, has there been a group of more disinterested individuals with greater capacity for work, privation and physical suffering than those men who ran the *Antares Press* in the Calle de San Francisco.

The appearance of a paper known to be controlled by the communist party produced a public sensation. None of the political parties on the left had its own paper, and the founding of the communist press was proof of its growth and political power.

On the afternoon in September, 1936, when the first copy of *Frente Popular* came off the press, the long shed on San Francisco Street was invaded by thousands of people.

"It's true," laughed the communists. "It's a miracle."

"It's an omen," said the beautiful women, the distinguished lawyers, the thirsty candidates, the anxious aspirants to high office with the aid of the communist party. This beginning, which had managed to overcome the initial difficulties, influenced all the politicians on the left and widened the communist sphere.

The communist enterprise got long-term credit from the banks.

The biggest Chilean banks authorized large loans to a journalistic organization which fought them hardest. Importing firms quarreled for the *clientele* of a paper which had the political support of the Chilean section of the Communist International!

The enterprise grew and prospered, but no business ever paid less for longer hours in worse conditions; in very few did the workers ever have to struggle with such antiquated machinery. I did not let the thought reach consciousness that all that sacrifice, that titanic struggle, the sufferings and the privations were but a part of the fuel to maintain at high pressure the boilers of an engine on which was riding the bloodiest dictatorship in history. What a paradox! Free men, dedicated to freedom and the liberation of man, working so hard on the fortifications behind which there grew to life and power an ominous and sadistic dictatorship!

The non-communists who had cooperated in the endeavor celebrated each of its successes as if they were receiving dividends; as if they had been partners or shareholders. Yet it was the sole property of the communists, and its sole destiny was to serve the purposes of the Comintern, of Russia and the illustrious comrade Stalin.

One day the cable despatches of the United Press flooded our desks with the news that revolution had broken out in Spain. The military had risen against the Republic. The people had invaded the Montaña barracks in Madrid. There was fighting in the streets. The revolution in Spain further vitalized the Popular Front and was a tonic to communist activity. The heroism of the Spaniards, their astonishing courage and the valor that sent chills up the spine of the whole world were transformed into political capital by the communist party.

Meanwhile, parliamentary elections in Chile showed the incontestable power of the Popular Front, its electoral strength and the great contingent it could muster. The communist party won the Senate and the Chamber of Deputies; a representation no one could have dreamed of, two years earlier.

One of the important conquests was the enormous trust that we had won from the radical party, whose most outstanding leaders were our friends. And as the promoter and standard-bearer and witness for the purity of our motives appeared Gonzáles Videla who would later be President of Chile, thanks to the support given (in exchange for favors, past, present and to come) by the Chilean communists. He was considered our best friend, our most generous and loyal ally. And indeed he was, in those days. Thanks to the support of Gonzáles Videla the stubborn resistance of Schnacke and Hidalgo—of socialists and trotzkyites—was broken.

When our team passed the doors of Senate and Chamber, arm in arm with the leading radicals, I knew the meaning of bitter victory. Here was political victory, but my spirit was not at peace. I felt myself sliding down the inclined plane of treason to myself. The Yenan Way was defrauding the workers. The victories were for a small group of leaders only, at the price of vaster misery for the people. I was arranging and cooperating, without wishing to, in an immorality —for the successes of the Comintern were paid for by the Chilean workers with strikes withheld in agreement with the government, with effective diminution of salaries, with social appeasement, with greater misery and less bread for the people.

And yet that victory was intoxication to me as it was to the workers, the employees, the thousands of young men who followed our banners with such enthusiasm. For most of us the minor evil then seemed Moscow, with its sadistic Stalin, its Road of Yenan, its Popular Fronts in which radicals and communists triumphed together, rather than Nazism with its bloody oppression and its dictatorship enforced by Storm Troopers.

4

As I have mentioned previously, we had set up "study groups" in which were offered indoctrination courses adapted to the tastes and abilities of different groups. For the workers—the socratic method, the lesson without any previous plan, the answer to any question the individual might care to ask. For the students—an imitation of a university lecture, with a full discussion afterwards. For the ladies, the lessons were more like the classic French *salons,* and took place in the homes of respected Chilean families. Here marxism, dialectical materialism, world-wide political developments, life in the Soviet Union, and interpretation of national events in the light of all these, were all discussed. The people who attended these meetings were, for the most part, honest folk who came to learn, but who also agreed with the communist party in its preaching against injustice and the economic evils that afflicted so many people in the world. Most of our students would not have accepted the advisability of violence nor of the Stalinian purges, executions and assassinations. But consciously or not they were adherents to the ideas, the work and the tortuous infiltration of the communists.

Young girls of good social position came to those meetings, who had not the slightest proletarian link but who were drawn by the strange, mysterious and sometimes forbidden thing called communism. Some came to impress their fiancés and suitors with the fact that they were, different; others to shock their grandmothers. And in a few the religious spirit operated, the desire to relieve human misery and to bring about a better world. Among them there was a couple known as "La Chita" and "La Lela," family nicknames such as often cling to a person throughout his life. Each was a perfect foil for the other, as different as day and night, and never apart. La Chita was fascinating, mocking, with a keen sense of humor; La Lela was serious, with an acute critical sense, and prone to take other people and life itself very seriously indeed. This couple came closer and closer to the party. One fine day their baptismal names—Lucía Acuña Sepulveda and Delia de la Fuente Smith (La Lela) were inscribed in the party register as members.

Delia stood out among all the others by her eagerness to learn, by the punctuality with which she turned in her work, and by her devotion. She had been educated in a school run by German nuns; of her religious background there remained only her ardent devotion to a cause, the habit of discipline and a feeling for organization. One of the nuns, knowing of the antagonism between our two countries, had always predicted for her a Peruvian husband. And little Delia would cry at the prophecy of so hideous a misfortune.

Months after meeting her I realized that between myself and this obedient lover of obscure Hegelian philosophy and polished conversation, a link was being forged. Ours was an idyll of the mind in which our bonds were intellectual rather than sentimental. She was drawn by my methodical explanations, my reasonings in which each statement was illustrated from reality; she reveled in new ideas, the invitation to a dangerous life, and action risked for a heroic end. I was captured by her simple obedience, her fresh candor free from tenderness and her sharp critical judgment, her great capacity to see the essence of defects under words, gestures and appearances, the inconsistencies and fragility in events and characters.

I knew that Delia did not come to the party from snobbery or a desire to draw attention to herself, nor even through any identification of herself with the proletariat or personal social resentment. It was rather, as with many young people, from a yearning for something better than the world around her, the tendency to endow life with a superior meaning, the desire to serve others and to find one's own happiness in theirs. In me the adherence to communism had come from the suffering I had seen around me. In her it was an interior need to realize herself in something worth while, an urge to live more fully.

Throughout this idyll, which was more reasonable than sentimental, we spoke little of love and much of our conceptions of the world, the meaning of life and the path we sought. She introduced me to her parents. Her mother adored art. The father was a happy student of spiritualism, rosicrucianism, jainism and yogi practices. We became good friends, and one day her name and mine were inscribed on the marriage register.

We planned a vacation—a trip to the lakes in southern Chile which offer the most enchanting views in the world, especially in summer. We planned to intoxicate ourselves with love, with Chilean wines and with the beauty and witchery of nature. And when our plans were about to materialize, came a message from Moscow.

"The Spanish civil war needs the help of all who are able to go there. Not only does the republic need the blood of soldiers; the communist party has to have cooperation from those most experienced in political struggle. This is not an order nor even a suggestion. It is only an authorization to take the most appropriate and practicable path for the interests of the party and the International. If you wish and if you can; if the work in Chile will not suffer seriously; if the program of the Popular Front will not be impeded; if you feel that you can be spared, then see if it suits you to go to the Spanish Front."

Delia was excited. In Spain the revolution was a living thing; in Chile it was not. Liberty was fairly secure in Chile, while it was constantly more threatened in Spain. Drawn by the heroic vision of Madrid, by the greatness of the task, the importance of the struggle, we decided to go. We gathered together our few possessions and obtained papers and documents. Through the intervention of the republican ambassador Rodrigo Soriano and the cultural and press attachés of the Spanish Embassy, the writer Maria Zambrano and Luis Aldalve, I got the necessary documents to enter republican Spain and a job as war correspondent for the Buenos Aires *Critica*, authorized by Natalio Botana.

In the March fog we flew over the majestic mountain ranges on our way to Buenos Aires and Spain, the last refuge of all our hopes as communists.

As shepherd of the Comintern delegation in Chile I never used either my own name or the name on the passport with which I had travelled from Moscow. In the party and outside it I was known by the pseudonym of "Jorge Montero."

"Comrade Jorge Montero" figured in Chilean police annals only after he had disappeared from politics. And this was due not only to careful and efficient clandestine work but also to the protection I received from outstanding and influential leaders in the radical party, and after their triumph, from the government itself.

Gabriel Gonzáles Videla, who later became President, was the foremost of these protectors. He and Justiniano Sotomayor were the outsiders who best knew and understood my background, the mission that I was carrying out, and the authority I held within the communist high command. Both shared responsibility for the success of the Popular Front in Chile, and above all for the nurture and flowering of the radical-communist friendship and cooperation.

It is almost sure that this knowledge was drawn on as the main source for a book which the government of Chile later published, dealing with the activities of those whom, generalizing, they called "instructors." In this book, published under the auspices of and edited by an official department, there is a long chapter on the activities, life and betrayal of "Comrade Jorge Montero" in Chile. Some passages are illustrative, and add a clarifying complement to what I have said:

"Comrade Jorge Montero" [I quote from a passage in the above book], "without loss of time assumed the direction of the Party, criticized the Line fixed by comrade Cazón and expounded the new tactics of the Popular Front, its fundamentals and objectives.

"Personal and direct knowledge of almost all the party leaders in the country and especially of the members of the Central Committee led him very soon to the conviction that they were for the most part sectarian, devoid of imagination and full of animosities. Very deficient human material with which to carry out the task which had been assigned to him. While he was making an effort by systematic education to bring about a change in the mentality of these leaders, he did not for an instant neglect the practise of the 'New Line.' For this he formed a sort of team of agile and teachable collaborators, preferably young, without removing anyone from his post. For example, he respected the position of Contreras Labarca; but the effective agent of his final decisions became Marco Chamudez. He did something analogous in all the 'independent organizations' which took their orders from the Party. Once his bureaucratic machinery was in order, he devoted himself to guiding and reorganizing all the instruments of publication.

"From an introverted Party an extroverted one had to be created, broad, cordial, welcoming 'all the social strata.' A vast task which took several years and in which he reaped a great harvest in affection, envy, hatred and ingratitude.

"He replaced the 'International Red Relief' by the foundation of a 'League for the Rights of Man' with a program that included all political and religious opinions. He opened the doors of the party to intellectuals, doing away with the emphasis on labor; further, he used them as an attraction in the proselytizing work of his organization. He was responsible for the opening of the 'Casa America' on the corner of Arturo Pratt, an institution with a character as much social as political. He demanded that the Communist Party and its allied organizations should use the national flag in their public demonstrations. The Peruvian Montero taught the Political Bureau of the Communist Party to sing the Chilean national anthem.

POPULAR FRONT

"In the matter of publicity he suppressed *Crimson Banner*, a leaflet which was the official voice of the Chilean Section of the Third International and *Only Front*, organ of the Workers Federation of Chile. In their stead he created *Popular Front* with its own press at 347 San Francisco Street, with broad informative journalistic features. He contracted for the telegraphic services of the North American United Press instead of the Soviet agency Tass. He founded small papers in the minor cities; and the party headquarters and publishing house included a broadcasting station *National Radio;* all this was through the intermediary of Sociedad Barra and Company, Limited, founded especially for the purpose.

"In external action he organized the members of parliament and the best elements of the Party in accordance with their especial talents to carry propaganda to all political, social and intellectual circles. They were real commandos operating in No Man's Land, among friends and enemies, not to destroy, but to carry the brotherly word of communism redeemed of its past intemperance. The Uruguayan poetess, Blanca Luz Brum, came to be in intellectual, political and artistic circles the messenger dove of the new popular faith. This concentrated infiltration by comrade Jorge Montero quickly brought its first fruit: a resounding speech by Deputy Justiniano Sotomayor Perez Cotapos, which gave its start to the Popular Front in Chile.

"His first harvest was the senatorial triumph of the opulent landholder of Cautin, Cristobal Sáenz, with the decisive and enthusiastic support of the Chilean section of the Third International.

"Comrade Jorge Montero, as the guardian of the Communist Party, operated always in the shadows and kept his adopted name, although it was he who put an end to the custom that communist leaders had of using battle names. Finally he introduced another innovation when he offered a course of Marxism in the house of a respected family in Cienfuegas Street of this capital. Students of both sexes, of every shade of political opinion attended. In those days it was fashionable to be communistic. A charming girl, Lala de la Fuente, wished one day to hear the marxist professor about whom everyone was talking. The lessons moved on to the Forrestal Park and, passing by way of the Marriage License Bureau, are continuing today in the City of the Viceroys.

"To sum up, the instructor, acting on every possible front, was able to take the Communist Party out of its illegal status and make it into what was almost a historical party. With clarity, flexibility, culture and audacity the Peruvian Montero transformed the Communist Party in Chile from a persecuted nomad into a settled group with a home of its own, with leaders and members who used their own names, and who actually felt emotion on hearing the national anthem.

"When this talented masterpiece of Jorge Montero was at its height he received an order to transfer to Spain, now destroyed by Franco's revolution. . . .

"One day Andres Nin was found mysteriously assassinated in a suburb of Barcelona. The writer Victor Serge accuses Codovila directly of having ordered the crime. Montero, who had felt certain of being able to defeat Nin decently with the weapons of intelligence and talent, expressed his disapproval of this act in the only way that was possible within the organiza-

185

tion to which he belonged. He asked to be transferred; and Dimitrov sent him back to Chile."

The chapter about me closes with the following words:

"The reasons for Montero's expulsion from the Party have never been published. There are those who maintain that it was inspired from Buenos Aires by Vittorio Codovila on assuming the functions of delegate extraordinary of the International with discretionary powers over all of Latin America."

Such is the general opinion of the Chilean government and of the distinguished director of the radical left who cooperated energetically and intelligently in the joint work of the radicals and communists. Later, President Gonzáles Videla harshly and eloquently corrected his bearings and his political attitude to the communist party. He became, under the pressure of experience and proof of the most shameless and virulent fifth columnism, one of the strongest and without doubt one of the most sincere adversaries of communism in the Hemisphere.

In what I have quoted, there are inexact facts and some exaggerations and omissions; notwithstanding which, it has documentary value, and a greater value still, in that it shows how the most progressive Chilean radicalism has reversed its erroneous stand of yesterday, recognizing the great danger of infiltration.

CHAPTER VII

Spanish Ordeal

1

I HAD read Clausewitz, Ludendorf and von Schlieffen. I had, therefore, a general idea but no concrete one of what a country was like in wartime. With this idea I approached the Spanish frontier. We arrived at Cerbere, crossed the dividing line and entered Port Bou—a peaceful provincial town, a quiet place without any sign that it belonged to Spain or that the four walls of Spain were ablaze. Normal village life went on; people walked calmly and the routine of peace seemed undisturbed.

On one of the rocks of a cliff, a couple of men were drilling, trying to pierce the stone and humming fandangos as they worked. Approaching, we asked them what it was going to be.

"Can't you see? A shelter."

We didn't object. A shelter on the surface of the earth, a sort of open cave in the wall of rock! That pair had not the remotest idea of what a shelter was, or of the way in which a bomb exploded. It was enough, they thought, to cover their heads.

While we were waiting for the train to Barcelona, the sirens sounded; an airplane was approaching the town, probably to bomb it. The people who, like us, found themselves in the station restaurant, ran to a place under one of the arches of the station. It had only the name of shelter, with which to console these poor folk; indeed it was the more dangerous, for if the town were bombarded the bombs would surely be dropped on the station and on that very masonry. My wife pointed this out to me.

"No, you don't know what you are saying," I answered. "This is the safest place of all, not because it's a shelter or because that stone vault is over our heads, but because it is the target for Franco's aviators and they will never be able to hit it."

The Spaniards who heard me immediately opened conversation with us and spoke quietly of the war and its consequences. The airplane arrived, a tiny machine like the ones leaflets are scattered from;

187

nevertheless, it was said, it was bringing its load of bombs all the way from Mallorca. It dropped them on the town, producing half a dozen reports and a few holes in the fields. My wife remarked:

"It is the first time I have ever heard a bomb go off. Why haven't they shot down this horror; why don't the anti-aircraft guns of the republic get him?"

"The republic is not prepared," I said. "They will be setting up their defenses to shoot them down soon."

"That little airplane with its fuel capacity never came from Mallorca—no!"

"Little airplane—what do you know about it, little one? That is an airplane to cross Europe and back again."

"No, my boy. I tell you, no. That machine comes from near by; from France perhaps."

So the people commented, until our train arrived: and after a long journey we reached Barcelona.

On the avenues the street-organs played and the monkeys danced to the notes of *Bien Paga* and *Maria de la O.* The cafés were crowded with patrons, quiet and happy; they were ordering liquors of all sorts, various little concoctions and soft drinks, coffee and sandwiches. Had it not been for the uniformed militia going in every direction and the freedom of the Spanish women, which made the Avenue of Flowers resemble Montmartre, Barcelona would have had the appearance of a normal city miles from any war.

We had interviews with a few party directors who assured us that the situation was very serious. Later, the rumor spread that the alliance of anarchists and the workers' party (the FAI, the CNT and the POUM) had got hold of a cargo of arms sent by Russia across the Mediterranean; that the captain of the Soviet ship had lifted anchor and withdrawn, refusing to unload the whole cargo until the government offered the necessary guarantees.

The anarchists and poumists swore that all this cargo was destined for the communist party; that the communists would arm themselves and fall, without pity, on all their adversaries as they had in Russia—especially on the contingents commanded by the FAI, the Anarchist Federation of Iberia.

"Such a ship may exist, but all this about the arms it brings is just a story," said the Catalans in the cafés, who were not members of any party. A week later, in the early hours of the night, shots could be heard on all sides. Cafés and homes closed their doors; the streets were almost empty, though lighted. About midnight we heard the noise of trucks, and of men screaming and shooting. Anarchist militiamen were fighting in the streets, not against Franco but to determine whether the FAI, the CNT and the POUM or the "Stalinists" as they called the communists, were to be the ruling party.

The battle, which seemed to have no precise objective, lasted for three days. Hundreds of dead, thousands of wounded! Great quantities of ammunition used up, cars destroyed and time wasted! A chaotic situation which did the republic absolutely no good. On the fourth day, the combatants began to withdraw and the storm troops sent from Valencia by the government of Largo Caballero arrived. The arrival of the troops was peaceful, the revolt died down and the insurgents went back to wherever they had come from. The affair seemed to have no sense to it.

"Franco will win this war," said my wife with her usual acumen, the minute the revolt ended. "This way no army can win." There was a long heavy pause between us and she repeated as if waiting for an answer:

"This is lost! Lost!"

"Look, darling," I said, "the first thing you must learn here is not to make things difficult for us. When someone in a country at war says that the war is going to be lost, she is called a defeatist and can be accused as such." My wife swore she would never say such a thing again, but confidentially and between ourselves, the war was lost.

We left for Valencia. The central committee of the Spanish communist party was putting on a greater effort than the Comintern on a Congress day. And at its headquarters were to be found the outstanding figures of the communist international movement, many of them old friends of mine. Here was Palmiro Togliatti, the Italian who worked under the name of Ercoli; my French friends André Marti and Cogniot; Luigi Gallo with his Italian brigade, and the man called General Kleber who was having trouble with the party at that time. And here was Codovila, the same Vittorio Codovila who had run away from General Uriburu's bluff in Buenos Aires, and who had been segregated by Guralsky, only to land here in Madrid.

Some time before, Codovila, as delegate of the Comintern in Spain, had liquidated those of the party directors who did not docilely obey his commands. He invited Trilla Adame, Vega and some others to Moscow, where he had them given the *coup de grace*. On his return it was very easy to construct a docile and malleable group of directors.

The communist party had lauded Largo Caballero deliriously and long. He was hailed by the Central Committee as the "Spanish Lenin" —as the beloved leader, worthy of the love of the *Comuneros* of Castille—as the great chief who was leading Spain to victory. This overflowing love was changing to contempt, to sarcasm, to disgust. The heaviest and most virulent verbal artillery was now being prepared to work against the Prime Minister and his intimate collaborators. Speeches full of accusations, charges of negligence and treason would be made when the organ-stops should be pulled from Moscow. The highest directors of the communist party were like a pack of hounds baying at his heels.

Codovila, like the dwarf José Díaz with his falsetto voice, Dolores Ibarruri, the so-called Passionaria, Chueca the strong man of the central committee, Angelita the beautiful, cruel demon, swore an oath with their right hands on Stalin's "Fundamentals of Leninism," that Franco had lost the war and that the victory should be for the party of Marx, Engels, Stalin and Pepe Diaz. All of which could not be disputed short of incurring the risk of being called a defeatist.

In reality the faith and hope of thousands of combatants and millions of ordinary people, were fixed on a republican victory. We were sure that the indomitable Spanish courage would not be in vain, that the bravery of the thousands of men come here from every part of the world, some to fight with an altruism that was almost saintly, could not be lost. I felt an anguished need to believe in victory. I felt certain, as did all those who left their homes to come here to fight, that in Spain the decision was being made; that the land of the Catholic kings had become the pivot of human history.

I saw the reigning disorganization, the relaxing of all feeling for order, the harsh strain between the anarchists and communists, between Largo Caballero's socialists and the factions led by Prieto and Negrin; but the hope, the faith that this was temporary and would be overcome, soothed me.

A week after my arrival, having had friendly conversations with Codovila, I settled down to work. I would edit the daily *Red Front* and carry out also any political task that might be assigned to me. Before a week was over, I had been introduced with great precautions into what might be called the "sancta sanctorum" of the party. My surprise was immense when I found there, leaning back in a wide armchair, comrade Stephanov, one of the few old friends of Lenin who had escaped the purges and who was, with Manuilsky, one of Stalin's closest friends and who had also the prestige of having for many years directed the revolutionary movement of Chinese communism.

190

"Comrade Moreno wants to talk to you," said Angelita, taking me to the inner room where Stephanov was. "You understand? Comrade Moreno!"

Stephanov laughed, rose to greet me and embraced me gaily.

"How are you, man? You came with your wife, eh? Are you comfortably settled? How is everything? They tell me you have been successful!"

"And you, comrade Moreno?" I asked smiling and looking at Angelita who was surprised by Stephanov's welcome. Angelita was a beautiful woman, not without feminine appeal in spite of her hardness; she wore a pistol at her belt and carried a good supply of ammunition. I thought of the *Española* of Flemish art, with the knife in her garter, but I didn't say so, for Angelita wasted no time in jokes and was somewhat satanic. Later I learned that she had "given the shove" to many, and later still that she had died bravely before a firing squad.

Stephanov was the top leader of the revolution in Spain; of the war, and of the feints and attacks of the communist party. His word was received as the personal word of Stalin and his advice had as much value as if it came from the Kremlin.

We spoke of the progress of the war. Stephanov was not an optimist like the rest; on the contrary he harbored serious fears that it might end in a crushing and final defeat.

"We have lost a lot of time," he said, "in some most unfortunate mistakes which must be rectified if we are to win. This war is not being waged only against a military uprising; we are fighting against time. Our danger grows constantly greater."

We talked at length about Largo Caballero and about the crisis that threatened.

"Largo is a good man," said Stephanov, "an honest man who loves his people and the workers, but he is a fool. He is an eighteenth-century romantic; his thinking is subjective and arbitrary; he is sure that whatever he thinks is right, and that you organize a battalion in the same way as a union; that a strike and a battle should be led in the same way and that military discipline should be founded on workers' committees. Furthermore he is personally very vain, and what is worse, very difficult to handle. He is turning against us more and more, won't listen to our advice and refuses to adopt any measure that might lead to difficulties with the anarchists or the poumists." He paused, poured a spoonful of white powder into a glass of water and drank it down. "Largo doesn't realize that in wartime, politics must be for war. He tries to make normal politics, peacetime democracy—consulting with

191

anarchists, listening to the leaders of FAI and CNT and trying to please the poumists. And he has begun to mistrust us; he refuses to do as we say and even tries to oppose the party. We shall simply have to liquidate him."

"Liquidate him?" I exclaimed.

"Well," he smiled, "liquidate him politically, remove him from power. Nothing more." He lowered his voice, "We aren't in Russia."

"And who would replace him?"

"To succeed him? Why, Indalecio Prieto."

"How? Are you friends now?"

"There are no friends or enemies. There are people who serve us and people who do not serve us."

"And you think Prieto will serve us?"

"At least to neutralize Largo, yes. He is the only man who can destroy him. Anyone else would run the risk of failure. Prieto is dynamic; Largo is mild: Prieto works; Largo digresses."

He stopped speaking for a moment and said with a gesture of fatigue: "The ulcer keeps tormenting me." And after a pause: "For the moment you will collaborate on the newspaper. Then we'll give you other commissions; you will visit the fronts, make friends with the Spanish leaders. We'll see, we'll see."

Angelita came in with a cup of something which Stephanov drank. He was pale and his emaciated face showed suffering. I left, saying I would return soon. As I passed a door half-open onto the hallway a shout stopped me: "Madonna! You here!" And Marcucci rushed out and embraced me.

"Wait a minute. Don't go. Wait for me."

A few minutes later he joined me with his coat over his arm, smothered me affectionately in Italian curses and then in questions. He stopped for his revolver at the entrance and we went off together.

He had just got back from Moscow where he had worked for several months in the Comintern with Manuilsky and Dimitrov. In answer to my inquiries after several friends he answered:

"He is not there. You don't see him any more. People speak of him in a low voice," or "They shot him," or "It seems he's in a work camp," or "They are carrying out an administrative process on him."

I looked him in the eyes. He had become sad.

"You can't imagine," he said. "If you could see it! Moscow is a prison. If you were there your only wish would be to leave, to escape, to run away."

"What are you saying? I don't recognize you."

"Nor I. Each day I recognize myself less. This trip to Moscow, after the Brazilian failure, has about done me in. I have told Palmiro, I can't take any more. What's happening is horrible. Stalin is killing off half the party, or perhaps four-fifths. All Lenin's friends, all those who were with him in 1917, are underground, or prisoners in the work camps. Yes, my friend, either in jail or dead."

"But," I said, "the trotzkyites, the counter-revolution, the sabotage, the collaboration with the Nazis——"

"Do you believe, brother, that thousands of people who gave up their whole lives, their blood, everything they were and had to realize the revolution, would suddenly by a sort of collective madness—all of them—become traitors, spies, counter-revolutionaries and enemies of the working class? Do you believe that? Can you imagine it even? I can't."

We were sitting on a bench on the Plaza Castelar, at the door of a moving-picture theatre. Marcucci was horribly depressed.

"I grant," he said, "that Trotsky may be a fool and a knave and on his way to becoming worse. But not all of Lenin's friends can be traitors. Thousands of prominent members of the Russian party can't all be, even if Trotsky is."

"You must think like a European, like a Latin," I said. "If the Russians, with their special historical experience can accept a slave state, well let them. In our countries it will be different. Spain for example, won't accept it; the Spaniards are another thing again. They have neither the resignation nor the submissive spirit of the Russians. The Spaniard has, in addition to his temperament, some experience of liberty, some understanding of the democratic system, which the Russians have not."

"How you deceive yourself," he said, with pity. "You'll see; indeed there is nothing as different from Russia as Spain. There is no one more individualistic and stubbornly independent than the Spaniard. The Spaniard has defects but not the submissiveness of the Russian."

"Well, that's what I said."

"You'll see. In Spain the same methods will be used as in Russia; they are being used already. At this very moment in the communist party not only Stephanov rules and directs. You'll see the NKVD in action and you'll recognize its methods. The Soviets have not sent a single soldier to Spain; no, but they have sent thousands of police."

I was frightened. He traced lines on the ground with a little stick. Then he looked up, smiling sadly and said:

"In your America, there was a man, who after many battles, went off to die in a little town, saying he had ploughed the sea."

"Yes. Simon Bolivar."

"Well," and he laughed bitterly, "we too have ploughed, are ploughing the sea."

"WE?"

"Yes, man," and he laughed again. "We have ploughed the sea. You, I and a lot of other poor devils."

He got to his feet slowly, looked at me and said:

"How's Chile? Glaufbauf got caught, didn't he?"

"Yes, they caught him—and beat him up pretty badly."

"Poor old man. He always claimed to know all the rules of under-cover work. One day I urged him to write a book."

We spoke of unimportant matters, and after awhile there was nothing more to say. We parted; each went off slowly, worried, to his bed.

2

Not many days later Marcucci came to the printing room of the communist daily *Red Front* in Valencia. Bruno, the young Argentine who made the rotary press go round so fast he frightened the artisans of the peaceful old Mediterranean city, came to me as I was washing my hands with sand (we had no soap) to tell me.

I finished my unsatisfactory washing and left the darkness of the printing room, just as the sirens announced an air-raid. Marcucci was quietly reading the paper, still wet with ink, while men and women carried or dragged children off to shelter. We greeted each other and Marcucci said:

"Pierre has been looking for you for nearly four hours."

"Is he here?"

"He has been going over the fronts for several weeks. Last night he got back from Madrid, learned you were here and has sent me to get you."

The airplanes were over the city.

"I'd like to see my wife first," I said.

"Why first?" asked Marcucci. "Something important?"

"No. Because of the bombardment. She must be frightened."

"Don't be a child. By the time you reached her it would all be over. This happens all the time; you'd both better get used to it."

"Are there no shelters here?" I asked.

"Shelters? They have been building them for months and they'll be ready after the war. In time for the next one, as the French say."

"Then where is everybody running?"

"To the psychological shelter, which is all right too. Like religion, it consoles them and quiets their fears. These people are running to the basements of such houses as have them. They crowd together in them, sure of safety. I won't say what would happen in case of a direct hit."

We were walking towards the Central Committee. The reports rang out, now together, now separately, now near, now far. Most of the bombs exploded in Grao near the port; two fell on buildings in the Plaza Castelar.

"And how is Pierre?" I asked.

"Solemn as a church, austere, very demanding as to the political situation and the work each of us must do. He has as high a position now as Stephanov. He's much closer to Stalin and the Bolshevik directorate than when he was in America."

"And how do you get along with him?"

"Well, pretty well," answered Marcucci. "He is a decent fellow and that helps for a good relation with one's equals. He has a critical spirit and accepts my complaints in part, perhaps because he appreciates independence of mind, perhaps from sheer frigidity. Doesn't he seem to you emotionally absolutely frozen? He is all logic, reason, analysis."

"Yes, he has a knifelike mind; but he is gentle and clean and sane."

"I've heard him speak well of you and of your work. Of course he has some comments to make. He will tell you about them; you know he never hides his opinions."

We went into the Central Committee and Marcucci had to leave his gun and ammunition at the entrance. It was just like Moscow, and it was indicative how these indomitable Spaniards accepted and adopted the Muscovite methods. As we came in, there was Pierre standing in front of Stalin's picture. He did not smile, but embraced me effusively. His head was shaven and he seemed taller and more athletic than when I had seen him last. I was impressed by the warmth of his greeting. He was pleased by the success of the Popular Front in Chile and deplored the Brazilian fiasco.

"You were never in favor of the insurrection, were you?" he asked.

"No, I never approved."

"Don't repeat it," he said, as if it were an order.

Marcucci bade us goodbye; he was to leave that same night for Albacete. We remained alone, and plunged into an analysis of the general situation and that of Chile, going on to the economic, political and social failures in Peru, Ecuador and Bolivia. The lights were turned on and we went on talking in a suffocating atmosphere, due to the blackout. Pierre's way of presenting his disagreements was pleasant, and the smooth irony with which he attacked my reasoning when he differed with me was agreeable. He was not a man always set on being right, and sound reasons in opposition to his views were almost a pleasure to him.

"I shan't be in Valencia long," he told me. "I shall have to go to Madrid again and to the Aragon front; then even further. Let us eat together and talk all night. What you have to tell me will be very useful. Not only for my private information——"

"I understand. Thank you for your invitation. May I just stop on the way and see my wife?"

I knew that Pierre wanted a critical report to present to Dimitrov and Manuilsky perhaps, but in any case to the tight little inner circle of the Kremlin. In the car with Pierre, next to the chauffeur, sat a Russian dressed as a militiaman, armed with a machine-gun. Behind us followed another car with a crew of three men, all with machine-guns. Pierre saw that I noticed this and said:

"I doubt if this can protect me from bombs, or from a log in the road or a wire stretched across it. But one has only oneself to blame for being considered a personage."

We passed the building where *Red Front* was published, a lordly old mansion in one of whose rooms my wife and I lived. Then we left town, for Pierre lived in a mansion surrounded by orange groves and rice fields, beyond Albufera. We dined alone and Pierre introduced me to the excellent Spanish wines. Pierre's worst objection to my views had to do with my attitude towards the *Alianza Popular Revolucionaria Americana* in Peru.

"Have you got anything personal against Haya?" he asked, after raising his glass to my successes in Chile.

"No," I said, "nor against any of them."

"Are you sure?"

"Absolutely."

"I don't understand how you can accept the Chilean radicals as co-workers and refuse the same position to your countrymen, the *apristas*. If they are corrupt or candidates for corruption, so are the radicals. If the APRA is full of rogues, so is the radical party; and if Haya de la Torre is a knave, don't ask me for a list of Chilean knaves."

"In my opinion," I answered quietly, savoring my wine, "there are three essential differences between the two."

"Essential? That's interesting. Let's hear them," said Pierre, curling up in his chair likes a giant foetus.

"First, radicalism in Chile is not a vertical organization of a totalitarian type. There are no Duces or Fuehrers. It is democratic; in its bosom there is a right, left and center and even an extreme left; there is ideological elasticity. The APRA is not a democratic organization. On the contrary, it is a dictatorial structure and will lead to dictatorship. Haya de la Torre runs *aprismo:* the radicals run radicalism."

"Fine," said Pierre. "Have some more wine. It's very good. Did you ever think of being a lawyer?"

"Never. I liked philosophy and political economy."

"That's interesting. Go on to your second difference," he said with his chin on his knees.

"The second difference is that the APRA uses terrorist methods, and the Chilean radicals don't. The Peruvian *aprista* attacks his enemy with bullets; the Chilean radical prefers words, which may kill him politically but not physically. And for me this is very significant."

"The *aprista* uses terror as a reprisal against the brutal repressions of the dictator," said Pierre. "They may react primitively like the nihilists with useless crimes but——"

"No. *Aprista* terrorism is directed not only against the government but against anyone who opposes them, even against their own members. They punish their deserters with death. It is not like nihilism but a common criminality, vulgar sadism of the Nazi or the fascist variety."

"And the third difference?"

"The Chilean radical is a demagogue, promising what he can not give and has no intention of giving. He tells pretty stories to the Chilean *roto.* But the Peruvian *aprista* is a knave as well. Today he is anti-imperialist, tomorrow monopoly's servant. Today on the side of Russian communism; tomorrow with England; day after tomorrow, for the Nazis. Today he curses the Pope and tomorrow he bows down before the archbishop. Chilean radicalism fights, plays, wins and loses. *Aprismo* is always with the winner, whoever he may be. The radicals pay their debts when they can. Haya de la Torre and the *apristas* issue bad cheques; they make a pact in the morning to break it in the afternoon. It is the difference between a merchant and a swindler. Both may clear out your pockets, but one gives you something in return."

"I see you will never get along with the APRA," said Pierre, "but I assure you that I and a good many others believe that Haya is disposed to come to an understanding with us."

"With which of us?" I asked harshly.

"Why, with the International of course. With the Comintern."

I laughed. "Well that's an understanding I won't be present at."

"I know it. I know it very well." Pierre hit his chin against his knees and raised his eyes to mine.

"Do you think we are losing this war?" he asked.

"Yes."

He grunted, and I assumed he was agreeing with me.

"This matter of Spain," he said, "is a mere prologue. The real tragedy will come later. The alternative will be presented to every child of this century; fascism or communism. There will be no third road. And this is going to strengthen immeasurably the Soviet regime and the Stalinist sector."

"Why?"

"This Spanish war is consolidating Stalin's power. The Russian masses sympathize with the Spanish republic and are convinced that Stalin is giving it every help."

"But you yourself must admit there are no arms, no artillery, no tanks, no airplanes, nothing."

"Our armaments are being made," he said, "you know it, at an enormous sacrifice, not only of Russian bread, but of flesh and blood. They can not therefore be wasted or run the risk of falling into enemy hands. That is why the Spanish republic receives only small arms and second-class material."

"But surely, my dear Pierre, the cause of liberty must be defended everywhere, with every weapon."

"Spain," he answered, "is just a skirmish; it is not a war. And you must know that one can afford to lose one or a hundred skirmishes, if one ends by winning the war."

"We lost the skirmish of Germany," I objected, "and this war is being lost for lack of armaments."

"Yes, of course. There is no lack of courage."

"How could there be?" I asked proudly. "The Spaniard is the bravest human being in the world!"

"Have you heard anything of Guralsky?" he asked, evidently wishing to change the subject.

"No. You know we are not permitted to write. Where is he? And Inez, how is she?"

"Guralsky is not in the Comintern any more. He had a past you know, like beautiful women. That is, he had a debt to the party. And with us debts get paid, sooner or later."

"And Guralsky has paid his?"

"Look, comrade, it is better never to ask the fate of this or that Russian comrade."

He rang a bell and ordered the servant to tell the chauffeur to take me back to Valencia. He embraced me affectionately, saying:

"What we have said is entirely confidential."

"Of course. Don't worry."

As I drove back to Valencia in the car, driven by a Spaniard this time, and accompanied as before by a Spanish guard armed with a machine-gun, I brooded over the question of the armaments. Russia was trying out her new weapons, at the price of Spanish lives. The best were proven and then taken away; and the worst were issued to the soldiers who died with their fingers curled around them.

Such a policy was shameful and horrible, the sacrifice of men to try out things. Thousands of young lives were being lost so that comrade Stalin might know whether the infernal machine had been well or badly made by his Russian slaves in the work camps. Spain bled to death. And within me I felt a deep pain, as if my very depths were being torn by the harsh cry of wasted blood.

3

The civil war had brought to Spain a great tide of people, the strangest collection imaginable. On this flood rode like foam the extremes of ungrudging altruism and unrestrained banditry.

The International Brigades brought to Spain the best of militant communism from all the world. All, or almost all, the peoples on the globe were represented, with the exception of the Russians. For complex and subtle diplomatic reasons there were no Russian combatants on the earth or on the sea or in the air. There were Italians and Germans on both sides; on our side were Poles, Americans from every nation in the western hemisphere, Chinese and Danes, Hindoos, Egyptians, Belgians and French. There were blonds from Finland and negroes from Senegal, mulattoes from Cuba and *cholos* from Peru, blue-eyed and golden-haired boys from California and New England.

"This," said Marcucci, "let us not deceive ourselves, has not been organized by the Russians or by the great comrade Stalin. This has been done at great sacrifice by men like you and me. There are hundreds of men here who have come on their own savings. Comrade Stalin didn't help them to get here and he will not help those who survive to get back to their homes. And how beautiful it is to see them fight, transfigured almost, holding back the tide of fascism!" Indeed these combatants, come from the most distant places, fought with such valor that they all seemed Spaniards.

The men of the Central Committee made up slogans periodically and set them off like fireworks, one after another. They were given out to the press, sent out on the radio: "Madrid will be the tomb of fascism!" "They shall not pass!" "Better to die on your feet than to live on your knees!" Words, words, words—as Hamlet might say.

With the heroes and warriors, with those who had come to fight and die at the front, there had arrived at the same time and remained at the rear, thousands of adventurers of all kinds and conditions, with all sorts of backgrounds and purposes. Throughout the war, the cafés of Valencia, of Barcelona, of all the republican cities of importance except Madrid, were full of leisured customers who were café strategists, even when the last grain of coffee had disappeared from republican Spain and all the substitutes for coffee had been used up. There could be found every evening a crowd of people from every country. There was the man who bought jewels, any kind, from anywhere; he paid for them in pesetas which depreciated every morning, and when the advantage was very great, he sold them for dollars, for Swiss francs, for pounds sterling. There was the Hollander who was after antiques; the Belgian, probably a "rexist" and a Gestapo agent; the French woman who ran a boarding house, who made constant and furtive trips to France, moving with extraordinary facility; the Italian and the Swiss men, who always had neighboring tables, never missing a single day; the North American woman who called herself "the platinum blond"; the Japanese who sold "everything for a peseta," and the *marchands de tableaux* from Holland, Denmark and France. A whole motley army of traders, adventurers, rogues, spies.

"Why don't they clean all this filth out of the Republic?" some of us asked in the Central Committee. "Why aren't these people investigated—where they come from, what they are doing here, and by what means they are living? Send them back where they came from!" At first our criticisms were listened to and sometimes a vague resolution adopted, which remained on paper. Later, nothing was done at all.

The directors would repeat boastfully: "It doesn't matter. We can't lose this war. No, comrades, I tell you *no*. Because it can't be, it can't be. It just can't be." And the members of the Central Committee and those who heard the loudspeakers applauded.

"Before the fifth-column, we must deal with the defeatists," someone would say. "With those who think that we are going to lose this war just because there are a few adventurers in Spain, a few café strategists."

On the battle fronts was a courage without bounds, the highest of which man is capable. The terrible lack of every war necessity, the inferiority of armaments, the scarcity of munitions, the monstrous inexpertness and the grotesque mistakes of Colonel Lister and El Campesino Mayor, of a dozen men who wore uniforms and gold stripes—these were chasms which the Spanish people filled up with the sacrifice of its youth. There were mountains of difficulties, which the Spanish boys who were neither communists nor anarchists nor poumists but only fighters for freedom, overcame by the stoic surrender of the human animal's most precious possession, his life.

There are communist leaders who have studied and become experts in teaching youth how to die. It is not a natural talent but something cultivated in the Red Academies, which is learned and developed in the Soviet schools for communist leadership. It is like spying or the art of torture. The teachers of the art of dying brought films, made for the purpose in Russia, and showed them in the picture houses where the youth were rounded up and lectured to.

"Tanks?" asked the teacher of the art of dying. "Come on, there's nothing to it. The lion isn't as brave as he is painted. See how the brave Russian revolutionaries cope with the tanks of the invader."

In the film the Russian soldier sheds his coat, advances serenely and taps the eye of the tank; another soldier pours gasoline on it and lights it. The tank (in the film) burns as if it were made of dry wood. Its occupants leap out and surrender. The lights go on and the young men applaud.

"You see?" said the teacher in the art of dying. "What they did, we can do." And the audience rose to its feet singing war songs.

Frenchman's bridge, no one will cross you.

That same afternoon the boys would imitate the picture and of a hundred, one or two of them might immobilize a tank. The others perished under its gigantic treads.

The war progressed and human life was quoted lower and lower on what might be called the Moral Stock Exchange. To die meant almost nothing and to kill was no longer so serious nor so criminal. While the Spanish youth and the International Brigades fought with a courage that astonished the world, the traffickers took shelter behind the communist party card to carry out every kind of repulsive activity.

To die in the front-line trenches there was nothing like a party card; and to be comfortably installed in the rear, again nothing served so well as a card of the party of Pepe Diaz and comrade Stalin. It became a degradation, a filthy traffic in the noblest sentiments, a shameful concubinage with the worst forms of baseness. The communist leadership had become a vile sort of usurer who traded the heroism of some for the greed of the rest. And both, the heroes and the knaves, were made brothers by the symbol of the hammer and sickle, were yoked to the same defeat by the same worthy members of the Central Committee.

The political defeat of Largo Caballero increased the communist influence and gave it the halo, if not of power, at least of the administration of power. Communist adherents multiplied, coming from every field—from the republican army, from the employees of the Ministries and from the black markets, from the storerooms of spongers and speculators of every kind.

The Central Committee gave courses on all the Spanish problems of war and peace, made resolutions on the solution of the agrarian problem and the best way of filling tanks with gasoline, on fortifications and the price of eggs, on the promotion of officers and the songs that should be sung at the front. The meetings of the Central Committee gave a feeling of self-sufficiency and emptiness, of pedantry and ignorance. People who knew nothing about the subject under discussion gave solemn opinions and proposed as resolutions any idea that might happen to come to them. A wall painter laid down the law on strategy and tactics on the Estremadura front; carpenters became colonels and stonecutters were pronounced, in the name of Stalin, as generals superior to Alexander of Macedon. It was no longer a tragedy; it had become a burlesque drenched in blood and excrement, drunk with useless heroism behind which corruption rose like a sea at high tide, flooding it all.

In this madness, men who until yesterday had suffered prison and torture for the communist cause and for the defense of the workers' rights, were now become important communist directors with houses outside of town where they could sleep undisturbed by sirens, men who ate well while hunger brought the civil population to the point of exhaustion. They were members of a kind of confraternity of the elect, for whom this war provided the most comfortable hour of their lives.

When years later, after the defeat, I was speaking in Chile of the hunger and the privations that the Spanish people endured, Manuel Delicado, one of the grand dukes of the Central Committee of the Spanish party contradicted me:

"Look boys, why all this? To say we were hungry in Spain during the war is a lot of exaggeration. For my part I never ate better than in Spain during the war."

"You are right," I answered bitterly. "You are right. You are speaking one of the greatest truths that was ever spoken about the Spanish war."

But my irony was wasted; neither Delicado nor the others—a dozen or more refugee Spanish leaders—understood.

For the party leaders and for those of the so-called "auxiliary organizations" (a sort of title created to serve when the party didn't care to appear openly), the war was a period of great comfort. It was an easy life of which they had no doubt dreamed in their hours of misfortune. Comfortable dwellings, cellars full of fine wines, cars at the door, chauffeurs, beautiful women, blond and brunette, with green eyes or brown eyes, short-haired or long-haired, painted or not painted. For men like Delicado those were days of the fatted calf. But not for the Spanish people—not by any means.

The twelfth of October arrived, festival of the Race, which the Republic and the communists wished to celebrate worthily. I was called to go over the speeches written for the occasion and to give my opinion.

"They seem to me absurd, not just bad," I said to the communist minister and the members of the Central Committee. We were discussing the speeches which were to go by short wave to Latin America. "These speeches picture the Spanish conquerors as miserable adventurers and bloody oppressors. Here Cortez, Pizarro, Valdivia and Almagro are a bunch of assassins. And not only is it untrue, but it is an insult to the Latin Americans."

"Don't talk nonsense, my boy. You sound like a monarchist."

"Like a courtier of Charles the Fifth," added Angelita, laughing insolently.

"My opinion has been asked and my opinion is that neither Cortez nor Pizarro nor Almagro nor Valdivia nor Balboa can be treated as knaves."

A group of communist leaders who did not even know what

Cortez and Pizarro had done, opened an academic discussion to prove the speeches were good.

"You know something?" I asked. "The Spanish Americans to whom you intend to broadcast these speeches, are descended from the men you are insulting. Do you understand? And I think no one likes to hear his ancestors insulted, especially in celebration of a day that commemorates the very men you are accusing of villainy."

I began to laugh and Ercoli joined me. It was agreed that I should rewrite the speeches.

"But how is it," asked Codovila, "that these speeches are so bad? They were written by your own countryman Falcon. Are you prejudiced against him because of his dark skin?"

This nauseated me, but I answered quietly. "The speeches are phrased in this way because Falcon wrote them. In my country it is not the white men who hate negroes and mulattoes. It is they who resent the whites. Because Pizarro and the rest were white men, Falcon wishes to debase them."

A loud laugh greeted my answer and I was promised a fine supper if I would rewrite the speeches, substituting something better. By nightfall, the new speeches were approved. I had to work with the speakers to suit the style of each. From there I had to go to the broadcasting station to leave the texts for recording. When I finished it was after midnight. The speakers were pleased and one of the communist ministers said:

"I think you were promised a supper. You shall be my guest."

"Nothing could be finer," I said, "especially now when it is so hard to get anything to eat."

"My dear boy, are you serious?" he asked. "You must learn the ropes. In republican Spain there is everything—but everything."

I couldn't tell if he were joking or serious. But it was clear that these important communists were expecting a fine supper which would have no relation to the ration of lentils given out each day, one in the morning and the other at night. Those nightmare lentils which the people called, "Life Pills of Dr. Negrin—Resistance Brand."

We arrived at a mansion in one of those Valencian orchards, redolent with the perfume of orange blossoms, so popularized in Blasco Ibañez' novels. The mansion had belonged to Spanish counts before the revolution. An ancient dwelling, large and gracious, with neglected gardens and uncut lawns.

Other guests had preceded us, to judge by the cars drawn up at the door; more arrived after us. Soon the great drawing-room was filled and servants circulated with *hors d'oeuvres* and little drinks. One thing that was never scarce during the war was liquor, either Spanish wines or French cognac or Scotch whiskey.

"Gentlemen, supper is served," announced a white-gloved waiter who had obviously learned his trade serving the Spanish grandees, and now exercised it in the service of the big men of the communist party.

"It is for this that revolution is made in Spain," I thought against my will. "For this, boys die at the front; for this men left their own countries, their wives, mothers, sweethearts and children, to fight for liberty in Spanish trenches." My stomach was turned by the occasion and by the people around me.

We went into the great dining room, with its high ceilings and fine carved doors and exquisite chandeliers. Bottles of old wine, dusty with time, stood on the table; and there was half a lobster at every place.

"How about it, my boy? Is there or is there not any food in Spain?" asked my host. "What do you say?"

I didn't say anything. I only smiled. I couldn't have spoken if my life had depended on it. My throat was dry and my tongue choked me, but I had to go on smiling a greeting to the guests; many were not communists but important people from various political circles.

"This is indeed a supper representing the United Front," said Manuel Delicado. "All the republican points of view are represented here."

"Except for the poum," said a mature anarchist lady, smiling roguishly.

"The poumists are not republican," said one of the minister's upper secretaries acrimoniously.

There were perhaps forty persons at the table. After the lobster came a soup worthy of a fine French hotel; then fish, followed by what was only a dream to the people of Spain at that time—a *filet mignon* with fried potatoes as only the French can prepare them. The meal was generously accompanied by fine Spanish wines, hoarded through the years by the Spanish nobles. Dessert, ices, coffee followed; not the coffee served in the establishments where men and women came to talk about the war. No; real coffee such as they serve at the sidewalk cafés in Rio de Janeiro, Montevideo and Buenos Aires.

The host noted that I had not finished my generous portion of *filet*.

"You weren't as hungry as you thought," he said in a voice loud enough to be heard by all the guests. "You couldn't finish off your meat; and it was so good too." Everybody praised the meal and spoke of cooking and cooks. "Yes," said the host, "he was quite a find, my cook. He had spent a long time in Paris and understands the best cooking of both nations."

Fine French cognac, benedictine, cacao were served. Jokes were made about the abundance and great plans sketched for the future. The communist comrades spoke harshly of Largo Caballero, the ex "Spanish Lenin." The socialists and anarchists changed the subject.

At the moment when the talk was most animated a servant announced: "The ladies have arrived."

Eight or ten fashionably dressed and beautiful women, looking as if they had just left the beauty parlor, made their entrance. The conversation became general; the guests broke into groups to whom the servants continued to serve champagne, cognac and whiskey. I remained in a group with one of the new arrivals and as soon as I spoke she recognized my accent.

"An American, aren't you? Where from?—Oh, so far? Dear God! We used to say for something very distant that it was further away than Lima— And what have you come for? To fight? Are you with the brigades?"

"No, I am a newspaper man. I send news of the war to South America."

"And you send it——"

"In so far as the censorship permits."

"Then you are not one of this mob?"

"Mob? What mob?"

"Oh, all these communists, socialists, anarchists. All this gang?"

"But you then? Why are you here? Why do you come to their parties? You seem to be friends with this mob."

"At your age, such a question! Is not my head too pretty to be shot at? And Elena's hands, aren't they lovely? Can you imagine her hung up by her wrists? We must live, and as for this rabble— It won't last long. It will end soon."

"You think so?"

"Sooner than you or they imagine."

"I think on the contrary that the republicans are going to win."

"Oh, no," she laughed. "Take my advice and tell your paper that all this will soon end, and with a complete victory for Franco."

"Are you then a fifth columnist?" I asked, frightened.

Her laughter drew the attention of a neighboring group to whom she said in a loud voice: "Listen to this, comrade Minister, this is priceless. This comrade of yours says we are fifth columnists. What do you think of that?"

"Lord, comrade, but you're a wet blanket. We feed you and you say there is nothing to eat in republican Spain. We introduce you to beautiful women and you swear with your hand on your heart that you are face to face with the fifth column." And he slapped me on the back familiarly.

I said nothing, for there was nothing to say.

Word for word, scene for scene, I repeated it all to Marcucci the next day. I confessed to him that something in me was weakening. I showed him the fine cigarettes they had given me, all stamped "for the front." I told him I was beginning to think that everything was being run by devils; that I was being stopped at this bend of the road by a dark thought.

"What?" he asked.

"That we are wasting our lives. That all this sacrifice is useless or worse; that it is serving to consolidate an abominable regime. That all this altruism is turning into a bog in which man's best hopes are being sunk."

"You don't have to go so far," he said harshly, and stammered something else I didn't catch.

We were silent and walked slowly as if counting our steps.

"Where I do agree with you," he said with a sigh, "is that not only are we losing, but we have already lost this war."

"And whose fault is that?"

"Certainly not those who are fighting, or in the hospitals, or under ground. What fault can it be of theirs? It is the fault of the leaders. It is our fault. Yes, comrade, your fault and mine, because we haven't had the courage to cry out."

4

The communist party called for a vast mobilization. It declared the urgent necessity of establishing "the shock work of stakhanovist type," like that in the Soviet Union, with an end to winning the war. Work must be doubled. The republic was not losing the war. Oh, no. But it was losing its battle against time. And time must be won to consolidate the victory decreed by the Central Committee of the communist party and by its great director Pepe Díaz, through whose mouth spoke comrade Stephanov, who was in turn the friend and spokesman of the chief, of the supreme commander, Josef Stalin.

The meeting of the enlarged Central Committee was thick with smoke. Too late, theoretically and absurdly, the problem of hunger was finally being discussed. The Central Committee now at last recognized that the ration of lentils was insufficient. It was not only the people's homes that lacked food now, but those of the communists. All food was disappearing. Even the fish which was right at hand in the sea had risen to ten times its normal price. An egg now cost what six had, four months before.

"And this can't be, comrades," they ended all their speeches. "Because it can't, it simply can't."

"The fifth column is encouraging the black market, it is helping the speculators and organizing the starvation of the workers and peasants."

And so went the talk of Codovila, Delicado, Checa and the great captains of the party, Lister, El Campesino, Modesta, old Carmen and the others. Finally the floor was yielded to those who were not members of the Central Committee, and consequently had a voice but no vote.

We put the problem in the economic field, showed how it resulted from errors of the government—the uncontrolled inflation which resulted in the constant printing of more bills, the financial crisis, the economic unbalance and the absence of any sort of system. This, we said, was neither communism nor capitalism nor NEP. Our efforts were in vain. The leaders protested, denouncing us as intellectuals who were trying to be mysterious and incomprehensible to the comrades who were not "economic *bourgeois.*" When Marcucci and some others tried to defend our views, Delicado and Angelita screamed: "Enough! Enough! This is not an academy, but the high court of real proletarian opinion."

They toyed with their sabers and pistols. All attempt to correct their absurd point of view was useless; nonetheless, and in spite of physical fear, we tried. When they adopted a resolution to impose severe control on prices; to fix by decree the price of a dozen eggs, a pound of meat or a piece of fish, I interrupted without asking for the floor.

"This is madness! As soon as the government passes such a decree, the little there is now in the markets will disappear. The peasants won't bring their products to market and the hunger will get worse." Then Marcucci spoke, more calmly; his reasoning was less that of the economist than that of a householder. His speech was persuasive and I felt it must be reaching the minds of the leaders.

But when he finished, Stephanov said it was late and the discussion would continue the next day.

"By the members of the Central Committee only," Delicado announced.

"Exactly," agreed Codovila. "Since we have already listened to the opinions of the comrades who are in direct contact with the unions, the regiments and the popular organizations."

We did not even know, therefore, what resolutions had been adopted until five or six days later, when the government decree establishing severe controls and fixing prices and the penalties for violations was sent to the papers. Some cases were to be punishable by death. This decree was published and on the following day the markets were empty. They looked like churches burnt out by anarchists or barracks abandoned by their regiments. There was nothing, literally nothing. Just signs on the tables as if for a joke—"Meat"—"Vegetables"—"Fish."

Then the party called its most faithful, energetic and experienced workers to carry out the "shock task"—which meant to oblige the peasants to sell their products at the prices fixed by the government. For this one had to go into the country, into the villages, enter every house and as a last resort, with pistol in hand, force the peasants to sell. Shock troops would give one cover and support.

"This is a government measure," said the directors, "that it is essential to enforce. It is a war measure which must be carried out with war methods and obeyed with war discipline."

On the roads of Spain I became convinced that the Stalinist idea of collectives might be carried out at the equator or at the poles, but never in Spain. A woman with two baskets full of eggs was stopped on the road. The pistols were out and the rifles of the shock troops were pointed at her.

"You must sell those eggs at the price fixed by the government, comrade."

"With the greatest pleasure, as long as you give me a tip of forty pesetas a dozen, and, if you haven't the money, then that nice shirt you're wearing."

"You are going to sell them without any tip."

And the comrade would read the list of penalties while the old man who accompanied the woman, leaning on his shepherd's crook, watched with hard eyes, shining between wrinkles as sculptured as if they had been carved by Michelangelo.

The woman saw clearly that it was serious; that, as she might put it, politics had mixed itself into her baskets of eggs and could not easily be ousted. She understood—and made up her mind.

"The death penalty, the lad says?" she asked.

"Yes, comrade."

"And I must accept your wretched pesetas for which I may get a loaf of vinegary bread baked badly!"

"Well, comrade—we want to persuade you——"

The woman, laughing as if possessed, leaped on one basket and then the other, breaking all the eggs. She did it again and again, screaming: "Take the eggs for nothing, you sons of bitches! Take them and feed them to your bosses, choke the bastards with them, swell their fat bellies with them, the filthy crew of cut-throats!"

Her arms akimbo, her face twisted with fury, her voice sibilant, she stood in the middle of the road, defying the pistols and rifles of the republican government. She was the symbol of the Spanish people.

The soldiers wanted to arrest her. I knew it would be folly, since it would stir up the whole town. To arrest her would be politics and merely hasten the disaster. We left her there, standing between the baskets of broken eggs, hurling curses after us, her voice sharper with each imprecation. The old man watched impassively, as if he were a tree growing out of that earth.

In other places there were similar scenes. Members of our own cell told us about them. They had tried to take hams and sausages away from the peasants of Aragon, in exchange for the prices fixed by the government. They got nothing except threats.

"They would have lynched us if we had fired a shot," they said. "They would have torn us to pieces. They are like wild beasts."

"And what did you do?"

"What could we do? We didn't do anything. We left. And after we had left the village, from behind the fences and among the hedges, men, women, and children screamed at us: 'To hell with the republic! Long live Franco!'"

Such was the result of the wise Soviet policy which was arranged for Spain after a long analysis, which had been elaborated by the great Kremlin economists who brought to Spanish soil the systems, methods and procedures thought up by comrade Stalin himself.

5

The communist preponderance in the republican government increased its power and influence over the military to the end that the republican troops might be transformed into an authentic Red Army, which would take its orders from the party. At the same time an attempt was made to absorb, subjugate or liquidate the most important nuclei of the socialists and the anarchists. As for the Marxist Workers' party of Catalonia, the Central Committee declared them trotskyites and decreed that they should be dealt with as they had been in Russia.

The anarchists offered the strongest resistance. In the Republican Left something was happening very similar (always allowing for conditions and distance) to what had taken place in the radical party in Chile. There were even similar personalities. Kind, intelligent, ingenuous men had cooperated in good faith and given disinterested service, only to find themselves trapped and without the courage to shake off the communist yoke or to free themselves from their willingly contracted servitude. Besides these, there were rogues dominated by the desire for money, high position, good situations. These helped us deliberately, putting a price on their services, demanding more and receiving less each time. There were also thousands of poor devils who served humbly and devotedly without asking or receiving anything, on condition only of being left in peace in some little government post with a miserable little salary and haunted by the nightmare of dismissal. There were numerous traders of the type of Straperlo; traffickers in jewels and hunger, miniatures and narcotics, false passports and human blood. These knew well enough that help given to the communist party was at that time a good investment, which paid dividends and which at some moment might save them from ruin or even from death. With such filth the directors of the Central Committee and the Soviet leaders built up what they considered the greatness of the communist party in Spain, its undisputed and totalitarian authority.

The socialists had already abandoned all frontal attack against the communist party. Not because of any agreement but because the Spanish socialists preferred, under the circumstances, a poor settlement to a good case. They were tired of the long fight with its loss of so much blood. While their forces diminished or remained stationary, those of the communist party had grown by leaps and bounds. The socialists accused the communists, each time more weakly, of the crime of "proselytization." The communists denied it or promised to change, but they continued to use the most violent and shameless pressures to get new adherents. Everything served: the offer of a job in a ministry, the threat of dismissal, the hope of promotion, the promise of a transfer. Sometimes for six or seven hundred pesetas a month, paid out of the treasury, a whole family would join the ranks of the glorious party of Marx, Engels, Lenin, Stalin and Pepe Díaz. And always, without fail, the new functionary, like all the rest, must pay a monthly contribution to the party, thus reducing his wretched stipend.

Sometimes, on arriving at Madrid, on reaching Valencia, on spending a night in Albacete, one became involved in serious or trivial fights with socialists or anarchists. To the accusations that one or another of them made, the party replied shamelessly:

"And you? If you could, wouldn't you do the same thing? What bothers you is that you can no longer get away with these things, yourself."

Such reasonings often silenced the socialists and anarchists but morally they prevented any development in the republican process. It was clear that the large communist group was sunk in shamelessness, crime and cynicism. Facing the situation honestly, we could not help seeing that the procedures of fascism and communism differed only by a hair's breadth. It was becoming clearer every day that this violent terrorism was accepted without repugnance by constantly widening circles, as more and more people joined the victorious party.

A new enlarged meeting of the Committee was called, in which resolutions were to be drafted and slogans adopted which should be brought to the attention of the "political commissars" and others responsible for propaganda. The main manifesto was Colonel Lister's, with a subsidiary one from Modesto. Both spoke in detail of the fortifications of Belchite.

"They are impregnable," declared Lister, striking the table with his fist. "Understand, comrades? Impregnable."

He told how the fortifications had been built of steel and concrete by the best workers in the party, under the direction of Soviet experts of the *Trud*, which specialized in such things. They were the same men who had planned the giant dam of Dnieprostroi, and the canal which joined the Artic to the Baltic.

"So, comrades," concluded Lister, "the fortifications of Belchite are Stalinian. They shall not pass them! No, they shall not pass!"

Those dynamic words, reflections of Spanish courage and determination, had now lost the magic of the early days. We had seen in the environs of Madrid, on the hills of Estremadura, in the fields of Teruel, how the exhausted soldiers fell back under the fierce attacks and the superior arms of Franco's troops, retiring in disorder even as they cried, "They shall not pass."

We no longer believed in the miraculous power of these words. And the afternoon of Lister's boastful report, no one believed in the impregnability of the fortifications of Belchite, in spite of his oaths and Modesto's echo, and the miraculous intervention of the Soviet hand. Marcucci and I believed in them least of all, because we knew Soviet techniques at first hand. We had seen them in Tula, in Moscow, in Kiev, in Tangarova. We knew the way recently-paved roads cracked and how the toilet tanks overflowed; how the faucets would not turn off, so that the water ran out of the pipes day and night. We knew that there wasn't a single Russian factory or building or work center in which there were not many things "out of order."

What faith then could we have in these fortifications? But it had already been suggested that my position was defeatist; several comrades in the Central Committee had hinted that I had insufficient faith in a republican victory. And Manuel Delicado, who lacked the slightest interest in my opinions, had declared, not officially but extra-officially and in a friendly way, that I was no great supporter of Stalin. He didn't seem to think me a villain, but rather a nice dope.

"This guy," he would say, jokingly, "isn't quite a trotskyite, but he has no sympathy either for the Man of Steel."

After Lister's report followed by Modesto's and the praises of Codovila, Angelita, Carmen, Checa, and Morano, the Committee passed as a resolution: "THE FORTIFICATIONS OF BELCHITE ARE IMPREGNABLE"

Lister's words were echoed in the headlines of all the papers. And after that the cells repeated it: "The fortifications of Belchite are impregnable." In the barracks, lectures were given reiterating unceasingly that the fortifications of Belchite were Stalinian.

One evening, Queipo del Llano announced from the broadcasting station in Seville that within forty-eight hours Belchite would be attacked.

"Open your ears, you scum of the Mediterranean," he said. "You have said that the fortifications of Belchite were impregnable. Well, I assure you that they are not. They won't withstand a dozen shellings. They'll come crashing down like the walls of Jericho and you'll run like rabbits. And if you don't, so much the worse for you. We'll reduce your fortifications to dust and you with them."

Lister was called to the defense of Belchite. He chose the shock battalions, the most experienced with the most brilliant records; those who had held back the Italians at Guadalajara and the Germans on the banks of the Jarama, and the Moors in the University City.

Following the promise of Queipo, the newest German guns began to try out their powers on the fortifications at dawn, a cold milky dawn. The first shots were fired after three in the morning. By eleven o'clock under a bright sun, the fortifications were a pile of broken stone, of embrasures upside-down, of pillboxes like towers of Pisa from which it was impossible to shoot a cannon or a machine-gun. In less than eight hours the "impregnable" position at Belchite had become untenable. The Germans had had more cannons, more ammunition, more projectiles and had completely destroyed the perfect fortification of "the Stalinian type." Sandbags would have served better than did those fortifications. Before mid-day they had to be abandoned.

An order was given to withdraw. The proud boast of the communist party had come to hopeless grief; the military prestige of Lister sank with the crumbling fortifications. Lister learned of the disaster, swore, went to a high place, looked through his binoculars, received reports from the officers, contemplated the ruins and went away, without giving an order. He climbed, still swearing, into his armored car and drove away. Four cars went ahead, clearing the way; six others followed, and at the rear in a great omnibus went Lister's private guards, with their blue caps lined with white velvet.

The retreat took a long time. It was possible to save the small arms, the light machine-guns, the ammunition. The heavy arms were under the ruins, several meters underground, or made useless until it should be possible to destroy them. A little after noon, the troops were posted behind the hills around the battle-field of Belchite, but closer to the sea. For four days and nights there were advances and retreats. On the fifth day the air was tainted for miles around, due to the putrefaction of the corpses.

Belchite was lost. There was nothing to do but establish new lines much closer to the peaceful Mediterranean. Fifteen days later, the troops which had defended Belchite were retired to Valencia. There Lister gave the impression of a hysteric. He realized that his prestige as an invincible soldier had been destroyed, that his laurels were withering and his star paling as a result of the disaster.

"The fortifications were impregnable. They fell only because they were surrendered to the enemy," he screamed. "The cowardice of those who ordered the retreat lost us a Stalinian position. The most exemplary punishment must be meted out to those responsible."

At first we tried to persuade him that he was mistaken. "The fortifications weren't surrendered, Lister. They were destroyed. Reduced to rubble."

"It's a lie! Those fortifications were impregnable. The cowards surrendered them." He seemed insane, thirsty for communist blood. He repeated and repeated, and each time with more details, a long story of spies, sabotage and treason and began to point out the guilty ones.

The Executive Committee met. Those who had taken part in the earlier sessions were invited; and Lister, after a long speech full of violence and threats, pointed to those he accused. Brave men, active in the party since its earliest days, men above suspicion not only of disloyalty but of the slightest defection! Lister accused these men of cowardice and treason. In the highest spheres of the party the battle raged.

"It can't be true. Lister must be wrong. Today he wants to shoot young officers, perhaps for putting him in the shade. Tomorrow it may be us. The party can not support him."

The other side answered with insults. "Intellectualoids! *Petits bourgeois! Cowards!* Traitors to your class! We welcomed you from your little class, took you under the broad wing of the proletariat and now you come with your whining sentimentality—your cologne-water revolution!"

It was stupid, cruel and sickening.

Marcucci had been to Madrid. Now he returned and we ate together. I told him what was happening. That night he came to the meeting.

"There is no need for you to be here," said Codovila. "Your job is elsewhere. Were you called here?"

"And may I ask where you think I should be?"

"At the front."

"I came from there. Nothing is happening there; the soldiers are bored. So I came back. I think I am more needed here."

"You are not the one to decide where you should be," Codovila shouted in Italian, his face red with rage.

"Nor do I think that you, Vittorio, have the authority to order me around like a corporal. You're wasting my time, Codovila, and your own. I'm going to stay and I'm going to oppose this plot of yours."

"And what am I plotting?"

"Murder," Marcucci said.

They were interrupted by the arrival of a group of people. The meeting was about to begin; the members of the Central Committee were already seated. Lister was pacing the floor, muttering unintelligibly. The report on the Belchite fiasco was read. The accusation had been written out and signed by Lister and various political commissars of his division. When the reading of this document came to an end none of the top men said anything.

Carmen spoke (the fat old Russian woman who called herself that), and backed up the accusation as "cadres commission" of the party. She spoke of the social origin of each of the accused and showed that they were all sons of *bourgeois* or *petits bourgeois;* there was not one among them who had proletarian parents. Therefore they were, of course, corruptible and undependable; from such people a stab in the back was to be expected. Lister gesticulated, swore, repeated everything again and again. The fortifications had been given away. Yes, comrades, given away. And this was treason and counter-revolution and cowardice and crime and connivance with fascism. He asked the death penalty.

Then Marcucci spoke.

"These comrades whom Lister accuses so unjustly are not to blame because Soviet cement can not stand up under German cannon. You can't hold up a fort with will-power."

Lister, fat Carmen, Angelita, everyone interrupted. The president asked for order and Marcucci continued:

"Belchite became untenable. Too many men fell. To have held out would have been stupid. Furthermore the purpose had been accomplished, since the Soviet comrades had found out that their fortifications couldn't stand up to the German guns. Wasn't that the reason for the experiment?"

A howl drowned him out.

"Listen to me. Hear what I have to say," Marcucci shouted. "Then do as you like with me."

"Let him speak," said Codovila, "and take a stenographic record of everything he says."

"Speak," said the president. "Say what you have to say. And let the comrades listen in silence."

Marcucci wiped his brow, took a sip of water and continued:

"The Soviet materials have been tried out and found wanting. A service has been rendered to the Soviet Union. I don't understand what the comrades are getting so angry about."

"You are hinting that Soviet materials are being tried out in Spain," said Checa. Again the president demanded silence.

"No, I am not hinting," said Marcucci. "I am stating a fact. I am saying nothing you haven't known for a long time. The government presided over by our comrade Stalin sent several types of airplanes to Spain. You know that they were all tried out, and that the best ones—

the fastest—disappeared; only the mediocre and defective ones were left. You know it. We have spoken of it often."

Codovila kept the others from interrupting. He wanted this to go on. The stenographers were taking it all down.

"I have said that Soviet materials were being tried out in Spain, and it is true. Modesto knows that he had those steel plates turned over to Gallo's Third Battalion to be used as armor on a train. And the party leaders know that they buckled under German machine-gun fire. Projectiles and explosives are tried out in the same way. And you all know that the successful ones are retired. Deny it if you can."

There was a new commotion. Lister and others advanced threateningly on Marcucci, who was delirious, transfigured.

"You have tried out the materials they sent you," he said to Lister. "Now you know that they are no good, thanks to thousands of Spanish dead. What more do you want?"

"This is infamy," shrieked Codovila, "the infamy of a traitor. I demand the expulsion of this man. It's time to employ Stalinist methods if we hope to preserve the unity of our great party, the future of its great work and the honor and glory of our venerated comrade Stalin."

The whole room applauded. Several men entered then and Marcucci's eyes widened at sight of them. My throat tightened with fear. For Stalin's policemen—the NKVD—had come to enforce the decisions of the Central Committee of the Spanish Communist Party. There could be no doubt: though they had changed their astrakhan jackets for Spanish workers' clothes, I recognized these men who now stood quiet and watchful with their hands sunk in their pockets.

Other leaders spoke. Delicado made a pompous declaration:

"We must enforce respect within the communist party. It has grown. All sorts of people have joined our ranks and they must be impressed by exemplary acts like the execution of these cowards. Let all know that he who defies the communist party dies. That we punish traitors, cowards, deviationists and enemies of the people. Then we shall have the love and respect of the Spanish people."

Delicado's speech made it clear that a line had been traced for the Central Committee to follow; that this meeting was only the chorus of the tragedy. Everything that followed was in the same vein, and the applause of the NKVD convinced me that all was lost. The police terrorism, the sadistic apparatus of torture and spying that ruled in Stalin's Russia was going to rule here. The nightmare had come to Spain.

217

All my doubts rose like a wave and I felt like Peter on the Lake of Tiberias crying, "Lord save me." But there was no one to hear.

Marcucci, with a courage that won my admiration, asked to speak again in defense of our comrades' lives.

"You are trying to subject our comrades to a police regime," he accused, but he was shouted down.

"If we are fighting here for the liberty of the world we should respect liberty enough to let our comrade express his opinion," I cried.

"Be quiet, fool! This is not a lecture for society women," they screamed at me.

"Liquidate them!" cried Angelita.

The president said, "Marcucci may not have the floor again." Two men led him out. I followed him, he was pale, his eyes inflamed, his lips dry. A group surrounded him at once. "Be quiet! Be quiet!" they said. "It is useless. You have lost the game. There is no help for it. They will kill you if you say anything more."

"Why not die this way as any other?" asked Marcucci.

"Don't beat your head against a stone wall," said someone. "You've done what you could for your friends. To go on is suicidal."

Inside, the meeting continued. It was resolved that the comrades who had "like cowards surrendered to fascism the impregnable fortifications of Belchite" must be punished. Lister was authorized to form a court-martial in his division; but of the fifty-three heads he had asked for, he was allowed only eleven. The rest would be merely expelled from the party and pointed out as cowards and traitors. It was agreed to take Marcucci's case to the Commission of Control. (In the communist parties, this is a sort of ante-room to expulsion in capitalist countries, and to execution in socialist states. It is a party tribunal which calls witnesses, collects proofs, judges like a court and sentences.)

On the following day Colonel Lister called his court-martial and passed sentence. Marcucci, as political commissar of the regiment, went to say goodbye to his comrades. I went with him, both of us with our nerves tortured by long nights without sleep. We reached the barracks at dawn. The lieutenant recognized Marcucci and let us in, compassionately, as if he felt sorry for us.

"Take them to the second patio," he said to a sergeant. We went in and saw only walls bathed in the morning light. We came out into a courtyard and joined other comrades, mostly military. We stood there for a long time but no one spoke, no one looked at anyone else, only at the wall in front of us, the large stones roughly hewn.

Why hadn't I stayed in my own country as a teacher in some little town, instead of trying to save the world? What was happening, what was going to happen was an irreparable thing. I would never rise above it nor erase it from my life.

Through the entrance arch came soldiers with drums and soldiers with rifles, their bayonets fixed. They placed themselves at intervals and stood as if nailed to the ground. After what seemed a long time, during which the drums beat dully like the pulse in an aching tooth, the soldiers came out who were going to be executed and those who must watch. They separated into two groups and I felt sure that every spectator was crying inside.

The victims smoked, laughed, were amazingly calm, though they were living their last minutes and they knew it. For them the morning light would go out forever and they knew it; and yet they maintained a serenity that was almost majestic. The condemned men refused to have their eyes bandaged.

"I have seen death before," said the major who had ordered the retreat from Belchite. "We are old friends. I want to see him come this time."

A lieutenant read off their names, then tore off their insignia one by one, while the eleven men sang the *Internationale.*

The major advanced as if he were leading a bayonet charge. He paused at the foot of the wall and turned to face the courtyard:

"Long live the communist party!" he shouted.

Twelve armed men entered the courtyard. All the condemned men shouted: "Long live the communist party! Long live the Communist International!"

The commanding officer of the firing squad lowered his sword and shots rang out. The major fell, transformed from a brave man to bloody carrion. Eleven times the crime was repeated. And so the communist party proved that the fortifications of Belchite were impregnable and had been abandoned by cowards who had retreated before the enemy.

That same night I heard that the trial of Marcucci had begun, which in view of his high rank was to be a comedy with many acts.

The next day Marcucci invited me to go to Madrid.

"Let us go to the front," he said. "It will calm our nerves and perhaps it will give us back a bit of our lost faith."

"But we will need passes," I said. "I have no safe conduct."

"I can still get them, and a truck to take us. Let's go today."

In the truck we were silent. We could not speak of what weighed

219

on our hearts and what we longed to share, crowded in as we were, with the others on the truck. I became obsessed by the idea that the truck was carrying us towards death.

Madrid was in total darkness. The streets within range of the 15-15 howitzers were deserted. The beautiful statues of the Retiro and the charming figures that adorned the city were buried under sandbags. Not a shot, not a siren.

We went to look for friends. There was plenty of liquor, for alcohol and war are inseparable. I drank with the soldiers but I couldn't get Marcucci even to moisten his feverish white lips. I was trying to forget my life. I was desperately tired, but not sleepy. We walked as far as the palace used as headquarters by the Association of Artists, Writers, Intellectuals—and what have you. They welcomed us, and we rested in the wide soft-cushioned chairs.

The next day nothing happened; the front was quiet. There were hours of absolute silence as if the combatants on both sides were having a long nap. We ate in the University City; at nightfall I asked Marcucci to find a place to sleep.

"Yes," he agreed. "Tonight I feel bad among all the uniforms. We shall have to sleep." So we walked in the dark slowly, our steps sounding on the pavement. Suddenly the sirens sounded.

"A bomb wouldn't be bad, especially if we never heard it," he said.

"How do you mean?"

"If a bomb hits you you never hear the explosion. And then you are no longer in the ranks of the glorious party of Marx, Engels, Lenin, Stalin, Pepe Díaz and Codovila. The members of the Control Commission and the clever members of the NKVD can't twist your nerves. You become a hero and the glorious comrades sing your praises."

The sirens ceased and a great cloud moved aside to let the moon shine through. We could hear the airplanes now as Marcucci hummed:

Frenchman's bridge, no one shall pass you.

A bomb exploded, then another.

"They are little ones," said Marcucci. "They don't shake the earth."

"There they come now, over us." More bombs exploded. The airplanes circled the city once and were gone. A little later an ambulance came by. We stopped it and went along to help with the wounded and to gather the dead. A bomb had fallen in a crowded group of wretched little hovels. The wounded were taken away by the ambulance, while an army truck gathered up the broken corpses with undertakers' great shovels. I picked up a little boy's head and a militiaman heaved it onto the truck. They let us ride back on the running-boards.

We went to the hotel where we always stayed on previous visits. There was no housing crisis in Madrid, as in Valencia or Barcelona; on the contrary! There is never a queue for the front line.

The doorman recognized us, embraced us and asked us if we wanted to go up to our rooms.

"Not yet, thank you. We'll rest here awhile first."

We sat down in the big chairs in the lobby. "Thank you, gentlemen. I'll leave you a candle then. You will find more in your rooms. A good night to you." And he went off, dragging feet heavy with fatigue.

"What time is it?" I asked, as you do in jail, without expecting or receiving any answer.

"When I was little," Marcucci said suddenly, "they didn't tell me stories like Alice In Wonderland or Aladdin's Lamp. An old neighbor in my village, for whom I did small chores like bringing water from the fountain or helping her to take her garden products as far as the highway, told me one story, though, that I've been remembering all day today. And yesterday too.

"There was a blind man, she said, who had lost his sight by looking at a great red star in the sky which the priest had told him not to. He went to quacks and magicians but none had the art to cure the divine punishment. He went to Naples and there, at the feast of Saint Januarius, he met an old man who listened to his sad story and said: 'Go to the great city where there are seven hills; when you set foot on the seventh hill beg pardon for your sins and there you will recover your sight.' So the blind man went from door to door, falling and getting up again, until at last he came to the city and climbed the seven hills and on the seventh he begged pardon for his sins. And he saw first a deep red light, like the star he had looked at, or blood. Then he saw more clearly the light, the countryside, the blue of the skies, and the distant purple of the mountains. And he saw what he had never seen before—what lay in his own heart, and in the hearts of other men."

Marcucci smiled, was silent for a long time and then stood looking at the candle, and sighed.

"I am there now, as if I had come to the seventh hill. I am seeing with miraculous clarity what lies in my own heart and in that of other men." He paused, as if waiting for me to speak, but I said nothing. If I had tried to speak I would only have sobbed. So I said nothing.

"I have been wrong, like a child, or like a fool," he continued in a low voice. "We have been wrong, you and I. Thousands of us have been wrong and are still wrong, knowing it inside." He waited for me to speak and still I said nothing.

"You are sleepy—are you very tired?" he asked gently.

"No. How could I sleep? I am listening. Go on."

"We are going on being wrong, and he who is wrong commits an error, and all errors, *mio caro,* like articles in a bazaar have a price. It is an inexorable law." He was silent again, then at last he went on hoarsely:

"I have been wrong. There is no doubt of it. With the best intentions in the world I have been the tool of a swindle, of the filthiest blackmail. But my good intentions don't matter, dear comrade. I will still have to pay."

"Man," I said, rising from my chair and pacing up and down, trying to regain my self-control, "I don't know why one shouldn't have the right, at any moment, to remake one's life, or at any rate to redirect it."

"Remake one's life!" he exclaimed. "Yes, it's possible, with great courage, defying everybody, putting your guts back after your belly has been split. Enduring the affliction and the despair of this remaking. But I wouldn't get anywhere trying to remake my life. It is broken on the inside. And that can never be mended. It's like someone with a broken spine. You know that if he lives, he will live paralyzed or in plaster. To live in plaster? No, comrade; much better to turn into plaster. Not to see, not to know."

"Your metaphor is a bit muddled," I said, to cut the line of his thought.

"All metaphors are muddled," he said. "But they express things strongly. Let's give up psychological subtleties. I swear to you as to a brother, I have seen and done such cruel things, I'm so soaked in crime, that all this is only the last drop in a brimming cup. But," he hesitated a moment and then said it, "I don't want to make you lose your faith. I know where that leads. I don't want to!" And he swore softly.

I insisted that he speak, confessing my own doubts, my terrors. I spoke of what I had seen and heard in the Soviet Union, of the hypocrisy, the lies, the lack of liberty, the farce of Russian socialism.

222

"You are wrong," he went on, "just as I was in thinking that it is a Russian evil; that we have before us a national weakness or a purely temporary one. I too thought it was a phase that must be lived through, that socialism might come. Remember, I lived in the Soviet Union for several years. I speak Russian as well as I do Italian and better than I do Spanish. I have lived among them, seen tens of their cities and hundreds of their villages. I have slept in their hotels and in the hovels of their workers, in the peasants' huts and in the directors' country houses and warm apartments. I have seen it all. I know."

He got up, paced the floor and said, in a much louder voice:

"The communist Bolshevik party founded by Lenin doesn't exist any more in the Union of Soviet Socialist Republics. Do you understand? Stalin has destroyed it; his policemen have liquidated it. There are thousands of old guard communists in the concentration camps. We scream to high heaven about Hitler's camps. Well, laugh at Dachau, laugh at the Gestapo torture chambers, laugh at Hitler and his band of cut-throats! All that is a bed of roses compared to what goes on in the socialist homeland. Those who haven't lived there as I have don't know, don't suspect and what is worse don't want to know and won't believe it if they are told. You for example, sitting there! You don't believe me. You don't want to believe me. Say it! Why don't you say it?"

I was silent.

"You don't dare believe me," and his voice was dim now. "We are all like that. It's faith, dear old boy. Faith is worse than life when it comes to dying, more selfish, more determined not to let go. When faith dies, it does all it can to kill us too. It tries to drag us down with it. And often it succeeds."

The candle was a mere stub which was rapidly dwindling.

He laughed gaily. Instead of being depressed, he now seemed animated. I thought it was from getting his troubles off his chest. He rubbed his hands and complained of the cold. The candle was sputtering.

"Let's go to bed," I said. "We'll talk in the morning."

"Tomorrow," he said in French, and then he repeated Hugo's verse:

> *Demain c'est St. Hélène*
> *Demain c'est le tombeau.*

"Stephanov can tell me nothing, nor our amiable Palmiro Togliatti either. I have seen what happens in Russia with my own eyes and it's worse than Germany. Neither can Codovila, that half-policeman, nor any of the other undertakers of the Republic, tell me pretty Russian stories. Especially Codovila, the noble proletarian, who never did a lick of work in his life! Do you know why the NKVD loves him? Listen.

"When Codovila came to Europe, thrown out of your America, the Spaniards knew all about it. But they shook his hand with that generous way they have, they protected him, were good to him. The communist party wasn't growing in Spain. It wasn't the police that hampered it but the hard, arrogant individualism of the Spanish people. While the CNT came up like boiled milk, while the poumists captured thousands of converts in Catalonia, the communist party was still-born. And do you know what Codovila did to save himself and the situation?

"Codovila knows all the back corners of the Comintern, all the hidden springs, the secretariats, the methods. He knows Dimitri Manuilsky, that cold, old goat, and above all, he has good friends in the NKVD. He knew he would find himself in a tight spot when he reached Moscow with his report on Spain. So you know what he decided to do? It's funny—and filthy. He invited four of the most prominent leaders of the Spanish party to Moscow. Trillo, Vega, Adame and a fourth who was to be his stooge. Once in Moscow, Codovila turned on them, accused them of all the mistakes he had made, presented a suitcaseful of what he called proofs. He pointed out his four guests as the ones responsible for the failure of the party to grow and said, knowing what he did, that they were friends of Andrés Nin, the poumist who had been Trotsky's secretary.

"Adame, Trillo and Vega tried to defend themselves. The stooge confessed his guilt and supported everything Codovila had said. There was no defense possible; the four Spaniards stayed in Moscow while Codovila returned to Madrid to find a new leadership. So arose Pepe Díaz, the Sevillan baker. And so it was, so it is—as you saw in the barracks two days ago. And so it will be tomorrow. And you know something?"

"What?"

"Watch out for Codovila. He hates you as much as he does me, or Sormendi, or Galan, or the major they just shot. The day he can, he will have you liquidated with the greatest pleasure."

"Let's go to sleep," I said. "It's four days since we slept."

"That's true isn't it? You won't believe me, but I'm not sleepy, not at all."

He sunk his hand into his pockets and stood in front of me.

"You know something else?"

"What?"

"Manuilsky doesn't like you, not one little bit. I think he'd give a good deal to be able to find the germs of trotskyism, zinovievism or bukharinism or some such obscure ailment in you. He'd liquidate you gladly. Did you ever criticize his plan for Brazil?"

"Not exactly. I didn't approve of it. It seemed irresponsible to me. But I never actually said so."

"Well, be careful," he advised. "When you opposed his Brazilian plan it didn't matter much, but now that it has turned out so badly he will never forgive you. He considers you an accuser and he'd give his right hand to have you silenced. Promise me you'll never say I told you."

"I promise."

Then he said, without sadness or despair, as if he spoke of something quite trivial:

"It is finished. I have completely lost my faith."

"Your faith?"

"Yes, *mio carissimo*, my faith. Faith in the communist party, faith in the proletarian revolution, faith in everything. We have been betrayed! All this is a fraud, a dirty miserable fraud."

The candle was out, the bit of tallow cold.

"Don't you think that the revolution in Europe will be different?" I asked.

"I used to think so," he answered, "and when I watched the Russians submitting to Stalin's tyranny I used to say they deserved it. Why didn't they rebel? Why did they tolerate this bloody regime? In France, in Belgium, in Spain the people wouldn't stand for it."

"That's my point."

"You can see you were wrong. In Spain the same thing is happening, exactly. Police, spying, NKVD, criminal trials and shooting, like you have just seen. Do you think this is socialism, or that humanity is being redeemed and mankind liberated?"

He came to me, put his arm around my shoulders and we felt our way to the stair. He yawned and said quietly:

"I am sleepy. Now I am ready to rest. I am going to sleep, very grateful to you. You have kept me company in these hours and it means a great deal to me. You might have stayed with them, making speeches, giving fuel to their rage. They are cowards. Oh comrade, how sickening it is. How sickening."

We had reached the door of his room.

"Have you got your gun?" I asked, in spite of myself.

"Yes," he said, "and it's loaded. Why?"

"Well, if you'd give it to me——"

"Give it to you? Why? Do you want to kill Codovila or blow your own brains out to see what they look like?" And he laughed. "This is no time to take my gun away from me. It's not the Moors, or the fascists, or the Gestapo any more. Now I have to defend myself from the brigades of the dawn and the NKVD." And he laughed harshly.

He opened the door and without turning on the light, entered the room in the semi-darkness of the morning. I heard him fall on the bed with a heavy sigh. I poured a glass of water.

"Here, man, give me that water. You made me thirsty when you poured it." He sat up on the bed, took the water and drank. On returning the glass he said, "Thanks, many thanks. You were always very good to me. Thank you."

I replaced the glass and as I turned to leave the room he embraced me warmly. His face was wet with tears.

"Thank you," he repeated. "See you tomorrow."

"See you later," I said and shut the door.

I walked quietly down the hall to my own room, speaking to the boy who was scrubbing the floor on my way.

I sat on the bed without turning on the light and began to undress, slowly. As I was taking off my shirt I heard a shot, and wondered if it were in this street or further off. Outside, the boy who had been cleaning the floor shouted. He was calling.

I ran out and instinctively turned toward Marcucci's room. The door was open. There was a smell of powder, and from inside the boy was calling for a match.

"A light please, comrade. Something has happened."

I had no matches. So I went to the balcony and raised the blinds. The manager came in and lit a candle. Marcucci was stretched on the bed, without his coat; beneath his head and shoulders spread a great blood-stain.

"He has killed himself. Jesus, Joseph and Mary!" exclaimed the manager. The boy crossed himself.

I went to the bed. One of his legs still trembled and his upper lip twitched ever so slightly. I called him, took one of his hands in mine, but he was still.

I knelt beside the body of the man who had left his life cursing his faith and protesting a fraud. And I stayed there crying, for Marcucci, for the thousands of Marcuccis who died this way. I cried for myself, for my life, for my youth burnt out in vain, sacrificed so that an infamous crew of murderers might prosper.

That night the Central Committee accorded honors to the brave comrade Marcucci, heroic fighter against the infamous tyranny of Benito Mussolini.

6

In Valencia there was general comment in political circles on the shooting of communists, carried out by communists. The people felt terror. The anarchists said it was like Saturn who devoured his own children, and the socialists did not hide their repugnance. The communist party was working now for the ousting of Prieto and his replacement by Doctor Negrin.

When I arrived, my wife told me the talk she heard in the cell, in the offices of *Red Front* where she worked, in the section of Anti-fascist Women, and in the circles of the responsible comrades.

"These are fantasies of our enemies," I answered.

"But it is our own comrades saying it."

"Well then, our comrades are dreaming bad dreams."

It was no longer a question, as before, of quieting her "defeatism," of calming her criticisms and her doubts. Now it was purely and simply a matter of fear. If she continued speaking in this way, one fine day they would arrest her as a "trotskyite," as an "enemy of the people." And the danger was greater because of the enmity of Manuilsky and the hatred of Codovila. As if she were trying to argue and convince me, I said:

"Look, my girl. The fifth column doesn't work only through the fascists and other agents. It operates also through communist charlatans who talk too much, who listen to all the rumors in the street and repeat them in the party. At this very moment the prestige of the party is increasing. It is natural that our enemies should attack us in every way possible."

That time was perhaps the only time I lied to her out of fear. We were expecting a child. They'll kill them both, I thought.

"But," she argued, "didn't the party say that the fortifications of Belchite were impregnable?"

"There is no impregnable position in a war, actually. There are victories and there are defeats, that's all. And in the end one wins and the other loses."

"And this time," she said bitterly, "it is we who are going to lose. They are going to clean us. Clean us."

"Only dirty things get cleaned," I said sharply.

"That's how they're going to clean us, as if we were dirt. Not because they're stronger but because we are defeating ourselves."

"What are you saying?" I asked, frightened. "Defeating ourselves?"

"Can't you see it? All those comrades getting rich in the black market and the leaders not only letting them do it but doing them favors as well? Don't you see the leaders living like kings while the people faint with hunger? The workers in the press rooms notice it, the doorman, even the messenger boys. There is nothing to eat. The markets are empty and the peasants curse the Republic. In the stores the comrade shopkeepers, sheltered by the party card, change the prices a dozen times a day. It's like that hymn to aviation—'Higher, higher, always higher.'"

"Listen to me quietly and don't talk nonsense. Inflation comes with every war and the communists are not to blame."

"Hunger will force the Republic to surrender," she insisted. "And if the communists aren't to blame that won't change anything. The result will be the same."

Her logic got on my nerves.

"Well, well," I said, "your reasoning is beautiful. But come, have you no faith in the victory of the Republic?"

"Faith? Yes, I have that."

"Well, that's enough. Be quiet then and don't repeat rumors or nonsense of café strategy."

"But they are comrades."

"Irresponsible comrades then," I said and changed the subject.

Days went by and weeks. The war news was the same. Fire on the Estremadura front and the enemy annihilated! Three soldiers came over to our side during the night. Quiet on the Teruel front where two soldiers came over to our lines. Period. And the radio played the *Himno de Riego*—the hymn of the republic which was crumbling.

I was typing on my machine—the same old stuff about the difficulties of attack, the bravery of our brigades, the virtues of Dr. Negrin's friends, the imminent transfer of the government to Barcelona. The telephone rang. It was André Marti.

"They want you in Moscow. Get ready to leave at once."

"I'll need a passport, comrade."

"You will get one. That's all. Congratulations and goodbye."

228

I was stunned. When my wife heard the news she asked: "And I?"

She was expecting a child, she could not remain there. The hunger, the cold with no fuel, the discomforts of every kind would be too much for her.

The government went to Barcelona. And the Central Committee, the newspaper, all the directing groups of the auxiliary agencies as well. We had to go, crowded together atrociously. We arrived and got settled. When we got there I went to the Central Committee to ask about a passport and to discuss my wife's situation. She was unable to work, so she might just as well go to Moscow.

Marti and Gottwald had gone with Ercole to the Teruel front where a new offensive was opening. I could see only Codovila. When I explained the situation and requested a passport for my wife he answered roundly: "No!"

I have never begged so hard for anything. Codovila only laughed, listened with a smile to everything I could say and answered smoothly: "In republican Spain hundreds of women are expecting babies."

"But she isn't doing anything useful here. Why should she stay? If they'll give me the *visa* I'll gladly pay her fare to Moscow."

"Oh, so we have savings! I see you haven't forgotten your *petit bourgeois* virtues. The passage isn't the problem. Moscow isn't asking for her, nor for both of you, but only for you. I can do nothing."

"But look. A telegram from you, or from comrade Stephanov, asking for her admittance, signed by two comrades from the International, Ercole, Marti or Gottwald——"

"They're at the front; won't be back for a month. Stephanov is very ill: his ulcer is hemorrhaging." And Codovila laughed again. "Don't worry, she'll be all right here. You always drown in a plate of soup."

I insisted, I argued, I implored. At last he answered angrily, "I really don't understand intellectuals. I never did. They're so sentimental, so complex, so full of whims."

"Why is it a whim to want my wife with me, so that I can be with her when the child comes; so that I can do something if anything goes wrong? Be human, man! Try to understand!"

"Stephanov is the only one who can help you. Try to see him. Maybe he will give you the authorization."

"But the Soviet consul said he would give me the *visa* on Stephanov's orders or yours."

"The consul said so?" said Codovila laughing. "It is impossible. I won't do what I think wrong. Try to see Stephanov."

Hope was born anew and I laid siege to Stephanov. I went to see him, waited, watched for him to come, lost hope and then went back next day. Five days, six, twenty; it was useless. He was too ill, they wouldn't let me see him or give him a message, or even tell me where he was. The Soviet consul repeated:

"An order from Stephanov or Codovila, and you shall have the *visa*. You ought to go, they are waiting for you. An enquiry has arrived as to when you were given the *visa* and in what name. You'd better get going."

Codovila laughed to the last. He was so sorry I hadn't been able to see Stephanov. Poor comrade! He was very sick and he might die. He must not be disturbed. And he laughed when he said goodbye.

I went to the houses of all my friends, to recommend my wife to their care. Something might happen when she was all alone. And one day with snow falling, a rare phenomenon, I went to the airport to fly to Toulouse in a tiny plane which held three persons. My wife, whose time was near, stayed on alone in Barcelona at the mercy of the bombs, the hunger and the cold.

And so I went to Moscow that winter of 1938. For the third time I entered the socialist homeland.

CHAPTER VIII

Moscow Revisited

1

ON MY third arrival in the Soviet Union there were further changes in Moscow. There was more asphalt, especially on the main avenues and on the one which ran along what used to be the "Chinese Wall." Along the avenue Ozhod-Niriat there were tall buildings in the modern style, apartment houses for the bureaucrats of the government and of the party. The outside of the walls was covered with marble from the Caucasus. Engineers were noisily and elaborately widening Maxim Gorky street, so as to line it up with the old three-story building called the "Tea Palace," said to date from the days of Ivan the Terrible.

In all this Muscovite transformation you could see the desire to make an impression, to give proof of magnificence, rarity or luxury. I was familiar with the process, since it is common to the dictators from whom Latin America has suffered and still suffers. While the people are sunk in starvation, filth and illiteracy, the dictators build wide, paved avenues and erect tall buildings to house the Ministry of War, the Police Department, the Ministry of the Interior or the Army Officers' Hospital.

The wide show-windows still displayed the paltriness and the poor quality of Soviet production. The portrait of comrade Stalin, enormous and bright-colored, presided over a few pairs of shoes which could not compare with the home-made products of the backward regions of Latin America. An enormous bust of the supreme chief of all the Russias rested on a dusty paper, on which were piled a few pieces of pottery, utensils and wooden toys. The slogans of the Five Year Plan for Art hung in print over a motley collection of musical instruments, still stamped with the names of those who had sold them in tzarist days.

In the morning very early, there was white bread in the stores and always a long line outside; this was entirely new. The press and the orators also declared that butter was sold, but I never saw any. Under the entry of a few stores hung a brilliant poster which said "Coopera-

231

tive Dairy," but as happens often in the vast expanses of the Soviet Union, these establishments were not open and therefore no milk was ever sold there.

The morning after my arrival I was surprised to see a truck delivering bread. I was delighted and said so, only to be told that the little truck delivered exclusively to the offices of the government and the party and the houses of a select few. What in backward capitalist countries was taken for granted, here in the land of socialism, twenty years after the revolution, was a special privilege only for the élite of the Soviet world!

In those days, there were very few foreign delegates in the Comintern. Spain was the center of attention and many Spaniards came and went, especially in the *dachas* where theoretical and practical military training was given to political converts. America was represented by Browder and Foster of the "Workers' Party," by three Chileans, Lafertte, Barra Silva, and Galo Gonzáles, three Argentines who were travelling with their wives, two Brazilians and two Cubans. The Chileans and Cubans enjoyed a privileged position in the Comintern. Chile was considered the champion of the Popular Front in Latin America; and Cuba was the scene of a wide and deep understanding between the openly communist party of Blas Roca, the disguised sector presided over by the writer Marinello, and the government of General Fulgencio Batista.

On the third day after my arrival I was summoned by Dimitri Manuilsky, who, notwithstanding the presidency of George Dimitrov, continued to hold a top position in the Communist International.

The old man, heretofore always crafty but gay, was peculiarly sour to me. I was already prepared by what Marcucci had told me on the night of his death, however, and was not disposed to let myself be crushed by his aggressive malevolence. When I came in, he was with the Chilean leaders, a Cuban who went by the name of Pérez, and the Argentines, Sommi and Orestes Ghioldi.

"Are you still alive, comrade?" was his cheerful greeting as he extended his hand.

"What do you think, comrade Manuilsky?" I replied smiling. "None of the bombs which have rained on Spain had my name on them."

The others laughed. I kept my eyes on Manuilsky's.

"Are you sick?" he asked. "You seem to me thin—too thin."

"Sick, no," I answered. "Just undernourished. There is very little to eat in Spain."

"Does one eat badly there now?"

"One doesn't eat badly, comrade. One simply does not eat."

"And why not?"

"There isn't any food."

"I've seen the Spanish comrades," he said, throwing back his head as if he doubted my words, "and they all look all right. They don't say what you do. Of course they admit it isn't always easy to get everything, but they have not gone so far as to say that people are hungry."

"Perhaps because they have not been," I laughed. "But I can tell you that the Spanish people are suffering severely from lack of food. There is a small ration of lentils, twice a day."

"And what are the people saying?"

"They endure. And they tell jokes. The lentils are called 'the Life Pills of Dr. Negrin; Resistance Brand.' "

"Resistance, that's it," said Manuilsky. "There is the secret. Resistance. Don't you agree?" he asked the others.

"Yes, yes," they echoed. "They must resist until the war is won."

"You don't seem very convinced that the Republic will win," remarked Manuilsky.

"I'm afraid we're going to lose," I said with emotion. "I'm afraid we have already lost."

There was a dramatic silence, which no one dared to break. Manuilsky nodded and said: "Others have told me that."

Again there was silence. He sat down at his desk, folded his arms on the plate glass that covered it and said:

"We are going to have some very interesting discussions. We are going to take up the most important questions in Latin America; Cuba, where our comrades are pursuing a very intelligent policy; Chile, where the Chilean comrades have achieved a maximum success; Argentina, where the party is failing. And if you will permit it we shall speak of Peru, whose leaders have contented themselves with imitating the South American cuckoos who lay eggs in the nests of other birds. And we might speak of Brazil too. What do you think?"

"It sounds like a very interesting program, comrade," I answered. "I think we could draw some interesting conclusions."

"Of course we can," he said smiling, and half-shutting his eyes, "and the first conclusion we'll draw will be that emigrants can not be tolerated in the Comintern."

"Emigrants?" I asked with surprise.

"Yes, emigrants," he said emphatically. "Like you, for instance."

"I have been wherever the Comintern sent me, or where the police took me," I answered firmly, "not where it has suited me to go. As to the cuckoo who lays eggs in the nests of others, so that they may hatch them, it seems to me that is wrong. I am more like those Argentine ostriches that hatch whatever eggs are put in their nests."

"Are you saying that for our benefit as Chileans?" asked Barro Silva.

"I say it in answer to comrade Manuilsky's insinuation, nothing more."

Manuilsky took a pad and pencil, made a note of something, agreed on another meeting with the Chileans and one with the Cuban. To me he said: "I'll call you when I need you." And the interview came to an end.

Since no work was assigned to me I wandered around Moscow. There were many old buildings pulled down and others going up. The rhythm of work was very slow and this was made up for by the numbers of workers. On every building there was an enormous crowd of men and women, old and young.

I tried to see my old Russian friends. Guralsky no longer lived in Ozhod-Niriat. My friend had been eliminated from the Comintern and even from all intellectual work. I was told he was in a shoe factory in a nearby town. Others said he was perhaps in a concentration camp. I never saw him again.

One afternoon I went as far as Pokrovsky Varoda to visit Dorogan. He had moved and they gave me his new address. I had brought him a few presents from the capitalist world—woolen sweaters, socks, stockings for his wife, caps for the girls and some big colored-silk handkerchiefs, which cost ten francs in Paris but were treasures in Moscow. I was sure they would be very pleased with all these, especially Mrs. Dorogan with her silk stockings—the dream of every Soviet lady.

Dorogan's wife received me as if she had completely forgotten me, my name and my face.

"It is I, comrade: don't you remember me? First at the foundry, later in your other house, four years ago! How are Lena, Natacha and Alyosha?"

The woman who had always been so kind seemed confused. She looked at me, plucking at her skirt, and muttering words I could not understand. At last she said that Dorogan wouldn't come till evening. I went away, thinking that Irene had forgotten me or else was losing her wits.

That evening I returned and found Dorogan and his two daughters. I came in, greeting him in Russian and Spanish, and with a great show of joy put my packages down on a table. Dorogan received me standing, with his arms folded. He was immobile. The girls, like statues behind him, had grown beautiful. The mother had apparently run away to hide.

"Why have you come?" asked Dorogan. "What do you want?"

"Dorogan," I said, upset by his reception, "you were always so good to me that I no sooner arrived than I wanted to see you and your family. I have brought you some little gifts."

He didn't move. "Why have you come? Go," he implored. "Forgive me, but you compromise me. Please don't come again. You are a foreigner and they may accuse us of something. I want no trouble with the party. And don't leave anything. Not anything, please!"

He took the package with both hands and held it out to me, forcing me to take it.

"Forgive me," he said again desperately. "Take your gift, comrade. I can accept nothing from you, not even your visit. Goodbye comrade, take care of yourself and I beg you to forgive us. Goodbye."

I was on my feet, shaken with fear, with disgust, with sorrow. Dimly I understood what was happening to Dorogan. "I want no trouble with the party," meant the NKVD, Stalin's police.

After a long walk I went back to the hotel with my package under my arm, wondering if this was all that the Russian workers had won after twenty years of sacrifice—hunger and misery—animal terror.

On the next day a man who spoke only Russian came to my room to summon me to a meeting with comrade George Dimitrov.

"Tomorrow at four o'clock sharp," he said and went away, leaving the signed and sealed pass with which I might take the omnibus which went to the Comintern building, now outside of Moscow and more than an hour from the Hotel Lux.

On my arrival at the Latin American section of the Comintern, I was given a piece of what looked like grey wrapping-paper, on which was written "three o'clock—Offices of the Cadres Commission in the Comintern."

I was on the dot. Ola Blagoieva, a woman of uncertain age, received me. She was badly groomed, with lank brown hair falling on her shoulders, dirty finger-nails and a few greenish teeth which looked infected. Her light eyes were gentle and the only fresh thing in her acid, withered face. Her manner was harsh as she began to fill out a questionnaire: age, nationality, number of times imprisoned, social class, parties worked in, union membership, parents' situation, social origin, occupation, means, method of support, number of children, degree of parentage with soldiers, land-holders, businessmen, money lenders. The woman wrote down my answers although I told her they were all on record, together with my biography at the Cadres Commission, and anyhow——

"Enough comrade," she said, rudely. "It is I who must do this work, not you. We are the ones to decide what must be asked or not asked of a comrade." Then she melted a little, smiled, showing her filthy teeth, and added: "You intellectuals are so difficult! Today more than ever, we must watch the conduct of our responsible leaders. The class enemy threatens us on every side. International fascism is waging a campaign of corruption."

From her tone and manner I realized that the upper circles were no longer favorable to me. I knew that from now on I might expect to run into difficulties of all sorts. But I was not going to give in easily. I matched my tone to hers and tried to give her tit for tat.

"If they had thought of that earlier, comrade Olessova, the directors of the German party might not have fallen so easily into the hands of the Gestapo. Nor would Prestes be a prisoner in Brazil, nor the rearguard of the Spanish army so full of spies."

She stared at me with what looked like admiration and, seeing that I was going to hold my own, she spoke pleasantly.

"They say that you are brave."

"Who says so?"

"The data we have here," she tapped some papers, "in your *dossier*."

"Every communist must be brave. Anything else, comrade?"

"Are you in a hurry?"

"Yes. At four I have an appointment with comrade Dimitrov in his office."

"Did you ask for it?"

"No. He sent for me."

"He sent for you?"

"I think I said it quite clearly, comrade."

A man entered the room through a concealed door at the side. This trick, I thought, is to frighten or to mystify. I rose and greeted him calmly. Comrade Olessova introduced us, giving his name as Andrei Bielov.

"Yes, yes," he said, in correct Spanish. "How are you, comrade? I saw you in Valencia in the Central Committee and in Madrid at the writers' congress with Ilya Ehrenburg and that French Catholic. Do you remember?"

"Julien Benda?"

"That's the one. And with the other one who screamed that he was afraid. Tall thin—what was his name?"

"André Chamson."

"That's the one. Well, comrade Olessova," he said, sitting down in an armchair and stretching out his shiny boots, "this poet was crazy with fear when the bombs fell. He would throw himself on the sofa and say he wished to die, that he was afraid and couldn't control it."

"What did he go there for, then?" asked Olessova.

"That's the sort of thing intellectuals do. Who can understand them, Masha Olessova, who?"

I was irritated.

"That man who was afraid and went to Madrid knowing there would be bombs," I said harshly, "is a poet, as Heine was. You know of Heine, the friend of Marx and Engels? When Engels, in one of his letters to Marx, complained of the outrages that Heine committed in the apartment they shared, Marx said he must forgive him; that poets were like that and could not be judged by the same yardstick as other men."

Bielov, obviously a member of the NKVD assigned to the Comintern, was vexed. He wriggled in his chair, lit a cigarette and cleared his throat noisily.

"And you think that poet was brave?" he asked.

"Of course. He had been wounded in '14. Yet there he was, fear and all, to fight for liberty. That is very brave."

"Brave to be afraid?"

"Yes, to be afraid and to keep on fighting."

"You see, Ola?" said the policeman. "That's how these intellectuals are."

Then he stood up, stuck his hands in his belt and paced up and down, clicking his heels on the floor.

"Did you take all the data, Ola?" he asked.

"Yes, I have filled out the questionnaire and added the extras especially requested."

"Have you told all the truth?" he asked me, frowning.

"Excuse me, comrade," I answered, "but I can not tolerate the insinuation that I might have lied."

"We want no fine speeches here," he said authoritatively. "This isn't a meeting of the Spanish or Chilean or Peruvian party. You don't need your talents for oratory here. Here you must answer the questions we ask, whatever they may be."

"I am prepared to answer them all, but I must demand that you assume I am telling you the truth until it is proven otherwise."

"It is not that you would lie or try to deceive us," he explained. "But everyone forgets, exaggerates, twists the facts. Our conversation is going to be long, very long, comrade. Much longer than you imagine, so you must be very patient."

I had chills down my spine, a contraction in my stomach, so that I feared my voice would tremble when I spoke.

"You have no reason to ask for patience. I shall be delighted to talk with you as long as you like if it contributes to the victory of liberty over fascism."

The policeman took his hands from his belt, letting a gun be seen. I thought he had done it on purpose. He slumped into the soft chair and was about to speak when comrade Olessova interrupted smiling: "The comrade hasn't much time now, because he has been summoned by George Dimitrov."

"By Dimitrov!" he repeated, surprised enough to pull himself up in his chair. "Did you ask for the interview?"

"No. He asked for it and named the hour; today at four. In fifteen minutes, to be exact."

"We'll see," he muttered. "Give me the telephone, Masha."

Olessova dialed a number and there was silence while she waited. She passed the receiver to the policeman who said he was speaking in the name of the Cadres Commission; that it was a delicate case, very urgent; that it was a matter of my political actions and of concrete data.

The voice at the other end, a woman's, could be plainly heard. She said yes, I had an appointment and that a translator and stenographers were waiting. The policeman made her consult Dimitrov. There was a long wait, hard for me to bear. Then she came back to the telephone and said that Dimitrov suggested that the comrades put off their inquiry to another day. Olessova, who had taken her eyes from the policeman, looked at him meaningly. The man nodded, sucked in his lower lip and looked disappointed. He sighed, stretched out his legs and said:

"Well, we have fourteen minutes. Have you seen Guralsky yet?"

"No, I couldn't. They told me he no longer lives in Ozhod-Niriat."

"Do you want to see him very much?"

238

"You understand I don't need to," I answered, all my composure regained. "Guralsky has been a good friend to me and it is natural I should wish to see him, but not if it interferes in any way with the Soviet police."

"Not at all," said the policeman. "Don't give it a thought. It just seems strange to us, all this courtesy of you Latin Americans. The minute you get to Moscow, you go visiting."

"Isn't it a Russian custom? Or are friendly visits contrary to socialist custom?"

"You are making fun of me," he said angrily.

"No," I answered, looking him in the eye, "I am just trying to get my bearings."

He got up, and standing in front of me, asked:

"What gifts did you bring to Dorogan?"

I tried to enumerate the things that I had brought and that Dorogan had refused to accept.

"You declared them at the border?"

"No. I was not asked for a declaration. This is the third time I have come to Russia and I have never had to declare anything. My baggage was presented for inspection, however."

He looked at his watch. "It's almost four o'clock. You must go to your appointment now. We will call you later."

I understood the cold threat behind his words. I knew where it might end, how far the NKVD went, when it persecuted someone. And in all this I felt the hatred of Manuilsky and the hand, or rather the claw, of Stalin. I thought of my wife, of the child who was going to be born, and my fear of being liquidated in Moscow grew.

The policeman said: "We will call you, comrade. We must talk a long time about you and your friends, about your bonapartism."

"Bonapartism?" I asked, smiling in spite of my growing fear.

"Dimitrov is waiting for you now. We'll talk later."

As I closed the door I heard him say to Olessova: "Call Manuilsky."

I went down the wide corridor as if I were walking a tight-rope. I had no sensation of the distance between my feet and the floor. I was spied on, followed, watched exactly as I had been under the dictatorships of the little Latin American tyrants. Humiliated, a prey to a bitter depression, I came to the large room where Dimitrov worked. The secretary announced me and a tall young man, dressed in a black suit of military cut, invited me to enter.

George Dimitrov was also in black, as before, except for his gleaming white shirt. I greeted him and stepped forward but he showed me no cordiality. He was affable and indifferent, as if we had met the day before, and he spoke as if he were renewing an interrupted conversation.

"Who do you think will win the war in Spain?" he asked.

I looked at him, then at the translator, smiled and did not answer.

"Forgive me," he said, "for not introducing you to comrade Lucas. He is not an official translator but a good comrade and my friend, who collaborates with me in delicate matters—like this one."

The tall thin man who had admitted me smiled in a friendly way and stretched out his hand. Then he sat down again at the little table, with pencil and paper.

I sat down then and answered the question.

"Not only do I believe, comrade, that we are going to lose the war in Spain, but I am convinced that we have already lost it."

"In spite of Negrin's accession to power?"

"Negrin can not make miracles," I said. "I think it is too late for anyone to save the situation."

"To what do you attribute the defeat?"

"To internal disorganization, to the Committee of Non-Intervention and the fences built around the Republic, and to the decided intervention of Italy and Germany."

"What else?"

"To the lack of armaments, the poor organization of the army, the uncontrolled espionage. And finally to the fact that there is at present no unanimous will to victory in republican Spain."

"No will to victory?" he repeated.

"No unanimous will to victory, which is essential. At the present time there are large groups who want only for the war to end. They believe and affirm that Spain has been used as a field of experimentation for new weapons, by outsiders. And they do not care to be guinea pigs."

"I understand," he said. "Are there other groups?"

"There is a very large one, a great part of which has been gathered under the communist wing, which is interested only in making money. They get rich on the black market: they make dark alliances to change the depreciated pesetas they take in, for foreign currency. They are busy with all sorts of piracy great and small."

"What are your differences with the makers of the war policy?"

"It seems to me absurd and criminal to sacrifice the lives of Spanish boys by sending them out on stupid offensives, knowing that nothing can be gained but failure. I think the party ought not to connive at corruption. Furthermore there is terror, by Lister, El Campesino and the others, by Codovila and the NKVD. I believe that the use of terror will not avert disaster; on the contrary it is hastening it."

There was a long silence. Then Dimitrov said:

"The versions coincide, don't they, comrade Lucas?" and without waiting for an answer, added, "It will be much better not to make comments on all this to the other comrades, to anyone at all."

"I won't, comrade Dimitrov," I answered. "And I want to say that I have never done so. I always give my opinion in the regular party meetings, assuming responsibility for my point of view."

"What more can you say?" asked Dimitrov.

I gave a long and detailed report of everything I had seen. The so-called socialism of factories and various establishments. The privileges accorded to the leaders and their friends, the manipulators of the black market. The collectivization of the barber shops, which consisted in each barber receiving ten pesetas a day while his receipts had to be turned in to the "Barber's Committee"—that is to say to a small directing group which practised extortion on the others. Also the "Committees" formed to administer the moving-picture theatres, hotels and cafés, which, having liquidated the capital on which these enterprises rested, lacked every means to offer even mediocre service. I even referred incidentally to the socialization of cats.

"Of what?" exclaimed Dimitrov in amazement. "Did you say cats?"

"The food situation in Spain is very bad," I answered, "and made worse by the economic disorganization. In every town the 'Committees' print money at the enforced rate of exchange and the peasants hide their products and use all sorts of animals for food. Among these the cat is very important. Well, to prevent their extermination, various Committees have socialized cats."

"How do you socialize a cat?"

"Well, the cats are considered as belonging to the Committee, and are all taken to a cat center and are fed there."

"And then?"

"Well, if a person needs a cat to catch rats and mice, he goes to the cat center to get one and pays a daily rent for it to the Committee."

"That's infantile!" exclaimed Dimitrov.

"The cat usually escapes to his old home. The man who rented it has to pay a fine or may go to jail, or even—so it has been said, but this I don't believe—may get the 'shove off.'

"The 'shove off' is death, I believe?"

"Yes."

After a long pause, during which a woman brought in tea, bread, ham, eggs, butter and fish, Dimitrov said:

"You won't speak of this either, will you?"

"No, I won't," I promised.

While we had tea he led the conversation to the over-all picture of Latin America and the work accomplished there.

"You have done a magnificent job in Chile," he said, slapping my back familiarly, and appearing cordial for the first time. "Your success has been beyond our fondest hopes. I must congratulate you, but unfortunately only here in private, between ourselves." And he laughed adding: "It is too bad that things have been so different in Peru. Is it perhaps because of your personal differences with Haya de la Torre?"

"I have no personal differences," I answered emphatically. "Neither rancor nor rivalry. The fact is that I don't approve of Haya's methods. They are very much like Lister's and Codovila's in Spain; full of contempt for the opinions, lives and liberties of others."

"Don't get angry," he said, patting my arm. "Tell me honestly: Don't you think Haya de la Torre's movement is democratic or could become so?"

"I am profoundly convinced that it is not and never will be. Within his party Haya is a dictator; he rules by his own law and tolerates no opposition. He has copied Nazi systems and methods. If he should win, my country would groan under a dictatorship just like those it has been suffering from for a long time. Haya de la Torre does not care for argument, nor the democratic battle. He prefers to words the bludgeon, the pistol and the dagger."

"A terrorist too, eh? Did you know that Haya has approached the Communist International again?"

"And what does he want?" I smiled. "Arms? Money?"

Dimitrov smiled too, sank his hands in his pockets and spoke as if in confidence:

"Haya de la Torre has approached us through Peskovsky. Remember him? Banderas Ortega; for a while he was the Russian ambassador to Mexico. He met Haya there, got to know him rather well, and helped him to come to Moscow. Peskovsky doesn't agree with you about Haya and *aprismo*. He is convinced that Haya would fall in naturally with our plans. Even while he passed for our enemy he would follow a political line parallel to ours—a line violently opposed to the rich in your country, and in favor of the great mass of Indians, mulattoes and *cholos,* who are, according to him, odiously discriminated against and passed over in favor of a small white minority. Peskovsky is trying to convince everybody that this campaign of Haya's is exactly what the International needs. I should like your opinion, comrade."

"You must permit me," I answered quietly, "to consider in this matter the interests of my countrymen, which mean nothing to Peskovsky. He has no doubt thought of all the angles, except the most important one—the best interests of the Peruvian people themselves."

"Do you sincerely believe," Dimitrov asked, kindly, "that the triumph of *aprismo* would be bad for your people?"

"I am sure of it, comrade."

"Well, you are right," he said. "That aspect had not been considered by Peskovsky, who has not the slightest notion of the life or the politics of your country."

"But," I said, "we could discuss the matter with him and those who hold his views."

"No," he said. "That won't be possible. Peskovsky has been imprisoned. Furthermore, Haya de la Torre puts a few conditions on his understandings with us. One of them concerns you. Do you know of it?"

"No, but I can guess."

"As one of the conditions essential to an understanding," he said, smiling deliberately, "he demands your removal in one form or another. He considers you Enemy Number One to a vast popular unity in Peru and in Latin America generally, and says he is willing to cooperate with all the communists in the continent except you. It seems he does not like you at all."

"I don't know why he bothers to work through you," I said, "when he is so used to eliminating his opponents by means of his gunmen without asking anyone."

"Comrade Manuilsky feels that it might be wise for the International—not now, but later when Haya succeeeds, if he does—to work out an agreement with him. Of course as long as Haya is failing, as he is at present, there is no need to take him into account, only perhaps later on— He has promised, for example, that as soon as he can he will demand definite recognition of the Soviet Union from parliament and the government."

243

"All that may be very fine, comrade," I rejoined, "but none of this proves that Haya de la Torre will be good for my country, or for its people. I am profoundly convinced of the contrary."

"In general I think your position unjust," said Dimitrov, "with a few reservations. Of course it is just from the nationalistic point of view which you adopt. But don't forget that a communist in case of conflict, must subordinate nationalism to internationalism. It is something you have never been able to understand or apply. Manuilsky has come to think of you as a stubborn nationalist and a very tepid internationalist. He thinks you are immoderately critical as well."

"Comrade Manuilsky likes men like Codovila."

"You may be partly right. Codovila cares neither for Argentina, Italy nor Spain; not for your country nor for mine. He cares only for Soviet interests; he has an oriental rather than a western mind."

"I can't be like that, comrade Dimitrov," I said, "even if comrade Manuilsky thinks——"

"No, no," he interrupted, "don't misunderstand me. Manuilsky appreciates your capacity for study and work, and the successes you have had in Chile. But he thinks that you have boasted about your opposition in the matter of Brazil, and even blamed him for the failure there and for its consequences."

"I thought the policy of insurrection unwise while we were promoting a Popular Front. That policy had authors and it is not my fault, you understand, that he was one of them."

"I am going to ask you another favor," said Dimitrov, "which you must grant me."

"You know it is my pleasure to serve you," I said, touched by the tact with which Dimitrov gave orders.

"Don't make any comments on the Brazilian situation, or compare it with that in Chile, or draw any conclusions from the Brazilian failure for the present Latin American policy. Your comments will do the situation no good and yourself great harm. Furthermore," he added with unmistakable meaning, "you might hurt some of your comrades."

"I promise, comrade Dimitrov."

"Good. Thank you very much. Now one more important and confidential question." He paced up and down again, looked up at the portrait of Stalin, then continued: "Comrade Manuilsky thinks that when the discussion of Chile comes up, the leading role should be given to the Chilean leaders as well as the praise and the glory. Do you understand? Before the members of the Comintern, the Chilean leaders must be given the credit for all the successes in Chile. You must disappear completely. You were never in Chile."

He looked at me steadily and shook me by the shoulder asking:

"Can you assist at the plenary sessions that we are going to have on Chile without speaking, or adding to the reports or correcting anything? I know it is unjust, but will you do it?"

"Results are what interest me," I answered, concealing my feelings, "and if this is the best way to get them, well, so be it." My voice roughened a little in spite of me. "I did not join the party to win decorations or honors. Manuilsky can have it his way."

"We have all joined the party to serve, to fight, to sacrifice," said Dimitrov. "Now another question. If it were necessary for you to go back to Chile to continue the work there for a little longer, would you be willing?"

"I should like to go to my own country," I said stubbornly, "to work for my own people—even if it does mark me as a nationalist, or as a cuckoo."

"That will be a bit later," Dimitrov suggested persuasively. "Right now we must consolidate what we have won. War threatens, and with war on the horizon the first consideration must be the defense of the Soviet Union. We must consolidate the positions from which this defense can be carried out. Chile is a magnificent position in South America. We can't lose it and therefore we need you there."

"All right, comrade," I agreed sadly. "It shall be as you wish."

"I expected you to be harder to deal with," he said gently, "but I see that my information was wrong. I think this conversation has helped us both and I am glad to have been able to speak with you so frankly."

I prepared to leave. Dimitrov was very cordial in contrast to his unfriendly reception. I realized that a great many decisions had been changed by this interview and that some devilish plans had been destroyed or at least laid aside. Before I spoke, he asked: "Are you comfortably housed? Is there anything I can help you with? I should like to be of service to you."

Moved by his kindness, I told him about my wife in Spain and Codovila's refusal to grant her the necessary authorization to leave.

"This personal pettiness," he exclaimed, "does a lot of harm in the party. They torture each other as if they were enemies; it should surely not be too difficult for them to get along together."

I tried to answer but he turned to Lucas and ordered that a box of food be sent from France to my wife in Barcelona. Then he promised me that he would see to it that my wife should have the necessary papers to cross the French border.

"Anything else?" he asked.

I told him about Olessova and the Cadres Commission and the man from the NKVD; of my attempt to visit Guralsky and the gifts for Dorogan. I gave him to understand that I felt a prey to constant vigilance.

"You had better speak less lightly than you do of the NKVD," he advised. "The man who questioned you in the Cadres Commission did so as a party member, not as a policeman. You must try to be more tolerant. There are grave internal difficulties and the Russians are suspicious by nature. Never mind. Go in peace. I will take care of all this. Sleep well."

His words calmed my anxiety. I felt light-headed with relief, now that I could hope to be free of the clutches of the NKVD.

Dimitrov looked at his watch and made a gesture of astonishment. It was later than nine o'clock and the omnibusses to the Lux had stopped running. He asked Lucas for a form and signed an order for a car and a fur coat for me. I clasped his hand effusively and he patted my back affectionately. Lucas showed me to the door and told me where to wait for the car. A few minutes after I reached the entrance, Andrei Bielov joined me. (In his capacity as a party member and not a policeman, I presumed.) He was smiling.

"Did you miss the bus?" he asked cordially.

"Yes, Dimitrov made me miss it," I said, drawing on my gloves. I laughed, sincerely gay.

"Was the interview so long?"

"Yes, we talked for a long time. What do you think of that, comrade?"

"You talked for more than four hours. Interesting, wasn't it?"

"Do you think so?"

"It is always interesting to talk for so long to a man like George Dimitrov. It doesn't happen every day, nor even every two years."

The chauffeur arrived, called me by name and asked for my permit. "Will you give me a lift?" asked Bielov.

"Of course, comrade," I said. He made me get in first, with marked courtesy, exchanged a few words with the chauffeur, looked at the signature on my card, and gave it to him.

"That card is historical," he said. "It is signed by Dimitrov himself. This never happens as you must understand."

"What a privilege," I said. "It means I am lucky, or perhaps that my luck in Moscow has begun to change for the better."

The policeman laughed and I joined him with a feeling of health and relief, burying myself in the furs that had been provided for me.

"It seems to be changing," said the policeman, offering me a cigarette and lighting one for himself. After that we pretended to doze in our respective corners.

2

More than twenty years had gone by since the successful October Revolution of the Bolshevik party. A series of Five Year Plans had been carried out with blood, agony and death. But in spite of everything the miserable conditions of the Russian people continued.

Stalin had announced (at the same time he was having Lenin's old friends liquidated) that the Union of Soviet Socialist Republics had abandoned all "capitalistic placentas" to enter with seven-league-boots into the new socialist life, happy, full of material and spiritual joy. He had declared that the USSR was entering on the stage in which the last vestiges of capitalism would be eradicated, not only from the lives but from the consciences of men.

The reality was opposed to the grandiose statement. The salary level had reached an incredible low, for it is infamous to pay a man the price of one egg for eight hours' work. A Russian worker earned a salary that would, if every cent of it were saved for eight months, buy him a suit of the kind you can get at a rummage sale in any capitalistic country. And this was twenty years after the proletarian revolution.

A common workman in the socialist homeland earned from five to eight rubles a day, and there was a day of rest each week when he got nothing. A little bun, of the kind served with coffee in western Europe, cost two and a half rubles; a piece of meat with some salad cost between twelve and seventeen rubles; a pair of shoes of unspeakably poor quality cost two hundred rubles. We delegates received, in addition to housing, food and laundry, fifteen rubles a day for eight hours of work, so that we were earning twenty or thirty times more than an average workman and we lived on a scale similar to that of a student of average means. Of course some among the delegates had better luck than others. Those who managed to be asked to collaborate on political, social or economic problems received from *Pravda*, *Izvestia*, the Lenin Academy, the Comintern review or the VOKS (the organization that linked the intellectual foreigners) four or five hun-

247

dred rubles extra, or the equivalent of from three to five months' pay
for a worker.

The same explanations were given me as on my former visits.
The workers earned so little because they could get everything they
needed so cheap in the cooperatives but this was not the whole truth.
There were in the cooperatives a few articles, mostly food of
poor quality. In the light-industry cooperatives, there was meat perhaps every nine days and in amounts proportioned not to the needs
but to the production of the individual. The best workers thus received a few ounces more of meat in their ration. The same rationing,
with variations depending on the season, applied to eggs, bacon, ham,
potatoes and dry vegetables. Bread was least restricted and dairy products were almost unobtainable.

The great agricultural production of Russia went to the European markets. French *épiceries* sold the violet Russian eggs cheap.
Wheat, fish, oats, and butter of various qualities were sold in Germany, England and the rest of Europe.

These products went to buy machinery, chiefly for the manufacture of armaments. It was essential to defend the socialist homeland;
it was imperative to protect the future of the proletarian revolution.
Russia had become a gigantic though inefficient armament factory.
Stalin's regime was and is a war machine, geared for war. The Russian socialist government had imposed slavery on the people so that
the army, the police and the upper circles of the communist party
should live in comfort.

One morning it was announced on the radio and in the press
that, within five days, five million tangerines would reach Moscow.
These tangerines were the product of the Stalinist production system.
They would be sold in stores open to all, since they were not an article
of prime necessity for the nourishment of the people. It had been
officially decided that a Russian could pass his life quite satisfactorily
without eating tangerines.

The news was commented on at the Hotel Lux by Spaniards,
Frenchmen and Latin Americans who saw only each other; since the
rest, because of the terror, never mingled with us. The day the tangerines arrived, we were up before the stores opened on Gorki Street.
No sooner had the doors opened than we went in exuberantly to buy.

There were the tangerines, brilliant and beautiful, in some baskets
tied with rope. There were twenty baskets, no more. I thought it must
be the show-case.

"Please comrade, we would like some tangerines."

"Tangerines?" "Tangerines?" "Tangerines?" The word flew from mouth to mouth until it reached the manager. Ceremoniously he drew near the show-case and said with exquisite courtesy: "The tangerines are all gone, comrades. Only these remain and they have been set aside for customers who will call for them later."

"All gone? How can that be, since the shop has just opened?"

"Yes, the tangerines are all gone," the manager repeated, smiling but authoritative. And since, in my surprise, I simply stood there with my mouth wide-open, he continued suavely:

"They bought them all. There was a great queue and none are left for you, comrade."

I looked the Cuban worker Pérez in the eyes. He was a great admirer of Manuilsky and I had never quite trusted him. I knew the manager was lying. There had never been any other tangerines than those in the show case. It was not true about the five million. So I just looked at the Cuban and smiled.

The Moscow radio announced that from the very earliest hours in the morning the workers in this happy socialist world had run to buy the tangerines of this Stalinian harvest, exhausting the supply in a short time; but it was announced that next week there would be ten million more. The people of Moscow fortunate enough to live under the Soviet regime would enjoy more Stalinian tangerines the following week. On the announced day I was up early, not to buy tangerines, but just to see what would happen. The day before, the papers had published the photograph of the "Hero of the Soviet Union, friend of comrade Stalin, Michurin," who had made possible this harvest of Stalinian tangerines.

I entered the store where the tangerines were to be sold. I asked for a dozen but got only two. There was no queue at the door and half an hour later the supply was gone, without so many as a hundred tangerines having been sold. All that about the ten million was another fairy-tale.

I made no comment, so as not to compromise myself any more than I had already. It was clear to me by now that I was completely isolated. The old Russian, Finnish, Polish and Hungarian friends who lived in the Lux scurried away from me without speaking, and pretended not to have seen me. Those who lived in Moscow and who were always up on new arrivals never called me.

One day I went out to buy a paper, and returning without it, found myself in the elevator face to face with the great General Kleber, defender of Madrid. Tall, white-skinned, with his clear eyes and athletic body, he looked different to me in mufti. He seemed a trifle hunched over and ill.

"General," I said. "My general, how are you? How happy I am to see you again! Where are you staying?"

Kleber said not a word. When I got out of the elevator he took me by the arm and drew me to a corner of the corridor. "Please," he said, "don't speak to me. Do you understand? Not a word. Not a greeting. I live here in the Lux. I knew you had arrived and I have seen you before. But please don't visit me or speak to me."

"All right," I said, grieved to see him looking as he did and to witness his fear. "I spoke to you because I thought you would be glad."

"Don't think badly of me," he implored. "You know that I am fond of you. But my situation in the party isn't good—and, I think, neither is yours."

His declaration froze my blood. I wanted to question him but General Kleber aroused my pity, trembling in a little corridor of the Moscow hotel, this man who had come to Madrid that seventh of November, in command of the International Brigades. There he cowered now, playing dead, as some insects do when they feel threatened.

I devoted myself to sounding others around me. The stenographers were magnificent antennae with which to capture confidential information; you only needed to greet one to know how the chief in her office felt about you. The translators were useful in the same way, and so too were the Latin American comrades. I soon discovered three facts. First, the Russians wished to have no dealings whatever with any foreigner. One morning I knocked at the door of a Soviet office and went in to get a copy of the *International Review*. The comrade who was inside shut the door and said: "I beg you not to come here again."

"Why not?" I asked. "Isn't this an office of the Comintern?"

"Don't take it like that, comrade," he answered. "You're a nice guy but you can compromise me. Do you understand? Don't come back. If you want something, ask for it by telephone."

"Why? It's the same thing," I said.

"No, comrade, it isn't. The telephone conversation will be recorded."

I went out depressed. Something in my conscience crumbled to dust. I was destroying myself. And although I was sorry for the poor Russian victims of fear, I was sorrier for myself. For I too was afraid.

What could I do alone? And so each one felt, and on this wretched and vile foundation of frightened men, the great Stalin was building his new and happy world.

The second discovery was that there existed two distinct views of my position within the Comintern. The employees in Manuilsky's office treated me with contempt, as if I were in the pre-liquidation phase. The people in Dimitrov's office, on the other hand, treated me with marked attention. The translator gave me his seat in the dining-room, the stenographer joined me for tea. The secretary smiled at me, with a joke, as she accepted a light for her cigarette.

The third discovery came by itself. Comrade Olessova had not summoned me to a new interview in the Cadres Commission. And one fine day when I met her casually, she smiled broadly, showing her few teeth fringed with green. She asked me if I was comfortable, not bothered by the cold, getting used to the food. This was definitive. I entered the dining-room radiantly happy, and spoke gaily to everyone. Just then Dimitrov's secretary called me.

"Good news," she said, "comrade Dimitrov has ordered a safe conduct and passport for your wife in Spain, so that she can move to France." My eyes filled with tears and to her great embarrassment I took both her hands in mine and kissed them. The next day Lucas confirmed the news officially, and I begged him to thank Dimitrov.

3

The criminality of the Soviet regime was rising, along with a great and violent cynicism. It was two years since "the most progressive constitution in the world" had been established, and in all their dramatic history, the Russian people had never been so physically and morally enslaved as they were under that very constitution. Russians were dragged from their beds, carried naked to the offices of the NKVD and sent to unknown destinations never to return. Under that constitution, the police arrested men and women, imprisoned them without trial, tortured them horribly, judged them in secret, condemned them without mercy, and ordered them executed.

On my third visit to Russia I could find none of the men and women who had worked in the Comintern since its inception. All had been liquidated, some by being removed to forced labor camps, others by being shot; in every case the accused were called the same names —saboteurs, spies, enemies of the people. One night in a solemn cell session the outbreak of the "third purge" was announced.

"The Soviet people and the foreign comrades who are in Moscow," said Manuilsky, "are to have the luck to assist at the most historically important trials of our time. Within three days in the Hall of Columns, Soviet justice as represented by our great and loyal comrade Vishinsky will judge Bukharin, Rykov, Krestinsky, Rakovsky, and other bandits, saboteurs, spies in the service of foreign powers and enemies of the Soviet people."

In spite of the insistent and energetic intervention of the puppet masters of the NKVD, the solemn words of Manuilsky were received without enthusiasm, as if the assembly were made up of befuddled men who no longer were impressed by the words of the Kremlin's grand vizier. The orators spoke one after another; they were all Russians and all in favor of stigmatizing—as they said—the nefarious activities of the people's enemies. At the end they submitted to the assembly a resolution in which they pronounced a terrible anathema on those whose trial was about to take place. For all of them the death penalty was demanded. The assembly on its feet unanimously approved the motion. Similar resolutions were voted that night in all the work centers of the Soviet Union, in all the government offices, in all the Soviet and party dependencies.

The Russian winter was ending. One morning, lit by the cold and attenuated sun, the major trial of the "Third Bolshevik Purge," opened; it was to run to eight or nine sessions. The Hall of the Columns, in the vicinity of the Bolshoi Theatre, was full. There was a special gallery for diplomats and another for foreign newspaper men; only those who had a special pass were admitted. Passes were authorized to the representatives of the party in the labor headquarters who were supposed to give a public report later, to the Soviet officials and to the representatives of foreign communist parties.

There stood accused of infamous crimes the outstanding theoreticians of communism, former Russian ambassadors to European countries, the last group of Lenin's intimate friends, the progenitors of the revolution. Bukharin had grown old and fat. He was serene, and from his words and attitudes there flowed a skeptical and contemptuous indifference; he spoke as if nothing which was happening had any interest for him at all. When Vishinsky dramatically raised his voice to taunt him, Bukharin would say quietly: "I permit myself to remind the representatives of Soviet justice that as yet I am not a criminal, nor a condemned man. I am still a Soviet citizen."

Rykov, Rakovsky, and the others listened indifferently. They were neither overwhelmed, nor sad, nor resigned, but rather stoical. Krestinsky seemed more upset than the others, when Vishinsky referred to the espionage that he had been guilty of in Berlin as ambassador of the Soviet Union. To the denials of the former diplomat, the answer was a rain of documents—letters, dated five, seven, ten years back, letters in which whoever wrote them had made an obvious effort to establish the existence of espionage and treason and the guilt of the accused, letters full of surprisingly precise data. All were signed by Krestinsky, by friends of his who had been tried, by communists who worked with him and who had disappeared. In these papers there was no ambiguous language, nor cryptic wording, nor vague insinuations. They were clear letters, rich in detail, abundant in descriptions; they seemed the carefully labored pages of an exciting detective story.

Vishinsky—the man loved by Stalin—would ask for the documents from the tribunal's secretary, indicating the numbers and directing the clerk to read them. Little pieces of paper written by Krestinsky were shown before this audience, in which he gave appointments to Germans under suspicious circumstances. Leaves from his own notebook were exhibited, in which he had made notes of large sums of money, specifying the currency—dollars, marks, pounds sterling. I asked myself how it had been possible for the Soviet police to collect so many treasonable papers throughout so long a span of years while the accused had continued to occupy high posts of responsibility. It was believable that the police should have got hold of one or two, or even ten, incriminating documents. But this collection from Berlin, Tokyo, Paris, Naples, Vichy, and St. Moritz, so marvellously catalogued over a decade and involving a man who had, until a year or two before been above suspicion—this, I could not accept.

Once the trial was over and sentences passed, the Comintern directors arranged for us to go on a tour of the factories and collective farms, the workers' clubs, and the house of culture in the environs of Moscow. On this tour I was able to compare what I had seen in 1929 and 1935 with the actual conditions in 1938. We travelled for ten days gathering impressions; I returned to Moscow tired, sick, and profoundly beaten down. What I had seen only increased my disappointment and struck harder at my battered and tormented faith. Not feeling like supper, I stretched out on my bed and dozed. I was awakened by a knock at the door and Dorogan entered, the same old friend who had thrown me out of his house, refusing my gifts and turning informer against me to the NKVD. There he stood smiling broadly, his arms open to embrace me.

"Are you angry with your old comrade? . . . I don't believe it!"

"What has happened?" I asked, sitting up on the bed. "Are you crazy or am I?"

Dorogan came towards me and put both his hands on my shoulders, holding me forcibly, and said in a low voice:

"We are neither of us crazy; but we are both cowards, which is worse. Shameful cowards—" and he spat, or made the gesture of spitting, three times on the floor. It was clear that he had been drinking; his breath was strongly alcoholic. I invited him to sit down, and put cigarettes beside him on a table.

"I have nothng to say to you," I said dryly. "Sit down. If you have anything to say I am listening."

"Good, very good," he said sitting down. "That is being a good comrade. I knew it, and said so to Irina and the girls. He won't be angry, I said. He will understand. Well, if he gets angry let him curse me all the way to America and back. So here you have me, come for my gifts. Have you got them?" and he laughed aloud.

"You must understand," he went on, taking off his coat and scarf, "that I was obliged to refuse your visit and your gifts and report you to the NKVD. You don't know what it's like for us Russians. The life of a communist isn't worth that"; and he flicked the ash off his cigarette; "and the liberty of a man and all his family isn't worth much more. I had to tell the NKVD because for quite a while I had been having my own difficulties, and, moreover, Aliosha was expected from Spain. You remember Aliosha?"

"Your son, the little one?"

"Little?" said Dorogan proudly. "If you could see him! A magnificent great boy, a good pilot; they chose him to go to Spain to try out the combat planes. Now he is back, he's here; right here in the Lux. We came to see him today. Since he knows that I like a bit of vodka now he had a good stock of it. After seeing him and talking with him, I said to myself, I'll go see that fellow; he must be pretty angry with me. I'll go see if he has given my presents to somebody else." Then he laughed again, and went on:

"How I have longed to talk with you, to speak with the same sincerity as that other time. How far away it all seems. . . . I wanted to talk to you about things which are impossible to discuss with Russians, not even with Aliosha, nor with my daughters, nor my wife . . . with nobody. Understand? With nobody! And now at last I have come to see you and ask you not to hold anything against me."

"No," I answered, "why should I? There are such strange things here that nothing surprises me; you Russians are dying of fear."

"Fear? Yes, you are right. But think, my Aliosha was expected! I did not know how he would come, nor how they would receive him. I only knew that some aviators who went to Spain to try out our war planes had been sent to concentration camps; some were shot, and some were simply never heard of again."

"But how is that possible?"

"That's how it is, my friend. Some say it is because they compared our standard of living with what the Spaniards were protesting against. Others, because they brought in valuable gifts without declaring them. They say so many things, but nobody really knows anything. . . . Have you nothing to drink?"

"No, I haven't."

"Well, look and see if there's anyone in the corridor." I opened the door and looked.

"There's no one," I said. Dorogan dashed out then, saying, "I'll be back. Leave the door ajar and put out the lights."

I turned off the switch and stretched out on the bed. Pretty soon Dorogan came back with vodka and some food. Then I shut the door, put out glasses, and we began to eat and drink.

"All this," he said, "was in Aliosha's room. How eager I have been to talk to you. We are sunk in filth and cowardice up to our necks. Because all we communists are cowards now. I, you, all of us, including Bukharin, Rykov, and Krestinsky."

"Why are they cowards?"

"Didn't you go to the trial? It was all a farce; it makes me want to vomit." Again he pretended to spit three times.

"What I don't understand about the trial," I said, lowering my voice, "is why they all lent themselves so plainly to their roles. I don't understand it!"

"You don't? Well of course you are not a Russian. But tell me—what is left to a Russian communist who has failed in Russia, who has fallen into disgrace and into the hands of the Soviet police? What is left to that man? Only to beg them to let him choose a comfortable way to die. Those men you saw have no hope at all inside the Soviet Union. And outside. . . ? Who is going to defend them? The communist parties? No! Who then? The catholics, the liberals, the socialists? Nobody, absolutely nobody. Then why fight? Why suffer uselessly?"

Dorogan took another drink and went on with his rambling explanations: "Each of the accused or condemned men has a family. If he cooperates in the farce of the trial, his family not only will not be touched but will be given a decent way to live by our glorious Soviet state. Under such conditions would you expect them to resist? Why? So that the persons they love will pay the consequences? Moreover, those who don't cooperate are simply liquidated in secret, without stage-sets or lights, or Vishinskys. Since they know that, why should they resist? The NKVD wants a letter—three letters? Let them bring paper and ink. They want two little papers, three compromising papers? All right, the prisoners write whatever the comrade policemen want. With papers or without them, the prisoner knows he is lost. If he does not produce the papers, he'll be liquidatd administratively; and his wife and children, his father and mother, will pay the consequences."

"But how could they liquidate administratively personalities like Bukharin, or Rykov?"

"Personalities? Nonsense. Here we are not dealing with *bourgeois* justice. This is proletarian justice. What a laugh, my boy! Don't you know what a lot of personalities, as you call them, have been shot, 'liquidated administratively,' by our great comrade Stalin?"

He opened another bottle of vodka, served it, and cleared his throat noisily.

"Drink, dear friend. I am saying to you things of which one or two would be enough to destroy me. I must talk; my guilt chokes me. And you must understand that I cannot speak of these things to my wife and children. I love them and my children adore me. But in Russia everything happens; they might inform against me. Horrible, isn't it? But it is the pure truth. And so I said, I'll tell him, he will have to know."

There was a noise outside. Dorogan signaled me to see what it was. There was no one outside; the corridor was empty, and all the doors closed.

"You remember Makar, from Magnitogorsk?" asked Dorogan.

"The architectural engineer?"

"Yes. He was a personality, wasn't he? Well, they shot him. And do you remember the time you ate with Mihailov, director of the Dnieprostroi dam, with Guralsky and with the German who had been a prisoner in Brazil?"

"Well?"

"Nothing, only they are all dead. Terribly logical. Bukharin and his tombmates, you and I. We have all failed, we who have lent our lives to this fraud, losing not only our lives but our souls. In the place of Rykov and the others what would you do?"

"I would fight."

"Sure. Outside—in the capitalist world, where you get defense even if you are a criminal, where even the worst regime won't liquidate your father and mother, your wife or your children; where at worst you would be dying for an idea. But here in Russia——"

"It is a horrible fraud."

"I knew you would see it that way." He began to laugh. "Then why don't you tell people outside? The duty of a decent man who has seen the truth is to report it. You saw Russia in 1929, again in 1935 and now today for the third time. What have you seen? That the whole Russian system is run by the police."

I didn't answer; a dark thought buried in my subconscious had come to light with his words.

"Answer me," grunted Dorogan.

"Yes," I said, "what you say is true."

"I knew it, comrade. I knew it. That's why I came, and why I told you all this. Any other man might denounce me, but I am prepared for that too, because I denounced you first. We have to think of everything in Russia. How vile to have sunk so low! But I had to protect myself."

He had another drink and then went on:

"In Aliosha's room there were two Spaniards and the Argentine delegate. He said you were an intellectual and had lost faith in comrade Manuilsky, and that you took pride in your independence of judgement. And I said to myself, this is it. This one won't approve of the way things are going. I was encouraged by the interest Bielov took in my denunciation of you."

"He was interested?"

"Oh, yes. He rubbed his hands and asked me lots of questions about what you thought about politics and comrade Stalin and Spain. What you liked best, liquor, women, parties? And he gave me an appointment to come back, but when I did he seemed to have lost interest in you. Then I knew they would let you go, and you would get outside where you could talk. And with the coincidence of my son's being here, the NKVD will never guess that I saw you."

I jumped off the bed. I felt feverish and paced the floor trying to throw off the anguish which was strangling me. Dorogan had stretched out on the bed. "Oh, how comfortable this bed is!" he said. Then he went back to the attack.

"Classless society! Here there is a caste which lives better, earns more, eats better, has precedence in all the rationing, lives in the best

257

houses, gets furniture, kitchen utensils, even bicycles for the children. This caste, my dear comrade, is the police of the NKVD.

"In Russia," he continued, nodding his head on the pillow, "the police is not, as in capitalist countries, an institution made up of people who openly belong to it. In Russia, the police is a vast web of agents, spies, informers, who invade everything. Factories and offices, collectives and unions, the barracks, the hotels, the cultural organizations, the Comintern itself! Every agent gets special favors, a better bread ration, or less people in his house, or a job as porter somewhere. In some cases the whole standard of living of a family is raised if a pretty daughter who speaks several languages agrees to be a prostitute in hotels where foreigners congregate. . . . You've been to a few collectives, haven't you?"

"Yes, about six."

"The most prosperous surely. You saw half a dozen persons, perhaps, in charge of things there, taking it easy. Well, they didn't get there by the sweat of their brows or by superior ability, but because they are informers. You saw factories too?"

"Yes, the most important ones in the environs of Moscow."

"Well, there it is much the same thing. The workers pay their union dues every week; not one escapes. All the money goes to the union cash-box, and out of that come the salaries of the directing comrades, and their helpers, who handle union affairs. These people spy on and terrorize the workers. And they are leaders precisely because the NKVD has put them there for that purpose."

"Why do the workers permit it?" I asked.

"There speaks a westerner, full of *bourgeois* prejudices and the thinking processes of the capitalist world! Ask a worker in a capitalist factory to be a spy and the chances are he'll sock you in the jaw and go off to another factory where he can work in peace. Here he would lose his union card, his work card, his ration card. No, you brilliant beacon of the Communist International in South America," he said with mock reverence. "Here we workers are slaves and have only one road open to us, to conform."

"In the capitalist world," I said, "the workers would declare a strike."

"And the laws and parliaments and courts, even the police, of the capitalist world permit you to strike. They even have the luxury of strike legislation; and they arbitrate quarrels."

"And here?" I asked, as if I did not know.

"Need you ask? Here the NKVD would come in with their machine-guns; and the workers would die, or be shipped off to the polar circle. No one would say a thing, and the travelling stars of the Comintern would go on making speeches against the crimes of Yankee imperialism, the piracy of English materialism, and the moral greatness of our glorious comrade Stalin. If some rumor did get out, you Comintern agents would get up a Congress of Peace somewhere and the rubles would be changed into dollars, and artists and novelists and poor fools, and rogues who enjoy free travel, would all go to it and launch invectives against the crimes of the capitalist world. While we, rotting away in our socialist paradise, would foot the bill to the last kopek."

"It is growing light," I said. "We have talked a long time and it has done me good, and also harm."

He talked on and on, along the same lines, repeating himself, harping on the tyranny of the system and the cynicism of those that went on supporting it. I felt I could bear it no longer.

"Perhaps there is still some hope," I said. "After Spain . . ."

"Spain! You were there; you know that it has been simply the field of experimentation for our arms. Aliosha almost cried when he told me. The war is lost; already the fighters are leaving for France. There they will be interned, but they won't be welcomed here; for Stalin will say that they lost the war by an agreement with the fascists."

"But if war comes and Germany attacks the Soviet Union are we to say 'Stalin is an assassin' and line up with the fascists?"

"No doubt Stalin is lucky to have found his match in Hitler. Each is a support to the other. Anyway, you are the third foreigner who has asked me that question."

"And what is your answer?"

"Nothing, because there is no answer. Perhaps after the war, who knows? I mustn't lose my faith in the Russian people."

There was a long silence.

"I am going," said Dorogan, putting on his coat. "Keep my presents for me. Don't go giving them to Bielov. I am going to my boy's room now to go out with him. See you later."

He left, shutting the door behind him. I washed hurriedly, before going out to wait for the bus which ran to the Comintern.

4

The meetings in the Comintern those days dealt with various Latin American problems; the achievement in Chile of a Popular

Front, the advances in Cuba, the concessions granted to the party in Costa Rica, the setback in Argentina, the possibilities in Peru, Ecuador and Colombia. Not a word about Brazil, which was *tabu* for comrade Manuilsky.

It was difficult for me to be silent when Chile came up for discussion, but I remembered my promise to Dimitrov. When Manuilsky smilingly turned to me during the meetings to ask any question, I always avoided answering, referring the matter to one of the Chilean leaders. Only once, when he insisted, I started to answer, but left it to them to develop. Manuilsky's behavior made me hope that the party's suspicions of me had abated.

Delegates from Argentina, Chile, Brazil, Peru, Cuba, and Uruguay were at the meetings. Browder and Foster were also there by special invitation. The Chileans received a great ovation from the greatest Comintern leaders—Dimitrov, Manuilsky, Togliatti, Browder, Foster, Gottwald, Broz, Kuüssinen, Pieck, Kolarov, Chou En-lai and minor leaders of Hungary, Macedonia, Spain and Indochina. Dimitrov painted vividly the prospect that lay before us—imminent war, the conflagration of Europe, Soviet isolation, the impossibility of communications and the likelihood, already envisaged by comrade Browder, of the disappearance of the Communist International.

"If the Communist International needs to be thrown overboard to save the ship," said Dimitrov, clearly and emphatically, "it will disappear as the First International, founded by Marx, disappeared once it had ceased to serve the purpose for which it was created."

"It will disappear formally," interrupted Manuilsky, "because the links we have formed across the world are now unbreakable. The Third International will die, but our bonds will grow stronger than ever, precisely because of that fact."

Actually the two men were disagreeing and their disagreements were the result of the discussion, notwithstanding the effort both were making to keep them unimportant. Manuilsky went on to another matter, saying:

"Never as in the present moment has it been so necessary to prepare for sudden changes and brusque reversals, as comrade Stalin has warned."

"Above all," said Dimitrov, "we cannot give concrete directions in each case, because we cannot foresee what will happen within six months. We cannot give even a cloudy picture of the next four weeks; the worst thing any of us could do would be to turn prophet." Then he went on to announce the resolutions which had been adopted, including one that I should go to Chile to work, at least until after the presidential elections, and to stay on until a favorable opportunity should arise for my entrance to Peru. Manuilsky had voted for it, he said, changing an earlier opinion that I should return to Spain.

"In Chile we can expect a radical President, can we not?" asked Dimitrov, turning to me.

"Yes," I answered.

"In Cuba," he continued, "we shall get closer to Batista and bring him round to our point of view. Won't we, comrade Pérez?" to which the worker who went by that name smiled and replied, "I think so."

"It is essential to go out of these meetings certain of one thing," said Manuilsky. "We are not liberals and are not going to fight for mere liberty. We must think first of gaining new positions. Freedom of the press, free elections, tolerance of the opposition must not be goals in themselves. Such things are unimportant unless with each step we are consolidating the party position. We have spent enough time waging war against dictators and their mistresses. Now we must be realists and see politics with one end only in view." He smiled, put out his cigarette, shook the dandruff off the collar of his hunting shirt, and continued: "If a dictator crushes democratic rights, or a general or a war lord seizes power, without any regard for the constitution, we are not inevitably to oppose him, providing he offers us advantages or opportunities, openly or surreptitiously. A comrade in the prefecture or parliament is worth fifty in jail, even if it means compromising."

We listened, astonished, thinking with no little fear how far this policy of sudden reversals was leading. He seemed not to notice our surprise and continued as if he were giving a lecture. "If the man in power offers something to the party in exchange for support, he must be dealt with discreetly to avoid shocking the crowd, covering our retreat if necessary by the sacrifice of one or two of our own comrades. Sometimes, painful as it is, one must throw one of the children to the wolves." Manuilsky looked at me when he said this, as if expecting me to comment.

"Perhaps, comrade," I said, "the workers won't understand very well why we fight fascism outside of our boundaries while cooperating at home with regimes which resemble it only too closely."

This criticism obviously irritated Manuilsky. Dimitrov didn't like it either. I was sorry I had spoken and wished I had had the sense to keep my mouth shut. But at the same time I was ashamed, because I knew that in former times I would have fought in defense of my point of view. Now I thought only of throwing in the sponge and escaping;

261

and I realized that the truth was that I no longer really cared. Nothing mattered to me any more.

"The workers," said Manuilsky, "will mutter a bit at first. We must manage to wrest a few concessions for them from the dictator or the winning general. If through communist intervention the most influential of the working class get a few advantages, they will be grateful to us and there will be no complaints. In Latin America the men in power are afraid of strikes among the electricians, the bakers, and the transport workers. Isn't that true?" he asked me.

"Yes indeed," I answered, seeing a chance to erase my former *faux pas*. "Comrade Manuilsky is well informed. They fear the strikes which are immediately felt by the public. On the other hand they don't worry about strikes in industries which have a less immediate effect."

"Hear, hear!" said Manuilsky happily. "If we can get advantages for the bakers, bus drivers and electrical workers, we shall have no worries. They will be happy and grateful and the rest will have to live on hope. Something for the white collar workers must be gotten too, but your peasants can be treated as if they didn't exist."

"You mustn't forget, comrades," said Kuüssinen, "that the workers in all countries, and especially in Latin America, are pure opportunists; they will follow the party that gives them tangible advantages. The great mass, comrades, and don't you forget it, doesn't see the problem of the liberation of the working class. Marx saw it, we see it, but they see only their daily bread. A loaf of bread more on the table, a pork chop, a bottle of milk or half a bottle of wine, will be enough to make them follow us. You can get this for them by maintaining cordial relations with the man in power, even if these are not entirely in the open."

"And will these Latin American rulers accept our support?" asked Gonzáles Alberti, an Argentine leader.

Manuilsky laughed aloud, joined by Dimitrov, Kuüssinen, Gottwald and Pieck but the Chinese Van Minh, who was present, remained expressionless.

"The Argentine comrade, with frightening *naiveté*," said Manuilsky, "asks if the Latin American rulers will accept our support. What says our Cuban comrade from his experience with General Batista? And the Chileans and the Peruvian?" And he laughed loudly again.

"They will do everything," interposed Dimitrov, "to achieve at least communist neutrality; they will pay our price, after much bargaining to be sure, and will try to deceive and betray us. We must get what we can. If the workers, the white collar group and the general public know that we have some influence in a government, however rotten, they will be coming to us for favors. In this way we can get new converts and servants, through greed or through hope."

"Above all," said Manuilsky, "our force must be used in defense of the Soviet Union. This is the first duty of the parties, of the individual communists, of our sympathizers, friends and followers. The mark of a good communist shall be precisely this: the fervor with which he defends the Soviet Union and its international policy, his eagerness to praise its works, the emphasis with which he teaches the people that the only just policy is that of the USSR and that all other nations are unjust, provoking wars, and leading to world wide conflagration." Manuilsky had been raising his voice progressively; now he almost shouted.

"The very soul of the communist's party strategy is the vigorous defense of the Soviet Union; there can be but one policy, that of Russia, of Stalin. No communist may have the right to defend any other. This must be clear to you all; remember it." There was absolute silence in the great hall of the Comintern. "Liberty," repeated Manuilsky, "interests us only when by defending it we can inspire the workers of the world with admiration for our great comrade Stalin." Manuilsky, Kuüssinen, Gottwald, and Pieck rose to applaud and the rest of us felt obliged to follow their example. But Manuilsky had more to say along the same lines. When he directed loyal communists to take their lines from reprints in the *bourgeois* press, from *Pravda*, *Izvestia*, or from Radio Moscow, a Chilean delegate, Galo Gonzáles, broke in:

"And if the Soviet Union is attacked, comrade?"

"Need you ask?" smiled Manuilsky. "It is no longer a mere danger that we shall be attacked. Indeed quite possibly the Soviet Union will be forced to take preventive action to defend its borders and to prevent a war. In such a case, the duty of communists would be to work for the defeat of capitalism in their own countries and the annihilation of their own *bourgeoisie*. Now if the socialist homeland should be attacked and the attackers were, for an example, an American nation; all the communists of America would be obligated to create the worst possible conditions for the action of the aggressor, and make every effort to facilitate the victory of the socialist homeland. There should be no scruple about methods and procedures; the basic centers of production should be hit and hit hard, the communications disrupted, production stopped and the loading of materials interrupted. Railroad lines should be blown up and a wave of terror spread as disruptive as possible. Bands of guerrillas should be organized, armed

263

and launched against the ports and oil wells, and all the vital centers of the country. This must be planned ahead and done without hesitation or fear, with your thoughts fixed on the motherland of socialism, whose soldier every communist must be."

Kuüssinen and Pieck rose and applauded feverishly; the others followed.

"Moreover, this is valid," said Manuilsky, "for today and tomorrow, and for five years from now, or ten years. It is valid for communists until we have crushed the last stronghold of opposition to the USSR. The tactics may change but the goal will not change nor the essential duties of every communist. Is this clear? Do you all understand?"

"Yes, perfectly," we all answered.

In successive meetings tactical questions and types of work were discussed.

"The Communist International," said Dimitrov in one of these, "has not attained complete success in its purpose of building up large parties in all the countries of the world. Only in France, and more recently, in Chile and Cuba (and because of the incandescence resulting from the civil war in Spain) has it been feasible to create important mass movements. In the rest of the world our comrades have had no success or too little, or the fiascos have been greater than the successes, as in Germany."

"I beg your pardon, please!" interrupted Wilhelm Pieck. "It is my duty not to permit so summary a judgment on Germany and the German people."

Dimitrov started to apologize and Manuilsky interrupted to minimize the importance of what Dimitrov had said; but Pieck was angry. He tore open the collar of his military tunic and shouted:

"This cannot be said, after the German communist party sacrificed itself to the last drop of blood to save the Soviet Union from destruction. Yes, it is time now to speak out in front of all these comrades, for we are tired of hearing it said that the German communists did not fight, that they gave in without a struggle. It was all so that civil war shouldn't break out in Germany, bringing about the intervention of the western powers, who might then reach the Soviet borders and bring Russia into the conflict. That's why we didn't fight."

"You're talking nonsense, Pieck," said Manuilsky.

"You know, Manuilsky, that I am not," Pieck retorted angrily. "The Communist International, you, and the Comintern ordered the sacrifice of the German communist party. Moscow told us to surrender!"

"Be still, Pieck," said Manuilsky. "Please, Wilhelm," pleaded Gottwald. "Sit down!" ordered Kuüssinen, taking him by the shoulder.

"No, no. I had to say this here, before these comrades," said Pieck, more calmly. "Because we are besieged with taunts: 'Why didn't you fight like the Spaniards? You are the disgrace of world communism!'"

"I beg you to sit down, comrade Pieck," said Dimitrov with firm dignity.

"Please be still, Wilhelm," repeated Gottwald and Kuüssinen.

"Surely it is not a crime to speak before responsible comrades of the enormous German sacrifice," exclaimed Pieck, his voice hoarse with emotion, "of all we had to do to save the Soviet Union from the possibility of war!" Then, turning to us, he exclaimed: "We Germans are not cowards, comrades; we are not unworthy to sit at the same table with Spanish or Chinese communists. It has been said that Hitler undermined our party and we fell without a struggle; but it is not true!"

Manuilsky called the German leader irresponsible. Since everybody was shouting, Dimitrov rapped his gavel and declared the meeting closed. We did not reconvene for two days. When we did, Pieck was the first to speak. He said he had been hasty and guilty of lightness in his accusations, and begged the delegates to forget what he had said.

"And never to mention it," added Manuilsky authoritatively.

"You must promise," said Dimitrov, "to say nothing of this in your respective countries. Not a word. Is it clear? All agreed?"

"All agreed," we chorused.

Then Dimitrov began to discuss the tactics and the type of work that lay before us. Our program must be to gain our ends through our friends, sympathizers and allies, while keeping ourselves in the background. "As Soviet power grows, there will be a greater aversion to communist parties everywhere. So we must practise the techniques of withdrawal. Never appear in the foreground; let our friends do the work. We must always remember that one sympathizer is generally worth more than a dozen militant communists. A university professor, who without being a party member lends himself to the interests of the Soviet Union, is worth more than a hundred men with party cards. A writer of reputation, or a retired general, are worth more than five hundred poor devils who don't know any better than to get themselves beaten up by the police. Every man has his value, his merit. The writer who, without being a party member, defends the Soviet Union, the union leader who is outside our ranks but defends Soviet international policy, is worth more than a thousand party members."

You could have heard a pin drop.

"Those who are not party members or marked as communists enjoy greater freedom of action. This dissimulated activity which awakes no resistance is much more effective than a frontal attack by the communists. The communist party of the whole world must learn the lesson of the Spanish war, where the efficacy of the fifth column was proved. Our friends must confuse the adversary for us, carry out our main directives, mobilize in favor of our campaigns people who do not think as we do, and whom we could never reach. In this tactic we must use everyone who comes near us; and the number grows every day. Particularly we must use ambitious politicians who need support; men who want to rise and lack a ladder, who want to get into the limelight and who realize that we communists can clear them a path, give them publicity, and provide them with a ladder."

"We'll provide the ladder today and take it away from them the moment it suits us," said Manuilsky.

"There are thousands of people, there will be millions later," said Dimitrov, "whom we can attract and domesticate. The application of the Popular Front tactics has shown it to be much easier than we'd imagined to domesticate the lower middle class and even a few of the upper middle class, and get them to follow us docilely. There are so many embittered persons, full of protest against something, and a prey to broken hopes. They long for something without knowing what, but something new and emotional and hopeful. There are thousands who don't know where they stand or what they want, but who long at any rate for a change in posture."

"And how far can we get, socially speaking?" asked the Cuban delegate who went by the name of Pérez.

"If in society there were infinite possibilities, we must achieve the infinite," answered Dimitrov.

"We have to get further than we did in Chile," said Manuilsky, sucking on his pipe. "We need to exploit the greed of the politicians on the left even more—or any politician we can work with, for that matter. Such men will sell their souls to the devil—and we buy souls. There are numerous ambitious generals in Latin America who are disposed to give us senatorships, seats in the house of deputies, mayoralties—to appoint our comrades Councilors of Social Security, Popular

266

Housing, Labor Arbitration, on condition that the communists refrain from attacking them or their anti-democratic procedures. We should organize crowds for them and praise them to the workers. Not only must we treat with the general in power, comrades, we must negotiate with him. We must try to obtain maximum advantages, large and small profits, from our cooperation."

"There are some generals," said the Cuban, "who don't want or need votes; they know how to get elected without them." Loud laughter greeted these words from General Batista's friend.

"Well, well," said Manuilsky, sucking on his pipe, "those who don't need votes, who stay in power by imprisoning their opponents, exiling their critics, killing those who get in their way, those men are always glad of our silence. Silence is golden, it is said, but in such cases our silence is worth diamonds, comrades. The general or the dictator or the aspirant to dictatorship will not want to have the workers complaining, or us talking to the workers. They will want us and our friends, people known to the public as leftists, swelling the popular demonstrations that applaud them."

"And if this official, once in power," asked the Chilean, Barra Silva, "turns against us?"

"Look, comrades," said Manuilsky persuasively. "Do you believe that with the forces at your disposal in your various countries you can prevent one of those generals from reaching the top? In Brazil, Argentina, Peru or Nicaragua? No, we cannot stop it; to try is to waste the energy we must save to defend the Soviet Union. I think, however, that if we don't interfere with these people, they will refrain from bothering us. Don't worry. They'll be careful not to!"

"Well then," said the Chilean, Lafertte, "must we get still closer to the Chilean radicals? And General Ibañez?"

"Of course," answered Dimitrov, emphatically. "Absolutely. Much closer!"

"Closer still, making sacrifices if necessary," said Manuilsky. "If one can cause a successful strike only by losing an influential radical ally it is almost always better to call off the strike. Here is a concrete, clear fact. The Chilean radicals are opposed to the unionization of the peasants; they fear that they may be asked to pay higher salaries themselves. Of course they are wrong, but it would obviously be a mistake for us to break our alliance with them. For the time being we must negotiate, seem to be trying for unionization so as to keep on the right side of the peasants, but carry the thing only so far as not to annoy the radicals. Leave them, of course, to carry the blame for it in the peasants' eyes."

Kuüssinen said then, after rather a long pause, "We must use people strange to us, who may or may not see eye to eye with us, but who see profit for themselves in cooperation. There are many union leaders in Latin America, pompous leaders without a following. We can build them up and use them very successfully in our campaign in favor of Soviet policy."

"The time has come, comrades," said Manuilsky, "when we must cultivate carefully all outstanding personalities—soldiers, painters with a reputation, writers and union leaders, musicians and sculptors of some renown, outstanding sports heroes and actors of stage and screen. In Mexico, we have Lombardo Toledano and his friends; they are not party members, but much more valuable for that very reason, and they render us greater service than the whole of organized Mexican communism. In Hollywood we have people who work admirably for the Soviet Union. Browder knows that. In Brazil, there is a group of writers and painters who are invaluable to us without a party card. And in Cuba, Juan Marinello is working out a more efficient policy than the whole communist party."

"Moreover," he added, "our attitude must be implacable against any newspaperman, intellectual, poet or writer who censures the Soviet Union or attacks us. He must be made an object of derision, his defects skillfully pointed out, his competitors or literary enemies built up at his expense. He must be attacked until he is discouraged or brought over to our side."

"In Chile, there are lots of poets, comrade," said Galo Gonzáles. "What is to be done with them? They are always quareling and are very puzzling to me."

"Poets," replied Manuilsky, "are versatile and full of complications. Be sure that our friends among them do not quarrel. Let them direct their animosity towards the enemies of the party and of the Soviet Union. Afterwards let them write poems in homage to comrade Stalin, the socialist achievements and Soviet victories and heroism."

"There are some who have political aspirations," said Lafertte. "They wish to be deputies and senators."

"Those," said Manuilsky roundly, "must join the party and appear as members, else some day they might turn to the church."

"As a general rule, comrades," said Kuüssinen, "intellectuals are very sensitive to praise. They like honors, applause and titles. Remember how pleased they are even here in Russia to be named 'Artist of the People.' Over there in your countries, because dictators and generals for the most part are dolts who have no respect for creators of culture, if you work cleverly, they will find among yourselves and with your friends the atmosphere that they lack and crave."

Manuilsky insisted again on how every communist was just a soldier of the Soviet Union, a guerrilla in the glorious Red Army, a hero on the outermost barricades of the revolution. Thus then, officially and by the voice of one of the top men of the Comintern, communists were changed from participants in the revolution of the working class of the world to become the fifth column of a power which was more ambitious than ever was Peter the Great, and which ran a police dictatorship which was absolutely totalitarian.

Communism was no longer a party or a doctrine, nor an ideal nor a philosophy; it was a bargain counter. The German people had sacrificed everything to the tranquility and greater glory of Stalin. Spaniards had served as guinea pigs so that the Stalinist regime could try out the quality of its weapons; and all the progressive men in the world, the most decent, the cleanest, the most heroic were to be changed by this crude and gigantic political swindle, into collaborators of tyranny.

5

In Spain, among the bloody corpses, I had felt my communist faith wearing thin. In Moscow, after the trials and these Comintern meetings, I felt only a cold calm emptiness. There was now neither faith nor convictions nor ideals; there was nothing except for a tense anguish like a pain in my vitals. And in that moment I thought I knew how the old Bolsheviks had felt, in their cells and in the dramatic trials.

When on the day following the last of the Latin American discussions Dimitrov summoned me to the Comintern, I went determined to agree to whatever he might say, with the indifference of a corpse at its own funeral. In the first place, I was now convinced that nothing of value about my country or the future of its people would be said. After long and bitter experience I had come to realize that no solution, no honest or disinterested advice, would be offered in the Comintern; since everything was being done for the benefit of the Soviet Union.

Furthermore I was anxious to leave the country alive, not to feel again the claws of the NKVD. I wanted to see my wife, to be with her when the child was born; and I longed to feel free of surveillance once more. The whole Russian atmosphere had begun to weigh on me so that I had an almost mad desire simply to get out and away, never to return, never, never any more. How painful it is to have come to hate so fiercely what one has once loved and trusted!

"Comrade," said Dimitrov, with his left arm around my shoulders, while his right hand clasped mine, "I hope you are going off without resentment or rancor, to work loyally." To which Manuilsky, who was also present, added: "The Communist International still trusts you, in spite of everything."

"You will go to Chile and not just now to your own country," said Dimitrov. "You know the next president of Chile must be a Radical. Moreover the Chilean comrades do not feel competent to carry on the newspaper that you founded. Your job must be to consolidate it on a firm base. We must get closer to the radicals, for the communist parties will be paralyzed once Russia's military strength makes itself felt. For the time being, we need more competent instruments with greater freedom, who inspire less resistance. People like professors in the University of La Plata, that famous Brazilian painter and his group, Lombardo Toledano and the fine men who surround him in Mexico, the leaders of Chilean radicalism, personalities like Batista, Lázaro Cardenas, the Colombian liberal Jorge Gaitan. You can see the task for yourself."

Manuilsky went on to speak of the Soviet Union and the glorious comrade Stalin, and I was filled with a physical disgust for everything. I might or might not leave the party; but at heart I was no longer a communist.

I returned to the Hotel Lux, my wits dulled as if by drink. I felt sunk in a boundless despair; my horizons lost sight of, I was absolutely alone, walking on the entrails of my faith and all my hopes. I thought of Marcucci's trembling lips as I threw myself on the bed. I dreamed of falling, falling into a soft chasm which had no ending anywhere.

There was a knock at the door and Dorogan's daughter Lena came in. I embraced her. "You have grown tall and beautiful," I said. She laughed gaily and broke into so rapid a torrent of Russian that I could hardly follow her. At last, however, she gave me to understand that she had come for their gifts; that Aliosha had been promoted; that there was to be a party to celebrate it and I was invited. I opened my suitcase, gave her the parcel, and promised to attend the party.

Her visit had done me good. I thought I must go to Aliosha's

room to congratulate him, but not before eating something. He would
doubtless press vodka on me, and in my present frame of mind it
could be very dangerous to be drunk. I lay there limply, in a half
twilight trying to make up my mind. Whether I slept or not I cannot
say; but as I lay there I saw the door open slowly, to admit a thin
man with a long black fur jacket and cap. "Comrade," said the man,
"I have come for you. Let's go."

"I don't understand," I said with my heart in my mouth.
"Where?"

"To the station. You leave tonight for Leningrad, and on to the
Finnish border. Pack your things."

I felt such joy sweep through me as almost to unnerve me. I
wanted to hug the man who brought me these tidings. Ironically
enough the thought of leaving the socialist homeland for the capitalist
world brought me now a great sense of freedom. I packed quickly,
trying to hide from this man the joy that bubbled up in me like a
great refreshing spring.

On the train I couldn't sleep. We stopped in Leningrad, the city
of Peter the Great, then rolled on to the Finnish frontier. The scenery
changed, the people, the guards. Now I was outside. Outside of the
country where the old Bolsheviks rot who had created the greatest
revolution the world had ever seen, where rots that revolution itself,
and the great idea which inflamed millions of minds, stirred whole
nations, made people believe in a nobler humanity.

I travelled torn between joy and sorrow. Joy at the thought of
leaving Russia and rejoining my wife, taking refuge in her arms, in
the clarity of her refreshing views, in her wise, obscure but nonetheless certain intuitions, and in our joint pleasure in the child that she
expected. Sorrow in the death of my great faith and in my broken
hopes. I had given up everything—the struggle for life, the building
of a future, security for old age—in the hope of finding some way
to lead my people out of their misery. And after long hard years here
I was, isolated, pathless without a compass, without even my dreams.
My people were in no better straits than they had been in 1919, and
as the train carried me through the clean enchantment of Sweden,
the terrible contrast with the filth of my own country struck me, perhaps with a little egotistic regret that I had been born in a land so
poor, so hard, among a people with so deep a capacity to endure
suffering.

Only he who has had a deep faith knows how tragic can be its
loss, how painful to have to stab it again and again as it tries to rise

271

anew. This grief was lessened for me by the joy of escape. I had walked the streets of Moscow with the chill breath of Stalin's bloodhounds at my back. I had been invaded by the psychosis of terror that dominates the average Russian, fear mixed with hate and disgust. I was escaping this and so was bathed in a glorious joy. I felt myself a free man in this capitalist world that I had for many years so fiercely attacked in my desire to forge happiness for my people.

To this world now I was returning humiliated, remembering the parable of the prodigal son and knowing that there was no hearth waiting to receive me. Some would see me as a deserter and others as a menace; but no one would ever trust me again. In spite of this, joy sang in me. I was going to have a child.

I arrived in Paris to find my wife in a sixth floor apartment in a sordid hotel on the left bank, happy too at the thought of our child, but very ill. Going to friends I was able to find a good doctor, Hertzog, who immediately made arrangements to place her in the Tarnier maternity home. She was by then in a very serious condition.

The day they took her to the delivery room was the longest of my life; and the night that followed was no better. The red tape of a French hospital is as immutable as the Soviet regime; try as I would I could neither see Delia nor learn from anyone how she fared. The next morning, only, I was informed that she would recover, but that the child was dead.

I wandered the streets that day a prey to sorrow and fury, feeling lost between two worlds to neither of which I belonged. My little son had died, at the hands it seemed to me, of my comrades. When they kept my wife in Spain with its lentil diet and its cold and bombardments and lack of medical care, they had made this thing possible. My little boy had died, had been killed by the iniquity, the pettiness, the sadistic cruelty of my own comrades.

Five or six weeks later we sailed for Buenos Aires, on the way to Chile. Of all our hopes there was nothing left. We had only each other.

CHAPTER IX

The Great Lie Revealed

1

IN CHILE, I was free to choose the path that should suit me best. I was free to abjure Stalin and the theories with which he cloaked his dictatorship; I was free also to remain in the communist ranks, the victim of a psychic inertia, pretending to a faith that was not only dead in me, but actually a decaying corpse. I could leave the party or remain in it. Which should I do?

At this crossroads, under the weight of indecision, the easiest thing was to wait for time to ripen my resolution as it ripens a vegetable; to let routine govern me, rather than my will. Then too I had still the duty to fight fascism. As a free man without any ideology I could not abandon the struggle, nor the others who were engaged in it, without falling into the fascist orbit. At that moment, to denounce Stalin and to expose his hoax would be to carry grist to the Nazi mill. Furthermore, deep within me there lingered a feeble flicker of hope. War might bring the downfall of Stalin and the triumph of some more truly progressive movement. Confused as this thought was, I cherished it. I was influenced also, let me confess it, by love of success; the triumph of the Popular Front in Chile and the prediction, "the next President of Chile must be a Radical." It was something purely sporting—to win for the pleasure of victory itself, the taste of triumph, a pleasure almost sensual, the joy of the gambler in the very turn of the wheel, the black dots on the dice.

I had also to consider what I owed the men who had put their faith in me as a leader. If it is cruel and painful to trample on one's own illusions, it is worse to destroy those of others, to show them by one's conduct that their trust has been misplaced. I was certain that the majority would join the chorus accusing me of treason. But I knew that in some there would remain a misgiving; they would feel defrauded and outraged, and this hurt me. I thought I must at least justify myself to the best and most honest among them, make them understand my ideological weakening and know the sordid reasons

273

that were compelling me to leave the communist party. I was, after all, the repository of something precious in these men—their trust.

Perhaps too, in a shameful fashion and without even admitting it to myself, I was motivated by fear of communist reprisal—the furious and persistent attacks, the insults and calumny that would result. And at the bottom of everything, as in Pandora's box, there was still hope. Perhaps there would be a change; a new movement by the Russians to throw off police tyranny, and a renewing current in the west which would destroy Nazism and bring a new life for all. By this sort of thinking, by these delusions, I resigned myself to continuing without faith, hope, or ardor, in the ranks of the party. I stifled my conscience by telling myself that I was only waiting for a favorable opportunity to break with it spectacularly. I know now that I was only lying to myself.

So I let the days pass, rescuing from disaster the journalistic enterprise I had founded and devoting myself to the cementing of good relations between the communists and the radicals. Neither the communist sympathizers, nor the popular enthusiasm or support, nor the powerful socialist party, were with Don Pedro Aguirre Cerda (nicknamed "Don Tinto" because of his swarthy complexion and the dark wine produced at his *hacienda*). Formerly Minister of the Interior under Arturo Alessandri, he bore the blame, rightly or wrongly, for what the Chilean people called the "Massacre of San Gregorio"—one of the hideous slaughters of strikers in which, in some Latin American countries, the army covers itself with glory.

Moreover, Aguirre Cerda and the outstanding leaders of radicalism had a good many objections to collaboration with the communists. I had to declare patiently and humbly, over and over again, the absolute hegemony of the radicals in the elections that were about to take place.

It was not easy to discipline and force to submission our own independent workers who were born fighters, but it had to be done. The communist propaganda was in favor of a vast unity of all leftist forces around the candidacy of Pedro Aguirre Cerda. Within the radical party, Gabriel Gonzáles Videla worked valiantly towards the same end.

The powerful forces on the right, notwithstanding the talent and sagacity of their leaders, strengthened the popular support for the left by their fascist parades, their defense of Franco, and the raising of millions of pesos with which to buy the election. Moreover, they had alienated the local national socialist movement by the needless slaughter of sixty-six boys, all under twenty-five, who had attempted a naive and absurd *putsch* against the government of President Alessandri. The Nazi group, therefore, voted for the Popular Front when the time came. Chile got a radical President. The Comintern Directive had been carried out, and from that moment communist power increased so much as to astonish its own leaders.

Aguirre Cerda never trusted the communists but he had no choice. In accepting our support, he gave us strength and prestige in political circles and an enormous influence with the workers, the white-collar groups, and the peasants. When the time came for the distribution of the prizes, the public posts, the communists' willingness to give the lion's share to the radicals strengthened the coalition and quieted radical fears. Aguirre Cerda, a short ugly man with exquisite manners, stoically accepted the criticism of his conservative friends, who blamed him for the growth of the socialist, and more especially of the communist, parties.

"Leave them alone," he would say philosophically. "These communists and socialists are not Russians, but Chileans. As soon as I am President, I'll let them manage the whole financial end of the government, the treasuries, the departments where money runs through the fingers—you'll see. These *rotos*, be they socialists or communists, catholics or radicals, will fall on the cash as a dog falls on a bone. They are Chileans, and they will soon discredit themselves and lose in sensuality all they have won by abnegation. I know them. You'll see."

And when some conservative would gently ask him, "What will it cost the country?" he would answer:

"It will cost something, but it must be paid. You conservatives are too stingy. In politics too, one must take out insurance and pay the premiums. Yes, sir; pay the premiums. And that is the premium we must pay. Anyhow, remember that 'in Chile nothing happens, and Chile has her star.' " And so it was. When the time came to divide the booty, men who had devotedly sacrificed everything for principle became only too easily corrupted.

It is a fact that a political party cannot jump with impunity from one side to another. In Chile, this was the result of the sudden shifting of the communist party line and the political moves from the extreme right to the extreme left, casting all principles aside. "Don Tinto," taciturn, patient, and thoroughly Chilean, gave the most heady posts to the communists and socialists.

The communist party was asked to nominate one of their men

for the post of councillor in the National Labor Insurance Fund of Chile. In spite of my warnings, our leaders chose a nice, good, unselfish man whose only qualification was his loyalty to the party—Muñoz Sandoval. Aguirre Cerda was delighted with the choice and named him to the post, where he would sit among his peers, all top radical leaders. Carlos Contreras Labarca, a simple man, loved the spectacular and the dramatic. He, therefore, wanted Muñoz Sandoval to enter his new position with *éclat*, making a defiant, aggressive, and stirring speech which would shake the foundations of an institution that was doing little in fact for the workers. I was opposed to this idea as being meaningless and apt to irritate the radicals.

When comrade Muñoz Sandoval presented himself to the directing council of the Workers Insurance Fund he was formally welcomed. He read an aggressive speech accusing everybody and announcing himself as the harbinger of a new day. The radical leaders laughed happily and had all the account books brought in for him to see.

"Never in my life, comrades," he told us later, "have I seen such big books. A man could hardly open them. Lines and numbers enough to make you dizzy. None of you, not even the intellectual comrades, ever saw so many numbers! The accountants talked of assets going up, and liabilities coming down. Now and then they talked about 'actuary indices.' What are actuary indices?"

"And what did you do?"

"What should I do in that briar patch of numbers? Nothing, of course," said the communist councillor, "I said it was good; it seemed very good to me. After that they made me sign, and I signed."

"What did you sign?"

"How should I know? Didn't I tell you it was all just numbers? I don't know what it was."

Months later the Central Committee of the communist party of Chile expelled from its ranks, dramatically, as "incompetent, dishonest, and a traitor to the working class" poor Muñoz Sandoval, who went from door to door begging to have his case reconsidered. When I intervened, blaming the leaders themselves for having chosen a good but stupid man for such a position, they answered that the prestige of the party had suffered and someone must be sacrificed.

Meanwhile our journalistic enterprise was in a critical condition. The newspaper was dying; the printing had gone as low as two thousand copies. Everyone expected me to revive it; as the founder, they felt it was up to me.

"Moreover," said Galo Gonzáles, with the authority that his trip to Moscow had given him, "comrades Dimitrov and Manuilsky wished it; the Comintern directed you to handle this matter."

The approval of the Comintern no longer meant anything to me, though I was still carried by the inertia of my dead faith. It is so with love, with friendship, with grief, with fear. They survive in us for a time, even moving us to action, before extinguishing themselves completely. So I accepted the task.

"How long will you give me?" I asked. They discussed it backwards and forwards.

"Can you do it in two years?"

"I'll try it in one."

My words were greeted with an ovation which seemed almost affectionate. Then I sketched out an optimistic plan: First, to get hold of a large building, where the editorial offices could be on the ground floor, with the party offices above; second, to get a rotary press that could put out twenty or thirty-thousand copies of thirty or forty pages; third, to obtain at least six linotypes, and to have a newspaper plant which could run off sixty to a hundred thousand copies in the morning, and twenty or twenty-five thousand in the afternoon. I recommended selling out everything in the Calle San Francisco where *Frente Popular* was now being published. The reception of my specific plan was none too cordial. Where was the money going to come from? As I saw it, the time had come to present a bill to all those who had benefited from party support, and to take advantage of our power, of the fear we inspired, and of the meekness of the Chilean financiers.

We got paper on credit in large shipments which we deposited in a warehouse, from which we sold it to the businessmen of the city and of the nation. We got long-term loans, discount of notes with prolonged maturity, and generous contributions from rich sympathizers. Doors opened to us with surprising ease. The Bank of Chile was honored to count our communist press among its preferred clients. The savings banks and other institutions were pleased to discount the notes issued by Barra & Cia, Limited. The bonds of the communist organization rose steadily in value, as the party rose in political power.

La Nacion, the government newspaper in Santiago, had several rotary presses. We acquired one of these cheaply because it was supposedly defective; we had it repaired by a German communist who came from Buenos Aires for the purpose. The linotypes and other minor equipment were obtained in the same way. I spent hours every day playing with credits, and passing the debt from one bank to another. Rich people hastened to give us short-term loans, and we paid

277

off one with what we got from another; and so, gradually, having started off without a cent, we paid our bills and built up a permanent capital.

With the guarantee of a rich Chilean businessman, we got title to a house for the party and the newspaper. On the corner of Moneda and Miraflores streets, over a large handsome house, shone in red neon lights the Soviet star. Below, in what had been the courtyard, our rotary press rolled out thousands of copies to the public.

The world situation had turned more complex. It was necessary to fight, and to use all the influence of Gabriel Gonzáles Videla, to get the government to admit several thousand Spaniards from the concentration camps in France. Pedro Aguirre Cerda dwelt on this at length; but it all came to a simple conclusion:

"But my boys, why should Chile hold the baby? It is up to Stalin; after all they fought for him."

Hitler's aggression, moreover, had reached its climax. The Munich pact and the policy of appeasement had only encouraged Nazism and incubated war. Czechoslovakia had been surrendered for peace in our time, and now Poland was threatened by the motorized divisions of the German dictatorship. War had come! A new war. What would the socialist homeland do now, with its great Red Army nourished at the price of Russian hunger? It was ready to move at any time. Now the moment had come. In my heart the fires of my sympathy for Russia that had seemed to die, smouldered anew. My hopes rose again before the prospect of the total war which the Soviet regime seemed prepared to wage against Nazism.

2

I myself took on the telephone the "urgent" United Press message: Hitler and Stalin had come to an understanding! Germany and the USSR had signed a Pact of Peace and Amity; Ribbentrop was flying to Moscow to sign the accord and seal the agreement. Hitler and Stalin were walking arm in arm onto the stage of History, and the proletarian revolution had served as a monumental pimp for this unspeakable traffic of flesh and blood.

The words of Manuilsky in the Comintern, his villainous cynicism, should have prepared me for this, but the news was absolutely unbearable to me.

The German-Soviet pact put the Chilean party leaders into a quandary. Party members besieged them for an explanation; meetings were held in an attempt to understand the reasons for the event. Those closest to me came to me for my opinion; and I answered that it was up to the leaders to give out the line on so serious a matter. I could say nothing.

The cells all voted resolutions asking for an explanation of the pact. In the labor headquarters, the workers asked what was going on, especially the socialist workers, who turned very sarcastic indeed. When the leaders came to me in despair, asking me to draw up some sort of statement for them to give out to the party cells, I refused.

"I have not come to carry out a political task," I answered. "I am here only to help you in technical aspects. Now that the President has been elected and the newspaper is on its feet, my mission here has ended."

Contreras Lebarca, Galo Gonzáles, Barra Silva and Fonseca begged me almost hysterically to find some explanation for the situation or to be responsible for the crisis within the party which must result. I wanted to laugh at their weepings and wailings, as I realized that now the last bond that had tied me to the party was broken. I cared about the world, the turn of the war, the future of humanity; but for what might happen to communism or the Chilean communist party, I cared not at all.

Before the insistence with which they besieged me, I had to say at last:

"There are things so monstrous, comrades, that they can never be equalled, and this pact is one of them. But why worry? In the past, the purges, the sudden shifts of policy, the assassinations have all been explained. Now, the Stalin-Hitler embrace will be explained in the same way."

"You have no right to speak in that way," said Contreras Lebarca. "We have a great responsibility here, especially you—who have the confidence of the International."

"The International may have confidence in me," I retorted, "but I have no confidence in the International."

"Quit the clowning," said Barra Silva, "and remember that our people may disband. We must give them some sort of explanation."

"They will not disband," I said contemptuously. "The party is at its height; it is powerful. Remember that the communist parties did not disband anywhere after the capitulation of the German communists, nor after the liquidation of the old Bolsheviks, nor after the defeat of Spain, nor after the refusal of your Papa Stalin to let the republican fighters from Spain into the Soviet Union. They will not disband now; your poor communists are prize suckers."

This moment, I was thinking, was one from which I could not escape. In spite of everything, until now I had rationalized my support of the party by the excuse that a united front must be maintained against nazism. Yet here went the two, hand in hand. Hitler and Stalin! I felt my own vacillations and hesitations fall from me like dead leaves from the trees in autumn.

"I don't approve of the Pact," I went on. "Yet it seems to me understandable, logical, absolutely in accord with Stalinist behavior. But it runs against every decent feeling a man has, and is a path I cannot follow. I am sick of this, sick."

"What has come over you?" asked Contreras.

"You must calm yourself," advised Barra Silva, "and stop this nonsense. For all of us, this news has been a blow. But we mustn't demoralize the comrades."

"Do you think the Hitler-Stalin pact is calculated to raise the communist morale?" I demanded. "Look, comrades, let's not argue. You must look on me as lost. I have no longer any faith in Stalin nor in the Soviet Union, nor in the glorious Bolshevik party, nor in the socialism of the NKVD."

"What are you saying?" asked Galo, indignantly. "This is to offer oneself up for crucifixion."

"Heresies, old Galo, heresies," I laughed. "If I had spoken them in Moscow, we wouldn't be talking together today. Your NKVD comrades would have shot me in the back of the neck."

"A comrade like you shouldn't say such things, especially in front of other comrades," said Galo.

"You are ill, ill," repeated Contreras, while Barra Silva, Chacon, and Abarca stared at me in silence, appalled.

"If you don't make a scandal," I suggested, "neither will I. I am tired of fighting and morally undone. I have no interest in opposing anyone or anything. I want a quiet withdrawal, silent and quiet. What do you think?"

My words made a profound impression. They were frightened by them, but took them as a reflection of the state of mind into which the pact had plunged me. None of them suggested any punishment for my conduct; even Galo seemed to abandon his post as high priest of the Control Commission.

I left them quietly, by myself, possessed of a new sad peace. I would not follow Marcucci's example and blow my brains out; nor would I make any scandal. I would go quietly, without saying anything. It was finished.

Contreras Lebarca came to see me the next day, bringing me a rough draft of a "strictly confidential internal document," according to the title, in which it was declared that the pact had been signed in the interests of peace, and with the concrete end of postponing war as long as possible.

"It is a moving little piece of sentimentality," I said bitterly, after reading it. "There should be some corrections, especially in your grammar."

"But," he asked, smiling and unusually agreeable, "does it seem to you that it will do for our followers?"

"I repeat," I said, "that anything you want to tell them will do."

"Then it might be better to say nothing."

"That's it, much better. Then they would say nothing. They would mutter for a couple of weeks or months even, and then they'd forget. After such a pact, much more important things will happen."

"Won't you correct it?" he asked, timidly.

"No!"

The Central Committee began to discuss and correct the document. Although I was repeatedly summoned, I did not go. I knew they were meeting on the floor above, all the while I was receiving telegrams downstairs. And such telegrams! Hitler invaded Poland; the armored divisions rolled across the land of Pilsudsky. I went up with all the telegrams to the room where the Central Committee was sitting, and asked for permission to read them. I never saw a group of people so bereft of bearings or plans. The document they had worked on for the better part of a week was now worthless since it was obvious the Hitler-Stalin pact had actually precipitated the conflict. The Central Committee of the Chilean communist party never did get around to giving any explanation of the pact, or the splendid banquet offered to Ribbentrop by Stalin.

I began at once to draw up a financial statement of our publishing venture, so as to present it on the last day of the year. I was anxious to turn over the newspaper in perfect shape, for I was sure that the slightest irregularity would give occasion for future calumny. I had to account exactly for every penny, and that year the enterprise had assets of five million pesos. My final accounting could not be rendered until the thirteenth of June of the following year. As I was turning over the business, the arrival of Vittorio Codovila in Santiago de Chile was announced. I was summoned twice to see him but I did not go. One day he came to my house, fat as ever, smiling, rosy-faced, and curly haired; his paunch had grown and he looked a little older.

He informed me that he came on a special emergency mission to all of Latin America.

"I've just come from Mexico," he said, "and there I conducted a cleansing purge, quite in order. We have had to expel Hernan Laborde, Campa, and an unserviceable nucleus. The new party secretary of Mexico is Dionisio Encina; I had him chosen because he seemed a proletarian we can trust." Then he pulled out a great portfolio full of documents accusing Laborde, Campa, and the rest. It was the old familiar stuff, the same wording, the same phrasing, the same mendacity, the same insults.

Codovila was very kind and patient with me. "You've always been a great talker," he said, "and now you are so quiet; what's the matter?"

"I'm pretty tired," I said. "Winding up the financial affairs of the enterprise has kept my nose to the grindstone. Fortunately, I've almost finished. At last I shall be free," I added, desiring to create an immediate break.

Codovila seemed to understand and led the conversation into trivial channels. Some messages to me from Thorez, Duclos and Raymond Guyot, the regards of Cachin and Cogniot! I saw he wished to avoid the issue, and the thought left me completely indifferent. I was resolved, but there was no hurry. He took a most cordial leave of me, as if we were good friends.

A week later, he begged me to come to him, since because of the Chilean police he could not seek me out. He must be careful not to be seen in public with known communists. As a proof of trust, he gave me the address of his secret lodgings. I went there and found him more cordial and amiable than ever. He spoke at length and I listened in silence. I did not agree or disagree; I just let him talk. He spoke about trotskyites and the perils threatening the Soviet Union, the situation of the party in Mexico, the reasons why he had not remained in Peru, his fear that the police would interfere with his work, his ideas about what should be done in Chile at that time.

"I plan to stay here for awhile," he said, "there is a great field here. But we must restrain the excessive opportunism of the Chilean comrades. Don't you think them too opportunistic?"

"Oh, I don't think so," I said indifferently.

"Do you think that I should stay here? What do you think?"

"The climate is agreeable, although there are bad periods, but they are short. It is pleasanter than Buenos Aires, certainly. The Chileans say that in Chile one earns little but enjoys much."

Codovila was not amused. He stared at me long and fixedly. As I said nothing more, he opened his first guns.

"There are comrades who have had their doubts and suffered a veritable crisis over the German-Soviet pact, but the wide-awake among them must realize——"

"Look, Codovila," I interrupted, "the matter of the pact doesn't interest me, especially after the division of Poland. I wish neither to know nor even to guess why such a pact was made. It was done and that's all there is to it."

Codovila went right on talking as if I had not spoken, with a patience that astonished me. I would never have expected this suavity in him. After he had finished all his reasoning I returned to the charge, as if I feared he might persuade me.

"I tell you, my friend, the matter fails to interest me."

I expected him to jump at this, threatening me with excommunication, a decree of expulsion dictated by Manuilsky and all the Moscow powers. Contrary to my expectation he seemed perplexed and even confused. He changed the subject, talked of Peru, of *aprismo*, of the advances made to him by Manuel Seoane and Luis Alberto Sánchez.

"They have sent me confidential messages asking for an interview. What do you think of them? What would they want?"

"I have had several meetings on various occasions with Sánchez, Seoane and other *aprista* leaders. They are disposed to come to an agreement with the communist party on a monetary basis."

"Monetary! How do you mean?"

"Talk to them. They'll ask you to get Moscow to give them thirty million dollars to finance their revolution. In return, they offer legality and a few positions to the party."

"Just what Haya de la Torre proposed to Lossovsky."

"That's right; they are incurable. They'll die as they were born and will never improve. Haya and his close collaborators, whom he controlled through blackmail and threats, have lost all moral feeling, erased all boundaries between politics and banditry, between a struggle for power and the drug traffic, assassination of their opponents and the sale of their country to the highest bidder. They are sick with the worst sort of adventurism."

"Don't you exaggerate a bit, comrade? Aren't you perhaps a trifle prejudiced?"

"I don't care to discuss that either. Time will tell whether I am right or not."

"But a communist fighter," said Codovila, pleasantly, "a leader like you with your talent, should not put things that way. It is a desertion, cowardice, flight before the enemy."

"Perhaps it is all that and so what?" I said, rising to my feet and pacing the floor. "Look, Codovila, I no longer feel like a member of the communist party, much less like any kind of a leader. The reasons I joined the party no longer exist. The faith and infinite hope with which I worked for it have rotted inside me. Now I feel that I have nothing to do here."

"Are you crazy?" he said, without changing countenance, so that I knew he had for some time realized the state of affairs. "You have the least right of any to say such things!"

"I am not crazy," I said in a loud voice. "And I have a right to say that I can bear no more. I bore the liquidation of the best people in the International. I bore the defeat of Spain, the death of all Lenin's friends, the founders of the revolution. But this, I can no longer bear; it is not to be borne!"

"You are ill. You must not go on working. You need a rest. Do you know that in spite of the war, it is possible to reach Moscow?"

I looked him in the eye seeking something in his glance that might betray the satanic character of his proposal. But Codovila seemed tranquil and friendly. I began to laugh. A little trip to Moscow, eh?

"I cannot bear for every commnist party to become a little nazi-communist fifth column," I said, "a brigade of spies, a group of terrorist bandits ready to blow up bridges, set fire to buildings, burn up oil wells, wreck machinery, and give information to the invaders, all that Mr. Stalin may sit comfortably in his dictatorial saddle. What I have done here is bad enough. I do not choose to take part in another Spain, nor play the Madam to another Chile. It is finished; you can do what you like. I, for my part, shall do nothing, shall say nothing, and shall slip away like a fugitive. If I am hit, I shall hit back. It shall be blow for blow. I shan't be pushed around, I promise you!"

Codovila was sitting at the table. He said nothing; he did not even make a gesture of any kind. Nor did he seem surprised.

"I am going to ask a great favor of you," he said.

"What's that?"

"Draw up a report for me on Peru. I know so little about it," he said dully. "You are the only person who can clearly see Peru; we must know what is really happening there."

"Just what Manuilsky prescribed is happening there," I said bitingly. "The party is collaborating with the government. Repressing strikes, putting smoke screens around conflicts, having secret understandings with the clandestine *aprista* movement, all without bothering the government."

"Yes, but for the first time we have our own elected deputy."

"Yes, comrade Juan P. Luna—but not elected."

"Hasn't he been elected?"

"He has been appointed, named by the government of General Benavides. Ask Luna to send you a report of his collaboration. I don't know anything about it, and I don't care."

"We must talk more, much more," said Codovila pleasantly. "You will do me the favor to come again."

I took my leave when it was dark. On reaching the street I was dizzy and saw a kind of colored fringe around people's faces and clothes, around the edges of things. I thought I must have been smoking too much, but I felt at peace, superbly and dynamically at peace.

3

A few days after the conversation with Codovila, I learned officially that the Italo-Argentine was not alone in Santiago. He was a member of a delegation sent by the Comintern, which was headed by Pierre, my advisor in the South American Bureau in 1930, and the pleasant and hospitable friend whom I had met again in Valencia in 1937. Second in command to Pierre was a North American who went by the name of "Jimmy." Contreras Lebarca assured me that Jimmy was one of the trusted lieutenants of Earl Browder. The Chileans, adopting it from the Cubans, called Browder the "Viceroy." He told me that he had learned to say in Spanish: "Regal Envoy, Hearer and Corrector of the Royal Audience," picking up the joke from the Cubans and the Chileans. Vittorio Codovila, the Tunisian Nemo with his adolescent ingenuousness and his great corpulence, and the Paraguayan student Oscar Creydt, made up the delegation.

The afternoon of the day that I heard of their arrival, the Pierre of the old days came to see me at the newspaper office. He was just as I had known him in Buenos Aires, just as I had seen him in Spain. The ten years had passed over him without leaving him another wrinkle, or a grey hair, or any change of his face or body. He looked as if he made new blood for each day, not just new blood but young blood like that of Doctor Faustus. I told him so, and he answered, affectionately but firmly:

"I assure you, I have not sold my soul to the devil."

"Sit down, Pierre, if you want to talk."

"No, no," he said. "I can only stay a moment. Understand, dear comrade, that I take a risk in coming to you now. This will prove to you how much your spiritual state concerns me. No one perhaps understands you as I do. We must talk."

"Whenever you wish."

"Tomorrow at three?"

"All right."

"Well then, you will wait here, and a comrade will come to pick you up. Agreed?"

"Agreed, Pierre."

The meeting took place in the house of a rich Chilean business man, owner of a sugar refinery which was not working. The door of the house had a knocker in the shape of a lyre, which struck the mouth of a bronze lion's head. I went to that reunion convinced that any benevolence that they might show would be purely fictitious. Furthermore, I knew that Pierre would be supplied with many penetrating arguments; as a result it was not a question of my persuading anyone but of confirming my break with them. The chasm between us was now too apparent; there was no other recourse but to act openly without making any excuses. I was too far from Pierre, his position and his arguments, his Stalinism, and it was stupid to think of piercing Codovila's closed mind. As for Nemo, he so lacked all political sense of smell that it was absurd to expect him to notice the stink of the corpses Stalin marched over. Jimmy—but who could this Jimmy be, Browder's friend?

I entered a house which smelled of time, of age. In the great rooms filled with old furniture floated a rancid odor which seemed to rise like a vapor from the rug, from the wallpaper, from the dark pictures of saints that hung on the walls. I crossed the wide hall. When I appeared at the door, Jimmy, Codovila, and Nemo were already together. On a sort of footstool lay a Mexican hat, and there I dropped my own, as well as my coat and gloves. When I went in, Codovila was making the gesture of stowing away a pistol in his right-hand pocket. He kept his hand there, as if he wished me to notice it, so I made a point of not doing so.

After a while Pierre arrived; he greeted me warmly. The meeting became official. Pierre invited me to speak first.

"Anything I might say I have already told Codovila. If you wish, he can repeat it, and I will rectify any errors or omissions."

"But Codovila," said Nemo, "had no authority to handle the matter at all, or any matter; he must have done it in a personal capacity, as a friend."

"A friend? Come, come, great Nemo! Comrade Codovila did not say it was personal. On the contrary, he posed as the agent sent to Latin America by the Communist International."

Codovila watched me with all the impudence he possessed, his face creased in a cynical smile. The silence was tense and angry between us; it was cold too, which was as bad as the silence. A soft knock was heard on the door and the owner of the house came in. He begged to be excused, greeted us, and apologized for not having lit the fire in the fireplace. He would do it at once and bring whisky, sherry and cognac. While he squatted to make the fire, he asked if we preferred soda or water with our whisky, and did we care for ice? Codovila asked for black coffee, the rest for whisky and water.

We chatted idly of the weather, the beautiful view. One would have taken us for a group of friends about to settle down to a game of poker. The owner of the house left us then, saying, "You shall be quite alone. I will return at night to serve you a country supper, if you are still here."

"With some good Chilean wine," said Nemo.

"With whatever you prefer," agreed our host, and left us.

When the street door had closed behind him, Pierre spoke:

"We have come here to talk together like good friends. This is neither a tribunal, nor a Control Commission, nor a Comintern delegation demanding an accounting. It is a friendly meeting to discuss our doubts and worries; we all have them. A communist leader is not a vegetable or a mineral; he is a man with feelings and a complex psychology full of moods, with hours of enthusiasm and minutes of discouragement. Come on, man. Tell us what ails you. We wish only to help you, to convince you that you are among friends."

Nemo and Codovila spoke along the same lines and begged that we forget anything that had tended to separate us from each other.

"It is clear and certain," I said, trying not to let my voice break, "that Codovila has already told you of our conversation. Whether he was authorized or not makes little difference. Everything he has told you is true. Why repeat it?"

"If you take that attitude, we'll never get anywhere," said Pierre, gently.

"I'm not trying to get anywhere, Pierre," I answered, "after having landed where I am now."

Pierre looked at me a long time, drumming his fingers on the table. Codovila was doodling, while Nemo passed a paper to Jimmy on which he had written something in English. Codovila's black coffee was getting cold.

"The German-Soviet Pact," said Pierre, as if he were lecturing, "is a historic necessity. It is not a caprice of destiny nor a resolution worked out by Stalin and Hitler. It is dictated by events which we must obey if we wish to save the Soviet Union from becoming involved in a destructive and bloody war. I don't exaggerate when I tell you it is a question of saving the October Revolution."

He was silent, watching me, awaiting my answer. I returned his look impassively and said nothing.

"We are simply not ready for war," he said, almost tearfully, "and this has been proved in Spain and in Finland; you know the inferior quality of our production. Although we have poured everything into munitions, in spite of all our sacrifices, there are defects, dangerous weaknesses. Our artillery is as good as any, but our aviation is still very deficient; so are our means of transportation—all of them without exception. We have one good type of tank, but the others are bad. You saw that in Spain."

He walked to the window and looked out at the mountains.

"Of course we have a lot of men. Millions of men and women, tens of thousands of soldiers. Under any circumstances our defense may be weak in armaments, but it will be a giant ant-hill in regard to manpower, waves of men, mountains of men, hordes of men. Just like that," he said, pointing to the great range of the snowy Andes that rose like a wall behind the city of Santiago.

"Do you think that Stalin and his Bolsheviks can be so stupid as to send that great human mass into war now? No, comrade, no! Let them cut each other's horns and hack each other's livers. The Soviet Union must save herself for the future, for the last hour, for the *coup de grace*."

I was shaken with indignation. I was angry and had to express it, in spite of the role of impassivity I had planned for myself.

"What Stalin and the Russians want is for the other nations to be their sepoys." Jimmy asked for the meaning of sepoy.

"Hindu soldier of the British army," said Nemo.

"Another meaning," I suggested, "is soldiers who kill and die for the advantage and victory of others. And what Pierre is maintaining here is that for the sake of the stability of Stalin's regime, Latin America should fight to the last Indian; the Chinese to the last coolie; the Spaniards to the last gypsy, and so on with the Hindus, the

Italians, and the Cochin-chinese. Everyone—except the Russians."

"The Russian comrades have already had their revolution," said Codovila. "It's up to us to defend it, and the best way is to follow the line laid down so wisely by our comrade Stalin."

Pierre interrupted:

"Sepoys! Soldiers who kill and die for the victory of others. Well, so what? Why shouldn't Poland or Turkey, Finland or China, be the shield of the Soviet Union? Why is it better for Russians to die than for Arabs, or Manchurians, or Indonesians, or Americans? Why?"

And Pierre looked at me defiantly for the first time.

"Because if it is a question of defending man's liberty in this world, fighting Nazism and conquering it," I answered, "it is monstrous that the Soviet Union should refuse combat in this way, and should ally itself with the Nazis at the very moment when others go to fight against them. Actually Stalin is helping Hitler. While Hitler sets fire to the world Stalin brings him the fuel. That is an alliance with Fascism!"

Codovila got up shouting, but Pierre made him sit down again. "An alliance with Fascism," he said quietly. "That's just where you're wrong; The Soviet Union has just signed the pact. I tell you, that pact will be broken on the day it suits Stalin and the Soviet Union. As long as we are weak, we will comply with it; as soon as we are stronger than our ally, not only will we cease to comply, we'll make him swallow the pact, signature, seals, diplomatic ribbons and all. You must understand for once and for always that between us and the capitalist world there is only one question—that of force and violence."

"Magnificent!" I said, letting myself be carried away. "When it is necessary to oppose Nazi violence with Soviet violence to save men's freedom, Stalin and the Russians renounce their Sorelian fine talk to become pacifists and friends of Hitler. No, Pierre; this is fraud, deceit, a piece of rascality!"

Jimmy had risen from his seat. He approached the chimney and stirred up the coals, adding new logs to the fire. In the red light of the flames his ruffled light hair looked like a brush.

"Fraud, deceit, rascality," repeated Pierre. "But who is being defrauded? It is not a question of deceiving the workers; no. If we manage to trick the imperialists, the lords, the great magnates, why not? If they are stupid enough to believe in pacts, treaties and papers, they'll sink that much sooner." He moistened his lips with the whisky and went on: "Who believes in pacts or treaties, comrades? They are like the laws which are obeyed by poor devils who haven't the strength to overthrow them. What you've got to remember is that Stalin and the Soviet Union will treat with the devil and his mother-in-law and be ready for a stab in the back or the breast, no matter which, since both kill equally well."

He paused and came over to where I sat; then crossing his arms he declared: "What we are doing now with the Molotov-Ribbentrop pact is to deceive, delay the shock, win the battle against time, since time makes us stronger every day. And when we are strong enough, it will be over. Pacts, treaties, Leagues of Nations, pacifist speeches! We'll crush them."

"And afterwards, Pierre?" I asked hoarsely, "afterwards? Subjugation of the peoples by Stalin's methods, NKVD brigades in every country, every party, every little ghost-government? Inventions of deviations to right and to left as an excuse for the assassination of leaders, officials, and any man who has a mind of his own? The transformation of the world into a concentration camp like Russia? You know, Pierre, how to suborn the labor leaders with half-pounds of butter or a rasher of bacon; how to make the policemen the highest human type, and how to set up the spy as an example to the world's youth; how finally to bring the cultivated men of Europe and America down to the level of the Russian, stupefied with terror."

Since Codovila and Nemo were trying to stop me, I yelled now at the top of my lungs, "Yes, that's how it is. And also how to transform the assassin who ties up your arms and shoots you in the back with your face to the ground, into the hero of a universal drama. Isn't it so?"

"I told you," said Codovila, "he is a renegade, a deserter."

"Look, Codovila," I shouted, "I am not Julio Antonio Mella whom you pushed into liquidation. I am not Andres Nin, or the unfortunate poumists whom you had killed in jail. No. I am not one of the officers in Lister's division whom you had shot in the Valencia barracks. This is another story. Here, if you attack me, come what may, you'll get as good as you give. I won't consent to a single blow, without returning at least one more. And you'll remember me!"

Codovila was as yellow as broom; his eyelids twitched, and his lips were white. Pierre went towards him and forced him down in his chair.

"Vittorio, please," he said, "do me the favor, please." Then he turned to me.

"Look, comrade, you are in an exalted state which I understand very well and forgive absolutely. You need to talk a great deal more, to see more clearly, above all to rest. The struggle has unstrung your nerves. Your imprisonments are telling on you. You need rest and freedom from responsibility."

"Thank you, Pierre," I said dryly.

"I have something to propose to you as a friend who appreciates your work and recognizes your sacrifices and the unselfishness with which you have served the party. Do you want to go to Moscow and discuss all this, and have a rest in a good sanitarium in the Crimea or wherever you please? I am offering you one of the solutions proposed by the International. If you wish it can be guaranteed by Dimitrov who esteems you very highly."

"For a communist," said Nemo with his absolute lack of intuition, "it is a piece of luck to be able to go at this time to the Soviet Union. My disinterested advice, comrade, is that you should accept the offer we are making you in the name of the Comintern."

Their voices were so silky and smooth that I joined in the game to see just how far it would go.

"But," I objected, "a trip to Moscow in wartime. How———"

The faces of three of the four lit up. Even Pierre's was shining with pleasure; Codovila beamed. Nemo looked pleased also; only Jimmy went on drinking, seemingly indifferent.

"It can all be arranged," said Pierre. "If you wish, you may take your wife. There are two Chilean comrades due to leave; you could go with them."

"Andrés Escobar is one," said Codovila. Like a heavy curtain after a scene of a play, silence fell on the room.

"What do you say?" asked Pierre. "Do you accept, or would you like time to think it over?"

"Look, Pierre," I said with emotion, "I made up my mind a good while ago. I don't believe in your gory socialism. Stalin fills me with the same hate and disgust as any other sadistic tyrant or cowardly bandit who has people shot in the back. I am convinced by facts that the Soviet regime is a system of monstrous extortion, of human abasement, of total privation of liberty and of permanent injury to thought, culture and intelligence."

"It is a pity—I say it in all sincerity—to hear you speak in this way," said Pierre, in the tone of a doctor to a patient in a critical condition.

"It is a pity," I said, almost between sobs, "to have reached this wretched state—to have endured the sacrifice of the German party and the thousands of Spaniards to Stalin's tyranny, to have endured without shrieking it from the housetops, the conversion of Russia into a slave state. It is a wretched thing to have authorized suffering and martyrdom so as to consolidate a police regime in which a man is worth only as much as a dirty rag."

"You cannot talk like that," shouted Nemo. "That is counter-revolution."

"I don't give a damn what you choose to call it. I am fed up! I have borne with all this infamy out of fear of a fascist triumph. Now that they are allies, it is finished. To hell with Stalin and all his crew!"

Pierre signaled to Jimmy and they withdrew to a corner of the fireplace, for private consultation. After a few minutes they came back to their seats. Jimmy said firmly:

"You have not convinced me that your resolution dates from very far back. You have convinced nobody. You have made up your mind recently for reasons that no one understands."

"Stalin or the Comintern," I retorted, "needs a delegation to enforce directives in Latin America; and he chooses four men. Here they are: Pierre, the Eyes and Ears of the Kremlin; Jimmy, representing the smallest communist party in the world if one considers the population of the United States, its electorate, the social groups which are interested in politics, and the size of organized labor."

"It's called the Workers Party," said Jimmy in fairly intelligible Spanish.

"The label doesn't make the whisky, comrade Jimmy," I answered. "The fact remains that you represent the smallest communist party in the world. Next comes Codovila from the smallest, most divided, and most useless party in Latin America; and then here is Nemo, citizen of Tunis, where there is no party at all, not even one communist to put up a poster. With the exception of Pierre, three generals without troops! These are the men trusted by the Comintern, valued because they are putty in the hands of Stalin, Manuilsky, and our friend, Pierre."

"I am shocked by the way you run on," said Pierre. "You are thinking emotionally and not historically. Today the North American and the Argentine parties may be small, but you forget that they are feeding the sacred fire, keeping the coals alive. Someday, after this war is over, there will be another depression."

"The economic crisis of capitalism," I quoted.

"All right. All we're doing now is collecting the strength with which to strike. When the United States, England, or Germany as the case may be, is weak after a depression, then the troops of Jimmy and Codovila will come out of the woodwork. Fire will break out, and the role of our staff will be to extend it. The embers of today will be the conflagration of tomorrow. Then the imperialists will be up against solid strength. We well know how much the *bourgeois* love their comforts, their good life, their summer vacations, and their weekends. They'll be frightened, and once frightened they will surrender to the armies of Jimmy, Codovila, and Nemo."

"When they have their armies, they will be generals; today they are merely recruits, who obey your voice, Pierre, and carry out your orders. You need only to suggest something for them to shout, 'Moscow speaks, comrades. Moscow speaks.'"

"All right," said Pierre, "we're going to stop now. You know that in the party we permit no resignations; anyone who wants to leave us is expelled."

"I know it," I answered. "Do as you please; but if you strike, I'll strike back."

"Have you seen the documentation on the Mexican leadership, on the expulsion of Laborde, Campa, and the others?"

"Yes."

"What do you think of it?"

I laughed. "The same old villainy. Take out the Mexicanisms and it is what the party has said a thousand times, in a thousand cases."

"All right," said Pierre, "I propose that nothing be said publicly in your case. It will merely be announced that you are leaving the paper; and you will of course receive no thanks for services rendered. No praise, no attack, perhaps some small criticism. Arrange quietly to turn over the enterprise, leave everything in running order, and when everything can go smoothly without you, you simply withdraw, without explanation or comments or mention of any misunderstandings. Are you agreed?"

"Agreed. But won't it be like the Soviet-Hitler pact?"

"There is nothing worse than useless words."

"All right," I said. "I have finished."

I put on my coat and said "Good night." No one answered, but Nemo saw me to the door. I was weighed down by depression; but I did not think of the day as one of misadventure. On the contrary, I felt serene and proud. I knew my situation was bad and my future lamentable, but I felt strong to face whatever lay before me. Outside it had sleeted, and now it was raining hard. As Nemo slammed the door behind me the cold bit into my bones. I pulled down my hat to keep the rain out of my eyes and walked to the street-car stop. At last I was out of the party.

4

I worked for more than a month getting the paper in order, and asked the Central Committee to call a meeting at which I might turn over the publishing enterprise. It was a long meeting and very boring. The leaders were all there; it was more like a joint session.

They offered me the floor and I gave a report on the general situation of the business. I reported the assets, the liabilities, the inventory, the current accounts in the banks, balances, circulation, turnover. I saw that they were bored and I tried to be brief. I too wished to go, to get through for good that night. My personal situation was now difficult, since I entered and left everyday without speaking to the leaders, like the ghost of the printing room.

By midnight I had completed my report, and I asked for an approval of my accounting. When I finished, the silence was uncomfortable, heavy, thick. Contreras Labarca offered the floor but nobody wanted it. There was another pause during which everybody lit cigarettes, exchanged hypocritical smiles, and even began to talk to each other. Finally the Spaniard, Manuel Delicado, spoke:

"We have been told here tonight about the publishing enterprise as if it were a matter of showing an accounting of a silk business or a paper factory. The comrade, however, has not spoken of the newspaper's political position or its long silences on matters of great interest to the workers, and that is what the Central Committee wants to hear about."

There was another silence. I purposely did not speak, creating tension deliberately. Contreras Labarca very courteously invited me to speak.

"I have nothing more to say," I spoke clearly. "I have reported to the Central Committee on the work I have accomplished. I am not interested in what might interest Delicado. I want my accounts approved."

"We need some self-criticism here," shouted Delicado, "and I demand that we shall have it!"

"If you enjoy self-criticism," I retorted, "go in for some of it yourself. Start with your own responsibility in the Spanish disaster."

Then the storm broke. Everyone spoke at once. Delicado was

white and furious; and I must have been too. Contreras Labarca brought order and asked me to apologize for insulting the memory of the Spanish fighters.

"Enough, man," I said. "Don't be childish. How long are you going to speculate with the blood and sacrifice of others? How long are the opportunists going to live on the heroism of those who fought? I make no apologies; this sickens me!"

Again a storm of voices broke out, exclamations and threats. Some begged for a calm discussion between comrades.

"I ask for a vote on the accounting," I said. "Is it approved or not? That's all I care about."

There were more shouts:

"This is for the Control Commission!"

"You can't demand a vote on what you want!"

"You'll have to explain this to the party!"

I gathered up my papers slowly, closed my briefcase and, before leaving through the nearest door, I said "Good night."

I felt thirty stares concentrated at the back of my neck, instead of the NKVD bullet. No one dared to stop me nor to offer an insult, nor to say in fact anything at all. The members of the Central Committee and the Spanish communists who enjoyed protection from the Chilean command knew quite well of my break with the Comintern delegation.

I awaited anxiously and patiently the resolution in which my expulsion from the ranks should be decreed. I was quite sure that some morning a long text full of shocking adjectives would appear in the communist paper. In spite of Pierre's promise the universal rule of the Comintern must not be broken. They had proceeded so with the entire leadership of the Mexican party, publishing the expulsion of Laborde, Campa and the others in the communist paper and reprinting tens of thousands of leaflets for distribution all over Latin America. In my case there could be no exception. No expulsion was ever kept secret. The rigorous custom of the party was a stormy scandal let loose against the reprobate. The policy was to make of him who was expelled a "stick in the barnyard," so that no one could use him, nor he be of use to anyone ever again. As the weeks and months went by in silence I decided that my case had been taken to Moscow.

Pierre left Santiago; so did Jimmy, and Nemo was getting ready to go. Only Codovila would remain with his Paraguayan assistant, Creydt. All this strengthened my notion that my expulsion and the resolution on it would be drawn up by Manuilsky in person. Months later, Codovila and the Chilean leaders brought a communist delegation from Peru for an interview with me.

My situation with the Peruvians was difficult, because of the collision of sentiments. It grieved me to know that they thought me a deserter. It didn't matter to me what the Comintern might think or say, Manuilsky, Pierre, Codovila or the Chilean leaders. But that my own people, whom I had converted, who had followed me with love and trust, should think me a deserter or simply "a *petit bourgeois* tired of fighting," to quote Codovila—that hurt. Something occurred to me that seemed an inspiration, opportune and useful.

"I am ready to discuss my case at length with the Chilean leaders, with Codovila and the Comintern delegates who are still here, in your presence. Propose this, and name the day, the hour and the place; and I promise you that it will be a battle that will teach you a great deal."

They were enthused and tried to arrange it, but every possibility was rejected, the Chilean party and Codovila keeping absolutely silent about my desertion. Pierre had kept his word. It was not until two years later, when all hope of my return was abandoned, that the Chilean leaders, Contreras Labarca, Ricardo Fonseca, Andrés Escobar and Vargas Puebla, were sent to Peru to announce formally my expulsion from the communist party. I was invited to defend myself or to send someone in my place to defend me. My answer was verbal: "Do as you please. But don't forget, I shall return blow for blow."

On leaving the communist ranks I had to face absolute poverty. It was very difficult to find work and to remake my life in business or journalism. The party fenced me in implacably, fiercely. Whoever promised me work was besieged by communist threats and the assurance that I was a dangerous man. Each attempt of my own to find work ran up against a greater obstacle raised by the communist leaders. I thought of emigrating to another country, but how and with what? I hadn't even carfare. The party was using against me the power that I myself had forged for it. And my feeling of guilt grew and crushed me psychologically to a point that seemed unbearable.

I turned to journalism and offered to work for miserable salaries. The newspapers rejected me, as much for my past connections as for the present enmity the powerful communist party bore me. My radical friends did not wish to make enemies by helping me out of my situation. They were sorry, they really were, but political reasons prevented them from offering me work or having anything to do with me at all. It would be dangerous.

The owners of the newspaper *La Opinion*, however, former friends and allies of the communists, were moving further and further out of their orbit. This made it possible for me to become an editor of Juan Luis Mery's paper. It was there that one morning I felt born anew the hope in me which I had thought forever dead. I was shaken as if by a great wind. Hitler, in spite of the pact, had attacked Russia that morning. German divisions were advancing, *en route* to Kiev and Dniepropetrovsk. From that moment Russia must line up alongside of England and France. I knew that now the foreign communist parties would abandon their "anti-imperialist" campaign to fight the Nazis.

When the attack came on Pearl Harbor, I went around to the North American Embassy to offer my services. For four years, I collaborated with Harrison Biddle and with Ziffren and Tomlinson, who headed the United States press campaign. Here was I, then, an ex-communist, working for the same cause in which both Russia and the United States were fighting. In spite of all the efforts of my former comrades to have me eliminated, I worked in the cause of the United Nations from Pearl Harbor until the fall of Berlin. That same day, at last, I returned to Peru.

5

Nazism and fascism had sunk in blood, and fear filled the hearts of the Latin American dictators, their police, their mistresses and their agents. In Peru there was a tempestuous swing to the left. The *apristas* and the communists took advantage of the situation. The communists hung literally from the coattails of the Soviet marshals, trying to reap profit from the battles of Stalingrad and Berlin.

The APRA and all the casual left set up a clamor for their share in the liquidation of fascism; and to hear them howl one might have supposed that these men had really shed some blood for the victory.

The oddest of these groups and the most insistent was the highland landholders, the feudal lords of the plateau who had been chilled by the suggestion that their unproductive lands should be partitioned. It was funny to hear them attack capitalism and complain of man's exploitation by man. For the Andean landholders of Peru the great enemy is the inventor of the salary, which is why they make their Indians work for nothing. It is the *corvée* of the pre-revolutionary period in France. And the worst thing in the world, to hear them tell it, is the *hacienda* on the coast which raises cotton or sugar, paying wages to its workers and complying with the labor laws.

All this amalgam, a motley socially and politically, united in 1945 under the ex-dictator Marshal Oscar Benavides and the *aprista* leader, Victor Raúl Haya de la Torre, into a sort of popular front to announce the candidacy of Dr. José Luis Bustamante y Rivero, and to elect him to the highest office in the land with virtually no opposition from anybody. A man of no political distinction, a careful and polished writer, a provincial lawyer completely unused to the ways of the capital, a sincerely democratic, devoutly Catholic, and certainly incorruptible man, he was entirely unfitted for the role his country was asking him to play. Circumstances, over which he had no control and never would have, had forced him into it, the pawn of destiny.

Never, as on the occasion of this great coalition, was there more talk of democracy, of civil liberties, of the rights of man. Never had there been, since Pierola, so much hope among men of good will for real democracy in Peru. Yet never was there so skillfully forged or so widely established a terrorist movement, supporting a regime of armed bands and controlled by unprincipled and undisciplined ruffians. Of course, this was not Bustamante's doing, but he was incapable of firm action. The APRA, which had given him his popular backing, had from the first gained control of the important posts and the positions of power in the nation. Little by little, they crowded out the sincere and honest liberals who had thought that in this new regime there was hope for decent and progressive democratic growth and gradual reform.

Meanwhile the communists proceeded to carry out Manuilsky's orders, with the help of the Chilean leaders, Contreras Labarca and Ricardo Fonseca, who had by now achieved the status of continental directors of the party. The Peruvian communists held a congress, and to their closing session they invited the President himself, who not only accepted but made the meeting an occasion for one of his fine speeches. In this speech he thanked them for their cooperation in his election and said he looked forward to the support and collaboration which they had promised his government.

For what strange reasons would Bustamante do so dangerous a thing? To me it seemed inconceivable that an intelligent lawyer could be so naive, so rustically simple as not to realize what profit the communists would glean from his action. To others, a bit removed from the political scene, it seemed strange that a devout and practising catholic should give his blessing to an excommunicated body. The wisest politicians wondered at his lack of political acumen. His friends tried to justify his act, but could not. Only the communists

298

failed to question, for they were far too busy harvesting the seed the President had sown.

The popular masses looked with new respect on these poor devils who had suddenly been raised to the level of an important political force by the blessing of a religious man devoted to the Virgin of Caima and the Lord of the Earthquakes. The old communists, who had joined the party in my day, and who had renewed their friendship with me on my return and complained to me of their dissatisfaction with their leaders, broke with me again after that speech, seeing the communist star once more in the ascendant. The workers who had hitherto been least drawn to communism, those who simply wanted bread for their children, argued in their own practical fashion: "If the President goes to greet the communists it must be because he respects them, and accepts their collaboration and is prepared to reward it. And if that is so, we had better play in with the party, so that we can receive our share of the benefits which its power can give us." To such men the theories of communism meant nothing but its practical power everything.

In this way the scholarly and gentle President helped the communist propaganda in Peru, like many another leader who for reasons of his own has used and been used by the party. I could see that I must get out in front, denounce the communist advance, destroy its position, tear off the mask and let the face be seen. I knew that no one could do it better than I, since, to quote Martí, "I had lived in the monster's bosom and I knew its entrails . . ." But I hesitated to reenter the political field or to appear openly as anti-communist.

The communists, however, were not the only danger to my country, as I saw it. Haya de la Torre and his party, emerging after eleven years of resistance, had emerged openly as the representatives of the popular will, had dyed their banners red again and were advocating recognition of the USSR. While they gave lip service to democracy they were organizing armed bands not unlike Hitler's storm troops.

In the labor unions they were dividing up the spheres of influence with the communists, exactly as had in times past the Chilean socialists.

The friends of Mariátegui who had, like me, left the communist ranks, regrouped themselves for action. "No one wants to fight," said Portocarrero. "The country is afraid; there are no organized political parties, no civilian forces, capable of enforcing a democratic way of life, so the field is free for both the *apristas* and the communists."

"They have the force," added Lino Larrea, "and are disposed

to use it without pity. They have made a mixture of Stalin's methods with Hitler's, so we'll soon know what the Germans and Russians had to suffer."

"We must go out to battle against them somehow," said Portocarrero, "though I doubt if we have the strength to hold them back."

"We cannot stay with our arms folded," said the labor leader Pedro Parra, in a low voice, turning on me his kind clear gaze, "but though our duty is to face them, we must also face the fact that it means danger."

After a good deal of talk of this kind we worked out a plan. One day at noon, towards the end of a damp sticky Lima winter, there appeared and circulated in city and country a four page weekly called *Vanguardia*, entirely dedicated to an attack on both *aprismo* and communism.

Our attack against communism suffered from our own susceptibility to the soothing and pacifist propaganda of Stalin. We still did not wish to see the world divided in two, but believed that capitalism and socialism could live side by side in peace, each making contributions to the other in mutual tolerance. When our second number was torn up and burned in the streets, we met to confess our fears to one another and renew our determination.

"If we show courage," said Lino Larrea, "it will prove contagious to others. Of course we are afraid, but we may be able to draw others to us and then we shall be less alone."

"You should have seen," said Carlos Barrantes, a former anarchist, "what a hundred brave men did in Barcelona. We are a few more than ten, but we can emulate them."

Portocarrero was interested in the political position. "Courage, of course," he said. "But the nature of our attack must be considered. It must come from the left, from our own position. The arguments of the right—calling them leftists, marxists, revolutionaries, disturbers of the peace—have strengthened both the APRA and communism in the people's eyes."

"Yes," agreed Donayre. "After a quarter of a century of dictatorship, and in the political corruption that has ruled this poor country for so long, anything that suggests change or renewal is bound to seem attractive."

"We are agreed then to attack them. By showing the people the truth—that there is nothing new either in the APRA with its violence, nor in communism with its total subservience to the wishes of the great Stalin. That the ideas, be they good or bad, of Marx, Engels and

Bakhunin, have nothing to do with the facts—which are that communism has converted itself into a traitorous fifth column, a group of agents in the service of a foreign power."

"As for the APRA," added Pedro Parra, "we must prove that the *apristas* are not reformers, but merely Nazis, and that far from extirpating the old dictatorial system, all they propose is to institute a new and violent dictatorship of one party."

"We must discuss each fact and expose the truth. Confound them out of their own mouths and show them untrue to the doctrines they themselves profess."

So, in the desolation that surrounds the fighters of a lost battalion, we began the fight against the savage horde that paced the city streets and the country roads with menacing feet. Communism was of the two far easier to combat. The resistance they tried to offer was quickly destroyed; their ideological positions could not be supported when attacked from the arsenals of Marx himself. We won very quickly in this way the workers whose faith was healthiest and most sincere, because they believed in Marx and Engels but not very much in Codovila and the other communist party leaders in Latin America.

Our campaign against the APRA was longer, more painful, and required more thought, more skilful arguments. At last, however, it was crowned with success. *Aprismo* sank ingloriously and cravenly in a bloody decline, without glory or grandeur. Before this, however, *Vanguardia* had some difficult days. The little paper had begun without support from any rich sympathizer or generous bank, like that which had backed the reviews and newspapers which I had published in Santiago. On the contrary it existed precariously, and suffered the pressure not only of its enemies but also of those of the newspaper *La Prensa*, in whose shop it was published, of the paper shortage and of the tactics of the distributors of periodicals, most of whom were controlled by the APRA. Each week seemed like the last for the little sheet that waged its fight implacably on a double front.

One day came what seemed like the final blow—a rumor that *La Prensa* was changing hands. I felt as if my last hope were gone. Then, miraculously came relief, cooperation, even help. The new director of the enterprise and of the paper proved to be Francisco Graña Garland, a young industrialist and *entrepreneur* who was seriously concerned for the welfare of Peru and disturbed by the terrorist methods of the APRA. He had not been long in charge before I realized that I had a friend in him and support for my *anti-aprista* views.

He was also in favor of the fight against communism, with no appeasement of Russia and no faith in the promises of Stalin.

"You are still hynotized; you are like a former drug addict," he said to me, "held by the late effects of the drug; there are in you still bonds, painful to cut, to the old ideas. Stalin is a miserable pirate, who has defrauded and deceived millions of idealists. You are suffering from the same illness as Henry Wallace. You'll see for yourself some day."

I had definitely left the ranks of the Communist International. I was opposed to the party and its policies, but I still thought it feasible to combine a condemnation of the hypocrisy, the cynicism and the vileness of the Yenan Way and moral collaboration, with the good that the Soviet Union might yet bring to the cause of the world's unfortunate. Between the fall of Berlin and the red invasion of Czechoslovakia, I went through a period of appeasement, believing Stalin's words which seemed to promise the organization of One World collaborating fraternally instead of two worlds at war with each other. I lent new faith to the promise of the Soviet dictator which offered a peaceful cooperation between capitalism and communism.

The events in Czechoslovakia and Yugoslavia destroyed these illusions. The peaceful little country, governed by President Benés, friend of Soviet Russia, defender of Stalin and his policies, was occupied by force. A murky *coup d'état* and a bloody rosary of assassinations, among which the terrible fate imposed on Masaryk cast a sinister glare, proved that the criminal wave had not been kept within Russian frontiers and that the peaceful words were merely the infamous Yenan Way again. Stalin's dictatorship was becoming more cynical, more pitiless, an avalanche threatening the entire world. The attitude of the Soviets towards Tito's regime proved that the Kremlin policy was entirely unprincipled and had no relation to the real good of the worker. Therefore the world had to face a historic phenomenon as hideous as that of fascism or nazism. These events destroyed in me forever every vestige of hope that I still had in a change of direction on the part of Russia. Thus I was left with only one road open to me, that of denouncing the danger, attacking the menace, and exposing in all its rottenness the Yenan Way, in all its horror the Soviet preparation for unleashing on humanity a Third World War.

There began for me then a friendship which grew out of a common struggle. A realist, friend to new ideas of all kinds, and compassionate before the sufferings of his people, Graña Garland appeared, from the first moment, as the head of a truly new and progressive movement, as the logical leader to unite the varied and scattered forces of the opposition. He had political gifts, mental agility, generous disinterestedness, and a mind open to social renovation and to the wretchedness of a people weighed down by economic contrasts and racial hatreds. He understood with delicacy and sensitivity the whole harsh complex of social contradictions, and seemed to have the capacity if not to find solutions, at least to seek for them.

He gave me conditions that permitted the little paper to live, and soon began himself to collaborate in the writing of it. Day by day he became more clearly the logical and effective opponent to Victor Raúl Haya de la Torre. For me and for many others he had arisen as the organizer of a vast new political movement, honest and sincere; for Haya, he became an inevitable pretender to the presidency, that is to say, his only real and dangerous contender.

Haya saw with his usual lucidity, his marvelously hypersensitive vanity, and his exaggerated ambition, that Graña Garland had not only the equipment but also the support adequate to fight a successful battle. Not strong enough to defeat him, he decided to have him killed. The *aprista* press tried by threats to intimidate Graña. "Panchito," it said, "take care! This campaign may cost you your skin." This of course, in the name of democracy, under the shelter offered by the judicial indifference of a democratic government presided over by the legalistic Dr. Bustamante y Rivero. Gay, full of joyous life, with confidence in his destiny and in himself, Graña Garland, unafraid, was nonetheless spied upon by the terrorist gang, his steps marked and his days numbered. The net was stretched out for the victim, the marksmanship of the assassins rehearsed, the false trails laid and the plan securely made. One warm summer night, at the wheel of his own car, Graña Garland received the shots in his breast which removed him from Haya's path and his country's service forever.

Peru was shaken with fear. This force of *aprismo* had shown itself truly to be a native version of the totalitarian parties of Stalin or Hitler, which would eliminate in one way or another anyone who got in its way. Out of the bosom of a sad people, weighed down with misery, tortured by dictators, embittered by the grievances of centuries, this evil thing had surged, and threatened to destroy every decent liberty which it had promised to establish.

The nation reacted with courage. Men of conscience and good will rose to their feet in answer to the entreaty of Pedro Beltran,

spoken over the still-warm corpse of the democratic martyr that
Graña had become, that the crime be condemned and the cowardly
government be compelled to declare itself from henceforward, opposed
to terrorism. Tens of thousands followed Graña's bier. *Vanguardia*
appeared in the streets, naming the criminals. Knowing them all, and
being familiar with Haya's mental processes, I knew that he would
have planned a perfect crime whose tracks would be carefully concealed by the police itself. This meant that the organizer must be not
only a killer, but an intimate of Haya, with the coolness and judgment necessary for the execution of a well-thought-out scheme. Alfredo
Tello Salaverría was such a man, cold, sadistic, intelligent, almost
rash, with a rich history behind him of unpunished *aprista* executions.
Vanguardia, therefore, openly accused this man in big black headlines, demanding the deputy's punishment as the organizer and planner
of the crime. Our campaign, after much delay, met with success, both
judicial (in that the man was tried and found guilty), and political,
in that many idealists left the *aprista* ranks after this. But every
success has its price. I guessed that I must pay it.

Mass explosions are just that: explosions. I foresaw that the
popular feeling of grief and indignation around Graña's bier was
ephemeral; its moments were counted. Now the fight in defense of
democracy, against APRA terrorism, was to be a long fight, difficult
and vigorously opposed. For this reason the attitude of Pedro Beltran
at the tomb of the murdered journalist had the virtue of uniting all
those of us who were waging the same fight. Around Beltran, notwithstanding differences in ideas and in points of view, there formed
an invincible field of gravitation which attracted strongly all those
who were trying to defend democracy, the dignity of man and the
elementary freedoms of the individual. Towards this field I too was
drawn, to give my most energetic collaboration, even to the point of
assuming the direction of the *Prensa* in Graña Garland's place. Under
my direction the *Prensa* defended, under all circumstances, even under
very adverse ones, the cause of democracy and human rights and
attacked openly communist activities, whether open or disguised.
As a consequence, I was punished for having denounced elections in
my own country which resembled those held by Stalin in Eastern
Germany, for having called attention to communist intrigues, for
having defended the right of every people to a democratic government, by being exiled once more from my country, and in exile I
remain.

Meanwhile, the *apristas* had decided to seize by force the power that their former friend and protector was now less eager to give them. They had wealth at their command, for in the shade of the government they had found many ways to enrich themselves, and from abroad came funds from the secret organization of the cocaine traffic which had flourished undisturbed under the legalism of the democratic government. Eduardo Balarezo, friend and accomplice of Lucky Luciano, had become one of the outstanding figures of the APRA and a member of Haya's intimate circle. Seeing ahead of it probable political liquidation, the APRA thought it wise to embark once more on a revolutionary adventure.

At dawn one day in October, the insurrection broke out. Sailors in Callao Bay mutinied against and killed their officers, landed successfully, and offered arms in abundance to the *aprista* crowds. It would seem that on this occasion every element of success was present, except leadership. Ironically enough, this one thing was lacking. None of the great APRA party chiefs was available to assume command in the hour of danger. They contented themselves instead with issuing orders and counter-orders by telephone, urging the rebels to advance. They tried to direct a revolution by remote control, like all the colonels and generals of Latin America, forgetting that it was not troops they were leading but civilians, who were waiting for their personal appearance to act. For fifteen or twenty hours the leaders watched the fight through long range binoculars, and the *aprista* revolution went down to defeat in a river of young blood—with the sterile sacrifice of a despairing youth in a bog of cowardice and wretchedness.

After this the cold President saw himself forced to act at last. He abandoned the rigidity of a juridical customs inspector and decreed measures against his former friends and allies. Like all weak men, he made his decrees in a loud voice and with insufficient practical results. His inept, if correct, democracy changed overnight to as rustic a dictatorship as that favored by any little Latin American general or colonel.

He ordered the closing of all APRA headquarters, and all its newspapers; his police arrested hundreds of suspected people while permitting most of the leaders to escape from the country, taking with them the large fortunes they had amassed while in power. As if trying to make up to the party for outlawing it, and as if to throw a sop to the communists at the same time, he ordered my imprisonment and exile to Mexico. In a full press conference, he declared that he acted in this way out of deference to the warnings of a "friendly government," and because he had in his possession abundant documents proving me to be an agent of the Cominform. The Minister said that I had been acting in connivance with a Russian couple, the Kosselevs, who lived in Arequipa.

I wasted my time in challenging the government of Bustamante to present their proofs. They never did. Furthermore, the Kosselevs whose name had been linked to mine no doubt because it was Russian, continued to live peacefully in Arequipa under the full protection of the authorities in some small official capacity. In a book published in Montevideo, Bustamante, that conspicuously distinguished man of law, declares that he ordered my exile not as a journalist but as a political danger. What beautiful and democratic jurisprudence!

My exile was short. One October midnight, a military *coup d'état* overthrew President Bustamante y Rivero, obliging him too to fare into a foreign country. There came to power a military council, presided over by General Manuel Odría. I returned to Peru, resolved to fight for the establishment of a democratic regime, the recognition of civil rights, respect for a free press and the defense of the famous Four Freedoms. My campaign lasted for more than a year, only to be interrupted by a new exile. My democratic campaign was not to the liking of the military council, or of the government which grew out of it.

In this very compressed story of my postwar activities, it can be seen that Catholics beyond suspicion of communist sympathy, and military men who are actively opposed to communism and who have not hesitated to outlaw the party, become the unwitting protectors and tools of Stalin when they persecute enemies of communism. The governments in our hemisphere lack the vision to weigh and measure the communist danger. They lack the will to resist and are guilty of yielding to communist tactics. Our people generally lack the aggressiveness that has become essential at this moment in history to confront the greatest danger to menace humanity since men came out of caves.

The real struggle against communism in Latin America demands above everything respect for public opinion, true concern and austere observance of inalienable principles. The peoples of Latin America are not easily persuaded of the advantages of the democratic over the communistic way of life so long as they observe that, whereas the democratic countries condemn on the one hand elections such as those in the Russian zone of Germany, where there is but one list and compulsory suffrage with the elimination of any contender, liquidation of all opposition, prison, exile for the troublemakers—on the other hand they recognize as democracies governments in Latin America which have come to power in exactly the same way.

Quite reasonably, surely, it occurs to people that political logic, morality which shelters the dignity of man and the democratic way of life, can hardly change in essence, content and standard merely by crossing the ocean. It becomes incomprehensible how dictatorship can be abominable in Eastern Germany, or Asia, only to be praised as a fine government in diplomatic speeches in America.

To a simple and honest citizen these practices seem the battle tactics of two equally fraudulent powers, each accusing the other of condoning undemocratic procedure on its side of the curtain, while practicing them quite happily, one in Eastern Europe and Asia, the other in our hemisphere.

It is this monstrous inconsistency on the part of North American diplomats which is actively helping the communist propaganda to reach the hearts of ingenuous and long suffering people, who, knowing North Americans so much better than they do Russians, often tend to prefer the unknown evil. There cannot be an effective struggle in our hemisphere against the Soviet fifth column until these people see some hope that democracy can free them from the dictatorships under which they suffer. The democratic propaganda must seem honest and consistent with the dignity of man if it is to be made attractive to the Latin Americans, who have been disillusioned too often by what they have seen.

Once again, as in the disastrous days of Munich, the western world is sick with appeasement, and we in Latin America are the sickest of all. There is no understanding of the magnitude of the menace and no one seems to realize that in the Soviet system everything, absolutely everything, is organized for the purpose of war. Russia is totally and totalitarianly organized; its production, its civil life, the rationing of food and the smallest daily activities of the tiniest village, are part of the gigantic machine. We Americans fail to see that never were Marshal Goering's words so true: "We have no butter, but we have guns." It would seem that we refuse to accept the harsh and overwhelmingly logical conclusion, which must result from a mature consideration of the facts. Communism equals war. It is this terrible conclusion which every free man must face whether he likes it or not. And in view of this conclusion all appeasement becomes a crime.

Mexico, May, 1951

Aguirre Cerda, Pedro. Chilean leader of the radical party, elected President in 1938 by the combined efforts of heterogeneous forces united in a Popular Front.

Alessandri, Arturo. Chilean leader of the liberal party who was elected to the presidency on a great wave of promises, supported by a vast coalition of leftist forces, only to lean later to the right and depend for support on the conservative and liberal parties.

Barbusse, Henri. Contemporary French writer, author of *Under Fire,* and other works. He became an active member of the communist party, a friend of Stalin and an outstanding figure in the Communist International.

Kun, Bela. Leader of the communist revolution in Hungary in 1918-19, friend of Lenin and president of the Soviet Hungarian Republic until the defeat of communism in Hungary. He fled to the Soviet Union where he worked in the Comintern until his imprisonment and murder by Stalin's police.

Benavides, Oscar. Peruvian dictator who rose to power by a *coup d'état* in 1914-15, and again after the murder of Sánchez Cerro in 1933. In 1939, his candidate Jorge Prado Ugarteche was elected president. In 1945 he deserted Prado to support Bustamante y Rivero, and died during his presidency.

"Búfalo." Nickname of the *aprista* worker Barreto, who led the attack on the Trujillo barracks in 1932 and fell in action. The name was used afterwards to designate a Peruvian imitation of the Nazi Storm Troopers, called the "Búfalos."

308

DRAMATIS PERSONAE

Bukharin, Nicolai. Bolshevik ideologist, Lenin's friend, author of several works, among them *The ABC of Communism*. Stalin removed him from post after post; finally he had him arrested, tried by Vishinsky and condemned to death as a traitor, a counter-revolutionary and a friend of the Nazis.

Bustamante y Rivero, José Luis. President of Peru, elected in 1945 by a coalition of the APRA and the communists, as well as others who wanted a democratic government in Peru. Overthrown by a military coup in 1948.

Cachin, Marcel. French communist leader, founder of the French communist party, directing member of the Communist International, considered a "relic" because of his "rightist deviations."

Cazón, Manuel. Party name of a young German communist who was very important in the organization of the communist parties in Brazil, Argentina, Chile and Ecuador. Member of the Comintern delegation in Latin America in 1934-38.

Chu Teh. Chinese communist, friend of Mao, a product of the Red Army academies. Enthusiastic advocate of violent liquidation of all who differed with Mao.

Codovila, Vittorio. Italian-born, naturalized Argentine, founder with José Penelón and the Ghioldi brothers of the Argentine communist party. When Penelón left the party, Codovila rose to the highest position in the Comintern in South America. Has been for a quarter-century in the confidence of the NKVD. In Spain along with the Russian command, he exercised dictatorial powers.

Cogniot. French communist deputy, one of the leaders of the "Internationale des Travailleurs de l'Enseignement," an international organization of teachers, dominated by communists. Collaborator of Leon Vernochet.

Díaz, José. Secretary-general of the communist party in Spain. Docile and obedient to the dictates of Moscow, he became the puppet of the foreigners who controlled the destiny of Spain and the conduct of the civil war.

Dimitrov, George. Secretary-general of the Bulgarian communist party. A refugee in Germany, he was accused by the Germans of causing the Reichstag fire. He stood up to the German prosecutors in such a way as to bring attention to himself, and then became one of the world figures in communism. Stalin was forced to accept his supreme leadership of the Comintern. Dimitrov later became leader of the Bulgarian government.

Dorogan. Pseudonym given to conceal the identity of a once important Russian leader. A real person, but with the events of his life distorted in such a way as to prevent his recognition by the Russian authorities and reprisals against him or his family.

Droz, Humbert. Swiss communist, friend of Lenin in his exile, one of the founders of the Third International, formerly a pastor of the Lutheran Church. Outstanding member of the supreme command of the "Profintern," he was next to Lossovsky the leading figure of world syndicalism. As a delegate of the International Red Syndical, he assisted and led the CSLA (Latin American Syndicalist Federation) in Montevideo, using the name of "Louis."

Fernández Oliva, Bernardo. Chief of Police during the dictatorship of Leguía in Peru (1919-1930). A specialist in torturing political prisoners, he boasted that "no prisoner ever died on his hands."

Ghioldi, Rodolfo and Oréstes. Argentine communists, brothers, founders with Codovila of the Argentine party and submissive to his orders. Rodolfo was one of the mentors of the armed insurrection that failed in Brazil.

Glaufbauf, Frederick. Czechoslovakian communist, especially trained in Moscow for work in Latin America. Active for a long time in Uruguay, Argentina and Chile, directing the schools of indoctrination, he was finally informed against and after a short imprisonment was exiled. He returned to Moscow where he continued working in the Comintern.

Gonzáles, Galo. Chilean worker, wagon driver in the port of Valparaiso and one of the important leaders of the Chilean communist party. A docile follower of Codovila.

Gonzáles Videla, Gabriel. Chilean radical leader, disciple and friend of Pedro Aguirre Cerda. Active in the promotion of the Popular Front, advocate of cooperation with the communists, when he reached the presidency he named three communist ministers, the first in America. However, after some experience he became convinced that the communists were not acting in accordance with Chilean interests but with those of Soviet Russia. He broke with them then, outlawed the party, and bore down on the leaders, propagandists and organizers of communism.

Gottwald, Clement. Czechoslovakian communist, member of the Comintern, entirely submissive to Manuilsky, along with Kuüssinen, Pieck, Togliatti, Kolarov and Van Minh. He triumphed over all his opponents in Czechoslovakia, gaining the confidence of President Benes only to betray him, and playing a part in the "suicide" of Jan Masaryk.

Graña Garland, Francisco. Young Peruvian politician, director of La Prensa and stubborn opponent of the APRA and its leader Haya de la Torre. After failing to heed several threats from the APRA, he was assassinated by a band of gunmen who killed him as he sat at the wheel of his automobile in front of one of the industrial laboratories he directed. After a long trial the murderers were proved guilty and are at this moment in prison.

"Guralsky." Lithuanian communist of Hebraic origin, active in the Lithuanian revolution of 1917. Arrested and condemned to death, he was pardoned because of his youth (fifteen years). Escaping from jail he reached Russia, joined the Red Army and fought in the invasions. Lenin gave him high positions in the communist youth movement. He directed the South American Bureau of the Comintern from 1930-1934, in Brazil, Argentina, Uruguay, Chile and Paraguay. His fate is unknown.

Haya de la Torre, Víctor Raúl. Peruvian political leader, founder and leader of the APRA or Alianza Popular Revolucionaria Americana. A fighter who began with liberal and leftist tendencies, he came later to use all the methods of Nazism and Stalinism. Several insurrections which he initiated failed. Outlawed by previous governments he remained in hiding until the presidency of Bustamante y Rivero, whom his party had supported. He had for a few years a great deal of power which he abused, and after the defeat of an armed insurrection in Callao his party was again outlawed and the leaders prosecuted. He took refuge in the Colombian Embassy in Lima, where he still remains, the center of an international controversy which has been taken to the International Tribunal of The Hague.

Ingenieros, José. Argentine writer, author of *The Mediocre Man* and other works of a social character. He was among the advanced thinkers who defended the Russian revolution in 1919. One of the most distinguished figures of Argentine thought in the first quarter of the century. Committed suicide in 1926.

"Jimmy." North American communist leader whose real name I never knew. He travelled with "Pierre" and Codovila through Latin America, in 1939-40. He organized and presided over the secret conference of leaders which took place in Buenos Aires and Montevideo, with a view to meeting the crisis produced in the communist ranks by the Hitler-Stalin pact.

Justo, Juan Bautista. Argentine politician, founder and director of the socialist party there, translator of Karl Marx' *Das Kapital* into Spanish.

Kalinin, Mikhail. Metal worker, second-rank leader of the Bolshevik party in Russia, President of the Soviet Union.

Kirov, Serge. Communist leader of the new generation that arose with the revolution. A strong personality, a party chief and head of the Leningrad government, he was in 1934 second in power to Stalin himself. In spite of his high position and the precautions with which he was supposedly surrounded, an unknown man entered his office, found him alone and killed him. Only the police of Stalin ever saw the assassin, who received no trial. It was given out that he was a Zinovievist and had been shot, along with eighty other "class enemies." It was persistently rumored however that Stalin himself had ordered the assassination.

Kuüssinen, Otto. Finnish communist leader, intimate of Stalin and Manuilsky and prominent director of the Comintern. He broke down all resistance within his own party after the fashion of Thaelmann and the Poles, sending his opponents to Moscow where they were frustrated for a long time and finally liquidated.

Laborde, Hernan. General secretary of the Mexican communist party who fell into disfavor with Moscow because of his restlessness under the direction of Lombardo Toledano. When the party which he directed refused to carry out certain demands of Lombardo's, Moscow sent Earl Browder to Mexico to subdue him. A short time later, Laborde and the men who surrounded him were all publicly expelled from the communist party by order of the delegation headed by Pierre with Jimmy and Codovila as his assistants.

Lafertte, Elías. Chilean worker leader, companion of Luis Emilio Recabarren, founder of the Chilean communist party and one of the most important leaders of the labor movement in Chile, Lafertte became a mere ornament, submissive to Russian dictates.

Largo Caballero, Francisco. Spanish socialist, organizer of the General Union of Workers in Spain and its ablest leader. A left-wing socialist, he sought the support of the communist party and used it to fight the right wing of his own party, receiving the title of "the Spanish Lenin" from the communists. Head of the Spanish Cabinet during one of the most unfortunate stages of the Spanish civil war, Largo Caballero refused to become a mere instrument of the party, with the result that he was attacked and finally overthrown.

Larrea, Lino. Labor leader and organizer in Peru. Member of the communist party, he occupied high posts in the executive committee and secretariat and made a trip to Russia where he worked in the Comintern. In 1940 he left the party and became one of the most energetic fighters against its fifth column activities in Peru.

Leguía, Augusto B. Peruvian politician, and constitutional President of Peru in 1908-1912. He rose to power again by a *coup d'état* in 1919 and dominated the country thereafter until 1930, when he was overthrown by a military *coup* directed by Lieutenant-Colonel Luis M. Sánchez Cerro.

Li Li Siang (also Li Li San). Chinese communist leader, founder of the Chinese party. He worked with "Borodin," the Russian agent, during the insurrection of Chiang Kai-shek and was one of the collaborators in the policy of the Kuomintang until the fall of Shanghai.

Lister, Enrique. Spanish stonemason, member of the communist party who rose to be a colonel during the civil war. He directed the violent repressions ordered by the Communist International to impose their will on the various groups that went to make up the Republican faction. He worked at all times under orders from the NKVD which was sent to Spain with the specific purpose of "purging Republican Spain of class enemies."

Litz Arzubide. Mexican poet, member of the communist party who visited the Soviet Union in 1929.

Lombardo Toledano, Vicente. Mexican politician whose influence has somewhat waned. Organized the CROM (Regional Confederation of Mexican Workers) in the days of Calles, from whom he later parted. Without being a member of the communist party he helps it in many ways and is well received in Moscow. Head of "Partido Popular" which tends to follow the party line. Seems to have lost the support of most *bona fide* labor in Mexico today.

Lossovsky, Alexander. Russian labor organizer who joined the Bolshevik party in the days of Lenin, and who held important posts among them. President of the "Profintern" or International Red Syndical. Author of several books, among others, *From the Strike to the Seizure of Power*. In the speech he gave before the last session of the Profintern, Lossovsky makes a direct reference to his correspondence with the Peruvian political leader Haya de la Torre.

Luna, Juan P. Peruvian communist leader, member of the executive committee of the party and agent of Vicente Lombardo Toledano in Peru. Communist deputy to Parliament from 1939-1945 and delegate with directive powers to the congresses of the Confederation of Latin American Workers, presided over by Lombardo and communist in organization. Actually he has been again named deputy by the present regime in Peru presided over by Manuel Odriá, despite the fact that the communist party as such is outlawed in that country at the present time.

"Magyar." Pseudonym of an outstanding Hungarian leader who participated with Bela Kun in the Hungarian insurrection of 1918-

1919. His articles, which appeared in almost every issue of *International Correspondence* served as a guide to the world communist movement. His final post, after the murder of Kirov, was to be an *agent provocateur* for the police of Stalin.

Manuilsky, Dimitri. Ukrainian communist, President of the Comintern for a long period, and in Stalin's confidence. He dominated the Comintern even after the presidency passed to Dimitrov, and saw to it that even the foreigners conformed to Stalin's wishes in everything. He was intimately bound up with the NKVD. After the war he represented Russia at the San Francisco conference and was the Ukrainian delegate to the United Nations.

Mao Tse-tung. Chinese communist leader, trained in Moscow. Unconditional slave of Stalin, he acted always as Manuilsky's agent in the bosom of the Comintern. During his stay in Moscow he received special treatment and was distinguished above other foreign delegates, was received by Stalin and was able to discuss with him personally the problems of the Chinese party. His opponents in China, who were not in accord with his policies, were called to Moscow and liquidated, one by one, over a long period.

Marcucci. Top leader of the Italian Communist Youth. He came to occupy the highest posts in the KIM and his opinions were considered by the leading circles in the Comintern. For a long time he was active in South America, and later in Spain participated in the actual fighting of the civil war. Committed suicide in Madrid in 1937.

Mariátegui, José Carlos. Peruvian writer, author of various works, notably *Seven Essays on the Peruvian Reality* and *Defense of Marxism*.

Martínez, Ricardo. Venezuelan communist, resident almost all his life in the United States. He waged a few skirmishes in the A F of L in the time of Gompers, then joined the communist party in the United States and appeared in Moscow in 1927-28. He always worked as an agent of the "Profintern."

Mella, Julio Antonio. Cuban communist student leader.

Mery, Juan Luis. Chilean journalist of leftist leanings. Owner and director of *La Opinion* in Santiago in whose pages he waged a vigorous campaign for civil liberties and for the economic independence of Chile.

Munzenberg, Willy. Outstanding theoretician and finance expert of the German Communist party. Opponent of Thaelmann, he was in favor of a foreign counterbalance to the Russian hegemony in the Comintern. He was important in German communism until 1930, when his star began to fade.

Negrín, José. Spanish politician who played a conspicuous part in the last stage of the civil war. A friend of the communists, he received their full support in exchange for important political power in the republic. Under his presidency of the Republican cabinet the absurd and unfortunate crossing of the Ebro took place, an engagement to which the Russians forced the republican army so that the Russians could try out some of their weapons.

Odría, Manuel A. Peruvian general, Minister of Government under the constitutional President Bustamante y Rivero in 1947 charged with the duty of clearing up various assassinations. In October, 1948, the general overthrew the government by a *coup d'état* and formed a military government with himself at its head. At this moment he is President of Peru, supported by a Congress whose members he himself appointed.

Orrego, Antenor. Peruvian senator, one of the leaders of the APRA, and one of its most competent intellectual interpreters.

Pardo, José. Peruvian politician, son of the Manuel Pardo who founded the *Civilista* party and cooperated with Piérola in the defeat of General Cáceres in 1895. He ran against the same Piérola in 1908 as a conservative, and defeated him. Elected president again in 1915, he was overthown in 1919 by a *coup d'état* directed by the dictator, Augusto Leguía.

Parra, Pedro. Peruvian labor leader. Member of the communist party and held high positions in the executive group. Resigned in 1940.

Piatnitzky, O. Russian revolutionary leader, collaborator of Lenin in the original organization of the Bolshevik party. One of the outstanding specialists in organizational matters, he directed this work in the Comintern. Differing with Stalin's policies, he was arrested and accused of sabotage and counter-revolution. Refusing to lend himself to the absurdities of a public trial he was secretly killed or "submitted to an administrative process."

Pieck, Wilhelm. German communist belonging to Thaelmann's group. During the war, Pieck remained in Russia where he became an influential man and intimately tied to Manuilsky. He is at present Stalin's puppet in East Germany.

Piérola, Nicolás. Peruvian politician, founder and leader of the democratic party. United with Manuel Pardo to overthrow militarism and was the hero of the bloody insurrection in 1895 after which he became President. During four years he initiated great reforms and advanced the country along democratic lines. Defeated in the elections of 1908 by the *Civilista* Pardo, son of Manuel, he never again reached power, but remained until his death in 1913 an ideal to democratic Peruvians.

"Pierre" (Pierre Austin). Pseudonym of a very important Russian leader whose real name I never knew. One of the youth group who enjoyed Stalin's favor and confidence, he worked with "Borodin" in China, then with Guralsky in South America. During the war he was in Cuba, in Mexico and Costa Rica, and has more recently been in Chile, Argentina and Uruguay.

Portocarrero, Julio. Peruvian labor leader, organizer of Peru's first unions, and associated with every struggle for the advancement of labor in Peru. Disciple of Mariátegui, under whose influence he came into the communist orbit, he was founder and leader of the Peruvian communist party. After the Hitler-Stalin pact he left the party, of which he was at that time Secretary-general, and became one of the opponents of the communist fifth column in Peru.

Prestes, Luis Carlos. Brazilian revolutionary who started as an army engineer. He took part in the insurrection of Getulio Vargas. Famous for a march across the interior of Brazil known as the "march of the Prestes Column." Won by Guralsky to communism, he went to Moscow in 1933 and studied in the Oriental University where he knew Mao Tse-tung and Ho Chi Minh. Returning to Brazil, he organized the ill-fated insurrection of Rio de Janeiro and the Northeast. After a term in jail he came out to organize the Brazilian communist party of which he is the supreme leader. He was named a member of the executive committee of the Communist International.

Radek, Karl. Russian revolutionary, member of the Bolshevik party, one of its most brilliant publicists in the early years. Accused as a counter-revolutionary he was condemned to ten years of prison. It is said his life was spared because by his denunciation, the movement of Marshal Tukhachevsky against Stalin's tyranny was crushed.

Rolland, Romain. Outstanding French writer, author of *Jean Cristophe*. Pacifist and a man of advanced ideas, he romantically sought the reconciliation of French and Germans. Due to his poor health he lived isolated in Switzerland for a long time. In his last years, he drew nearer to communism but was always suspicious of Soviet policies.

Sáenz, Cristobal. Chilean politician, rich wheat-grower, the first successful candidate for office of the Popular Front. Later he was a minister in Aguirre Cerda's cabinet.

Sánchez Cerro, Luis M. Peruvian military man. Elected President in spite of the opposition of the APRA, in trying to crush this opposition he unleashed a bloody repression on Peru resulting in the death of between six and seven thousand victims. On April 30, 1933, he was assassinated by an *aprista* fanatic. He was followed by Benavides.

Seoane, Manuel. Peruvian politician, second to Haya de la Torre in the APRA. Author of various books, vice-president of the Senate in 1945. After the failure of the Callao insurrection, he took refuge in the Brazilian embassy and later emigrated to Chile.

Sinani. Tzarist officer who went over to the Red Army, becoming later a party member. Had a brilliant political career ending in the post of Secretary to the Latin American section of the Communist International. Had great influence on Latin American communist officers until his death in 1935 at the hands of the Soviet police.

DRAMATIS PERSONAE

Sotomayor, Justiniano.   Young politician of the Chilean radical party. Very influential in the radical assembly of Santiago. Deputy and youth leader until 1936.

Stephanov, Mikhail.   Russian communist leader. He took part in the revolution of 1917 and collaborated with Lenin in the organization of the Bolshevik party. Member of the so-called "Old Guard" he managed to escape the persecution of Stalin, perhaps because of being abroad so much. He worked in China in the twenties and in 1930-31 was entrusted with the analysis of conditions in the semi-colonial countries for the Comintern. During the Spanish civil war he acted in Madrid under the name of "Moreno."

Thorez, Maurice.   French metalworker, whom Guralsky raised to the head of the French party.

Togliatti, Palmiro.   Known as "Ercole" during Mussolini's domination of Italy, a time which he spent in Moscow, and in commissions abroad for the Comintern. Trained in Russia and docile to the official line, he was a Manuilsky man in the Comintern.

Van Minh.   Pseudonym of Chinese communist leader who was a delegate from his country for many years to the Communist International. He was an adherent of Manuilsky and an opponent of what he termed the "nationalist" tendencies of Li Li Siang.

Vernochet, Leon.   French communist, Secretary-general of the teachers' union called "Internationale des Travailleurs de l'Enseignement."

Vishinsky, Andrei.   Russian communist politician. Mouthpiece for Stalin on numerous occasions, notably in the United Nations.

Zinoviev, Gregory.   An outstanding figure of the Russian revolution and collaborator of Lenin in the organization of the Bolshevik party. He was at one time President of the Communist International. Under his command the Comintern moved into other countries and began to organize parties everywhere.

Date Due

Demco 293-5